Women and Gender in International History

NEW APPROACHES TO INTERNATIONAL HISTORY

Series Editor: Thomas Zeiler, Professor of American Diplomatic History, University of Colorado Boulder, USA

Series Editorial Board:

Anthony Adamthwaite, University of California at Berkeley (USA)
Kathleen Burk, University College London (UK)
Louis Clerc, University of Turku (Finland)
Petra Goedde, Temple University (USA)
Francine McKenzie, University of Western Ontario (Canada)
Lien-Hang Nguyen, University of Kentucky (USA)
Jason Parker, Texas A&M University (USA)
Glenda Sluga, University of Sydney (Australia)

New Approaches to International History covers international history during the modern period and across the globe. The series incorporates new developments in the field, such as the cultural turn and transnationalism, as well as the classical high politics of state-centric policy making and diplomatic relations. Written with upper-level undergraduate and postgraduate students in mind, texts in the series provide an accessible overview of international diplomatic and transnational issues, events, and actors.

Published:

Decolonization and the Cold War, edited by Leslie James and
Elisabeth Leake (2015)
Cold War Summits, Chris Tudda (2015)
The United Nations in International History, Amy Sayward (2017)
Latin American Nationalism, James F. Siekmeier (2017)
The History of United States Cultural Diplomacy, Michael L. Krenn (2017)
International Cooperation in the Early 20th Century, Daniel Gorman (2017)
Women and Gender in International History, Karen Garner (2018)

Forthcoming:

International Development, Corinna Unger
The International LGBT Rights Movement, Laura Belmonte
Reconstructing the Postwar World, Francine McKenzie
The Environment and International History, Scott Kaufman
The United States and Latin America in the Contemporary World, Stephen G. Rabe
The History of Oil Diplomacy, Christopher R. W. Dietrich
The Nineteenth Century World, Maartje Abbenhuis
Global War, Global Catastrophe, Maartje Abbenhuis and Ismee Tames

Women and Gender in International History

THEORY AND PRACTICE

KAREN GARNER

BLOOMSBURY ACADEMIC
LONDON • NEW YORK • OXFORD • NEW DELHI • SYDNEY

BLOOMSBURY ACADEMIC
Bloomsbury Publishing Plc
50 Bedford Square, London, WC1B 3DP, UK

BLOOMSBURY, BLOOMSBURY ACADEMIC and the Diana logo are trademarks of
Bloomsbury Publishing Plc

First published in Great Britain 2018

A catalogue record for this book is available from the British Library.

A catalog record for this book is available from the Library of Congress.

ISBN: HB: 978-1-4725-7612-5
PB: 978-1-4725-7611-8
ePDF: 978-1-4725-7613-2
eBook: 978-1-4725-7614-9

Series: New Approaches to International History

Typeset by Deanta Global Publishing Services, Chennai, India

For Penny and Guy, and a safer and fairer world in the future

CONTENTS

6 Women, gender, and government leadership 199

7 Women, gender, and diplomacy 251

LIST OF FIGURES

LIST OF TABLES

SERIES EDITOR PREFACE

New Approaches to International History takes the entire world as its stage for exploring the history of diplomacy, broadly conceived theoretically and thematically, and writ large across the span of the globe, during the modern period. This series goes beyond the single goal of explaining encounters in the world. Our aspiration is that these books provide both an introduction for researchers new to a topic, and supplemental and essential reading in classrooms. Thus, *New Approaches* serves a dual purpose that is unique from other large-scale treatments of international history; it applies to scholarly agendas and pedagogy. In addition, it does so against the backdrop of a century of enormous change, conflict, and progress that informed global history but also continues to reflect on our own times.

The series offers the old and new diplomatic history to address a range of topics that shaped the twentieth century. Engaging in international history (including but not especially focusing on global or world history), these books will appeal to a range of scholars and teachers situated in the humanities and social sciences, including those in history, international relations, cultural studies, politics, and economics. We have in mind scholars, both novice and veteran, who require an entrée into a topic, trend, or technique that can benefit their own research or education into a new field of study by crossing boundaries in a variety of ways.

By its broad and inclusive coverage, *New Approaches to International History* is also unique because it makes accessible to students current research, methodology, and themes. Incorporating cutting-edge scholarship that reflects trends in international history, as well as addressing the classical high politics of state-centric policy making and diplomatic relations, these books are designed to bring alive the myriad of approaches for digestion by advanced undergraduates and graduate students. In preparation for the *New Approaches* series, Bloomsbury surveyed courses and faculty around the world to gauge interest and reveal core themes of relevance for their classroom use. The polling yielded a host of topics, from war and peace to the environment; from empire to economic integration; and from migration to nuclear arms. The effort proved that there is a much-needed place for studies that connect scholars and students alike to international history, and books that are especially relevant to the teaching missions of faculty around the world.

We hope readers find this series to be appealing, challenging, and thought-provoking. Whether the history is viewed through older or newer lenses, *New Approaches to International History* allows students to peer into the modern period's complex relations among nations, people, and events to draw their own conclusions about the tumultuous, interconnected past.

Thomas Zeiler,
University of Colorado Boulder, USA

ACKNOWLEDGMENTS

My sincere thanks go to Thomas Zeiler for including this work in his series "New Approaches to International History," and to Bloomsbury Academic Press Editor Emma Goode. Their support and encouragement over several years that I spent developing and writing this textbook has been greatly appreciated. My thanks also go out to the anonymous reviewers of earlier drafts of this text, as well. Their thought-provoking questions and insightful suggestions have most definitely improved my work and I'm very grateful for the time and expertise they contributed to this project. Any errors or shortcomings in this work are all my own.

Last but far from least, I appreciate my daughters and my sweetheart who cheer me on and bring me joy, and who share their loved ones in our wonderful extended family.

CHAPTER ONE

Introduction

Foundational questions

How have "women," dominant Western constructions of "male/masculine" and "female/feminine" genders and male-over-female gender power relations, shaped states' foreign policies, the formation and operations of key intergovernmental bodies, and the selection and conduct of elite government leaders across the twentieth and into the twenty-first centuries?

In other words, how have "women" and gender power relationships mattered during recent international history?

Key concepts

Gender as the term is used in this textbook refers to the socially constructed roles that define the characteristics, appropriate behaviors, realms of activity, and roles assigned to men and women, in relationship to one another, within a given historical, cultural, and sociopolitical context. The dominant white, heterosexual, middle and upper classes in modern-era Western industrialized societies have historically recognized two-gender "norms," that is, white, heterosexual, middle- and upper-class "male/ masculine" and "female/feminine," and have delineated two separate spheres of society, each linked to one of these gender norms. In Western societies, the "public" sphere of paid work, government, politics, and war making has historically been designated a "male/masculine" and privileged realm of human activity; the "private" or domestic sphere of the home and family that focuses on nurturing and caregiving has historically been designated a "female/feminine" and subordinate realm. Moreover, particular things (such as armaments), institutions (such as militaries), nations (such as the United States or Great Britain), or regions of the world (such as the global North) that have wielded "more" power than their categorical counterparts are coded with a "male/masculine" gender as opposed to a "female/feminine" gender. In the contemporary Western and non-Western worlds, there is growing recognition of the fact that the strict separation of public from private realms of society does not represent lived experience and that gender identities today are in fact more fluid, layered, and more diverse racially, sexually, and economically than advocated by dominant Western stereotypical gender norms. Nonetheless, these historic two-gender distinctions retain their normative status and their influence on elite states' policy makers' perceptions and behaviors; and, the relative gender power relationship—male-over-female—remains intact within international systems and intergovernmental institutions into the twenty-first century.

International History focuses on gathering documentary evidence in relation to international events and the interactions of governments, their leaders, and other key nongovernmental organizations (NGOs) and actors, within intergovernmental bodies or with each other, within a particular historical context. International history is concerned with determining what happened at specific moments in the past, who was involved, how it happened, and why particular events unfolded as they did in the international arena. Traditionally, international wars and dominant Western states' foreign policies, diplomatic and trade relationships, and studies of elite government leaders dominated international histories. In recent decades, however, cultural studies, social themes, and non-Western perspectives have expanded and redefined the field of study.

International Relations is a branch of political science established in the twentieth century, which starts with broad theoretical explanations of how and why international systems and institutions, and the people who created and led those systems and institutions, operate as they do. International Relations (IR) accounts identify common features of states', organizations', and leaders' behavior to build theory or normative rules. IR scholars then test those theories and analyze case studies from across historic periods. When exceptional behavior occurs, IR accounts seek to explain these deviations from the theory-defined norm.

> International politics is a man's world, a world of power and conflict in which warfare is a privileged activity. Traditionally, diplomacy, military service, and the science of international politics have been largely male domains. In the past, women have rarely been included in the ranks of professional diplomats or the military; of the few women who specialize in the academic discipline of international relations, few are security specialists.
>
> J. ANN TICKNER (1991: 27)

This textbook examines how Western normative constructions of masculine and feminine genders and women's subordinate relationships to male power within those constructions have influenced the metanarrative, or the grand arc, of international history and the trajectory of IR theories in the twentieth and twenty-first centuries. In these centuries, most states' governments and global governance bodies have been disproportionately dominated by male leaders and by gender power structures that have institutionalized white, heterosexual, elite, Western male privilege. This text reveals, however, how a small number of women who have held government and nongovernment leadership posts have participated in and influenced the course of international history, even as the metanarrative generally has not acknowledged their presence *as women* or recognized that gender difference determines a fundamental and unequal power relationship. From the early twentieth century onward, Western and non-Western women have participated in state-to-state relations and in decisions about when to pursue diplomacy or when to go to war to settle international conflicts. Western stereotypical masculine and feminine gender constructs have also influenced the establishment and evolution of key intergovernmental organizations and their political, social, and economic policy-making regimes as well as their security and development agencies. Additionally, Western and non-Western feminists have critiqued male-defined IR theory, and male-dominated states, foreign policy making, diplomatic regimes and protocols, and the functions of male-dominated intergovernmental organizations, and have proposed alternative theories and practices. These feminist prescriptions for more inclusive, socially just, and transformational politics regarding the conduct of international relations are more relevant than ever in the world today. They deserve further attention and analysis in international studies classrooms and in global policy-making chambers.

This textbook draws on the recently published work of global scholars in the fields of women's and diplomatic history, international relations, and gender and feminist studies, synthesizing their contributions to a new international history. It starts with the foundational question posed by IR scholar Cynthia Enloe in her seminal study *Bananas, Beaches & Bases: Making Feminist Sense of International Politics,* published in 1989: "Where are the women?" (1989: 1). Then it elaborates on this question, as Enloe and many other scholars have done, to ask how particular women are situated in international history with respect to the men of their generations, and how specific historic gender power relations have impacted the determination, implementation, and consequences of states' foreign policies and the workings of intergovernmental bodies. Through historic examples, this text aims to get to the heart of the ways that gender power has been distributed and how it has operated in the international political arena, and then to challenge the Western-defined status quo regarding male-over-female gender power relations that still prevails at the elite level of global politics and that is interconnected with historically based colonial power hierarchies of race, sexuality, and economic control over the world's resources.

To be sure, as many historians and gender studies scholars remind us, we need to challenge ourselves to question universal gender categories such as "male/masculine" and "female/feminine" when we are in fact referring to gender in a much more specific cultural and historical context. In 1992, historian Elsa Barkley Brown asked her colleagues to strive for a deeper understanding of the diverse life experiences and consciousnesses of those often referred to collectively as "American women" in their historical and feminist scholarship in order to challenge existing structural inequalities. She identified a key problem underlying many scholarly studies that focused on "women" and "gender":

> The overwhelming tendency now, it appears to me, is to acknowledge and then ignore the differences among women. . . . The effect of this is that acknowledging the difference becomes a way of reinforcing the notion that the experiences of white middle-class women are the norm; all others become deviant—different from. This reflects the fact that we still have to recognize that being a woman is, in fact, not extractable from the context in which one is a woman—that is, race, class, time and place. We still have to recognize that all women do not have the same gender.

> (BARKLEY BROWN 1992: 300)

With these considerations in mind, this textbook aims to integrate "women" and "gender" analyses into the study of international history, and to identify clearly which "women" and which society's specific gender constructions are under discussion. Women's history and feminist studies generally, as well as studies focusing on race, sexuality, and class, have questioned the metanarratives of many fields of study including common understandings of "world" history. All these scholarly fields have challenged universal claims to define "knowledge" and what is remembered and valorized in the human experience. This has led to many collections of local histories and sociological and political case studies that have foregrounded difference and distinctions. This textbook intends to provide a more synthetic account that engages with the metanarrative of international history. It highlights episodes where "women" and feminist theorists and activists from a wide range of ideological perspectives have challenged and transformed the very global events where men's experiences have been privileged and deemed the drivers of history. Geopolitical developments of the twentieth and twenty-first centuries, including the two world wars, the establishment of key intergovernmental forums, the Cold War, global economic development and "sustainable" uses of resources, "new" wars, and transformation of global security policies, have all involved "women" as they have involved "men." In all these global developments, gender power resources have been in play, in ways that have often impeded, and in ways that have sometimes promoted, social justice and human security. This textbook examines some of the ways that "women" and gender power relations have intersected with the metanarrative of twentieth- and twenty-first-century international history. It aims to produce a broader understanding of the people, institutions, and power structures that have shaped international relationships in the past, and to present new approaches to transform those relationships in progressive directions in the future.

No history textbook that is intended for undergraduate classroom use as this one is can be all inclusive. The histories that are recorded and remembered are always partial histories, selected by those who study and write about the past, often to address questions that historians have about their own societies and the times in which they live. This text focuses selectively, but also representatively, on "women" and gender power relationships that have informed the course of twentieth- and twenty-first-century international history. Each chapter begins with some key questions that have guided historical, IR, and gender studies research for the theme under consideration and defines key concepts discussed within the course of the chapter. At the end of each chapter additional references to recently published scholarship and selected internet-based resources are identified to encourage further exploration of textbook themes. A final reference section lists the works that were consulted in the writing of each chapter.

The six substantive chapters of this text focus on "women, gender, and ...": IR and critical theory (Chapter 2), war (Chapter 3), intergovernmental organizations (Chapter 4), global development (Chapter 5), government leadership (Chapter 6), and diplomacy (Chapter 7).

Chapter 2 introduces major IR theories as they have been developed at specific historic moments in the twentieth century to explain the interactions of states (usually) and the interventions of non-state actors (sometimes) to respond to international conflicts or to take collective action in areas of common interest. This chapter also presents a variety of feminist critiques of classic IR theories and concepts, explaining when and why they emerged. Finally, it examines a new critical concept, a "feminist foreign policy," which is being defined in terms of its principles, values, and practical applications. Several historic figures including the former US secretary of state Hillary Clinton (2009–13) and Swedish foreign minister Margot Wallström (2014– to date) have been linked to feminist foreign policies. Their records will also be discussed here in order to offer some real-world examples that expose the limits and highlight the possibilities of new directions for IR.

Chapters 3, 4, 5, 6, and 7 provide historical overviews of the themes under consideration as filtered through a gender-conscious lens from the First World War era to the present. These chapters also present several more in-depth examinations of specific historic events or figures. Chapter 3 examines in a broad historic sweep how "women" impacted the conduct of the two world wars and the Cold War superpower relationships, and the ways in which national- and human-security issues have been linked to unequal gender power relations during times of war. This chapter also identifies some of the instances when gender has been linked to unequal power relations based on race, ethnic, class, or religious differences during times of war. This chapter then focuses attention on "women" and gender power relations during the post-Cold War conflict in Bosnia-Herzegovina that erupted in 1992. During this "new" war (1992–95), and in the "post-conflict" aftermath, Yugoslav and international women activists and academics, as well as judges at the International Criminal Tribunal for the Former Yugoslavia (ICTY), effectively directed international attention to condemn wartime rape of women, which was used as a gendered weapon of war to achieve the "ethnic cleansing" of a population. Due to actions perpetrated by warring forces during this conflict (and during the concurrent ethnic war that took place in Rwanda from 1990 to 1994), global populations and the majority of states' governments recognized the systematic use of wartime rape as a gross violation of human rights to be prosecuted as a war crime against humanity in the temporary international tribunals established in relation to the Bosnian and Rwandan conflicts, and in the permanent International Criminal Court that the Rome Treaty established in 1998. At this time, a gender consciousness (and sometimes a feminist consciousness) seemed to be growing among world leaders regarding the conduct of war. However, women were almost entirely absent from the deliberations that led to the brokered ceasefire of the war in Bosnia-Herzegovina through the Dayton Peace Accord of 1995, as they have been excluded from most formal political roles in the postwar state, divided into Serbian-dominated Republika Srpska and the Bosnian Muslim- and Croat-dominated Federation of Bosnia-Herzegovina. These contradictions and gender power implications will also be examined here.

In Chapter 4, "women" and historic gender power relations that have shaped the establishment and evolution of the major intergovernmental organizations of the twentieth and twenty-first centuries, the League of Nations, and the United Nations (UN), are the topics of study. This chapter compares men's and women's roles in establishing and attempting to use the League of Nations forum to promote peace, security, and justice as revealed through an examination of the League's history during the 1920s and during and after the Conference on the Reduction and Limitation of Armaments that was convened in 1932. It also considers the roles of men and women in establishing a new intergovernmental body, the United Nations Organization, which was formed in 1945 as the Second World War ended. Within this new intergovernmental body, women's NGOs and women who served as government delegates and in the UN Secretariat recognized opportunities to link their efforts to promote "women's equality" with efforts to expand the notion of "universal" human rights to encompass "women's" human rights. Their efforts came to fruition with the four UN Conferences on Women (1975, 1980, 1985, and 1995). These conferences produced new global agreements and established new international norms and practices that represented real transformations in gender power relations and real challenges to other linked global power relationships based on race, class, and colonialism. A concurrent regional development beginning in the 1970s, the rise of an effective European "women's equality" lobby, resulted in substantive gender equality policies and practices within the European community and succeeding European Union (EU). Some of the most significant results of these feminist collaborations will be examined here, including a focused discussion of the UN Security Council Resolution 1325 on Women, Peace, and Security adopted in 2000.

In Chapter 5, the connection between the historically male-biased global economic and social development policies pursued by First World nations, financial institutions, and the United Nations, and the unfulfilled quest to substantially diminish global economic inequalities to promote peace and human security are explored. This chapter discusses the gender power relations inherent in Western-defined "modernization" and "socialist" development models. It provides an overview of the Western normative gender power relations that underlay post–Second World War reconstruction projects in occupied Germany and in Europe through the Marshall Plan and in occupied Japan through the Supreme Command of Allied Powers. As this chapter explains, gender power constructions defined by the West and Cold War superpower relations continued to shape the UN intergovernmental development efforts throughout the 1950s and 1960s. But by the 1970s, Western and non-Western feminist researchers and activists were beginning to challenge male-biased development models. This included subjecting UN-sponsored "basic needs" development theories and programs, neoliberal economic theories and policies, and "sustainable development" theories and programs to First and Third World feminist critiques, thus challenging Western colonial biases embedded in these development policies that had been formulated earlier.

Feminists have proposed alternative development models to First World donor governments and UN agencies aiming to better address the needs of "women" and other perennially impoverished groups who inhabited Third World *and* First World nations. However, even as various global aid agencies and Western governments implemented some programs based on "Women in Development," "Women and Development," "Gender and Development," and ecofeminist development theories in the 1970s, 1980s, and 1990s, gendered and other global inequalities persisted into the twenty-first century. More recent UN-sponsored development efforts, as articulated in the Millennium Development Goals (2000–15) and the Sustainable Development Goals (2015–30), represent, at the very least, the slow transformation of global development normative treaties and aid-agency resource allocation. This chapter explains how global feminist theories have impacted intergovernmental development efforts, incorporating "gender equality" as a necessary component of development program design and aid administration to improve the outcomes of global poverty-eradication initiatives, to improve health and welfare of global populations, to promote environmental sustainability, and to achieve lasting peace and human security.

Chapter 6 focuses on the few Western and non-Western women who have held elite government leadership roles in the twentieth and twenty-first centuries. It examines some of the ways that Western-defined masculine and feminine gender stereotypes have influenced the construction and conduct of elite government leadership and executive institutions in the realm of international politics. This chapter examines the legal and social barriers to "women's" political leadership, which have been the most difficult to breach at the highest levels of political power in most nations of the world, and evaluates the successes and failures of feminist challenges to break down those barriers. It also explores the proposition that "women" as national leaders can bring about transformational change in global politics through their gendered practice of international relations. To conduct this exploration, this chapter considers the foreign policies and international relationships cultivated by a few women leaders: Indira Gandhi, Margaret Thatcher, Michelle Bachelet, Ellen Johnson Sirleaf, and Angela Merkel. As there have been relatively few women who have served as heads of government over the past century, the focus here is on the exemplary experiences of these selected female leaders, compared with each other and with the male leaders who were their contemporary cohorts or adversaries. These examples reveal some of the ways that Western-defined male-over-female gender power relations have operated in foreign policy discourse and institutions that have shaped and reflected ways of thinking about elite global leadership.

Chapter 7 addresses the roles that "women" have played as diplomats, representing their nation's interests to resolve international conflicts from the First World War era up to the second decade of the twenty-first century. As with women who have held other elite leadership posts in international politics, the numbers of women serving in their nation's elite diplomatic corps have been small. Moreover, throughout this period, Western-defined gender role expectations have followed women from all nations into the halls of intergovernmental bodies and into formal international negotiations where global conflicts are resolved. This chapter examines the experiences of women diplomats from Western and non-Western nations who engaged with their male counterparts at the League of Nations and the United Nations from the 1920s to the present. To examine how women's diplomatic roles have expanded over the course of the last century, this chapter focuses attention on a few women diplomats whose ideas and activism have influenced the goals and conduct of their nations' diplomatic negotiations. In considering the historic examples of the few women who have served in elite diplomatic posts, this chapter addresses the question of whether "women" should be called upon more often by nations to apply their gender power in ways that might transform twenty-first-century conflict resolution. The conclusion to this chapter and to this textbook does not, by any means, conclude the scholarly conversation regarding the roles of "women" and gender power relationships in twentieth- and twenty-first-century international history. Instead, it summarizes chronological developments, exposes some historic patterns, and discusses implications for the future.

References for further study

Boylston, J. (2009), "Gender as a Question of Historical Analysis," *Gender & History*, 20: 558–83.

Nadell, P. S. and Haulman, K. (2014), *Making Women's Histories: Beyond National Perspectives*, New York: NYU Press.

Strasser, U. and Tinsman, H. (2005), "Engendering History," *Radical History Review*, 91: 151–64.

Youngs, G. (2004), "Feminist International Relations: A Contradiction in Terms? Or: Why Women and Gender are Essential to Understanding the World 'we' Live in," *International Affairs*, 80: 75–87.

Web resources

Cynthia Enloe, Research Professor, Clark University, Worcester, Massachusetts interviewed by Elisabeth Prügl, Professor of International Relations and Deputy Director of the Graduate Institute of International and Development Studies, Geneva, Switzerland. January 17, 2012. https://www.youtube.com/watch?v=DbEJ3RESlf0 (Accessed July 9, 2017).

Hutchins, K., "Feminism and International Relations." Open University. October 3, 2014. https://www.youtube.com/watch?v=ajAWGztPUiU (Accessed July 9, 2017).

Women in Politics Global Map 2017. United Nations. http://www.un.org/sustainabledevelopment/blog/2017/03/womens-political-parity-slow-to-grow-as-un-launches-latest-women-in-politics-map/ (Accessed July 9, 2017).

Bibliography

Brown, E. B. (1992), "What Has Happened Here: The Politics of Difference in Women's History and Feminist Politics," *Feminist Studies*, 18: 295–312.

Enloe, C. (1989), *Bananas, Beaches and Bases: Making Feminist Sense of International Relations*, Berkeley, CA: University of California Press.

Enloe, C. (2004), *The Curious Feminist: Searching for Women in a New Age of Empire*, Berkeley, CA: University of California Press.

Hudson, V. M. and Leidl, P. (2015), *The Hillary Doctrine: Sex & American Foreign Policy*, New York, NY: Columbia University Press.

Olcott, J. (2014), "A Happier Marriage? Feminist History Takes a Transnational Turn," in P. S. Nadell and K. Haulman (eds.), *Making Women's Histories: Beyond National Perspectives*, 237–58, New York, NY: New York University Press.

Peterson, V. S. and Runyan, A. S. (2009), *Global Gender Issues in the New Millennium,* 3rd ed., Boulder, CO: Westview Press.

Shepherd, L. J. (2015), *Gender Matters in Global Politics: A Feminist Introduction to International Relations*, 2nd ed., New York, NY: Routledge.

Sjoberg, L. (2013), *Gendering Global Conflict: Towards a Feminist Theory of War*, New York, NY: Columbia University Press.

Steans, J. (2013), *Gender and International Relations: Theory, Practice Policy* 3rd ed., Cambridge, UK: Polity Press.

Strasser, U. and Tinsman, H. (2014), "World History Meets History of Masculinity in Latin American Studies" in P. S. Nadell and K. Haulman (eds.), *Making Women's Histories: Beyond National Perspectives*, 187–210, New York, NY: New York University Press.

Tickner, J. A. (1991), "Hans Morganthau's Principles of Political Realism: A Feminist Reformulation," in R. Grant and K. Newland (eds.), *Gender and International Relations*, 27–40, Bloomington, IN: Indiana University Press.

Tickner, J. A. (2001), *Gendering World Politics: Issues and Approaches in the Post Cold War Era*, New York, NY: Columbia University Press.

Williams, A. J., Hadfield, A., and Rofe, J. S. (2012), *International History and International Relations*, New York, NY: Routledge.

CHAPTER TWO

Women, gender, and IR and critical theories

Foundational questions

How have key IR theories—liberalism, realism, and neoliberalism—been both state-centric and male-gendered in terms of philosophical and political traditions, theoretical assumptions and central categories of analysis, and in defining substantive topics and areas for empirical research?

How have constructivist approaches that recognize how state and institutional identities are socially constructed as well as historically specific challenged traditional ways of understanding international relations?

How have feminists built critical feminist IR theory to expose male privilege and marginalization of women's roles in international affairs and defined a "feminist foreign policy" that has the potential to transform the values and practice of international politics in the future?

Key concepts

Feminism(s) analyze the privileges of hegemonic masculinity that dominate and subordinate "women," based on gender. There are many disagreements among feminists regarding the sources of and remedies for women's oppression that represent liberal, radical, essentialist, Marxist-socialist, postmodern, postcolonial, multicultural, and intersectional theoretical perspectives, thus the acknowledgment that there are many feminisms. Nonetheless, all feminist theories assert women's personhood and equal value as human beings vis-à-vis men.

Hegemonic Masculinity is a term that sociologist R. W. Connell has used to describe "the most honored or desired" form of masculinity, which has a preponderance of power over all other masculinities, at specific moments in history (2000: 9–10). As the term is used in this text, hegemonic masculinity refers to the dominant or "ideal" form of masculinity as modern Western societies have defined it, or the masculine "norm" against which all "others" are judged. Western-defined hegemonic masculinity exhibits characteristics of autonomy in decision-making and freedom of action, rationality, ambition, assertiveness or aggressiveness, competitiveness, and physical strength expressed in heroic achievement or domination of the weak. In the international political realm, hegemonic masculinity is associated with white-ness or Caucasian ethnicity, Western culture, material wealth or upper-class status, and heterosexuality, that is, all the twentieth- and twenty-first-century markers of race, nationality, ethnicity, class, and sex and gender privileges.

In the elite realm of twentieth- and twenty-first-century international politics, males who lack any of these markers of privilege are subordinated or "feminized" in relation to their privileged male counterparts. All women are subordinated in relation to Western-defined hegemonic masculinity; however, some women may exhibit ideal masculine characteristics and some women may exert their race, nationality, ethnicity, class, or heterosexual privileges over some subordinated masculinities or femininities.

IR Theory provides a framework or a lens through which scholars and students of international relations can describe, analyze, and predict how individuals, states, intergovernmental organizations, NGOs, and transnational corporations understand the international political system and interact within it. IR theory prioritizes and links a set of ideas and behaviors of selected international actors to help make sense of complex world systems.

In contrast to IR theory, feminist theory seeks to identify and analyze gendered systems of power and oppression in terms of why they exist and how they operate. Feminist theory also provides a vision of the world free from gender oppression and other systems of oppression that are linked to gender oppression and proposes strategies to realize that vision.

The Nation-State is a modern cultural and political construction. Nations are defined as groups of people who share common histories, values, traditions, languages, and ethnicities. States are defined as groups of people living under a single political system and established government, delineated by territorial borders. Nation-states or "countries" as they are understood in the twentieth and twenty-first centuries, are made up of the people living within the state's territorial boundaries, under a single government. These people may have different religious or cultural backgrounds but they share some values and practices and a common "national" identity.

Historically, the field of IR has defined the role of the nation-state as the primary actor in the international system. In other words, the international system is a "state-centric" system. However, contemporary IR studies do incorporate a range of nonstate actors.

Feminists assert that modern nation-states are male-gendered in that, historically, they have been defined, governed, and defended by (mostly) men, in the interests of men.

Sovereignty is claimed by the governments of separate and autonomous nation-states. Claims of sovereignty grant governments the single legitimate political authority and right to use force within their territorial borders and to assert that no external power has the right to interfere in the nation-state's internal affairs. Nation-states recognize the sovereignty of other states when their governments establish formal diplomatic relations with one another (known as reciprocal recognition), when they assume responsibility for government debts and when they are admitted as members into formal intergovernmental bodies, such as the United Nations.

The concept of state sovereignty is also male-gendered, as it assumes the state's autonomy, independence, and authority to use force, characteristics that are associated with the masculine norm as defined in modern Western cultures.

In the post–Cold War era, limits on state sovereignty have been recognized when a state's government violates the human rights of its own people and practices or allows genocide or other crimes against humanity to take place within its territorial borders, thus calling into question the government's legitimacy. When those events occur, international coalitions of states or member states of intergovernmental organizations may determine that there is a justification for "humanitarian intervention" to halt human rights abuses.

Power as it is understood in the elite, state-centric system of international politics is usually defined as a coercive means of exerting domination and control, and associated with the Western masculine-gender norm as defined above. Feminists assert the legitimacy of another feminine-gendered definition power, usually referred to as "empowerment," as it is used positively to increase the capacity of all peoples and empower individuals within communities.

Introduction

Theory enables us to see immediate needs in terms of long-range goals and an overall perspective on the world. It thus gives us a framework for evaluating various strategies in both the long and the short run, and for seeing the types of changes they are likely to produce. Theory is not just a body of facts or a set of personal opinions. It involves explanations and hypotheses that are based on available knowledge and experience. It is also dependent on conjecture and insight about how to interpret those facts and experiences and their significance.

CHARLOTTE BUNCH 2000: 12

Conventional wisdom [of mainstream IR theorists] has it that [the international system] is a world of states, nonstate actors and market transactions. It is a world in which neither men nor women figure per se, the emphasis being on impersonal actors, structures, and system processes. Yet in the theories that depict this abstract system, there seems to be a structuring-out of women and their activities and an implicit structuring-in of men and their activities. There is a hidden gender to the field, and it affects how we think about empirical international relations and political economy. It inspires those of us who notice it to question the extent to which discontinuities in the global economy have cast shadows over gender continuities, transformed gender relations so that we no longer think of sex roles, or maintained and transformed this realm of system structure simultaneously.

CHRISTINE SYLVESTER 2001: 161

This chapter defines several key IR theories that have been used to make sense of the international political system in the twentieth and twenty-first centuries—liberalism, realism, neoliberalism, and constructivism—and explains their historic roots and their evolution. Beginning in the 1980s, feminist critiques of these conventional IR theories emerged. These critiques exposed the Western normative discourses of gender power that predominated within the international system (as well as the linked discourses of power and privilege regarding race, class, national identity, and heterosexuality) and how these discourses have shaped the ways male and female foreign-policy makers and international organizations have institutionalized and perpetuated male privilege and female subordination in international politics over the last 100 years. In other words, none of the mainstream IR theories are gender-neutral. Nor are any of the interactions between states or their representatives gender-neutral. Nor are any of the foreign policies devised by state powers or the effects of those policies on human populations gender-neutral.

Feminist scholars have also expanded the topics of inquiry and the types of sources that are used to address IR research questions. For example, feminist IR researchers may study elite or non-elite actors; they may utilize ethnographic participant-observer research methods, or examine cultural production such as art or literature or focus on discourse analyses to understand the location, expression, and uses of power in the international system. This chapter also provides an overview of various feminist theoretical prescriptions for redefining the study and practice of international relations by interjecting feminist values and principles into intergovernmental, governmental, and nongovernmental forums, institutions, agencies, treaties, policies, and programs. Finally, it introduces the twenty-first-century conceptualization of a "feminist foreign policy" as it has been theorized, embodied in a few individual elite policy makers, and practiced within a Western-defined masculine-gendered and state-centric international system.

Liberalism

The modern disciplinary study of international relations and its principal theories that have been aimed at understanding how states and other actors interacted to make war or resolve conflicts within the elite international political system emerged in the early twentieth century. IR studies and theories, however, were based on historic Western political and philosophical traditions dating back to ancient Greece and the formation of the "city-state" or the *polis*. In ancient Greece, the city-state established internal or domestic political, judicial, and social institutions and practices within its defined territorial borders, as well as external relations or international relations with other city-states and non-Greek states. Citizenship and political roles in Greek city-states were defined in gendered ways. The "public" male roles of soldier and protector of the state legitimated men's exclusive claims to citizenship and to the formulation of state policies to deal with other states in war or peace. The "private" female roles of nurturing the family and performing domestic work within the home, with no prescribed soldiering roles to secure the state's borders during war or peace time, precluded women's claims to citizenship. Classical political theory, emanating from the writings of ancient Greek philosophers Aristotle and Plato, and later echoed and developed by early modern-era European philosophers, such as Thomas Hobbes (1588–1679) and John Locke (1632–1704), defined "political *man*" as rational, independent, autonomous, and "free" to engage in formal politics, while emotional, interdependent, and unpredictable females were excluded from the public sphere and from political power.

Twentieth-century IR theories drew on these Western political foundations to explain state-to-state relationships and to respond to a new era of total warfare as it was waged during the First World War. Grounded in liberal philosophical traditions as they were articulated by John Locke who postulated the "natural rights" of all *men* to pursue "life, liberty and property," as well as on the "rational" liberal philosophy of Immanuel Kant (1724–1804), who hypothesized a "perpetual peace" that could be based on international cooperation among a confederation of democratic states governed by the rule of law, liberal IR theory proposed methods for promoting and preserving the greatest levels of individual freedom, equality, and prosperity for independent, democratically governed states in the international political arena. Liberal IR theory of the First World War era asserted that increased cooperation and collaboration among interdependent states was both rational and necessary because, as history had proven, exaggerated nationalism and imperialist rivalries between states had only led to a massively destructive war. Increased cooperation and collaboration among states would create conditions for the expansion of international trade, with economic benefits to participating nation-states. Increasing contacts and collaboration among states would lead to the evolution of common human rights principles and development of shared cosmopolitan values. Cooperative and collaborative collective security agreements among nation-states would increase the likelihood of international peace.

Liberal IR theory asserted optimistically that nation-states and other nonstate global actors shared an enlightened self-interest in seeking out cooperative international relationships to achieve the greatest good for the greatest number of people. US president Woodrow Wilson's "Fourteen Points" speech to US Congress in 1918 elaborated a doctrine of "liberal internationalism" based on optimistic liberal IR theory. Wilson's Fourteen Points outlined the goals for which the United States would fight when it entered the First World War, allied with the great European democracies Britain and France, and proposed conditions for the postwar peace settlement, correcting what had gone wrong within the nineteenth-century imperialistic international system. Many US and British liberals of the early twentieth century had asserted the principles of liberal internationalism that were included in the Fourteen Points, although Wilson was their "prime publicist" (Williams 2006: 21). Liberal internationalism promoted "open" diplomacy and an end to private and exclusionary agreements between states; freedom of passage on the seas for trade or travel; removal of restrictive trade barriers between nations; reduction of offensive armaments to reduce the likelihood of resorting to war to settle international disputes; democratic self-determination for all nations and an end to colonial relationships; and establishment of an intergovernmental organization whose member states would promote global peace through collective security arrangements and international treaties based on just, democratic values. Well-known advocates of liberal internationalism included British liberals E. H. Carr, Alfred Zimmern, Norman Angell, and Philip Noel-Baker and American liberals Edward House, Robert Lansing, Paul Kellogg, Charles and Mary Beard, and Jane Addams, among many others who supported the newly formed League of Nations. Many advocates of liberal internationalism joined liberal think tanks such as the British Royal Institute of International Affairs, and the American Carnegie Foundation for International Peace, and the Council on Foreign Relations. These First World War era liberals hoped the Fourteen Points would lead to a peaceful and progressive "new world order" that was in fact "faithful to the Anglo-Saxon" political democracy, capitalist market economy, "manly," and "muscular Christianity" traditions (Williams 2006: 40–41).

Realism

The political thought developed by English Enlightenment philosopher Thomas Hobbes provided the foundational principles upon which twentieth-century realist IR theory later developed. Hobbes understood human nature to be individualistic and self-interested, driven by fear and suspicion to compete with others for resources. The only escape from perpetual struggle and conflict was to join in a common society, bound together and governed by a single, sovereign authority (or a "Leviathan," as named by Hobbes) that maintained order and security and thus assured freedom. Twentieth-century IR "realists" adopted Hobbes's view of human nature and projected it onto the behavior of modern states. Realists had become disillusioned with the "idealism" of liberal IR theory after collective security based on international cooperation between nation-states failed to prevent the rise of aggressive fascist states in Europe and Japan in the 1930s, or the outbreak of the Second World War.

Realist IR theory accepted the prevailing world power relationships of the mid-twentieth century as a given and sought to explain the state of the world "as it existed" rather than providing a vision of what could exist in a cooperative "utopian" future world, as liberal IR theory had been criticized for doing. Postulated most famously by Hans Morganthau in his classic text *Politics Among Nations* (1948), realist IR theory asserted that struggles to maximize power governed the behavior of autonomous nation-states in an "anarchic" international system that lacked a single, sovereign authority to impose order over all. Each state struggled to maximize its relative "power" over others—usually defined as "hard power" in masculine and military terms but also measured in economic strength, industrial capacity, and sometimes in the power of ideas. Realist IR theory conceptualized the arena of world politics as a "zero-sum game," that is, what benefited one state signaled a loss for another state. Nonetheless, realist IR theory also recognized that states could and did enter alliances with others when it suited their national interests; sometimes these fluid alliances were referred to in gendered terms as "marriages of convenience." Moreover, the Great Powers could and did provide protections for their client states in the international arena in exchange for strategic advantages or to expand their moral or ideological influence. These power calculations were, theoretically, based on rational, unemotional, and objective measures. Additionally, international norms could be developed, such as the concept of state sovereignty with its attendant obligations and privileges, which also governed some aspects of states' behaviors. At the most extreme end of the spectrum in terms of emphasizing states' superior power within the international system, realist IR theory dismissed the importance of international organizations or other nonstate actors in world politics. According to realist theory, because those nonstate actors lacked military power to enforce international agreements, they lacked any "real" power; they merely possessed "soft power," that is a "feminized" version of power, to influence, but not to determine, states' behavior.

In the Cold War era that followed the Second World War, realist IR theory seemed to describe accurately the bipolar international system when the two global superpowers, the United States and the Soviet Union, were locked in a struggle for power and influence, but only if "world politics" were very narrowly defined and circumscribed. "Peace," narrowly defined as the absence of open global warfare between the United States and the Union of Soviet Socialist Republics, was maintained through a global balance of power between the "East" (Soviet-dominated socialist states) and the "West" (US-dominated democracies and client states), and through nuclear deterrence, or the notion of mutually assured destruction if either superpower unleashed its nuclear weapons arsenal on the other.

Realist IR theory provided the intellectual justifications for the Cold War–era strategic foreign-policy of containment by the United States to halt the expansion of socialist states and the power and influence of the Soviet Union. Suspicious of what they defined as expansionist Soviet intentions in Eastern Europe post–Second World War, conservative anti-communist policy makers in the US State Department who were backed by elected officials in Washington DC agreed with the conclusions of George Kennan, an analyst who worked at the US embassy in Moscow. In 1946, in a long telegram sent to his State Department superiors in Washington, Kennan asserted that the Soviet leaders were poised for an aggressive and global power grab, and advised that they must be opposed on every front. In accord with these conclusions, US president Harry S. Truman announced the "Truman Doctrine" in March 1947, and pledged US aid to those "free" peoples of the world who were resisting internal or external pressures from "totalitarian" socialist or Soviet-inspired armed forces. Kennan elaborated the policy of containment implied by the Truman Doctrine in a seminal essay on "The Sources of Soviet Conduct" published in the Washington journal *Foreign Affairs*:

> Soviet pressure against the free institutions of the western world is something that can be contained by the adroit and vigilant application of counter-force at a series of constantly shifting geographical and political points, corresponding to the shifts and maneuvers of Soviet policy, but that cannot be charmed or talked out of existence. The Russians look forward to a duel of infinite duration, and they see that already they have scored great successes.

(FOREIGN AFFAIRS JULY 25, 1947: 576)

The zero-sum game between Washington and Moscow policy makers was on for the next forty years. As realist IR theory defined it, this was the only game that mattered during the Cold War era.

Neoliberalism

Neoliberal IR theory, not to be confused with neoliberal economic theory, which will be discussed further in Chapter 5, emerged as a response to realist theory as the Cold War bipolar international system was beginning to break down during the 1970s. This was an era of *détente*, or a brief period of relaxed tensions between the United States and the Soviet Union when nuclear weapons' control agreements were negotiated through the Strategic Arms Limitations Talks and when the US Congress temporarily approved wheat sales to the Soviet Union. Neoliberal IR theory is sometimes referred to as neoliberal institutionalism or rational institutionalism. It explains how international organizations, institutions, and regimes play an important role in promoting international cooperation. While neoliberal IR theory concedes to realist theory that states are "unitary actors," meaning that states act individually and "rationally" in the international system, neoliberal theory asserts that cooperation among states in fact occurs quite frequently because it is the most rational choice for long-term absolute gains in power. According to neoliberal IR theory, this is particularly true in terms of social and economic transactions where global governance bodies and institutions that enable states' cooperation to mutually increase trade, for example, also serve an individual state's self-interests. In addition, long-term absolute gains in states' power achieved through cooperation also applies to results that can be gained through participation in collective security treaty organizations or in other states' membership organizations such as the International Criminal Court that discourage individual state's aggressions. The costs of discouraging those individual aggressive states can thus be shared by many.

Constructivism

As an approach or framework for understanding international relations, (social) constructivism focuses on the behavior of states or international organizations or nongovernmental organizations, and the individuals or international "agents" who represent them, as their behavior is shaped by shared beliefs, rules, conventions, regimes, or institutions that are all socially constructed. This core premise of constructivism has been articulated by IR scholar Nicholas Onuf (1998, 2013: 4): "Constructivism holds that people make society and society makes people. This is a continuous two-way process." Onuf linked the constructivist framework to the study of international relations by asserting that international politics operate in a "self-contained world" of our own making, with sets of rules that states and international agents devise and abide by, to help them reach their self-defined goals. Constructivist analyses recognize that nation-states do not have fixed identities or fixed national interests and that rules governing international relationships change over time because of the ongoing interactions between nation-states and other international agents. Despite their fluid nature, rules present states and international agents with certain choices, and patterns of rules and related practices establishing norms, conventions, or regimes such as those governing "sovereignty" set up certain expectations for states' and agents' behavior within the international realm. How and when and why these norms, conventions, or regimes are defined and how they evolve are the subjects of constructivist IR analyses.

Constructivist IR analyses gained saliency in the late 1980s and 1990s, as the Soviet Union dissolved and as its military alliances and ideological dominance over socialist states collapsed. At that time, the Cold War bipolar international order broke down rapidly and without much theoretical explanation by prominent realist or neoliberal IR models that had focused on military aspects of national security and on balance-of-power calculations by rational state actors. Why did the breakdown in the bipolar international order occur when it did? How did it prompt both democratic and capitalist economic transitions in former Soviet and Soviet-satellite states? What was the connection to outbreaks of ethnically driven genocidal warfare in various regions of the world that seemed to be based on shifting "national" or "cultural" identities rather than on "rational" or military power considerations? What role did these "new" wars and the forces of expanding economic, political, social, and cultural "globalization" play in transforming notions of inviolable state sovereignty into "weaker," or "feminized," definitions of sovereignty that justified "humanitarian intervention" into intrastate conflicts? These and other questions based on close observation of states' and international agents' behaviors and how to interpret them inspired constructivist analyses of international relations that took into account not just materialist structures and interests such as the relative strength of a states' economy or military or its geographic location, but also intersubjectively shared ideas, such as who is worthy of a state's protection or which genders should serve in a "modern" state's military.

Critical feminist IR theory

Feminist IR analyses locate their intellectual roots in historic feminist theoretical traditions that date back to Renaissance- and Enlightenment-era Western European feminist pioneers who identified male-over-female, power-and-privilege hierarchies as a problem to be rectified through social, economic, political, or legal means. The relative influence of feminist principles valuing women as "equal" to men in terms of their human worth and human rights, and the cross-cultural reach of feminist social movements determined to challenge masculine dominance, have ebbed and flowed during the modern era. However, a multiplication of feminist critiques of dominant and oppressive manifestations of male power, or "patriarchy," and other linked forms of oppression, and a global surge in feminist activism beginning in the 1960s has since undermined male dominance in every realm of social interaction, including elite academia, the source of IR theory, as well as the arena of international politics.

The end of the Cold War era that inspired constructivist analyses of international relations also inspired critical feminist analyses of conventional IR theories that had failed to explain the connections between states' foreign policies and a society's domestic gender power relationships and

Table 2.1 Feminist theories of IR

Liberal (or Western "Enlightenment") Feminism: asserts the "equality" of men and women in terms of their physical and intellectual capabilities and their rights to participate in the public realms of society, including male-dominated government leadership, domestic and foreign-policy-making roles and military roles. Liberal feminists argue that excluding the female half of humanity from these public roles is unjust and irrational. Gender segregation deprives global society of half its talent and, when given equal opportunities historically, women have proved their equal worth.

Radical Feminism: challenges male aggression and dominance, the devaluation of women, and the denigration of the feminine perspective in societies throughout the world. Radical feminists argue that this denigration and subordination of women allows dominant males to exert physical violence as well as to enact structural violence that threatens women's security in domestic private spaces and in national and international public spaces, during wartime and during peacetime.

Essentialist (or "Care") Feminism: asserts the value of women as women, who hold different values, adhere to a different ethics of care, and therefore exhibit different cultural behaviors in society than men do. Whether these gender differences are biologically based due to women's roles in reproduction, or whether they are socially constructed and culturally learned, essentialist feminists argue that "women" emphasize interdependent relationships and exhibit life-affirming, nurturing, and caring behaviors, and when given the opportunity they will be more successful peacemakers and peacekeepers than men.

Marxist-socialist Feminism: asserts that capitalist economic relations and patriarchal power relations are linked in ways that oppress most women. As capitalist organizations' mission to maximize profits relies on men's ability to focus on paid productive work in the public sphere and on women's unpaid reproductive work in the domestic sphere for its smooth operations, and justifies women's lower paid work in the public sphere because of women's domestic care-work obligations, Marxist-socialist feminists challenge the global capitalist economic order and the socially constructed public/private boundaries that privilege men and subordinate women in capitalist societies.

(*Continued*)

Table 2.1 Continued

Postmodern Feminism: asserts that gender roles for men and women are constructed through language and that language has the power to legitimize or delegitimize actors or their actions. Postmodern feminism rejects the false dichotomy set up by the unitary and biologically determined categories of "man" and "woman" and argues that real men and women "perform" gender differently with their bodies, based on situational contexts, and based on class and race and sexual orientations.

Postcolonial and Multicultural Feminisms: reject the often-unacknowledged privileges claimed by white, middle-class Western women, and the "othering" of all non-Western peoples in the dominant modern Western world order. Postcolonial and multicultural feminisms criticize the racist and imperialist assumptions inherent in the expansion of global neoliberal capitalism that subjugate and exploit women and men of color living in the global South, and poor and migrant populations living in the global North. Postcolonial and multicultural feminists assert that "women" must challenge gender discrimination and other forms of oppression in ways that make sense within their own cultural contexts, rather than following a Western feminist model for women's emancipation.

Intersectional feminist analyses: assert that there are multiple gender identities affected by an individual's intersecting race, class, national, and sexual identities. Power and privileges or discrimination and disadvantages adhere to these different identities in different social and global contexts. Consciously performed intersectional analyses can reduce reflexive gender stereotyping and can lead to more nuanced and effective policy making in complex world systems.

Sources: Steans, J. (2013), *Gender and International Relations: Theory, Practice, Policy*, 3rd ed., Cambridge, UK: Polity Press. Peterson, V. S. and Runyan, A. S. (2009), *Global Gender Issues in the New Millennium*, 3rd ed., Boulder, CO: Westview Press.

their combined impact on human security, both inside and outside states' borders. Whether approached through liberal, radical, essentialist, Marxist-socialist, postmodern, postcolonial, multicultural, or intersectional feminist theoretical frameworks, feminists have focused critical attention on the socially constructed nature of sex and gender roles. In recent years, feminists, especially those intellectually grounded in postcolonial, multicultural, and intersectional analyses, have acknowledged and theorized a broader range of multiple genders (multiple masculinities as well as multiple femininities) and multiple sex identities, mediated by factors of race, ethnicity, nationality, class, and sexuality, with different degrees of privilege attached to them, as well. As critical theorists, feminists have also challenged the power differentials between privileged male-gendered arenas of work, politics, the military, and paid economic activities over subordinated female-gendered arenas.

As IR scholar J. Ann Tickner has put it, Western culturally defined "gender symbolism" shapes our normative ideologies and pervades our institutions.

Masculine characteristics "such as power, strength, protection, rationality, and warrior" are juxtaposed and privileged over feminine characteristics "such as weakness, protected, emotionality, and passivity" (Tickner 2006: 389). Since the 1980s, feminist IR scholars have applied gender analyses to international studies. They have challenged the assumption that "international politics is a man's world" (Tickner 1991: 27), and have expanded the subjects of IR studies to include women as international agents. They have engaged in new initiatives to quantify and document "women's" roles and the presence of "women's" bodies in international relations. For example, feminist IR scholars and researchers associated with the WomanStats Project have produced a database that collects cross-national data on women's status and women's relative levels of "security" in 175 societies around the world and collates that data with a society's level of prosperity and peacefulness. Through its website, the WomanStats Project makes that data freely available to other researchers, national and international policy makers and to global media outlets. Feminist IR critiques have also redefined concepts that nonfeminist IR theories and studies had treated as gender-neutral, such as war, power politics, national and human security, human rights, international organizations, and transactions in the global labor market and global economy, and have exposed their masculinist biases.

In addition, feminist IR scholars have expanded their inquiries into topics previously ignored in studies of international politics. While nonfeminist IR studies had focused on the "high politics" of elite government policy makers or international organizations and multinational corporations and were primarily concerned with public and male worlds, some feminist IR studies have taken a "ground up" approach to studying how international politics and relationships impact the everyday lives of "ordinary" people. Cynthia Enloe's now-classic collection of analytical essays, *Bananas, Beaches, and Bases: Making Feminist Sense of International Politics* (1989) was one of the first IR texts to ask "where are the women?" and to look beyond elite IR policy-making circles. As IR scholars V. Spike Peterson and Anne Sisson Runyan have pointed out: "This seemingly simplistic question has yielded many insights" into the ways power operates in international relationships (2009: 8). In *Bananas, Beaches, and Bases,* for example, Enloe illuminated the roles of women as sex workers in the global sex tourism industry, as colonized subjects in Hollywood film's manufactured and masculinized nostalgia for Western empire, as prostitutes servicing Western soldiers on foreign military bases, as Western diplomats' wives promoting their nations' foreign policies, and so on. These non-elite activities located particular "women" within the field of international relations and revealed in specific ways how Western hegemonic masculine power has been projected onto the world politics arena. Moreover, these examples helped to break down what feminists saw as false divides between "international" and "domestic" politics, and between public and private gendered spheres. The outpouring of feminist IR scholarship over the past few decades has followed Enloe's lead and expanded the range of IR topics to include those previously dismissed as "marginal" to world affairs and has explained their relevance.

Feminist IR scholars have also employed methodologies borrowed from other disciplines such as anthropology, sociology, and cultural studies. In an early and often-cited example, Carol Cohn examined the "rational" world of "defense intellectuals" during the late Cold War era. As she explained their socially constructed world, these policy makers discussed the waging of nuclear warfare "dispassionately" (in their view), in "technostrategic" language that was "sanitized" and presented as gender-neutral, but was nonetheless gendered and sexualized (Cohn 1987: 687–718). Cohn analyzed the defense intellectuals' language, their social relationships, and social status by adopting ethnographic research methods and engaging as a "participant-observer" at a Harvard University summer workshop on nuclear strategy in the mid-1980s. As Cohn shared in one of many examples she recounted, she was most interested in the way that the language "functioned" for defense intellectuals in creating their hyper-masculine world views as they discussed the use of weapons that could annihilate humanity:

> Much of the sexual imagery I heard was rife with the sort of ambiguity suggested by "patting the missiles." The imagery can be construed as a deadly serious display of the connections between masculine sexuality and the arms race. At the same time, it can also be heard as a way of minimizing the seriousness of militarist endeavors, of denying their consequences. A former Pentagon target analyst, in telling me why he thought plans for a "limited nuclear war" were ridiculous, said, "Look, you gotta understand that it's a pissing contest—you gotta expect them to use everything they've got." What does this image say? Most obviously, that this is all about competition for manhood, and thus there is tremendous danger. But at the same time, the image diminishes the contest and its outcomes, by representing it as an act of boyish mischief.

> (COHN 1987: 696)

Cohn found that when she used similarly dispassionate language when discussing nuclear warfare, or adopted the "expert jargon," she was accepted into the defense intellectuals' male-gendered world. However, the abstracted language also transformed (temporarily) her own way of thinking, and she became disconnected from thinking about the human lives that nuclear weapons would claim if they were actually deployed. Cohn's ethnographic research taught her in an experiential way "something about the militarization of the mind" that took place in male-dominated IR policy-making circles (1987: 714).

Feminist IR theory has also included an activist dimension that has proposed strategies to interject feminist women into international realms and institutions where Western-defined hegemonic masculine power predominates, in order to transform and humanize those realms and relationships. Or, as Cohn has put it, feminists have engaged in a "deconstructive" as well as a "reconstructive" project—deconstructing the masculinized practice of international relations and reconstructing "compelling alternative visions of possible futures" of a "more just and peaceful world" (1987: 717–18). Whether feminists advocated "mainstreaming" strategies that positioned feminist women "inside" male-dominated governments or intergovernmental organizations where international institutions, regimes, and policies were constructed, or whether they proposed oppositional strategies that focused on the roles played by nonstate actors and on critical theories that challenged the dominant gender order from the "outside," diverse feminist perspectives have focused on transforming conflict-based international relations into "peaceful" and mutually beneficial international relations (in the broadest definition of "peace" as explained further in Chapter 3).

Regarding the often-conflict-based interstate or intrastate interactions, IR scholar Kimberly Hutchins has explained a major point of difference among various feminist theoretical approaches that have addressed the problem of political violence in the conduct of international relations. Although feminist scholars recognize that "women" can be aggressors during times of war and "women" may engage in violence themselves or support the use of violence by others to achieve political goals, feminists have fundamental disagreements regarding the ethics of political violence. "Liberal" feminists, or "enlightenment" feminists as Hutchins refers to them, trace their intellectual roots to Western Enlightenment values such as expanding universal human rights based on international laws that guarantee equality of status and privilege for men and women and individual freedoms for all. Liberal feminists reject the exclusion of women from all public realms of society, including exclusion from equal participation in "just" wars, and so they sometimes support the use of political violence. The concept of "just" wars will be discussed further in Chapter 3. Here it will be noted that Hutchins explains how liberal feminists draw distinctions between ethical and unethical political violence and legitimate and illegitimate targets of violence. Liberal feminists are open to engaging in interstate wars and support "humanitarian intervention" into intrastate or interstate conflicts. They accept the use of violence as a political means, to halt violence toward disempowered groups for an ethical end (2007: 93–95).

In contrast with liberal feminists who accept that women's participation in state-sponsored political violence may be necessary, Hutchins identifies "care" feminism, or what this text refers to as "essentialist" feminism, that always opposes political violence as a male-gendered act of force. Care feminism, like liberal feminism, postulates a "universal" code of ethical values, applicable across historical eras, cultures, and geopolitical boundaries. While liberal feminists assert that "equality" of opportunity for women and men to participate in all social and political realms has universal ethical value, care feminists emphasize the important ethical value of "care" for others, based on a "female" model of humanity that universally nurtures and cares for others, as mothers care for their children. This "essentialist" understanding of gender difference asserts that "women" are essentially different from "men" in their motivations and behaviors. Care feminists therefore cannot sanction the use of violence, as violence "perpetuates [Western-defined hegemonic] masculine behaviors and excludes women" from public policy-making spaces (Hutchins 2007: 93–94, 98).

Hutchins defines a third feminist theoretical perspective on political violence, a "postcolonial" feminism, which "challenges the ethical universalism of both enlightenment and care feminisms." Postcolonial feminists focus on "the ethical significance of context" and assert the ethical necessity of recognizing the differences among "women" around the world. Women's gender identities and access to "power" are based on their particular historical and cultural locations, and the ethics of engaging in political violence is connected to those differences (2007: 94, 96). From the postcolonial feminist perspective, women's participation in acts of political violence can be ethically justified in wars for national liberation or struggles for self-determination that revolt against colonial (and neocolonial) power relations (2007: 97).

Liberal feminists who assert the democratic principle of "women's" necessary and equal participation in all realms of society, and postcolonial feminists who emphasize political and historical contexts that justify "women's" participation in international relations, are also joined by essentialist feminists who make their own arguments for women's necessary participation in elite international political arenas. Asserting that "women" (generally) possess unique and valuable qualities of nurturance, cooperation, and high regard for human life, essentialist feminists argue that these "feminine" qualities are also necessary for preservation of all life on the planet. Therefore "women" must be integrally involved with global policy making as it relates to security, human rights, environmental sustainability, social and economic development, and so forth. While contemporary academic feminists and other scholars sometimes dismiss essentialist arguments for, or against, women's participation in international affairs, IR scholar Jill Steans has observed that "gender essentialism is far from dead in 'real-world' politics" (2013: 11). The international episodes recounted and issues raised in this textbook confirm that observation.

Feminist foreign policy

In the last few decades a new concept, a so-called feminist foreign policy, has entered the realm of international studies and the wider public debate, as scholars and activists have attempted to link feminist theory to practice. The foundational principles of a feminist foreign policy have been drawn from feminist IR critiques of conventional gender-blind IR theories and the entrenched power structures that have privileged Western-defined hegemonic masculinity in the contemporary international system. With those criticisms in mind, a feminist foreign policy must be transformative and reject the usual practice of elitist power politics. A feminist foreign policy elevates human security and freedom from physical or structural violence for all as the goal and raison d'etre of international relations. A feminist foreign policy, therefore, is based on an ethics of care and justice for all human life, and for all other forms of life on the planet. A feminist foreign policy includes women and other marginalized groups and their needs and concerns as participants and guiding subjects of international policy making, recognizing, and challenging linked hierarchies of power and oppression based on gender, race, class, nationality, sexuality, and so on. A feminist foreign policy champions human rights for all, with no distinctions between men's human rights and women's human rights. A feminist foreign policy promotes cooperative relationships, collective security arrangements, corporate social responsibility, and environmental sustainability. It criticizes militarized states and militarized economies that enable a first-resort response to violence to resolve conflicts at all levels of social interaction.

Feminist foreign policy as embodied and practiced by US secretary of state Hillary Clinton and Swedish foreign minister Margot Wallström.

A few of the world's global policy makers, including US secretary of state Hillary Rodham Clinton (2009–13) and Swedish minister for foreign affairs Margot Wallström (2014–to date), have articulated the fundamental principles of a feminist foreign policy in recent years. As secretary of state, Hillary Clinton expressed the feminist maxim that IR scholar Valerie Hudson and feminist journalist Patricia Leidl have dubbed "the Hillary doctrine," that is, "the subjugation of women is a direct threat to the common security of the world and the national security of the United States" (Hudson and Leidl 2015: xiv, quoting Clinton 2010). Margot Wallström, when she became foreign minister in 2014, announced openly that, moving forward, Sweden would pursue a "feminist foreign policy." These foreign-policy makers have also taken steps to put feminist principles into practice in the masculine arena of international politics.

Hillary Rodham Clinton grew up in the 1960s as a broad-based feminist social movement was beginning to challenge masculine privilege and sexism in every realm of American society, public and private. As a graduate of Wellesley College and Yale Law School, Clinton entered the nation's educated elite. Her interests in social justice, women's rights, and children's welfare led her to pursue work in American politics and law circles, first in Washington, DC, and then in Arkansas. After her husband, William Jefferson (Bill) Clinton, became governor of Arkansas in 1978, she served as an activist first lady. She led a task force to improve education in Arkansas and served on national boards for the Children's Defense Fund, the Child Care Action Campaign, and the Children's Television Workshop while she also practiced law in a private firm. When Bill Clinton was elected president of the United States in 1992, Hillary Clinton breached many of the traditional gender expectations for the nation's first lady, going far beyond the bounds of attending ceremonial functions and acting as official hostess to White House visitors when the president appointed her to lead a national health-care policy reform task force in 1993. She also acted as one of the president's close advisers on foreign-policy matters, weighing in on US military interventions into Haiti, Rwanda, and Bosnia, for example. By 1995, Hillary Clinton was engaging in more overtly feminist activities at the national and international levels, advocating for women's and girl's "empowerment" through education, enhanced economic opportunities, and expansion of legally protected human rights and anti-violence and anti-trafficking measures. Hillary Clinton's plenary speech at the UN Fourth World Conference on Women held in Beijing in 1995 established her global stature as a liberal feminist spokeswoman when she declared: "If there is one message that echoes forth from this conference, let it be that human rights are women's rights and women's rights are human rights, once and for all" (Clinton 1995). Throughout Bill Clinton's second term as president, Hillary Clinton joined the president and his secretary of state, Madeleine Albright, in supporting women's human rights and women's empowerment through various State Department initiatives that included a global program offering support and training for women's political involvement in societies undergoing democratic transitions and a global anti-trafficking campaign. As President Clinton finished his second term on office in 2000, Hillary Clinton entered electoral politics and won a seat in the US Senate representing New York State in 2000, and was re-elected in 2006. In 2008, she campaigned for the Democratic Party nomination for president, but lost to her opponent Barack Obama. When he was elected president, Barack Obama appointed Hillary Clinton as secretary of state in 2009.

As secretary of state, Hillary Clinton served in an administration and presided over a State Department that established policies and funded programs to promote women's rights nationally and internationally and that foregrounded attention to women's roles in US National Security Strategy documents. To institutionalize her liberal feminist goals to advance gender equality and justice, she elevated the status of the State Department's Office of Global Women's Issues, significantly increased its budget, and appointed her former chief of staff and feminist ally, Melanne Verveer, to head the office at the rank of ambassador. She also pushed for the integration of gender analyses and attention to women's rights and status in every political and economic policy office within the Department, a practice known as "gender mainstreaming" that will be discussed further in Chapters 4 and 5 ahead. Regarding US development policy as advanced through the US Agency for International Development (USAID), Clinton announced that investment in the education and empowerment of women and girls would be one of the six foundational principles guiding US development strategies to lead to "a safer, more prosperous, more democratic, and more

FIGURE 2.1 UN 464917 *Hillary Rodham Clinton, secretary of state of the United States of America, addresses the opening of the 16th session of the Human Rights Council, in Geneva, Switzerland. February 28, 2011. Credit: UN Photo/ Jean-Marc Ferré*

equitable world" (Clinton 2010b). Through her speeches and published articles Clinton supported the establishment of UN Women in 2010, a UN agency that consolidated and strengthened the efforts of four previously established UN agencies dedicated to women's advancement, gender research, women and development, and integration of women's issues in all UN agencies. Hillary Clinton also used her global bully pulpit as US secretary of state to advocate for women's necessary and equal involvement in peace negotiations and peacekeeping operations worldwide, supporting UN Security Council Resolution (UNSCR) 1325 on Women, Peace, and Security, as well as related Security Council Resolutions 1820, 1888, 1889, and 1960. In the United States, she led efforts to develop the US National Action Plan to operationalize the goals of UNSCR 1325 and to promote gender equality in US foreign-policy-making and national security branches of government. Justifying her liberal feminist positions and their translation into State Department practices when she was secretary of state in rational and "realist" terms, Hillary Clinton asserted:

> The United States has made empowering women and girls a cornerstone of our foreign policy, because women's equality is not just a moral issue, it's not just a humanitarian issue, it is not just a fairness issue, it is a

security issue. It is a prosperity issue and it is a peace issue. And therefore, when I talk about the need to integrate women's issues into discussions at the highest levels everywhere in the world, I'm not just doing it because I have a personal commitment . . . I'm doing it because it's in the vital interest of the United States.

HUDSON AND LEIDL 2015: 278, QUOTING CLINTON 2010

In their analysis of "the Hillary doctrine," Valerie Hudson and Patricia Leidl acknowledged the important feminist theory–inspired rhetorical, resource allocation, and programmatic shifts in US State Department under Secretary Clinton's leadership. They also asserted that far more fundamental cultural shifts and much broader reformulations of gender expectations had to occur in order to consistently implement the feminist foreign policy that the Hillary doctrine implies. For example, in terms of how the United States (or any nation) determines when to go to war, for it to be a legitimate decision, the decision makers must include women who participate fully and on an equal basis with men. The rules for waging war must include effective protections for civilian lives and absolute rejection of sexual violence and rape as weapons of war. In post-conflict zones, the protection of women's and other vulnerable population's physical safety must be included in states' and the UN's postwar reconstruction plans. None of these fundamental shifts occurred to truly transform US foreign-policy-making or US actions in the global arena during Clinton's tenure as secretary of state. Despite her energetic advocacy of feminist foreign-policy principles, Hillary Clinton faced, as one reviewer noted, "the sclerosis of the U.S. policy making bureaucracy and the opposition and indifference of foreign governments to women's rights and gender equity concerns" (Nossel 2016).

Moreover, Hillary Clinton's critics have sometimes accused her of being a "hawk" when she served as secretary of state, because she advocated for the use of military force and supported expanding military interventions in Afghanistan, Libya, and Syria during President Obama's first term in office (Zenko 2016). Feminist critics have documented the many ways that women's experience of wars is qualitatively and quantitatively distinct from the ways that men experience wars. They argue that very few, if any, of women's wartime experiences promote human security or shift the gender power balance toward more social, economic, or political equality for women. During Hillary Clinton's tenure as secretary of state, US State Department programs and engagements with foreign governments elevated the importance of women's rights and status, the State Department rhetoric was changed to make "women" more visible in international politics, and the US government increased the resources that were dedicated to women's development programs. Nonetheless, US engagement in foreign wars was not diminished and Clinton did not back away from the use of political violence to achieve US security objectives.

Margot Wallström, born in 1954, entered political life through Sweden's Social Democratic Party Youth League. She was elected to Sweden's national parliament, the *Riksdag*, representing the Social Democratic Party in 1979 and served until 1985. Following that service, she held several high-level appointments in Sweden's national government, as deputy minister for civil affairs in the late 1980s, then as minister for culture, followed by minister for social affairs during the 1990s. Wallström's political career took an international turn in the late 1990s, when she was appointed as European commissioner for the environment (1999–2004). She then served as vice president for the European commission in charge of institutional relations and communication (2004–10), and then as the first special representative of the UN secretary-general on Sexual Violence in Conflict (2010–12). When Sweden's Social Democratic Party leader Stefan Löfvan became prime minister in October 2014, he brought Margot Wallström, who had proven herself to be a strong advocate for gender justice, into his government to lead the Foreign Ministry. Following her appointment as foreign minister, Wallström announced that Sweden would follow a "feminist foreign policy." She has asserted that, "It's time to become a little braver in foreign policy. I think feminism is a good term. It is about standing against the systematic and global subordination of women" (Aggestam and Bergman-Rosamond 2016: 1, quoting Wallström 2016).

In Sweden's "Foreign Service Action Plan for Feminist Foreign Policy, 2015–2018," Sweden's Foreign Ministry laid out its plans to make gender equality a reality, asserting that gender equality is "essential for the achievement of the Government's other overall objectives, such as peace, security and sustainable development." As feminist theorists have argued the point elsewhere, Margot Wallström has also asserted in her public speeches that discrimination and violence against women threatens global peace and human security (Rupert 2015). Sweden's Foreign Ministry announced that all foreign policies were to be based on sex-disaggregated data that was subjected to gender analysis, and Swedish policy would adhere to the myriad international laws and EU gender-equality agreements that were already in place. Those agreements began with the 1948 Universal Declaration of Human Rights and have been elaborated in many subsequent human rights agreements among UN member states and EU countries. They include, notably, the landmark UNSCR 1325 on women's full and equal participation in all international peace and security operations, and have expanded with further measures that guaranteed protections from gender-based violence in time of war, and inclusion of women and gender analyses in disarmament and arms control negotiations and counter-terrorism measures. Sweden's Foreign Service Action Plan for Feminist Foreign Policy also pledged adherence to the 2030 Agenda for Sustainable Development that UN member states adopted unanimously in September 2015. The 2030 Agenda (to be discussed further in Chapter 5) outlined

FIGURE 2.2 **UN 711690** *Margot Wallström, minister for foreign affairs of Sweden and president of the Security Council for January 2017, addresses journalists with Secretary-General António Guterres on the Council's open debate on conflict prevention and sustaining peace. January 10, 2017. Credit: UN Photo/ Eskinder Debebe*

seventeen Sustainable Development Goals and 169 specific targets related to protecting the global environment and to establishing a global economy, global society, and global governance bodies based on principles of gender equality and economic justice. The Foreign Service Action Plan pledged that Sweden would continue to play a leading role in implementing the gender-equality goals within the 2030 Agenda for Sustainable Development, as it had played an active and "often decisive" role in formulating those goals. Following Sweden's 2016 election as one of the non-permanent members of the UN Security Council for a two-year term from January 2017 through December 2018, Foreign Minister Wallström is expected to advance her deeply held feminist foreign-policy principles within the most elite decision-making chamber of the United Nations, among the world's most influential leaders. Wallström's feminist principles would be consistent with what IR scholars Karin Aggestam and Annika Bergman-Rosamond have described as "Sweden's sense of self-identity as a 'humanitarian superpower'" (2016: 4).

Margot Wallström has already acted on her feminist foreign-policy principles, as the following example demonstrates. In 2015, the foreign minister reformulated Sweden's relations with Saudi Arabia and with Swedish arms manufacturers, based on the Löfvan government's pledges to promote gender equality, human rights, and human security in its international affairs. In February 2015, Wallström frankly criticized Saudi Arabia's dictatorial form of government, legal and social discriminations against women, and harsh suppression of Saudi social and political dissidents. She also characterized Saudi Arabia's social relations as "medieval" (Nordberg 2015). In response, Saudi Arabia temporarily cut off diplomatic relations with Sweden; Saudi Arabia's ally, the United Arab Emirates, followed suit. Löfvan's government, influenced by Foreign Minister Wallström, also determined that it would not renew a longstanding bilateral arms sale agreement with Saudi Arabia. Swedish arms exporters, a significant corporate business interest, objected, as did many other financial leaders and diplomats in Sweden, but the decision of the Social Democratic coalition government held firm. In many instances, the government's foreign policy has been implemented in ways that were consistent with the foreign minister's stated feminist foreign-policy principles. Nonetheless, Sweden's foreign policy is not without its contradictions. Feminists have criticized Sweden's immigration policy for disproportionately restricting the admission of women immigrants and for redirecting development funds that would have aided women in Third World nations to managing the post-2015 influx of immigrants into the nation (Aggestam and Bergman-Rosamond 2016: 7–8).

Summing up

IR theories have emerged at specific historical moments throughout the twentieth and into the twenty-first centuries. These theories have been based, in part, on close observations of states' behavior and on the behavior of other nonstate actors who have engaged in international politics. Some elements that have determined this behavior have been acknowledged by theorists in the past, and the relative importance of these various elements—such as states' "power" in terms of military strength or industrial capacity or geographical location or control over natural resources or ideology—have been debated and foregrounded by different theorists, depending, in part, on the global historical context. Until mid-twentieth century, however, the gender power exerted by male leaders who most closely identified with white-ness or Caucasian ethnicity, Western culture, material wealth or upper-class status, and heterosexuality had not been acknowledged as an integral component that determined the behaviors of states or other actors in global politics. Feminists and other critical IR theorists introduced gender power into the equation, identifying Western-defined male privilege as fundamental to explaining how international relations have operated and have perpetuated global maldistributions of power. Feminists have also raised these criticisms with a purposeful action agenda: to advocate for radical transformations of international power relationships in order to achieve greater measures of human security and planetary security, and to achieve equality of human rights for all.

References for further study

Blanchard, E. M. (2003), "Gender, International Relations, and the Development of Feminist Security Theory," *Signs: Journal of Women in Culture and Society*, 28: 1289–1312.

Enloe, C. (1989), *Bananas Beaches and Bases: Making Feminist Sense of International Politics*, London, UK: Pandora.

Hudson, V. M. and Leidl, P. (2015), *The Hillary Doctrine: Sex & American Foreign Policy*, New York, NY: Columbia University Press.

Lobasz, J. and Sjoberg, L. (2011), "The State of Feminist Security Studies: A Conversation," *Politics & Gender*, 7: 573–604.

Web resources

Clinton, H. "Remarks at TEDWomen Conference," December 8, 2010. http://blog.ted.com/ted-blog-exclusive-hillary-rodham-clinton-at-tedwomen/ (Accessed July 11, 2017).

Ministry of Foreign Affairs, "Swedish Foreign Service Action Plan for Feminist Foreign Policy 2015–18, Including Focus Areas for 2016." http://www.government.se/contentassets/b799e89a0e06493f86c63a561e869e91/action-plan-feminist-foreign-policy-2015-2018 (Accessed July 11, 2017).

Wallström, M. Swedish Minister of Foreign Affairs at Georgetown Institute for Women, Peace and Security, Georgetown University, April 3, 2016. https://www.youtube.com/watch?v=wE7R-Y8gXfo (Accessed July 11, 2017).

Wilson, W. "President Woodrow Wilson's Fourteen Points, 8 January 1918." http://avalon.law.yale.edu/20th_century/wilson14.asp (Accessed July 11, 2017).

WomanStats Project http://www.womanstats.org (Accessed July 11, 2017).

Bibliography

Aggestam, K. and Bergman-Rosamond, A. (2016), "Swedish Feminist Foreign Policy in the Making: Ethics, Politics, and Gender," *Ethics & International Affairs*, 30: 1–12.

Blanchard, E. M. (2003), "Gender, International Relations, and the Development of Feminist Security Theory," *Signs: Journal of Women in Culture and Society*, 28: 1289–1312.

Bunch, C. (2000), "Not By Degrees: Feminist Theory and Education," in W. Kolmar and F. Bartkowski (eds.), *Feminist Theory: A Reader*, 11–15, Mountain View, CA: Mayfield Publishing Company.

Clinton, H. R. (1995), "Remarks," *United Nations Fourth World Conference on Women Plenary Session*, Beijing, Peoples Republic of China.

Clinton, H. R. (2010a), "Remarks," TEDWomen Conference, Washington DC (Accessed July 13, 2017).

Clinton, H. R. (2010b), "Remarks on the 15th Anniversary of the International Conference on Population and Development." (Accessed July 11, 2017).

Cohn, C. (1987), "Sex and Death in the Rational World of Defense Intellectuals," *Signs: Journal of Women and Culture in Society*, 12: 687–718.

Connell, R. W. (2000), *The Men and the Boys*, Cambridge, UK: Polity Press.

Diez, T., Bode, I., and Fernandes Da Costa, A. (2011), *Key Concepts in International Relations*, Thousand Oaks, CA: Sage Publications.

Garner, K. (2010), *Shaping a Global Women's Agenda: Women's NGOs and Global Governance*. Manchester, UK: Manchester University Press.

Garner, K. (2013), *Gender and Foreign Policy in the Clinton Administration*, Boulder, CO: First Forum Books, Lynne Rienner Publishers.

Goldstein, J. S. and Pevehouse J. C. (2006), *International Relations*, 7th ed., New York, NY: Pearson Longman.

Grant, R. (1991), "The Sources of Gender bias in International Relations Theory," in R. Grant and K. Newland (eds.), *Gender and International Relations*, 8–26, Bloomington, IN: Indiana University Press.

Handler, S. P. (2013), *International Politics: Classic and Contemporary Readings*, Thousand, Oaks, CA: CQ Press Sage Publications.

Helbich, W. J. (1967–68), "American Liberals in the League of Nations Controversy," *The Public Opinion Quarterly*, 31: 568–96.

Hoffman, J. (2001), *Gender and Sovereignty: Feminism, the State and International Relations*, New York, NY: Palgrave MacMillan.

Hooper, C. (2001), *Manly States: Masculinities, International Relations and Gender Politics*, New York, NY: Columbia University Press.

Hopton, J. (2003), "The State and Military Masculinity," in P. R. Higate (ed.), *Military Masculinities: Identity and the State*, 111–23, Westport, CT: Praeger.

Hutchins, K. (2007), "Feminist Ethics and Political Violence," *International Politics*, 44: 90–106.

Karns, M., Mingst, K. A., and Stiles, K. W. (2015), *International Organizations: The Politics and Processes of Global Governance*, 3rd ed., Boulder, CO: Lynne Rienner.

Kaufman, J. (2013), *Introduction to International Relations: Theory and Practice*, Lanham, MD: Rowman & Littlefield Publishers, Inc.

Kennan, G. (1947), "The Sources of Soviet Conduct," *Foreign Affairs*, 25: 566–82.

Mattina, A. F. (2004), "Hillary Rodham Clinton: Using her Vital Voice," in M. M. Wertheimer (ed.), *Inventing a Voice: The Rhetoric of American First Ladies of the Twentieth Century*, 417–34, Lanham, MD: Rowman & Littlefield Publishers, Inc.

Miller, F. (1999), "Feminisms and Transnationalism," in M. Sinha, D. Guy, and A. Woollacott (eds.), *Feminisms and Internationalism*, 225–36, Malden, MA: Blackwell Publishers, Ltd.

Morganthau, H. J. and Thompson, K. W. (1948, 1985), *Politics Among Nations: The Struggle for Power and Peace*, New York, NY: Knopf.

Nordberg, J. (2015), "Who's Afraid of a Feminist Foreign Policy?" *The New Yorker*.

Nossel, S. (2016), "A Feminist Foreign Policy," *Foreign Affairs*, 95: 162–67.

Onuf, N. (1998, 2013), "Constructivism: A User's Manual," in N. Onuf (ed.), *New International Relations: Making Sense, Making Worlds, Constructivism in Social Theory and International Relations*, 3–20, New York, NY: Routledge.

Peterson, V. S. and Runyan, A. S. (2009), *Global Gender Issues in the New Millennium*, 3rd ed., Boulder, CO: Westview Press.

Rai, S. M. and Waylen, G. (2008), *Global Governance: Feminist Perspectives*, New York, NY: Palgrave MacMillan.

Rupert, J. (2015), "Sweden's Foreign Minister Explains Feminist Foreign Policy," *United States Institute of Peace*.

Stachowitsch, S. (2012), "Military Gender Integration and Foreign Policy in the United States: A Feminist International Relations Perspective," *Security Dialogue*, 43: 305–21.

Steans, J. (2013), *Gender and International Relations: Theory, Practice Policy*, 3rd ed., Cambridge, UK: Polity Press.

Sterling-Folker, J. (2013), *Making Sense of International Relations Theory*, 2nd ed., Boulder, CO: Lynne Rienner Publishers.

Sylvester, C. (2001), *Feminist International Relations: An Unfinished Journey*, New York, NY: Cambridge University Press.

Tickner, J. A. (1991), "Hans Morganthau's Principles of Political Realism: A Feminist Reformulation," in R. Grant and K. Newland (eds.), *Gender and International Relations*, 27–40, Bloomington, IN: Indiana University Press.

Tickner, J. A. (2001), *Gendering World Politics: Issues and Approaches in the Post-Cold War Era*, New York, NY: Columbia University Press.

Tickner, J. A. (2006), "On the Frontlines or Sidelines of Knowledge and Power? Feminist Practices of Responsible Scholarship," *International Studies Review*, 8: 383–95.

True, J. (2016), "Why We Need a Feminist Foreign Policy to Stop War," *Open Democracy*.

Viotti, P. R. and Kauppi, M. V. (2012), *International Relations Theory*, 5th ed., Glenview, IL: Longman Pearson Publishers.

Wibben, A. T. (2016), "The Value of Feminist Scholarship on Security," *The Journal of Turkish Weekly* (available online).

Williams, A. (2006), *Liberalism and War: The Victors and the Vanquished*, New York: NY: Routledge.

Youngs, G. (2004), "Feminist International Relations: A Contradiction in Terms? Or: Why Women and Gender are Essential to Understanding the World 'we' Live in," *International Affairs*, 80: 75–87.

Zenko, M. (2016), "Hillary the Hawk: A History," *Foreign Policy*.

CHAPTER THREE

Women, gender, and war

Foundational questions

How have "women" participated in and experienced the pivotal international wars of the twentieth century: the First and Second World Wars and the Cold War, and a critical "new" war of the 1990s, in Bosnia-Herzegovina?

How have governments or other warring groups constructed masculine and feminine gender roles to justify their decisions to go to war, or to define men's and women's participation in wars?

How have nonstate actors constructed gender roles to support or to oppose wars?

How were Western normative male-over-female gender power relationships transformed (or not) during these wars?

Key concepts

Militarism glorifies war making through words, images, and actions. Although states' militaries may necessarily take up arms to protect citizens and property from aggressive attacks, when societies and their institutions and populations are focused in their purpose, or structure or activities on war making, they are militarized. National economies can be militarized when military spending outpaces general-welfare spending and monopolizes government funds that could be applied for social purposes such as education, health care, poverty reduction, or environmental protection. National domestic politics can be militarized when national security concerns dominate all other social or economic policy issues. Linking the qualities of Western hegemonic masculinity such as heroism and "manly" displays of courage, stoicism, toughness, and dominance to soldiering, policing, and other security professions valorizes militarized activities; at the same time, these linkages devalue other non-militarized and feminized activities and populations. In militarized societies, women and other feminized populations can gain value and status through their support for war making, and political decision makers may recognize that these populations are vitally important to war making and other militarized social operations. But even when they take on soldiering duties, women and other feminized populations remain subordinated to the males in charge of the militarized realms.

Peace has been defined negatively as the absence of interstate war or violent conflict waged by armed forces in traditional accounts of international history or international relations. More recently, scholars and activists have defined the notion of "positive peace," which sets a higher standard for what constitutes a state of peace and the elements that are necessary for successful peacekeeping or peace-building efforts. Peace researchers such as Johan Galtung, for example, have defined positive peace as requiring the absence of "structural violence" as well as the absence of armed physical violence that inflicts bodily harm (2013: 173). When human populations are exploited or are discriminated against by institutionalized forms of racism, sexism, or coercive political repression, or when human rights are violated by structures of inequality that result in some populations living in abject poverty or in fear, they are subjected to structural violence that prevents the realization of peace. Ending open warfare without addressing the conditions of structural violence may result in a ceasefire but does not address the inequalities that cause violent wars or create the conditions for sustainable peace. Conditions of structural violence that are not addressed by state elite policy makers also diminish human security, and disproportionately so for women and other feminized populations, thus reflecting and perpetuating gender inequalities.

Security like peace, traditionally was understood by international history and IR scholars and government leaders in limited, sovereign state-centric, and militarized ways: as *national security* provided by the abstract, de-gendered state to protect citizens and property within its territorial borders from external state aggressors. Realist IR theories assert that national security is achieved through states' utilization, or threat to use, military force against external or internal aggressors. Liberal and neoliberal IR theories emphasize the rule of law and international cooperation among states formalized through collective security agreements to achieve national security. Critical IR theories formulated by constructivists and feminists have questioned states' roles and records as the sole protectors and providers of "security" for all populations, in all times of war and peace. Based on observations and analysis of the ways that coercive force is manifested and applied in the international system, these critical theories have expanded the goals of global "security" to refer more broadly to the security of human beings, as opposed to security of the abstract nation-state. As these critical IR theories explain, threats to *human security* may emanate from inside as well as outside state borders and may be perpetrated by states or nonstate actors. By promising to provide militarized national security, for example, masculinized states may abuse their power and oppress women and other feminized populations. Threats to human security may also be economic or environmental in nature or may be driven by racial or ideological or religious differences, but, they are always gendered.

War and its causes, conduct, and consequences have been central concerns of international history and IR scholars as wars force all combatants, and by extension all members of society, to examine their most fundamental beliefs and values and determine what they are willing to kill or die for. IR scholar Joshua Goldstein provides a concise definition of war as "lethal intergroup violence," that is, organized and sustained violence that occurs between states, communities, or ethnic or other groups who have opposing interests and who engage in violent resolution of those disputes with the intent to kill their opponents (2001: 3).

War making is a highly gendered activity. Historically and across cultures, male decision makers and warriors, mostly but not exclusively, planned and waged "interstate" and "intrastate" or civil wars. War makers have cultivated hypermasculine-gendered attributes—such as violence, aggression, physical strength, and misogyny—to win wars and force enemies to retreat. Nonetheless, war making requires the participation of all warring groups' members, male and female. Moreover, masculine- and feminine-gendered messages are used to mobilize groups to go to war and to fight with intent to kill opponents. "Women" may be portrayed as victims in need of male protection, as keepers of cultural traditions, or as symbols of national or group identities worth fighting for in war-mobilization messages. Or, "women" may be gender stereotyped as natural peace makers because women have the biological potential to give birth and therefore have a special interest in nurturing human life. These gender stereotypes of women as victims of wars, keepers of traditions, symbols of the nation, peacemakers, and nurturers predominate in many cultures even though women warriors who exhibit hypermasculine-gendered attributes can be found in nearly all societies.

Beginning in the twentieth century and because of the development of more lethal weapons and technology during the First World War, the waging of "total war" emerged as a war strategy. Total wars deliberately involved civilian populations in ways that previous centuries' wars that were fought by states' military forces on defined battlefields or at sea, and with less-destructive weapons, did not. Total wars aimed for total destruction of the enemy's war-making capabilities. Consequently, with the use of increasingly lethal weapons capable of mass destruction, and because of the greater frequency and regularity with which their combatants have transgressed moral boundaries, thus committing "crimes against humanity," total wars of the twentieth century have racked up huge death tolls.

IR scholar Mary Kaldor (1999, 2012) has asserted that a "new" form of war has gained prominence in recent decades. "New" wars are related to the emergence of the post–Cold War international system that lacked the bipolar superpower structure to enforce world order, as tenuous and narrowly defined as that "order" may have been. In explaining the causes, conduct, and consequences of new wars in theoretical and descriptive terms, Kaldor has noted that they most often pit intrastate groups against one another. New wars are often "caused" by particularistic ethnic, ideological, or religious differences between warring groups, rather than by more traditional interstate competition for territory or resources. New wars are often fought in decentralized ways, targeting civilians as well as opponents' armies or military installations. They also involve nonstate groups such as rebels, terrorist networks, or private military security companies, although any of these nonstate groups may have connections to international or transnational groups and resources. Finally, they are linked to post–Cold War globalization of the world market economy, and are often financed by global capital networks and supplied through a global legal or black-market arms trade. New wars, like old wars, are fought in gendered ways, with significant targeting of women and feminized populations through gendered forms of male violence.

Introduction

Historically, there is a reciprocal relationship between militarism and masculinity. On the one hand, politicians have utilized ideologies of idealized masculinity that valorize the notion of strong, active males collectively risking their personal safety for the greater good of the wider community, gaining support for the state's use of violence, such as wars in the international arena and aggressive policing in the domestic situation. On the other hand, militarism feeds into ideologies of masculinity through the eroticization of stoicism, risk taking, and even lethal violence. This can be detected in populist fiction and non-fictional books about war and weapons and in newspaper coverage of military actions.

JOHN HOPTON 2003: 113

Wars are often couched in terms of their protection of women, even when that is not their primary purpose or primary goal. What Just Warriors have defended, throughout history, is their women and children. Defining women and children in need of protection, then, is not only productive of gender subordination but also of war itself. Feminists have argued that "wars are humanized by their function of protecting women, because

Just Warriors make the world safe for their women and protect other women who are being abused."

LAURA SJOBERG AND JESSICA L. PEET 2011: 174

We will never usefully understand armed conflicts if we stubbornly focus our attention solely on the immediate war zone: we have to learn how to do gender analyses of refugee camps, of markets, of peace negotiations. . . . [Moreover] the months and years so comfortably labeled "postwar" in practice are riddled with wartime ideas about men-as-actors and women-as-victims, misleading ideas that serve to perpetuate the very conditions that set off the conflict in the first place.

CYNTHIA ENLOE 2013: XV–XVI

This chapter surveys the history of "women's" experiences in pivotal wars of the twentieth century, the First and Second World Wars, the Cold War, and the Bosnian War. During these wars, stereotypical Western gender constructions of "women" were contrasted with stereotypical gender constructions of "men" to generate popular support for war policies that required great human sacrifices at great economic cost. As Jean Bethke Elshtain has explained these two predominant but "mythical" female and male gender stereotypes: Western societies constructed "women" as "Beautiful Souls" who needed male protection and inspired male sacrifice by being innocent and pure of heart and by offering "succor and compassion" to the male warriors, and constructed "men" as "Just Warriors" who exhibited strength, emotional toughness, and other heroic characteristics associated with Western-defined hegemonic masculinity and fought with courage and conviction to protect "the homeland" and "innocent" women and children (1987: 4, 137, 140). In fulfilling the warrior role, boys completed their transition to manhood. These gender stereotypes prevailed in official Western government–produced wartime propaganda as well as in the popular imagination of Western societies throughout most of the twentieth century. The historical record of women's and men's actual participation in twentieth-century war making, however, reveals much greater diversity in gender roles.

Although this chapter examines gender stereotypes produced in globally dominant Western societies as they shaped the international systems within which the twentieth-century wars examined here occurred, cross-culturally the act of fighting in wars has often been conceived as a test of manhood and men's roles as warriors have justified their exclusive rights to govern and act in the public sphere in Western and non-Western societies. The extent to which these Western two-gender stereotypes resonate in Western and non-Western societies is because they have been perpetuated, in part, by dominant male-over-female gender power structures that have governed twentieth-century world politics in times of war and peace. Male leaders who determined war policies and who built military institutions drew on notions of Western hegemonic, heterosexual, and aggressive masculinity to cultivate male power and dominance, and utilized misogyny and homophobia to train military recruits (Steans 2013: 103). Warring groups have also employed gendered forms of coercive force to defeat their enemies and to overcome internal resistance to war within their own group. For example, the strategy to specifically attack civilian populations as "soft targets" with aerial bombings or with economic sanctions to win the war, or the tactic to use rape as a weapon of war to "emasculate" the enemy's men and to "spoil" the enemy's women, have all had gendered impacts on men and women in societies at war and gendered consequences in "postwar" periods. It is also clear from the lengths that twentieth-century governments and other wartime leaders have gone to induce their male group members to take up arms with intent to kill others—including "persuasion, sexual and other incentives, taunting and accusations, flattery and exaltations, and ideological equations of warriorhood with manhood"—that violence is not innate to "men's" nature (Kovitz 2003: 5–6). Yet, as feminist scholars have argued, militarized masculinity reinforces male dominance in a society in wartime and peacetime (see theoretical and empirical studies collected in Elshtain and Tobias 1990; Lorentzen and Turpin 1998).

To be sure, some "women" have historically advocated for war. In the twentieth-century wars discussed here, "women" fought alongside men or served in multiple combat-support and home-front–support roles that enabled their society's war making. At times, women's war-support work softened some of the rigidity of Western stereotypical two-gender constructions for specific groups of women, and these women were "rewarded" with more opportunities to participate in public sphere activities by the hegemonic masculine power holders. Moreover, certain essentialist gender constructions of women as "natural" peacemakers as well as "maternalist" critiques of violent and aggressive militarized masculinity made by certain women or men during these twentieth-century wars have also reinforced the dominant male-over-female gender power relations, even though they may have intended to challenge male dominance. Feminists have explained the conundrum: if "peace" is constructed as "feminine," then "war" is constructed as "masculine." This reinforces gender binaries in Western and non-Western societies between private, feminized spheres, and public, masculinized spheres, and justifies male-over-female gender power hierarchies (Goldstein 2001: 330–31; Kaplan 1994: 123–33). If women or men advocate for peace in times of war they are "feminized." They may be branded as unpatriotic or even treasonous and may lose their rights as citizens. Women as mothers may oppose wars based on their reproductive roles as givers of life, but they may also be called on by the state or warring parties, *as mothers,* to morally support *their sons,* who chose to fight, or to give birth to more sons to carry on the fight (Steinson 1980: 259–84). When the historic record is examined, biology is *not* destiny determining male or female participation in wars, as some culturally constructed gender role stereotypes would have us believe. Nevertheless, these problematic gender discourses have been employed in the wars explored here, and they have been the focus of much feminist criticism.

This chapter concludes with a gender analysis of the Bosnian War (1992–95). This "new" war provides an opportunity to analyze some of the ways that recent cultural constructions of masculinity and femininity shaped the narrative that explained how the war began, how it was conducted, and how the "international community" reacted to the war. Here, the term "international community" refers to the Western liberal democracies that defined the twentieth-century international system and its intergovernmental organizations. In theory and by their own self-definitions, these liberal democracies valued pluralistic societies, were tolerant of difference and promoted moral codes that respected human rights (Williams 2006: 20–21). During the Bosnian War, many expected and accepted gendered ways of waging war were followed. However, during this war and in the concurrent war that raged in Rwanda (1990–94), systematic rape was used as a gendered weapon of war to carry out a policy of "ethnic cleansing" in Bosnia and to perpetrate "genocide" in Rwanda. Feminist women's organizations based in the West, in the former Yugoslavia and around the globe directed the "international community's" attention to these systematic and gendered practices of wartime rape. Their campaigns to condemn these practices led to the subsequent definition and prosecution of wartime rape as a "crime against humanity" at International War Crimes Tribunals for the Former Yugoslavia and Rwanda established in the 1990s. This chapter analyzes these events and the subsequent efforts to establish "peace" and achieve postwar reconciliation in Bosnia-Herzegovina, and reveals how these efforts remain linked to male-over-female gender power relations.

Women, gender, and the First World War

The late nineteenth and early twentieth centuries witnessed an era of imperialist competition among the "Great Powers" of Western Europe, as they sought to expand their influence and territorial holdings in the Middle East, central Africa, and Eurasia, and by the United States, which focused its imperialist ambitions on territories in the Caribbean and the Pacific. In East and Southeast Asia, Japan also embarked on a period of colonial expansion following the Western imperialist model. The wave of Western-led imperialist expansion was both inspired by and was a consequence of great advances in science and technology, an acquisitive quest for natural resources and competition for new markets, a growing faith in "rational" social progress, and a firm belief in a "natural" racial hierarchy among the peoples of the world, with the European Caucasian race at the top of that hierarchy, so "proved" by Western colonizers who subjugated non-Western cultures.

Although expansionist urges were strong among military, industrial, and political leaders in all the Great Powers, a period of relative peace had been maintained during the late nineteenth century through their will to prevent the escalation of international conflicts that turned violent. This was done through diplomacy: either through direct negotiations between the conflicting parties or through arbitration managed by the "neutral" Great Powers. In addition, from the earliest years of the twentieth century, the Great Powers of Europe were enmeshed in two great alliance systems: the Central Powers of Germany, the Austria-Hungary Hapsburg Empire, the Ottoman Empire, and Italy, which soon left the Central Powers' alliance after the outbreak of the First World War in 1914, and the Triple Entente Powers of Great Britain, France, and tsarist Russia. These alliances established a balance of power that had prevented open armed-warfare on the European continent. Nonetheless, intense nationalist rivalries among the Great Powers over global trade arrangements including access to natural resources and markets for industrial goods, along with nationalist aspirations among the multiethnic peoples living within the reach of the extended Hapsburg and Ottoman Empires including, most notably, the Balkan state of Serbia, undercut the European alliance system. Moreover, the militarization of European societies was on the rise, evidenced by a competitive arms race among the Great Powers as well as by the outsized influence of military leaders and expansionist-minded industrialists on domestic-and foreign-policy-making.

This volatile mixture of circumstances established the conditions that led to the outbreak and rapid escalation of war in Europe in the summer of 1914. Triggered by the assassination of the Austrian Hapsburg Archduke Francis Ferdinand by a Serbian nationalist in the Bosnian city of Sarajevo on June 28, the system of Great Power alliances prompted a succession of declarations of war that by the end of August had engulfed the major and minor continental powers. Following the Archduke's assassination, Austria launched a military response to punish Serbia on July 28; this provoked Russian military intervention in support of ethnically Slavic Serbia against Austria and its ally, Germany. Soon after, on August 1, Germany declared war on Russia and launched a previously devised military plan to attack Russia's ally France as well. Germany declared war on France on August 3, planning on a quick defeat of France, attacking it through the neutral powers of Belgium and Luxemburg. At that time, Germany did not believe that Britain would honor its alliances and join France and Russia and go to war. Britain, however, recognized the threat that a European continent controlled by Germany and Austria posed to its national security. On August 4, Britain declared war on Germany. What became known as the "Great War" soon involved the European states and their vast colonial holdings in global struggles for power. The war was fought on all manner of battlegrounds, political, social, economic, and ideological, involving all members of society, from elite government policy makers, military generals, and civil society leaders to conscripted soldiers and civilians, in all the nations at war. War policy makers used every resource of power available to them to gain advantage and defeat their enemies, including the ubiquitous resource of gender power.

Gender and mobilization for war

The Western European governments and military establishments of the First World War belligerents introduced many war-making innovations in terms of new and increasingly destructive weapons in the new, twentieth-century era of "total war." They also utilized the mass media and mass culture in new ways to "sell" the total war to their literate citizens, generating messages that they were fighting "just wars" for righteous causes, not for self-interest or territorial gain, but to defend helpless victims from their enemies' aggression. Newspapers, journals, popular literature, educational pamphlets, and wartime recruiting posters created in Western Europe and in the United States relied in large part on nationalistic justifications that *their nations* were fighting to defend *their peoples* and *their values* against an aggressive enemy aimed at destroying their belief systems, ways of life, and their future prosperity. They also employed familiar two-gender role stereotypes in war-propaganda imagery and messaging, the male "Just Warrior" and the female "Beautiful Soul," inundating men and women with messages about how they should fulfill their gendered duties during wartime to generate popular support for their nation's war efforts. Scholars who have studied these media messages remind us that there is no reliable, objective instrument to measure how audiences received these messages. Nonetheless, Western war-policy makers employed some near-universal nationalistic justifications and two-gender stereotyping in war-mobilization campaigns, conveying, at the very least, the values they wanted their populations to hold and the behaviors they wanted their populations to display (James 2009: 16–19).

These official government mobilization messages were mirrored by wartime commercial advertisers who used patriotic images to sell products. In Britain in 1914, the famous stern and determined-male image of Secretary of War Lord Kitchener, looking straight at and pointing a finger at British men with the caption: "Wants You; Join Your Country's Army! God Save the King," was initially created for a commercial advertisement by graphic artist Alfred Leete. It was so effective that the British government adopted it to recruit British "Just Warriors." US artist J. M. Flagg adapted the image to recruit US "Just Warriors" when the United States entered the war in 1917. Flagg's version depicted a fierce-looking "Uncle Sam" who pointed his index finger out at American men and demanded: "I Want You For the U.S. Army." Private citizens and civic organizations were so moved to support the war that they also produced their own patriotic posters and banners and displayed them in businesses and public spaces such as libraries or in local parades and pageants.

In mobilizing men for war, wartime policy makers referenced constructions of hegemonic masculinity on recruitment posters and other print materials, using explicit and coded text messages to portray military service as an opportunity to prove one's manhood and fulfill one's patriotic duty to the protect and preserve the homeland under attack. In one variation, war-mobilization posters employed visual images and text to incite male rage when enemy attacks were made on *their women* and children, or on "innocent" women and children in victimized nations, and thus to inspire male military service to enact revenge for the attacks.

As the war dragged on after 1915, through three long years of stalemate and at a cost of millions of soldiers' lives on the battlefronts, government recruiting tactics evolved from enticing men to join the army with images of glory and valor on the battlefield, to using images of soldiers protecting women and children, to employing various coercive messages—as the British government also enacted conscription laws in 1916. Some propaganda posters mobilized men for military service by shaming them, taunting them with images of brutalized women and children, or with images conveying desecrated social institutions, to evoke feelings of shame that they failed to protect their nations' valued property. For example, both British and American propagandists used images that referenced Germany's brutal treatment of Belgian women to recruit male "Just Warriors" into military service. War-mobilization posters showed women and girls as the victims of German attacks, being raped and killed as Germany swept through the neutral nation to invade France during its western-front campaign in the fall of 1914. German soldiers were portrayed as brutes who invaded peaceful countries and violated international laws and universal standards of morality. Newspaper accounts in Britain and in the United States also reported on the German invasion of Belgium, using gendered language to depict Belgium as a small, defenseless, feminized nation and Germany as a brutish, barbaric, aggressive, hypermasculinized nation. Over time, British propaganda also feminized the British homeland, constructing the nation-in-need-of-protection, too, by reminding British men: "Remember that if they got the chance the Germans would destroy British homes [and assault British women] as ruthlessly as they have destroyed Belgian homes" (Albrinck 2009: 316–20).

To target men who had not immediately heeded their nation's call to enlist when the war broke out in 1914, mobilization posters and other recruitment efforts portrayed these male holdouts as shirkers of their patriotic duty, or as cowards, or as effeminate and impotent men, and dared these men to prove their manliness and virility. British recruitment posters posed questions such as "What did you do in the war, Daddy?," "You're proud of your pals in the Army of course! But what will your pals think of you?," and issued orders to the holdouts "Your friends need you. Be a man" (Albrinck

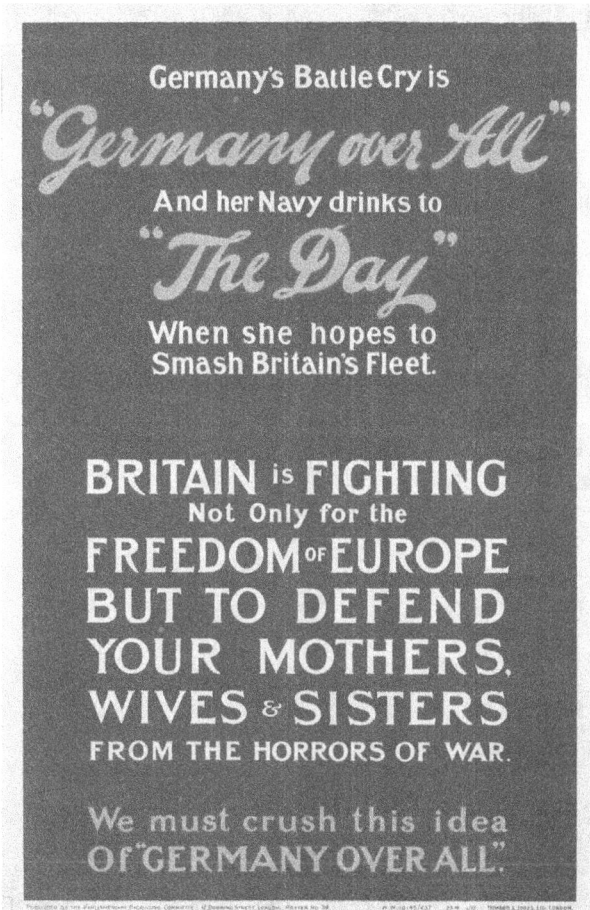

FIGURE 3.1 **IWM 5084** *Great Britain First World War poster Germany's Battle Cry is "Germany Over All." 1915. Credit: Imperial War Museums/Howard and Jones, Ltd., London, printer*

2009: 325–26). Some mobilization posters featured gender-bending images of women dressed in military uniforms and affecting provocative poses to taunt men, either to shame them or to seduce them into military service. The social upheavals that accompanied the war included a loosening of sexual mores. Young women seemed to be gripped by what the British press called "khaki fever," attracted to men in uniform as wartime propaganda linked soldiering with virility, and rejecting men who would not fight (Albrinck 2009: 331–32).

In contrast to the government propagandists' construction of men's soldiering roles, male war-policy makers often constructed women's wartime roles with a focus on motherhood. "Mothers" had a particular moral force in society, and when women were called upon *as mothers* to support their sons in war, mobilization messages were aimed at both young men and older women. Gendered messages sent to and about the "wartime mother" did not disrupt either of the Western-defined gendered spheres: the public and political sphere reserved for men or the private and domestic sphere reserved for maternal women. These messages elaborating the role of the "wartime mother" called up familiar sentiments and generated a great deal of support among society's traditionalists. Nonetheless, the demands of a total war, where *all* citizens were called on to contribute in extraordinary ways to the war effort sometimes challenged the gendered "separate spheres" formulation.

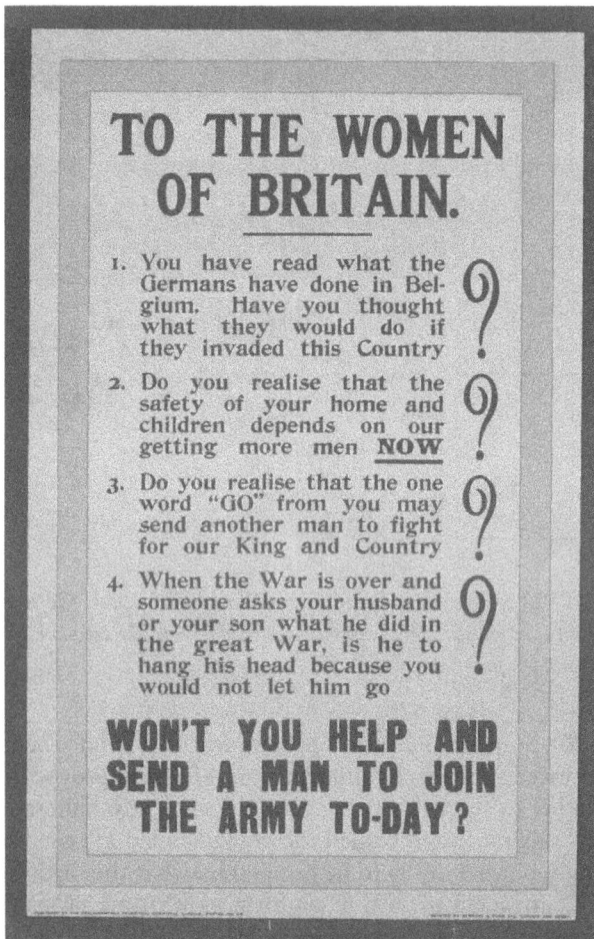

TO THE WOMEN OF BRITAIN.

1. You have read what the Germans have done in Belgium. Have you thought what they would do if they invaded this Country ?

2. Do you realise that the safety of your home and children depends on our getting more men **NOW** ?

3. Do you realise that the one word "GO" from you may send another man to fight for our King and Country ?

4. When the War is over and someone asks your husband or your son what he did in the great War, is he to hang his head because you would not let him go ?

WON'T YOU HELP AND SEND A MAN TO JOIN THE ARMY TO-DAY ?

FIGURE 3.2 **IWM 11675** *Great Britain First World War poster "To the Women of Britain." 1915. Credit: Imperial War Museums/Bemrose and Sons, Ltd. London and Derby, printer*

Although women have always participated in wars, historian Nicole Ann Dombrowski has asserted that the First World War, as a total war fought by thoroughly militarized societies, "marked women's definitive entry into the war machine" (1999: 7). During the First World War, Western nations also called on women to contribute to work outside the home, to "free-up" men to fight as an act of patriotism for the homeland and as support for the male warriors they loved. Mobilization propaganda directed at "women" urged women to work in war production and munitions factories, to join the general workforce and fill the previously male-gendered jobs that men left vacant as they went off to fight, to join their nation's "land armies" and fill the agricultural workforce, or to join the nursing corps or ambulance-driving corps to minister to wounded male soldiers. In many cases, the propaganda coincided with reality. Official portrayals of willing women workers mirrored women's actual enthusiastic participation in war-support work, as wartime photographs, news reports, and literature have documented. Women's wartime work and service to the nation reportedly gave them "purpose" as well as higher pay than they had earned before, or would earn after the war ended (Gilbert 2000: 278–80). During the war, Western European working- and middle-class women experienced "unparalleled opportunities . . . in work and family decision-making that made their experiences of war very different from men" (Boxer and Quataert 2000: 219). Working-class women moved out of domestic service and into munitions and other factories and into war-transport industries; middle-class women entered the nursing or other clerical or professional work previously dominated by men, and performed a great deal of necessary military-support voluntary service work.

Government war-policy makers were not the only forces actively mobilizing women for war-support work. Some liberal feminist women's suffrage societies, for example, identified the war as an opportunity to "prove" women's fitness for full citizenship rights and privileges by adopting a pro-war stance and demonstrating their patriotism. In Britain, the Women's Social and Political Union renamed the organization's newspaper to reflect their support for the nation's war effort. What had been named *The Suffragette* before the war became *Britannia,* with a new patriotic pledge as its motto, to work "For King, for Country, for Freedom" (Gilbert 2000: 285). Governments appreciated women's active support and the necessary wartime service they performed and many Western nations, including Britain, the United States, and Germany, passed women's suffrage laws during wartime or soon after the war ended. IR scholar Ann Towns has argued that through their war-support work, Western women's suffrage advocates successfully broke down some of the prewar notions of gendered "separate spheres" that prevented women from participation in their societies' public life. Before the war, most male leaders in Western nations believed that "civilized states exclude women from politics" because "women" were constructed as fragile, sensitive, nurturers of families in the private sphere. A new female-gender norm was emerging, so that "women's suffrage . . . became the expected behavior around the end of World War I. Suffrage became indicative of having reached a more advanced level of civilization and thus helped to set those states apart from presumably inferior states" (2010: 81–82).

Table 3.1 Timing of States Granting Women Suffrage in National Elections (limited in some instances by special qualifications)

State	Year	State	Year
New Zealand	1893	Luxemburg	1918
Australia	1902	Czechoslovakia	1918
Finland	1906	United States	1920
Norway	1913	Belgium	1920
Denmark	1915	Ireland	1922
Iceland	1915	Mongolia	1924
The Netherlands	1917	Spain	1931
Soviet Union	1917	Brazil	1932
Canada	1917	Cuba	1934
Estonia	1917	France	1945
Latvia	1917	Italy	1945
Lithuania	1917	Yugoslavia	1946
Sweden	1918	Romania	1946
Great Britain	1918	Bulgaria	1947
Germany	1918	Belgium	1948
Poland	1918	Albania	1958
Hungary	1918	Switzerland	1970
Austria	1918	Portugal	1976

Source: Boxer, M. and Quataert, J. (2000), *Connecting Spheres: European Women in a Globalizing World, 1500 to the Present*, 2nd ed., New York, NY: Oxford University Press.

Gender and war strategy, tactics, and weaponry

The First World War initially generated a great deal of national excitement and enthusiasm from the nations at war, with faith on all sides that the war would be concluded quickly and that war aims would be achieved with minimal sacrifice. These misguided beliefs were soon abandoned as new weapons technology and strategies used to conduct the war transformed the assumption of quick military victories achieved on the battlefield to the reality of a slow, deadly war of attrition fought by "anonymous, dehumanized" soldiers huddled in trenches, firing blindly across bombed-out and poisoned "No Man's Lands," using machine guns, zeppelins, tanks, artillery guns, land mines, and poison gas (Gilbert 2000: 275–76). These new weapons of war most certainly killed some civilians, as noted by British feminist pacifist Helena Swanwick in 1915: "When aviators drop bombs, when guns bombard fortified towns, it is not possible to avoid the women and children who may chance to be in the way" (quoted in Ashworth 2011: 30). The major targets of these particular weapons, however, were the foot soldiers stuck on the stalemated battlefronts. Historian William Keylor has described "the futility of hurling unarmored [male] flesh against the devastating firepower of the machine gun and heavy artillery." Nevertheless, war-policy makers continued to mount massive land-army offensives against one another, despite suffering huge losses of manpower of "almost suicidal proportions." For example:

> In the battle of the Somme from July 1 to November 18, 1916, the Germans and British lost 400,000 each and the French 200,000. The reward for the combined Anglo-French casualties of over 600,000 was a maximum advance of about 7 miles. In the same year, the Germans conducted a ten-month siege of the French fortress at Verdun at a cost of 336,000 men, while the French army's successful defense was paid for with 350,000 lives. At Passchendaele in 1917 over 370,000 British soldiers perished to gain 45 square miles of mud and shell holes.
>
> KEYLOR 2011: 58

The new methods of warfare disempowered male soldiers and rendered them "impotent." Many soldiers became emasculated victims of various feminized "hysterical" orders and neuroses known as "the burial-alive neurosis," "gas neurosis," "soldier's heart," and "hysterical sympathy with the enemy." As feminist cultural critic Sandra Gilbert has noted, "What had previously been a disease of women before the war became a disease of men in combat" (2000: 286).

German women and children comprised the largest group of civilian casualties during the First World War. Britain imposed a naval blockade along the European coastline to block supplies bound for the Central Powers in late 1914, following the realization that a protracted war of attrition was underway. British policy makers intended to starve "the enemy," to stop all goods, whether contraband or foodstuff, from reaching the German-controlled ports. As IR scholar Alexander Downes has documented, the British hoped "that the suffering inflicted would destroy [German] morale" (2006: 186). In addition, the British planned to burn and destroy all German and Austrian–Hungarian grain crops by dropping incendiary bombs on fields. The plan was aborted, however, vetoed by the French who feared German retaliatory attacks on their own wheat fields. The British public generally supported the blockade policy that continued during and after the war to punish and "starve the Hun," even as they knew that German women and children, not the elite male war-policy makers, were the major casualties of the starvation strategy (Downes 2006: 191).

Women's resistance to war: challenging the male state

To be sure, some prominent women, as well as some prominent male labor leaders and social and cultural critics, actively resisted the prevailing nationalist- and gender-power pressures to support the war. For one example, British journalist and feminist pacifist Helena Swanwick spoke out and published her arguments condemning the war and the gendered toll it exacted, or, in her words, the "horrors" that war inflicted on women. As previously noted, Swanwick criticized the use of modern weapons like aerial bombs dropped on cities and villages that killed civilian women and children, as well as male soldiers. She also exposed the fallacies of the arguments that male leaders used to justify war as a means to "protect" women and children:

> When the enemy invades a country, the men who talked in time of peace of protecting their women cannot do it. Either the army fights over its own land, reducing it to smoke and ruin, or it evacuates the place, leaving the non-combatants to the invader. Nothing that men suffer in war can compare in shuddering horror with what must be endured by a woman with child or a nursing mother who sees her home invaded.

QUOTED IN ASHWORTH 2011:30

In another effort to raise awareness of war's gendered impact on women, Swanwick also predicted accurately that at war's end, women would be ejected from their well-paid wartime jobs as men returned from the battlefields. She urged women engaged in war work to organize themselves into labor unions to prevent postwar job losses while they still had some leverage (Cooper 2002: 21). Swanwick spoke out on behalf of women's gendered interests during the war and in the decades that followed, until her death in 1939. She argued in Britain and at the League of Nations that women must assert their equal rights to participate in their nation's policy making. She believed that enlightened women and men should work together to oppose militarism and war, and to educate their societies to support peace.

During the war, peace activists included numerous leaders of Western feminist women's organizations who had long campaigned for women's political rights so that women could enter the realm of global politics and challenge the militarization of their societies as well as imperialistic international relations. Western feminist pacifist leaders including Jane Addams, Emily Balch, and Alice Hamilton from the United States, Alletta Jacobs and Rosa Manus from the Netherlands, and Emmeline Pethick Lawrence and Chrystal MacMillan from Britain organized a Women's Congress for Peace, which took place at The Hague from 28 April to 1 May, 1915 (Rupp 1997: 27–28). Despite opposition from the governments of belligerent nations and ridicule from international media that branded their efforts unpatriotic, treasonous, or naïve, 1,200 women from twelve nations met to express their feminist and pacifist convictions. The Women's Congress formulated what they believed to be a viable anti-war alternative to the war policies of male national leaders. With their anti-war proposals in hand, a Congressional delegation calling themselves the "Women's International Committee for Permanent Peace" arranged meetings with the heads of state or the foreign ministers of the warring European nations and with US president Woodrow Wilson, to argue their case for negotiating an end to the war and establishing the international mechanisms that might avoid future wars. As Jane Addams recalled the reception the women received from the male leaders as she looked back in 1922:

> Everywhere, save from one official in France, we heard the same opinion expressed by these men of the governments responsible for the promotion of war; each one said his country would be ready to stop the war immediately if some honorable method of securing peace were provided; each one disclaimed responsibility for the continuance of war; each one predicted European bankruptcy if the war were prolonged; and each one grew pale and distressed as he spoke of the loss of his gallant young countrymen, two of them with ill-concealed emotion referred to their loss of their own sons.

ADDAMS 1922: 11

Although the women's proposals made no headway toward ending the war in 1915, President Wilson brought forward many of the women's ideas with some modifications as he articulated his "Fourteen Points" to resolve the war in an address to the US Senate in January 1918. At that point, the United States had already entered the war in April 1917, on the side of the Entente and against the Central Powers. Women's peace advocates, including Jane Addams, no longer had the president's ear and he denied that pacifists had influenced his Fourteen Points in any way (Rupp 1997: 210–11). The press continued to damn the pacifists for their dangerous "isolationist" position, even though Addams asserted: "We were, of course, urging exactly the reverse, that the country should lead the nations of the world into a wider life of coordinated political activity" (Addams 1922: 64–65).

In nations at war, women who voiced their resistance to war, even when they drew on traditional gender expectations that "women," and especially "mothers," were by nature pacifistic and knew better than men the value of human life because they gave birth, were branded as dissidents, or even as traitors to the state. Britain, France, and Germany all considered the 1915 Women's Congress for Peace to be a national security threat, and French

Table 3.2 Principles of a Permanent Peace, as Outlined by the 1915 Women's Congress for Peace at The Hague

Respect for nationality, territorial sovereignty, and self-determination made mandatory by international law
Mandatory peaceful resolution of interstate disputes by arbitration or conciliation
States should exert social, moral, and economic pressures on states that use military force to resolve disputes
Foreign policy making should be under democratic control
Equal rights for women, including women's suffrage and rights to equal representation in governments
Establish an international "Society of Nations" to include a permanent international court to settle political disputes and a permanent general assembly
Establish a separate international court to settle economic disputes
Prohibit discrimination among nations in regard to trade and tariff barriers
Work toward universal disarmament; in the interim place all manufacturing and trade of weapons in the hands of government, not private businesses
Prohibit secret diplomacy and secret treaties among nations
Establish universal education for all children, including instruction on international law and peaceful values

Source: Baetens, F. (2010), "The Forgotten Peace Conference: The 1915 International Congress of Women," in *Max Planck Encyclopedia of Public International Law*, New York, NY: Oxford University Press.

Table 3.3 President Woodrow Wilson's Fourteen Points, January 8, 1918

Open covenants of peace, openly arrived at . . . .
Absolute freedom of navigation upon the seas, alike in peace or war . . . except as the seas may be closed in whole or in part by international action.
The removal, so far as possible, of all economic barriers and the establishment of an equality of trade conditions among all the nations consenting to the peace . . . .
Guarantees given and taken that national armaments will be reduced to the lowest point consistent with domestic safety.
A free, open-minded, and absolutely impartial adjustment of all colonial claims, ...
The evacuation of all Russian territory and such a settlement of all questions affecting Russia as will secure the best and freest cooperation of the other nations of the world . . . .
Belgium, the whole world will agree, must be evacuated and restored, ...
All French territory should be freed and the invaded portions restored, ...
A readjustment of the frontiers of Italy should be effected along clearly recognizable lines of nationality.
The peoples of Austria-Hungary, . . . should be accorded the freest opportunity to autonomous development.
Rumania, Serbia, and Montenegro should be evacuated; occupied territories restored; Serbia accorded free and secure access to the sea; and the relations of the several Balkan states to one another determined by friendly counsel . . . .
The Turkish portion of the present Ottoman Empire should be assured a secure sovereignty, but the other nationalities which are now under Turkish rule should be assured an undoubted security of life and an absolutely unmolested opportunity of autonomous development, and the Dardanelles should be permanently opened as a free passage to the ships and commerce of all nations under international guarantees.
An independent Polish state should be erected which should include the territories inhabited by indisputably Polish populations . . . .
A general association of nations must be formed under specific covenants for the purpose of affording mutual guarantees of political independence and territorial integrity to great and small states alike.

Source: "President Woodrow Wilson's Fourteen Points," The Avalon Project, Documents in Law, History and Diplomacy, Yale Law School, http://avalon.law.yale.edu/20th_century/wilson14.asp (Accessed July 7, 2017).

liberal feminist organizations boycotted the Congress to express solidarity with French war policy. Nonetheless during the war, one prominent French pacifist feminist, Helen Brion, who was also a socialist and a trade unionist, defied demands for loyalty to the French government and distributed pacifist tracts to soldiers. This action led to her arrest, trial, and imprisonment for treason, although she argued at her trial that she, as a woman, had no "rights," and was therefore "outside the law" and could not be "unpatriotic" (Grazel 1999: 188).

Gender power in the aftermath of war

After the First World War, women in Western nations joined in national and international politics as full citizens, having won, in many national cases, their rights to vote and participate formally in public policy making. They hoped to increase women's gendered influence on elite state politics as advocates for both peace and the application of international diplomacy to settle conflicts, and as "moral" forces interjecting new human-centered values into previously male-dominated political realms. A joint delegation of women's international organizations from the victorious Allied nations, the Inter-Allied Suffrage Conference, appealed to their national leaders as they deliberated the post–First World War peace settlement in negotiations at Versailles and pressured them to include provisions for women to participate in the proposed League of Nations (Rupp 1997: 211–12; Stienstra 1994: 56). Their efforts earned clauses allowing for, but not mandating, women's equal participation in the charters of the League of Nations and in the newly formed International Labor Organization, as Chapter 4 explains.

When women from the defeated Central Powers were initially denied visas to enter France where international peace negotiations were held, the pacifist feminist women's international organizations that had organized the 1915 Women's Congress at The Hague convened their own postwar conference in Zurich, Switzerland. The women's conference took place in May 1919, just after the Allied leaders announced the terms of the Versailles Peace Treaty that had been negotiated, largely in secret, by British prime minister David Lloyd George, Italian prime minister Vittorio Orlando, French premier Georges Clemenceau, and US president Woodrow Wilson (Keylor 2011: 72, 75–76). Many of Wilson's proposals to establish a "new" diplomacy and to usher in a new era in international relations were overridden during the Versailles negotiations; the victorious Allied Powers reaffirmed the supremacy of power politics in the postwar world. In the treaty, the Allied Powers held Germany largely responsible for the war and imposed crippling indemnities on the defeated Central Powers. They disarmed Germany immediately and gave only vague promises for future universal disarmament. They broke up the Austrian–Hungarian and Ottoman Empires and determined the borders of newly created states, denying the principle of self-determination for peoples in Eastern Europe and in Middle-Eastern Arab states in the process, while maintaining their own colonial holdings in Africa and Asia. The women at the Zurich conference heaped criticism on the Versailles Treaty for all its unprincipled failings and called it "morally indefensible," but they also pledged to engage in international politics with government policy makers in their home countries and at the newly formed League of Nations through their own newly formed feminist pacifist coalition, the Women's International League for Peace and Freedom (Haslam 1999: 140; Addams 1922: 88–93).

As traditional practices of power politics reasserted themselves at the Versailles Peace Treaty negotiations, traditional two-gender roles and male-over-female gender power hierarchies also reasserted themselves in American and European societies after the war ended. Even as women gained rights to vote in many Western and some non-Western nations, women's political power was circumscribed. Women in Western societies returned to their domestic duties, demobilized from war work (as Helena Swanwick predicted), just as male soldiers were demobilized from active military service and returned to "their" jobs in businesses and factories. As Western nations focused on rebuilding postwar economies, jobs in the wage economy were reserved for men who were the heads of households and soldiers whose sacrifices had earned them a privileged place in the labor sector. A renewed emphasis on women's reproductive roles, especially in Germany and Italy as fascist movements pushed for pronatalist government policies, also reversed some of the social gender role transformations that had taken place during wartime.

Women, gender, and the Second World War

With many of the nationalist rivalries that had caused the outbreak of the First World War still unresolved, the political and economic terms of the Versailles Peace Treaty, and the United States' heightened economic nationalism in the postwar period creating even more animosity between the Western European powers, the decades of the 1920s and 1930s can be most accurately characterized as a "twenty-year truce," rather than an era of "peace," in regard to relations between the world's Great Powers (Keylor 2011: 44). The unstable global economy of the 1920s devolved into worldwide economic depression after the US stock market crashed in 1929, plummeting prices of stocks and wiping out the monetary value of speculative investments and the cash supplies of financial institutions and individuals. The global depression only increased nationalistic foreign policies among the Western capitalist democracies and intensified imperial ambitions among the totalitarian fascist powers in Italy, Germany, and Japan, the rising Great Power in Asia. The League of Nations never fulfilled its promises to be an international forum for the peaceful settlement of interstate conflicts or to disarm its member states to prevent a future outbreak of war. The League's leading European member states, Great Britain and France, sometimes worked in concert with one another and sometimes did not as they maneuvered unsuccessfully to engage their First World War ally, the United States, as an active partner in managing Europe-centric global politics, to enlist Italy as their ally and abrogate its colonial expansion into Ethiopia, or to prevent the rearmament of Germany and resist German annexation of territories in the Rhineland, Austria, and Czechoslovakia. The Western European powers and the United States also failed to prevent Japan's colonial expansion into East and Southeast Asia.

Italy, Germany, and imperial Japan were inspired by fascist ideology and governed by patriarchal totalitarian dictators who represented political organizations that established a strict social order using oppressive force against all expressions of dissent. Each fascist state had set ambitious goals to acquire vast territorial empires, and articulated stridently nationalistic messages to expand the "living space" for "their" peoples and to gain access to raw materials and resources to enhance their economic wealth and global power; each fascist state pursued these goals through ruthless military campaigns that overran victim states and "other" ethnic and racial groups. During the period known as the Third Reich from 1933 to 1945, fascist Germany led by the Nazi Party and its Führer, Adolf Hitler, adopted a racist, anti-Semitic policy agenda that accompanied German imperial expansion. The Nazis promoted the doctrine of their own racial superiority, asserting that the Nordic or Germanic peoples, descendants of the Indo-European Aryan race, represented a "master race." They were committed to enslaving or exterminating all "undesirable" peoples within their imperial reach, which included a policy of genocide of the European Jewish population. Imperial Japan, too, adopted a doctrine of racial superiority over "lesser" Asian peoples. Japanese leaders constructed the Japanese people as "liberators" of other Asian peoples, freeing them from European colonial powers' exploitation. This national identity justified the domination of non-Japanese Asian peoples by the "superior" Japanese ruling class as they were absorbed into Japan's territorial empire, the "Greater East Asian Co-Prosperity Sphere."

Totalitarian fascist states of the 1930s were also fiercely anti-communist and were amenable to private, capitalist investments and market economies. These qualities initially dulled the Western democracies' perception of the threat that the fascists posed to their own populations, or to other victim states, or to fundamental democratic values of individual freedom and human rights. Western European governments' policies of appeasement and the US government's narrowly nationalistic political and economic policies prevailed during the 1930s, despite some challenges from more internationalist-minded men and women within their societies who understood the seriousness of the fascist threat to world peace. Consequently, the increasingly aggressive fascist states moved forward with their empire-building projects amid muted protests and ineffective diplomacy. In East Asia, the Japanese army occupied Manchuria in 1931, expanded its political and economic control over north China through the creation of puppet states governed by Chinese collaborators in 1933 and 1934, and finally declared war on China in 1937, when Chinese resistance seemed to be coalescing around a Chinese Nationalist Party–Communist Party united front engineered by the Soviet Union, as the Soviets feared Japan's rising power along its Asian borders. Italy succeeded in creating an African colony following its victorious land grab during the Italo-Ethiopian War in 1935 and 1936. Germany and Italy provided aid and aerial bombing support to General Francisco Franco's anti-communist forces during the Spanish Civil War from 1936 to 1939, and gained access to Spain's strategic raw materials when Franco's Nationalist Party government took control.

Germany's aggressive imperial project began in 1933, when the Nazi Party took control of the German government, and its leader, Adolf Hitler, became chancellor. Hitler's government flatly rejected the terms of the Versailles Peace Treaty, pulled Germany out of the League of Nations and openly engaged in rearmament. Launching its imperial expansion campaign in March 1936, the Nazi government remilitarized German territory in the Rhineland, which had been neutralized after the war. After settling on common interests in Europe in terms of support for General Franco in Spain, Germany and Italy concluded the Rome–Berlin Axis agreement in October 1936; one month later, Germany concluded an anti-Soviet pact with Japan. In March 1938, the Nazi government "peacefully" annexed ethnically German territory in Austria. Germany occupied Czechoslovakian territory that Britain and France bargained away at the September 1938 Munich Conference and seized the remaining independent Czechoslovakian territory by force in March 1939. As Germany prepared for further expansion into Poland, it signed a Non-Aggression Pact with the Soviet Union in August 1939, and agreed to a division of Polish territory with the Union of Soviet Socialist Republics to neutralize Soviet resistance to the rising Nazi power. Germany's swift, intense, and high-powered military attack on Poland following its blitzkrieg strategy in September 1939 finally prompted British and French declarations of war on Germany. In May 1940, Germany launched its western offensive according to imperial plan, once again overrunning The Netherlands and Belgium and occupying most of France by June 1940. With the installation of the collaborationist French Vichy regime to govern its occupied territory, Nazi Germany shifted its attention to Great Britain, unleashing an intense aerial bombing campaign of London and Britain's south-western coastline in September 1940 in preparation for a land invasion to complete the conquest of Western Europe.

With nearly all of Europe under fascist control, the United States amended its five-year-long policy of legislated neutrality that had prohibited sales of war materials and loans to all nations at war. In March 1941, the US

Congress approved the "lend-lease" of war materials to aid Britain, pushed the boundaries of US naval patrols far into the eastern Atlantic and ramped up its weapons and munitions production. A German about-face attack on the Soviet Union in June 1941 opened an eastern battlefront Europe, nullified the Nazi-Soviet Non-Aggression Pact and escalated the continental conflict. In August 1941, US president Franklin Delano Roosevelt met with British prime minister Winston Churchill in Newfoundland and the two leaders settled on joint declaration of the Western democracies' principles and values and war aims. Their joint statement, the Atlantic Charter, revisited Woodrow Wilson's Fourteen Points, envisioning a postwar international system based on free trade, freedom of the seas, and self-determination for all nations. It also asserted universal standards of human welfare to maintain the future peace. At the time, President Roosevelt was convinced that the United States must be an active participant in the anti-fascist war in order to play a leading role in determining the postwar peace. While not committing US military forces to the European War, Roosevelt's administration offered moral and material support to Britain.

In East Asia throughout 1940 and 1941, the US government increased pressures on Japan. The United States hoped to halt Japan's imperial advance by providing some minimal aid to Chinese resistance forces, freezing Japanese assets in US banks, and imposing an embargo on oil shipments to Japan. The added political and economic pressures prompted Japan to launch a surprise aerial attack on the US naval base at Pearl Harbor, Hawaii, on December 7, 1941, followed by attacks on US territories in the Philippines and the South Pacific and on British colonial holdings in Malaysia and Hong Kong. Immediately reacting to the punishing attacks on its territories and military installations, the US government declared war on Japan on December 8. On December 11, Nazi Germany declared war on the United States hoping to diminish US support for Britain and for the Western democracies' new ally-by-default, the Soviet Union. By December 1941, "the world" was at war again.

Gender and war strategy

Many histories of the Second World War focus on elite government and military leaders, all male, who seemingly acted autonomously to promote or protect their nation-states. IR scholar Laura Sjoberg has asserted that this historical treatment of the Second World War is common among war studies in general, in which "discussions of leaders' role in war-making often emphasize the advantages of characteristics associated with masculinity. . . . Much of this [war studies] literature . . . looks only at the individual with elite power and influence, and even then, only at the male individual with elite power" (2013: 158). Histories of the Second World War, especially those that focus on the "Grand Strategizing" of the Allied Powers at the major wartime conferences held in Casablanca in January 1943, in Teheran in November and December 1943, and in Yalta in February 1945, highlight the deals and decisions of the "Big Three" leaders of the anti-fascist alliance that emerged after 1941, British prime minister Winston Churchill, US president Franklin Roosevelt, and Soviet premier Joseph Stalin, as they calculated their collective and individual national security interests. Less-powerful feminized leaders who were brought into the anti-fascist alliance included Chinese Nationalist Government chairman Chiang Kai-shek and General Charles DeGaulle, leader of the Free French Resistance forces. These five leaders of the Allied Powers' "United Nations" receive the lion's share of attention in war histories, where their personalities and masculine-gendered leadership characteristics are the focus of intense comparisons and contrast analyses. Likewise, among the fascist powers, accounts of the hypermasculine imperial ambitions of Italy's National Fascist Party leader and prime minister Benito Mussolini, Germany's Nazi Party's Führer and chancellor Adolf Hitler, and Japan's prime minister and senior general Hideki Tojo, are often presented as synonymous with their nations' experiences during the Second World War. The war goals that these elite leaders pursued are often presented as unitary national interests, with dissenting voices or even whole populations who opposed their leaders' goals absent from historical consideration. According to many studies on the Second World War, these elite male government leaders and their military generals alone had wartime agency. They alone performed the cost-benefit analyses and made the decisions about when to employ various wartime strategies and how to use various weapons and their own peoples to wage war, making some of these decisions with explicit gendered intents in mind and discounting other gendered consequences.

The previous discussion of the First World War strategies examined some of the gendered aspects of fighting a total war. During the First World War, national government and military leaders sacrificed great numbers of male soldiers in air and naval battles and long, drawn-out trench warfare. War leaders also targeted civilian populations, predominantly women and children, with aerial and ground bombing or starved civilians by cutting off supply lines. Once again, all belligerent power leaders employed these gendered strategies during the Second World War. However, increasingly deadly weapons, efficient weapons-delivery systems, and egregious violations of human rights all took their toll on the human populations engaged in war so that estimates of casualties of the Second World War are usually figured at fifty-five to sixty million worldwide, or more if deaths from famines and diseases caused by the war are included in death tallies.

Gender, race, class, and mobilization for war

As a total war, the Second World War involved entire populations of belligerent nations. To mobilize mass support, government policy makers and nongovernmental groups that supported their nations' war projects targeted men and women in gendered, raced, and classed mobilization messages designed to appeal to selected population groups. All fascist and anti-fascist powers produced hypernationalistic, pro-war propaganda, and all powers silenced anti-war dissenting voices with varying degrees of force and brutality. War makers created and disseminated propaganda posters and pamphlets to mobilize their populations as they had during the First World War because these print materials continued to be popular communications mediums. They also used film to construct war narratives, to vilify their enemies, and to record massive pro-war rallies, military exercises, and parades of weapons to exhibit their national power. Wartime leaders delivered hyper-patriotic and, at times, vitriolic radio addresses and used their national presses to rally emotional support for the nation's war making and hatred for enemies of the nation. The messages delivered through all these mediums used the power of gender, race, and class stereotypes to generate military and other vital support from targeted populations efficiently and effectively.

With an aggressive territorial occupation and colonization project underway in Korea, China, Southeast Asia, and the South Pacific, the Japanese government needed to mobilize its entire population to achieve its war aims. As Japan had been building its territorial empire since the 1890s and fighting an imperial war since 1931, all able-bodied Japanese men and boys were drafted into the military to serve in combat and support roles. As Western societies had done in the early nineteenth century, when Japan industrialized in the late nineteenth century it constructed a gendered and classed division between the private, feminine sphere of the middle- and upper-class home and family and the public, masculine sphere of work, governance, and warfare. Japanese society defined gender roles for women of the privileged classes as the "good wives and wise mothers" who were focused on serving their families as their most important duties to the nation. Therefore, throughout the decade of the 1930s, war-mobilization campaigns directed at these women initially focused on persuading good wives and wise mothers to reproduce more male children who could participate in combat and colonization projects in the future. The Japanese government adopted pronatalist policies that included outlawing birth control and lowering the legal marriage age. It also enacted laws to support women *as mothers*, such as the Mother-Child Protection Law, passed in 1936, which provided social welfare to poor and widowed mothers (Bingham and Gross 1987: 231–36). War-policy makers directed propaganda campaigns at good wives and wise mothers, Japan's "reproductive soldiers," associating their fertility with the power of the state (Matsumura 2007: 80–81).

Many middle- and upper-class Japanese women supported their nation's war aims. Among them, Japanese suffragettes, who were generally more-educated and privileged women, had sought wider public roles for women in Japanese society beyond those of the good wife and wise mother during the 1920s. But during the long imperial war they suspended their active campaigning for political rights and equal rights in marriage. By the mid-1930s, nearly five million middle- and upper-class Japanese women had joined patriotic associations to support the soldiers materially and morally, rolling bandages and writing letters to troops in the field. This war work gave privileged Japanese women a public, if not political, role to play in the nation's war project.

As the war raged on, the imperial government was forced to recruit middle-class Japanese women to perform necessary factory work; working-class women, the "so-called female career factory workers" were already toiling in war production and other industries. Although middle- and upper-class men and women were dubious about putting more "sheltered" middle-class women into the workplace, side by side with lower-class women who were thought to have lower moral standards and to exhibit coarser behavior, war propagandists appealed to the middle class's patriotism. Mobilization campaigns focused on national "solidarity of the Japanese peoples," with slogans such as "one hundred million hearts beating as one" (Matsumura 2007: 91–92), or "labor in the service of the state," to persuade women that factory work was a patriotic duty (Miyake 1991: 281). By 1944, Japan enacted a conscription law requiring women of all classes between the ages of 12 and 40 to work in the war production factories that previously relied on a voluntary workforce. Resisters faced prison sentences and fines. As the United States began intensive bombing of Japanese cities, factory working conditions became much harsher and living conditions became miserable as food was scarce and women struggled to feed their families. By 1945, the government assigned some women to perform quasi-military duties, such as serving as fire marshals in cities like Tokyo where the United States began dropping incendiary bombs that killed an estimated 200,000 people (Bingham and Gross 1987: 237). Japanese women also dug trenches, constructed bomb shelters in targeted cities, and served on search-and-rescue teams for those buried in the rubble after bomb blasts (Miyake 1991: 287–89).

In Germany, the Nazi Party and the totalitarian fascist national government it created spread racist ideology, a message of Aryan–Germanic racial and cultural superiority, to mobilize German men and women and gain their support for the Nazi empire-building project. Nazi assertions of racial superiority were delivered during mass demonstrations and orchestrated spectacles such as those staged at yearly Nazi Party rallies in Nuremberg, and disseminated through religious, professional, and youth organizations. The Nazi Party promoted the message that war was necessary to fulfill Germany's racial destiny: to reunite racially pure Germanic peoples within an extensive territorial empire ruled by the visionary Nazi Führer, Adolf Hitler. Within this empire, extended into Eastern Europe and Russia, the Germanic people subjugated the "racially-inferior" Slavic people and attempted to exterminate the "impure" Jewish race (Findley and Rothney 2011: 128; LaFeber 1989: 366).

Nazi Germany employed traditional Western European two-gender role stereotypes as it rallied the German people to support its imperial project. German men were constructed as heroic warriors and political leaders in the public sphere and patriarchs in the private sphere; German women were constructed as supportive wives and nurturing mothers in the private sphere. With the message of German Aryan racial superiority so crucial to the Nazi imperial campaign, Germanic women also played a key patriotic role in bearing and raising the "pure race" children, who would build the empire. In German war-mobilization propaganda, women were portrayed as "guardians of racial purity, mothers, housewives, and bearers of the cultural heritage" (Rupp 1978: 166). As the war continued into the 1940s, Germany needed a larger labor force to fill the war production shortages as working-class men were conscripted into the military. Yet the Nazi government, in general, stuck to its ideology of separate gendered spheres ideology regarding German women's "proper roles." The Nazi government believed that German men would fight harder for their families and their nation if women's roles as wives and mothers were preserved as sacrosanct (Boxer and Quataert 2000: 249). The only professions open to German women during the 1930s were those linked to their roles as nurturing mothers in nursing or social-work fields. Nonetheless, by the mid-1940s and out of necessity, some German women were recruited into various support positions for the German military, such as clerical workers, ambulance and war-transport drivers, and so on (Anderson and Zinsser 2000: 309). Meanwhile, enslaved peoples from conquered territories filled factory labor needs.

British and American women and men saw some of the same war-mobilization propaganda images they had seen during the First World War repeated because the widespread demands on these populations to support their nation's total war projects were similar. American and British governments, militaries, industrialists, and their war-propaganda bureaus again constructed "men" as heroic, self-sacrificing "Just Warriors," who fought to protect all they loved and valued from an aggressive enemy. Wartime propaganda focused on cultivating male soldiers' feelings of personal obligation to protect "*their* women," with "*their*" women" portrayed in print media and on-screen images as "women-worth-fighting-for." These women were, most often, pictured as white and middle class. The pin-up photos of young and beautiful American actresses were one example of "women-worth-fighting-for," which the US military distributed to its soldiers during the Second World War; suggestive images of women who had been violated or were about to be violated by the enemy were another example of "women-worth-fighting-for." This so-called "rape propaganda" was designed to elicit male soldiers' hypermasculine urges to avenge *their* victimized women (Westbrook 1990: 589). Propagandists realized that constructing idealized images of women as "objects of obligation" was far more effective in mobilizing male soldiers, than persuading men to fight for an abstract and disembodied "state." Political scientist Michael Walzer has explained this phenomenon in theoretical terms as "the problem" of political obligation that liberal democratic states face during times of war in this way:

> Moved by love, sympathy, or friendship, men in liberal society can and obviously do incur ultimate obligations. They may even find themselves in situations where they are or think they are obliged to defend the state which in turn defends the property and enjoyment of their friends and families. But if they then actually risk their lives or die, they do so because they have incurred private obligations which have nothing to do with politics. The state may shape the environment within which these obligations are freely incurred, and it may provide the occasions and means for their fulfillment. But this is only to say that when states make war and men fight, the reasons of the two often are and ought to be profoundly different.
>
> WALZER QUOTED IN WESTBROOK 1990: 591

Protection and possession were powerful male urges that British and American propagandists directed in service to state war goals.

During the Second World War, war-mobilization propaganda created in the United States also employed racial messages, urging US soldiers to avenge their violated nation that had been attacked by a "sub-human" species swarming out of Japan. Japan's surprise attack on Pearl Harbor, its leaders' decisions to use rape and other brutalization tactics to terrorize civilian populations throughout the war years, as well as the suicidal military tactics employed in the final year of the war, including the Imperial Army's *banzai* charges and the Air Force's *kamikaze* pilots—all these war-making practices shocked the moral sensibilities of "white" Americans, who were already attuned to racial differences and had a long history of asserting their "white supremacy" over "non-white" races. American war makers denigrated and dehumanized the Japanese enemy through the dissemination of racially charged propaganda that portrayed the Japanese people as "beasts, vermin or devils" (Dower 1986: 294). Generating race hatred fueled white US soldiers' hypermasculine savagery, serving the purposes of the wartime policy makers who demanded "unconditional surrender" of their enemies. Imperial Japan's wartime propaganda likewise depicted US and British leaders and soldiers as "demonic others" on a mission to defile the Japanese "pure self" to inspire Japanese soldiers and civilians to fight to the death to defend the nation (Dower 1986).

British and American war propagandists persuaded women to join the war production plants and to serve their nations on the assembly lines "for the duration" of the war with images that highlighted women's capabilities, talents, and patriotism, such as the popular images of "Rosie the Riveter" disseminated in the United States. In Britain, larger numbers of women worked in war production plants during the Second World War compared to the First World War, comprising over 2.2 million of the 2.8 million workers who were "new" to the workplace. This was partly due to the fact that very early in the war, Britain had imposed a compulsory draft of single women who were between the ages of 20 and 30, for factory or military service. American women were not conscripted, but the US government's War Manpower Commission created a "Women's Advisory Committee" that focused on voluntary recruitment strategies; over 6 million women entered the wartime workforce (Matsumura 2007: 78). War-mobilization campaigns in the United States flattered women with high praise for those who joined the war production effort and glamorized their efforts in text and images. Other mobilization campaigns shamed US women who had not entered the war production work force, and branded them as "slackers," as the First World War posters produced in the United States and Britain had shamed males who did not join the military. These war-mobilization messages placed the responsibility for winning the war sooner and saving soldiers' lives directly on working women's shoulders (Rupp 1978: 95–97).

Military recruiters also sought to enlist American women into the newly created women's branches of the US military: the Women's Army Corps (WAC), the Navy's Women Accepted for Volunteer Emergency Service (WAVES), the Marine Corps Women's Reserve (MCWR), and the Coast Guard Women's Reserve (SPAR), as well as the quasi-military Nursing Corps. New uniforms were designed for each branch of service, and recruitment posters appealed to women's sense of patriotic duty with such messages as: "To Make Men Free: Enlist in the WAVES Today: you will share the gratitude of a nation when the victory is ours"; "Be a Marine, Free a Marine to Fight"; and "Are you a girl with a star-spangled heart? Join the WAC Now!" In addition, as wartime propaganda had done during the First World War, mobilization propaganda during the Second World War also repeated messages to women to persuade them to conserve war materials and food in order to support their nations in war. In Britain, messages to women proclaimed: "Food is a Munition of War, Don't Waste It." American women, outside of war zones were urged to produce and preserve more food: "Dig for Victory: Grow Your Own Vegetables" and "Can all you Can [of home grown vegetables]: It's a Real War Job!" Although studies of American women's contributions to the war effort reveal that patriotic obligations inspired women as the propagandists intended, more practical and "private" considerations also motivated women; they worked in war production plants or joined the military because they earned higher wages and received more respect than they had in prewar years.

Gender, race, and violations of human rights

The Second World War was fought in ways that violated human rights on a much larger scale than wars that were fought in the past. Wartime human rights abuses were gendered and raced in some obvious ways, and in some not-so-obvious ways, too. The few examples discussed here most certainly do not begin to cover the totality of the disregard for human life and human freedom that all belligerents displayed and all government leaders justified at one time or another during the long world war.

When Japan officially declared war on China, the Japanese army attacked and raped Chinese women in its bid to overcome the Chinese government's resistance and to terrorize the Chinese population. The brutal seven-week-long campaign by the Japanese to capture the Chinese national capital of Nanjing in December 1937, for example, became known as the "Rape of Nanjing." During the campaign, Japanese troops raped an estimated 20,000 women; they also murdered 12,000 civilians, and executed 30,000 defeated, and captured Chinese troops. After looting the city, the Japanese army burned much of it to the ground (Spence 1990: 448).

Rape and sexual abuse of women has been a common occurrence during times of war, certainly predating the twentieth-century World Wars, and occurring across cultures. Rape is a crime of domination, not an act driven by sexual desire. During wars, rape becomes a weapon of war often utilized to dominate the enemy (Goldstein 2001: 362–63). Feminist scholars who study aspects of militarized hegemonic masculinity, with its defining characteristics of male violence and its assertion of power over women and other feminized masculinities, define wartime rapes committed by soldiers under orders from their military leaders as "state-sanctioned institutionalized uses of force with the military as the ultimate exemplar of masculinity," that is, wartime rapes are "state violence" perpetrated by *militarized men*. Feminists who study the powerful homosocial bonds that military leaders deliberately cultivate in all-male militaries assert that the practice of gang rape creates a bond of loyalty among the male troops. They become an exclusive cadre of *"our men"* who rape *"their women,"* who are constructed as unchaste and depraved. The male bond created during a gang rape either alleviates a measure of an individual's guilt for the rapes that he commits, or he sedates himself in other ways to forget the guilt, or he turns his distress outward and becomes even more violent and aggressive toward his rape victims. These feminist analyses of wartime constructions of militarized masculinity dispel the myths that *all* men will commit *indiscriminate* rapes in times of war, but they also argue that "in wartime, perpetrating sexual violence—at least against the 'enemy'—becomes a more socially acceptable feature of (militarized) masculinity" (Alison 2007: 76–80).

The Japanese military also justified the exploitation of Korean peoples whom the Japanese considered to be "inferior" Asian peoples, following the logic of their doctrine of racial superiority. Japanese colonialists forced Koreans to produce food for the Japanese army, to deliver their nation's raw materials to Japan's production plants, and to labor in Japanese factories during the 1930s and 1940s. The Japanese army also "colonized" the sexuality of Korean women, raping women and forcing them into sexual service to

Japanese troops and civilian bureaucrats. Japanese officials screened the selected Korean "comfort women" for venereal and other diseases before they were posted to Japanese divisions. Initially, Korean comfort women were assigned to serve the Imperial army officers to reward their higher military rank. By the late 1930s, however, as the Japanese army occupied vast areas of China and started to move into Southeast Asia, the army enslaved Korean women and women from other occupied Asian nations and forced them into sexual service for the troops. Estimates of the numbers of Asian women who were forced into the ranks of the comfort women during the Second World War range from 150,000 to 200,000 or more; approximately 80 percent of these women were believed to be Korean nationals (Ramusack and Sievers 1999: 220–21). Testimony given by Korean women and human rights advocates to the UN secretary-general in February 1993, and at the 1993 UN Conference on Human Rights Nongovernmental Organization Forum in June 1993, noted that "genocide was not a goal" of the Japanese sexual assaults on Asian women, "but it is believed that 70 to 90 percent of these women died in captivity, and among the known survivors, none were subsequently able to have children" (Copelon 1998: 70).

The US military also "officially tolerated" prostitution in Honolulu as a service to its male soldiers when they served during the Second World War in the Pacific and were on leave in Hawaii. In this case, applications of race and gender power and abuses of human rights were sanctioned to serve site-specific military needs. With the male-to-female ratio in Honolulu being several hundred men to one woman, the male soldiers' "sexual release" was considered necessary to keep the peace, and, conversely, to maintain men's virility and "manly spirit" so that they would fight the Japanese enemy more fiercely. Honolulu brothels were also segregated in deference to the US white supremacist racial order, which had to be reinforced as US war-policy makers and propagandists constructed a race war against the Japanese "yellow hordes" to mobilize US soldiers. Brothels that housed "white" prostitutes who were recruited from San Francisco were officially regulated, and these white sex workers, constructed as "war workers," were somewhat protected. American military authorities inspected and certified the health of these women and sent those who contracted venereal disease to hospitals for medical treatment. Women of color who were prostitutes did not receive the same treatment. Women of color staffed the "local rooms," or unregulated brothels, where prices for their services were lower. Rates of venereal disease among these prostitutes were "astronomical." White US soldiers also had greater access to the brothels than US soldiers of color, who at times were barred from using the services of the white prostitutes (Goldstein 2001: 344–45; Bailey and Farber 1992).

The Second World War–era abuse of human rights that is seared into the collective memory of Western societies is that of the Nazi German policy of genocide against the European Jewish peoples. The source of this genocidal policy is usually traced to Adolf Hitler's racial theories, that Aryan Germany had to rid itself of "impure" and degraded racial groups. From the time of Hitler's ascension to power in 1933, the Nazi Party government singled out Jewish peoples for persecution and abuse, first stripping them of their citizenship rights and confiscating their property, then destroying Jewish businesses and homes. Following years of persecution, in 1938, the Nazi government began rounding up and incarcerating tens of thousands of Jewish peoples in concentration camps, where they were starved and forced to labor for their captors, with no distinctions in the treatment of male or female prisoners.

The US and British governments did not alter their immigration policies in the 1930s, when Jewish peoples fleeing from German persecution tried to leave their country and appealed to Western nations for asylum. In the United States, anti-Semitism, economic nationalism, and fear that Jewish communists would bring subversive ideas into US society weakened and restricted the US government's aid to the majority of Jewish refugees who were desperate to emigrate, although some of the most prominent Jewish scholars and scientists and their families were among the few thousand who were allowed to enter the United States under its immigration laws that strictly enforced a national quota system. Without material or moral support from the leading Western nations, the League of Nations Secretariat was also powerless to help the Eastern European Jews. The Secretariat was sympathetic to the Jewish refugees' plight but had no formal powers to move the Nazi government off its brutal racist mission after 1933. League member states would not provide funding for resettlement of the Jews who were not welcome in other nations without economic resources, and the Nazi government routinely seized money and assets from the Jewish people before they allowed them to leave the country. International women's, religious, and human rights organizations appealed to their members in Western states for aid, and provided what help they could to a few of the tens of thousands of Jewish refugees and displaced persons who fled from German-held territories in the late 1930s and early 1940s. They also visited the German concentration camps in the occupied territories where Jewish prisoners, and other "undesirable" and political prisoners were incarcerated when they could gain permission, but their actions had very limited impact and did not alter either the fascist or anti-fascist governments' policies (Garner 2010: 125–27).

After 1941 when Germany launched its attack on the Soviet Union, the Nazi government also enacted a policy of genocide, the "final solution" to Germany's "Jewish problem." Within the concentration camps—now "death camps"—in Germany and Poland, Jewish captives were gassed, shot, and buried alive. By 1942, the horrors of the genocide were known to Western Allied Power leaders and became public knowledge throughout the Western world as newspaper reports were circulated in London and other Western capitals (Garner 2010: 124). But even then, the Western Allies' war strategies were not amended to destroy German rail lines that transported the Jewish captives to the concentration camps or to launch other rescue missions. Anti-Semitic attitudes prevailed in the United States and Britain, in spite of continued appeals from human rights groups and Jewish communities living in the West. When the war ended and the death tolls were tallied, six-and-a-half million Jewish peoples had lost their lives at the hands of the German Nazis, a *holocaust*, or catastrophe, of deadliest nature (LeFeber 1989: 366–69). Following Germany's military defeat, Adolf Hitler's suicide, and the surrender to the Allies by the remaining Nazi government leaders on May 7, 1945, Western Allied troops "liberated" the Jewish survivors of the death camps. Only the highest-ranking Nazi leadership, twenty-two of the surviving Nazi generals and officials, would be held responsible for the genocide of the six-and-a-half million Jews and many more millions of European peoples killed in Germany's quest to build its "pure race" empire. These few elite male leaders were put on trial for their "crimes against humanity" at the War Crimes Tribunal convened by the victorious Allied Powers in Nuremburg, from November 1945 to September 1946 (Keylor 2011: 191–92).

Women, gender, and the Cold War

The US government and the Russian Bolsheviks who established the Communist Party–run state, the Soviet Union, had been locked in contentious state-to-state relations since the First World War era. In October 1917, the Bolsheviks staged a successful revolution and overthrew the West-leaning Russian provisional government that had briefly replaced the collapsed tsarist regime. When the Bolsheviks withdrew Russia from the Entente alliance and the Russian troops from the battlefield and negotiated a separate "peace" with Germany, the United States joined their British, French, and Japanese allies and sent troops into Russia to topple the Bolshevik government. After the 1917–18 anti-Bolshevik military mission failed, the US government refused to recognize the legitimacy of the Soviet Union until 1933. Government animosities between the United States and the Soviet Union temporarily abated during the Second World War, when the two Great Powers forged an anti-fascist alliance from 1941 to 1945 to defeat their common foes, Nazi Germany and Imperial Japan. That alliance ended abruptly with the defeat of the fascist powers and the US demonstration of its new and deadly nuclear-weapons superiority in August 1945, when the United States used atomic bombs to destroy the Japanese cities of Hiroshima and Nagasaki. Many historians and IR scholars date the onset of the Cold War to the days those bombs were detonated. They mark the end of the Cold War in December 1991 when the former the Communist Party–governed Soviet Union dissolved. It was replaced by a Commonwealth of Independent States, in which communist ideology and party dictates no longer reigned supreme.

The Cold War era is often studied in terms of the conflicts and interactions of the two global superpowers that heavily influenced international affairs from 1945 to 1991, with a focus on the elite government and military leaders who determined US and Soviet foreign policies during the long Cold War. During the Cold War, a struggle for global influence between the United States and the Soviet Union, the "superpowers" that emerged after the Second World War, was waged through rival military alliances, such as the North Atlantic Treaty Organization (NATO) and the Warsaw Pact, and through other strategic trade agreements, economic and military aid directed to client states in exchange for political loyalty, a massively expensive nuclear-arms race, "limited" regional hot wars fought with conventional weapons, espionage, and "illegal" covert operations, including political assassinations and widespread propaganda campaigns, to mobilize popular support for all these operations.

Some Cold War studies focus on determining which incidents or which leaders "caused" the Cold War, which of the two superpowers was most to blame for the continuation of the Cold War, or which state's leaders or state's global strategies were most responsible for ending the Cold War. Other Cold War studies have focused on specific Cold War–era conflicts and the creation and maintenance of two global spheres of influence, where the United States and the Soviet Union battled for the hearts and minds of peoples or for access to markets and resources of states in Eastern Europe, Asia, the Middle East, Africa, and Latin America. Or, Cold War studies have focused on the development of increasingly deadly weapons and weapons-delivery systems and on the nuclear-arms race that cost trillions of dollars in US and Soviet national treasures and threatened human security across the planet. Some of these studies have analyzed the Cold War era from the perspectives of the states or peoples of the Third World, either those aligned with the interests of the global superpowers or those that devised their own goals for national self-determination and remained nonaligned to either superpower. Some Cold War–era studies have focused on how US and Soviet government leaders used ideological weapons, or the power of ideas, to "win" the Cold War battle for the "hearts and minds" of the world's people. Gender power was part of the ideological weapons arsenal. The following section discusses just a few examples of how "women" and gender power operated during the Cold War era in the service of, or in opposition to, US or Soviet superpower goals.

American and Soviet policy makers used "women" and gender power relations to reinforce Cold War–era binaries: women versus men, "free" versus "communist" worlds, "East" versus "West," and "war" versus "peace" were all present in propaganda campaigns that were designed to generate support or fear among their own populations and to gain public approval for the allocation of national resources that fueled Cold War–era military engagements and the nuclear-arms race. Although some women and some feminized male populations opposed the Cold War international order, the hegemonic masculine state powers—the United States, the Soviet Union, and their state allies—successfully maintained the global superpower-run system for nearly five decades, shaping the world views of their peoples. Moreover, in the aftermath of the Cold War, they created a narrative that venerated the Cold War superpower relations that had "prevented" or "avoided" nuclear holocaust and maintained a "Long Peace" (Gaddis 1989).

Cold War, gender roles, East versus West

As discussed in Chapter 2, soon after the Second World War anti-fascist alliance broke down, US foreign-policy makers like George F. Kennan defined an irreconcilable conflict with aggressive Soviet power as a battle to be fought on all fronts to "contain" dangerous communist ideas and Soviet military and economic power. The US "Cold Warriors" who took over foreign policy making in the aftermath of the Second World War frequently used apocalyptic language to make their case that the "free world" was locked in a struggle for "world control" with the "slave world" that was overrun by "communist tyranny." The super-charged rhetoric of US male foreign-policy makers demonstrated, according to historian Christian Appy, that "the Cold War was, as much as anything else, a competition over discourse, a 'struggle for the word'," as well as for the world (Appy 2000: 2–3). How did US and Soviet leaders use their words to construct gender roles that would communicate the superior power of their worlds, for their own peoples as well as for international audiences?

Historian Elaine Tyler May has analyzed the relationships between constructions of class, race, and gender power in Cold War–era US society. In doing so, she described how US leaders sought to project an image of a materially prosperous US society, united in its love of freedom and democratic self-expression, that could be held up as a model for the rest of the world to aspire to, especially oppressed peoples living in Communist Party–governed nations. If the class, race, or gender conflicts that in fact existed in US society were exposed to public view, faith in the "American way of life" would be jeopardized. The nation would face a crisis of confidence and would experience a vulnerability that Soviet propagandists and other "enemies" of the United States could exploit to diminish US global power. The inviolable white, middle-class, affluent, suburban, nuclear American family became a symbol of US power both internationally and domestically. It became a bulwark against communist subversion and other dangerous forms of "perversion," such as homosexuality. One example of how Cold War–era propaganda utilized class, race, and gender messaging occurred when the US vice-president Richard Nixon showed off a model version of an "American home" to the Soviet premier Nikita Khrushchev at the American Exhibition in Moscow in 1959. Not only touting the superiority of the white, middle-class American home as a private "sanctuary" furnished with modern appliances that automated and streamlined domestic labor and provided a steady stream of news and entertainment, Vice-President Nixon also held up the white, middle-class, nuclear American family with its breadwinning male head of household and its homemaking female wife and mother as the "universal" human family ideal. America, according to Richard Nixon's narrative, took care of its women and made their lives "easier." Soviet premier Khrushchev countered with his own gendered propaganda message to praise Soviet women. He asserted that Soviet women were equal in all respects to Soviet men, and as they performed "productive" labor outside the home, they were liberated from their former lives of subservience and drudgery in the home (May 1999: 10–14).

Despite Khrushchev's confident assertions of Soviet superiority, during the Cold War–era Soviet leaders were nevertheless sensitive to Western criticisms that the communist revolution had neglected "human comfort" in its drive for economic and military advances. As historian Susan Reid has explained, by the latter half of the 1950s, Soviet policy makers were also focusing on the domestic sphere, where Soviet women had a gendered homemaking role to fulfill. The "modern" Soviet home of the late 1950s may have been an apartment, but it housed a single family in a "less cramped" setting than during the early decades of Soviet rule when multiple families occupied apartments together, and it was furnished in a less-austere, "cozier" style. State planners and architects of these new single-family homes had to accommodate the desires of the occupants of the new housing projects they were building, particularly the Soviet women. As Reid explained, Soviet "women were constructed as the primary consumers and homemakers and as such, their dominion and expertise within the domestic domain was acknowledged as a force to be reckoned with; women had to be brought on board the socialist modernising project if the new flats were not to become nests of regressive, petit-bourgeois mentalities" (Reid 2009: 470–71). Soviet women (and men) took pride in furnishing their homes. Most furnishings were created by the household members with beauty and comfort in mind, and according to state policy makers this should not be considered "counter-revolutionary." But official propaganda continued to direct gendered messages to women, to convince them that "the Soviet woman was not confined to her domestic role, but was also active in production and social life, which was vital to her self-realisation" (Reid 2009: 477–78).

During the Cold War, US and Soviet women also played their parts in the debate over the superiority of their nation's political systems, and they also linked their arguments to women's roles and status. The women's own constructions of feminine gender roles, however, were somewhat different from those of their male leaders. In the United States, primarily white, middle-class women were most often the ones who had the education and other social advantages to advocate for women's participation in international and domestic politics. These women-led international NGOs, and together with a few female government-appointed delegates such as the former first lady Eleanor Roosevelt, they constructed a discourse of women's equal rights within democratic societies at international forums provided by the United Nations. They presented their version of "women in U.S. society" as having equal opportunities to participate in politics and they advocated for international treaties that would make those opportunities and democratic privileges that they enjoyed universally available to women in all nations. They promoted a liberal feminist prescription for women's liberation that emphasized individual rights guaranteed by modern liberal democratic states, including property rights, voting rights, freedom of speech, freedom of religion, and freedom of association, and they supported liberal state intervention in the form of labor laws and social-welfare services to aid women and children. Women from the United States and other Western nations used the UN Commission on the Status of Women (CSW), which was formed in 1946–47, to propose a Convention on the Political Rights of Women, adopted by the UN General Assembly in 1952, a Convention on the Nationality of Married Women, adopted in 1952, and the Convention on Consent to Marriage, Minimum Age for Marriage, and Registration of Marriages, adopted in 1962 (Garner 2010: 168, 179–82).

Soviet women who were official delegates to the United Nations, and women from other socialist states and organizations that were sympathetic to the Soviet Union, formed the NGO Women's International Democratic Federation (WIDF) in 1945. They also used the CSW forum to criticize Western women's not-so-equal social status and to disseminate their alternative prescriptions regarding what women needed to be "liberated" around the world. Soviet women explained that the Soviet Constitution established their legal equality and included guarantees of equal pay for equal work, equal rights to employment benefits, paid maternity benefits, marriage based on mutual consent, and legalized abortion. But while the "woman problem" was officially solved according to Soviet state leaders and their female surrogates at the United Nations, in fact Soviet women performed an estimated 75 percent of the domestic work in addition to working full-time outside the home, and many Soviet homes lacked the "labor-saving" appliances available to Western women, despite the improvements in space and privacy described above. The only women's organizations allowed to form in the Soviet Union were those sanctioned by the government under the umbrella of the Soviet Women's Committee, and those organizations existed to communicate state messages to women rather than to facilitate independent women's activism. Nonetheless, Soviet women who served as representatives at the United Nations asserted the superiority of socialist states' treatment of women and they presented themselves as the champions of "peace," promoting nuclear disarmament and opposing the NATO military alliance, and advocates of human rights, anticolonialism, and women's and children's economic welfare. These arguments resonated with women from newly independent Third World nations, especially after delegates from the socialist states supported the "Group of 77" (G-77) nonaligned developing nations that formed in 1964 as an anticolonial voting bloc at the United Nations (Sundstrom 2010: 232–33; de Haan 2010: 550; Ilic 2011: 160).

"Supportive" versus "subversive" uses of gender power

Historian Laura McEnaney has examined the immediate "postwar" years and has argued that US policy makers and citizens experienced the early Cold War years as an era when society was neither fully demobilized nor fully militarized, but was focused on "national security" (McEnaney 2000: 4). The US government kept the nation "prepared" for nuclear war with the Soviet Union by creating a civil defense "paramilitary" program that mobilized men and women as members of "families" with distinct gender roles. The civil defense program defined special roles for *men as fathers* to protect their homes and families by building "private" nuclear fallout shelters and leading their families "as sergeants" in military-emergency drills, and special roles for *women as mothers*, to serve as their husbands' second-in-command corralling and calming the children in case of emergency, stocking the fallout shelters with food and water, and performing "light rescue" work if necessary to nurse the wounded (McEnaney 2000: 77). Women played leading roles in the government bureau, the Federal Civilian Defense Agency, which developed national preparedness plans and some middle-class club women embraced voluntary roles to assist the FCDA. Seeking to be of "service" to the nation as they had during the Second World War, the women civil defense volunteers instructed their counterparts—white, middle-class housewives— to apply their domestic organizational skills and traditional participation in community service work to perform "vital" national security support work. Despite the FCDA's clear messages that families were responsible for national security "at home," and notwithstanding that some women's volunteer groups embraced civil defense messaging, McEnaney notes that compliance with the messaging was far from universal: "It appears women behaved quite like men in the shadow of the bomb: as Cold War citizens and taxpayers, they generally endorsed the arms race and its premises, but as private citizens, they rejected a level of household militarization that asked them to arrange household duties around external threats" (2000: 120).

Gender power was also used to subvert the Cold War–era foreign policies of the global superpowers. American women who opposed the nuclear-arms race, for example, also used the power inherent in their gender roles as housewives and mothers to reject the superpowers' military strategy of "mutually assured destruction" (MAD). MAD compelled the superpower rivals to stockpile nuclear weapons and develop long-range missile-delivery systems in relatively equivalent numbers, each with the potential to annihilate their enemy (and the rest of the world), if the weapons were used in global warfare. As the superpowers developed and tested increasingly deadly nuclear weapons throughout the 1940s and 1950s, by the 1960s some US women, many of them white, middle-class, full-time homemakers and mothers, rejected the militaristic definition of "national security" emanating from policy makers in Washington and Moscow. A small group of mothers, along with some men, organized a one-day strike, known as Women Strike for Peace (WSP), in November 1961. The initial strike turned into a nationwide movement. WSP members waged a gendered antinuclear media campaign to disseminate their messages to the public. For example, WSP members wrote letters to Jacqueline Kennedy and Nina Khrushchev, which were published in newspapers, asking them to appeal to their husbands, the US president and the Soviet premier, to halt nuclear testing that would destroy the world for their children. As reported by WSP historian Amy Swerdlow, movement rhetoric was staunchly apolitical: "We're just ordinary people, not experts," "We're not politicians—we're housewives and working women. . . . We don't make foreign policy—but we know to which end we want it made: toward preservation of life on earth" (Swerdlow 1993: 19).

The WSP movement operated within the context of Cold War geopolitics when the US government routinely monitored all domestic political activities on the lookout for communist subversion. And, WSP criticized US foreign policy at a moment of extremely tense US-Soviet relations. As a result, the US Congressional House Un-American Activities Committee (HUAC) subpoenaed fourteen WSP women, some who had radical political associations, to appear at an investigative hearing in Washington DC in December 1962. Accused of political subversion, WSP members turned the tables on the male congressmen by transforming the hearings into a "contest . . . between masculine and feminine notions of patriotism" (Swerdlow 1993: 99). WSP activists played up their gendered feminine appeal to the media. They rallied support for subpoenaed members and packed the House hearing room with mothers and babies. In their testimonies, the women stated their morally incontestable concerns for human security and their fundamental faith in the United States' democratic principles and constitutional right to free speech. In the wake of the two-day-long hearings, national newspaper headlines declared the women's propaganda victory: "Peace Gals Make Red Hunters Look Silly," "Redhunters Decapitated," "Peace Ladies Tangle with Baffled Congress," and "It's Ladies' Day at Capitol: Hoots, Howls, and Charm" (Swerdlow 1993: 117). The antinuclear public opinion that was generated in part by WSP activism resulted in a nuclear test ban treaty between the US and Soviet governments that outlawed nuclear weapons tests conducted above ground. Nonetheless, nuclear-weapons stockpiling continued throughout the Cold War-era and underground weapons tests continued. WSP activists also turned some of their attention to protesting the escalating US war against communist expansion in Vietnam.

During these antinuclear and anti-war protests, some US women decided to enter national electoral politics, aiming to change the direction of domestic- and foreign-policy-making from inside US government. New York lawyer Bella Abzug, a WSP member since 1961, was elected to the US House of Representatives in 1970 and served until 1976. Regarding foreign policy making, Abzug vocally criticized Cold War anti-communism and militarism in all its manifestations. She was an avowed internationalist who believed that the United Nations was the best forum to work out global conflicts peacefully. She also believed that strategic use of economic assistance rather than military aid was the best way for the US government to encourage the spread of democracy worldwide (Jeffreys-Jones 1995: 137–47). From the time that she joined the WSP movement, Abzug never stopped denouncing the US stockpile of nuclear weapons or global nuclear-arms proliferation. Bella Abzug was also an early critic of the US military campaign to fight communists in Vietnam and Southeast Asia, and on the first day of her first congressional term in office she introduced a resolution calling for US troop withdrawals from Vietnam. Abzug was a strong supporter of the US participation in the United Nations International Women's Year conference and served as a member of the US delegation to the 1975 conference held in Mexico City (discussed further in Chapter 4). She also played a leading role in organizing the US National Women's Conference held in Houston in 1977, and led the National Women's Advisory Committee during the Jimmy Carter administration until 1978. In the years following her government service, as a "private citizen" Abzug nonetheless remained a "public figure" who criticized conflict-driven US foreign policy throughout the 1980s and into the 1990s (Garner 2013: 32–33).

During the 1980s, US president Ronald Reagan's administration ushered in an anti-feminist era in domestic-policy making and reestablished aggressive, masculinized US foreign-policy-making after a brief era of *détente* in Cold War relations with the Soviet Union. Regarding domestic policy, the Reagan administration called on Congress to expand neoliberal economic policies that privatized previously state-run human services and cut social spending. In 1982, Congress responded with cuts of "nearly $1 billion in Aid to Families with Dependent Children, $2 billion cut in Medicaid funding, $3.8 billion cut in job training funds, closing of child care centers serving low income women," and so on, funding decisions that had a disproportionately harmful effect on the lives of poor women and children in the United States (US Women's National Women's Conference Committee, 1982, quoted in Garner 2013: 52). The administration's foreign policy also supported congressional legislation to cut off US funding for global family planning initiatives. These cuts had a detrimental effect on women's reproductive health globally. At the same time, the administration advocated for dramatic increases US military spending, doubling the US defense budget between 1981 and 1984, and escalated nuclear-weapons development (Ferguson and Rogers 1987: 129–30). Moreover, high-level administration officials engaged in covert funding of anti-communist paramilitary forces known as the "Contras" in Nicaragua with funds they diverted from illegal arms sales to Iran.

To challenge the Reagan administration and congressional foreign-policy priorities and global actions, Bella Abzug organized the Women's Foreign Policy Council (WFPC) in 1987. Along with feminist activists in government and nongovernment roles, Abzug coordinated a WFPC campaign to expose the Reagan administration's illegal Iran-Contra activities. The WFPC also criticized the administration's nuclear-arms buildup and its proposed "Strategic Defense Initiative" to invest trillions of dollars in a satellite-based antiballistic missile defense system to counter a Soviet nuclear-weapons attack (Garner 2013: 55–58). At informal congressional hearings held in 1987, Abzug and members of the WFPC testified before sympathetic congressmen and women to outline "Women's Perspectives on U.S. Foreign Policy." Abzug articulated her views on women's necessary involvement in international affairs in opening remarks to the assembled hearing:

> The role of women in foreign policy is to create a different kind of structure that would enable women to secure a peaceful atmosphere, and also to change the prevailing thinking and perspective so that women can construct a world that will provide for equality, opportunity and social justice for their family and themselves . . . we're no longer prepared to just hoot and holler from the sidelines. The failure of our own policies in this country, as evidenced by the Iran-Contra Affair, as evidenced by events in the Persian Gulf, as evidenced by a whole series of failures in the international economy indicates that it's time for a new, bold approach. And I think women can make a difference.
>
> ABZUG TESTIMONY QUOTED IN GARNER 2013: 263

In addition to the hardships that Americans and global populations experienced due to neoliberal economic "austerity" policies and diversion of US government revenues to military spending during the decade of the 1980s, the Reagan administration's governing policies also increased pressures on the Soviet leadership. In response, the Soviets could either increase their military spending to keep up with the Americans or change the course of the Cold War policies and reduce military and other aid commitments to their socialist client states in Eastern Europe and anti-colonial allies in the Third World. Based on the strained state of the Soviet economy, popular opposition to the Cold War status quo in Russia, and a long, costly, and inconclusive war that the Soviets had waged to prop up a Communist Party government in Afghanistan in its fight against US-backed forces from 1979 to 1987, the Soviet Communist Party leadership, following the direction set by Party general-secretary Mikhail Gorbachev, transformed the Soviet Union's Cold War policies. Engaging in a domestic economic restructuring program known as perestroika, and a new policy of "openness" or glasnost between the government and the Soviet people, Gorbachev also opened nuclear-disarmament negotiations with the United

States and Western European democracies. In 1988, the Communist Party withdrew Soviet troops from Afghanistan and announced withdrawals of Soviet troops and decreased foreign aid to Eastern European socialist states, thus opening the way for popular uprisings in Eastern Europe that demanded more pluralistic democratic governments in Communist Party–led states across the region so that "by Christmas day [1989] virtually every Communist state in East Europe had announced plans for free elections by the spring of 1990" (Hartman and Wendzel 1994: 356). Eventually, liberalizing reforms led to the dissolution of the Soviet Republic in 1991. That revolutionary reconfiguration of global power marked the end of the Cold War world order.

Reacting to the swift collapse of Soviet power, the US government under the George H. W. Bush administration supported a "transition paradigm" that provided US aid and advisers to the former socialist bloc states in Eastern Europe and the Soviet Union as they transformed from one-Communist-Party-led state systems into pluralistic, democratic political systems, and from centrally planned, socialist command economies into participants in the global capitalist market economy (Pishchikova 2011: 40; 78–79). Nonetheless, the former Soviet and Eastern European nation-states did not follow a smooth or predicted path to open, democratic, economically prosperous societies that respected human rights, as the following example analyzing the Bosnian War illustrates.

Women, gender, and the Bosnian War

The war that broke out in Bosnia in 1992 was one in a series of wars that dissolved the socialist state of Yugoslavia, a state that had been forged during the Second World War Partisan resistance to Nazi German occupation as led by the Yugoslav Communist Party and Marshall Josip Broz Tito. After the German defeat in 1945, Marshall Tito, leader of the Yugoslav People's Army (JNA) became general secretary of the Yugoslav Communist Party. In the postwar period, he unified six populations of Slavic peoples living in Southeastern Europe: the Serbs, Croats, Slovenes, Macedonians, Montenegrins, and the Muslims living in the territory known as Bosnia-Herzegovina, to found the Cold War–era Socialist Federal Republic of Yugoslavia, a confederation of six socialist republics, based on ethnic-majority geographical territories. To rule over all, Marshall Tito established an authoritarian, Communist Party–led central Yugoslav government. To forge a multiethnic "national" identity among the various groups of Slavic peoples, his government combined anti-fascist purges with measures to earn loyalty among targeted groups. These measures included a propaganda campaign touting "Brotherhood and Unity," selective land redistribution, constitutionally guaranteed political and economic rights for women, and "market socialist" economic policies to moderate the ruling communist ideology. The federated Yugoslav state Tito and his compatriots established existed until 1991, over ten years after Tito's death in 1980.

Throughout the 1980s, however, renewed interest in separatist, ethnically defined "national" identities was expressed with increasing frequency in political discourse. The ethno-nationalistic revival seemed to be connected to a faltering economy and a waning faith in communist ideology. In 1989, Slovenia was the first Yugoslav republic to push for more autonomy, and then for secession from the federation. At that time, Slobodan Milosevic, head of the Communist Party in Serbia (the Serbian Democratic Party or SDS) opposed the breakup of Yugoslavia and promoted the reassertion of a centralized state and stricter Communist Party control over federated Yugoslavia, with SDS playing the leading governing role. While Milosevic's supporters were not able to overturn Slovenia's declaration of independence in 1991, a larger ethnic Serb population in Croatia who were backed up by the JNA and Milosevic and the SDS rejected Croatia's 1991 declaration of independence issued by ethnic Croatian "patriots" and their national leader, Franjo Tudman. At that point, a "civil war" in Croatia ensued: on the one side, Tudman's ethnic Croatian supporters fought for independence from federated Yugoslavia; on the other side, Croatian Serbs, who were members of the SDS with ties to Milosevic and JNA troops fought to annex a Serb-majority region of Croatia to a "Greater Serbia" ruled by Milosevic. Soon after the war broke out in Croatia, Bosnia-Herzegovina declared its independence from Yugoslavia. Ethnic Serbs in Bosnia-Herzegovina, allied with SDS and led by Radovan Karadzic, formed paramilitary groups. With encouragement from Milosevic and backing from the JNA the Bosnian Serbs began attacking Bosnian Muslims (or Bosniaks) in 1992, aiming to "remove" the Bosniaks from towns and regions that they renamed "Republika Srpska," which was also to be annexed to "Greater Serbia." By 1993, Croatian forces that previously joined with Bosniaks fighting in the Bosnia-Herzegovina Republican Army against the Bosnian Serbs and the JNA, also began fighting against the Bosniaks in the Croat-Bosniak War. Croatian forces also wanted to carve out an ethnic-majority Croat region from Bosnian territory, and annex it to the Croatian nation. This war lasted until 1994, when a new Croat-Bosniak anti-Serb alliance agreement was reached.

In waging these wars in Croatia and Bosnia, the rival fighting forces, and most often but not exclusively, those that were backed by Serbia and the JNA, employed brutal tactics that targeted combat forces and civilians in ways that violated "universal" human rights conventions formulated by the Western democracies who defined the common understandings of the "international community" at the United Nations, on a scale that had not occurred in Europe since the Second World War. Initially the European democracies and the United States resisted calls to intervene with military force to stop the atrocities that were issued by humanitarian aid workers and feminist NGOs, and that were publicized in the Western media. Leaders of the European democracies were divided about whether to intervene with military force in conflicts that were defined as "civil wars." Britain's prime minister John Major, for one, opposed any intervention beyond pushing for a negotiated settlement, and convened the London International Conference in fall 1992 that tried, but failed, to negotiate an end to the Yugoslav crisis. Other UN member states were slow to deploy UN peacekeeping missions, and the NATO alliance failed provide protection for civilians in designated "safe" zones or designated "no-fly" zones, until several years after the wars broke out. The US government, led by the George H. W. Bush administration until January 1993, applied non-military, diplomatic efforts to pressure the belligerents to enact a ceasefire. These included economic sanctions, arms sales embargoes, and refusals to recognize the newly independent states of Slovenia, Croatia, and Bosnia-Herzegovina until mid-1992, because the administration also interpreted these "new" wars as "civil wars," emanating from a "blood feud" that "[grew] out of age-old animosities" (George H. W. Bush quoted in Garner 2013: 81).

The Clinton administration that took office in 1993 also focused on ethnicity as the defining cause of the Yugoslav wars, and adopted views drawn, in part, from political analyst Robert Kaplan, who wrote a bestselling account of the outbreak of the Yugoslav wars, *Balkan Ghosts: A Journey Through History*. Kaplan's interpretation, too, characterized these conflicts as an inevitable eruption of "ancient ethnic hatreds" that the communist era masked, but did not eliminate. Some critics have identified these views as part of a post–Cold War "Balkanist discourse" that became popular in the 1990s, in which Westerners defined Western European societies as "superior" and more advanced, and Eastern European societies as "backward," "uncivilized," and homes to "a more primitive [European] self" (Björkdahl 2012: 302).

Gender, ethnicity, and constructions of the Bosnian "nation"

Despite Western leaders' dominant perceptions, ethnic rivalries were not consequences of inevitable, "natural," or biological imperatives, but were constructed and used strategically by the former Yugoslav government leaders to mobilize their peoples to take up arms and brutalize their enemies. These leaders included Serbian president Slobodan Milosevic, Bosnian Serb president of the Republika Srpska Radovan Karadzic, and Croatian president Franjo Tudman. These leaders defined their nations along strictly differentiated ethnic lines, and they asserted that their nations were under siege by their "enemies," that is, the members of "other" ethnic groups, who were unwelcome presences in their nations. The appellation of unwelcome "other" was directed most especially to the Bosnian Muslims, led by their wartime president Alija Izetbegovic. Examining at raw numbers of those killed in the Yugoslav wars reveals that the Bosniaks suffered the brunt of the attacks. Catherine Baker's 2015 study of *The Yugoslav Wars of the 1990s* includes statistics of war casualties compiled by the Bosnian War Research and Documentation Centre: 97,207 people had been directly killed by military violence; 39,684 had been civilians, and 57,523 were soldiers. Of those killed, 83 percent had been Bosniaks, 10 percent Serbs, and 5 percent Croats (Baker 2015: 95).

One of the effective ways to define "us," or the legitimate members of the in-group or "nation," is to highlight the distinctions and differences from "them," the excluded and illegitimate groups. "Race" as it was used in the Second World War, and "ethnicity" as it was used in the Yugoslav wars, were constructed as powerful "blood" distinctions among human groups, with behavioral characteristics and innate attributes attached to each race or ethnicity to justify dominance of one group over another. During the Bosnian War, the Serbs, Croats, and Bosniaks all attacked the "other" through physical combat and with sexual violence or other terrorizing tactics. They also attacked symbolic representations of the essential religious or cultural values that contributed meaning to the ethnic identities of their enemies.

FIGURE 3.3 **IWM 75050** *Bosnian Muslim civilians cross a temporary footbridge replacing the famous sixteenth-century Stari Most bridge at Mostar, shortly after it was destroyed by Croat tank fire in 1994. Credit: Imperial War Museums/Kevin Weaver*

All warring forces desecrated the sacred spaces of their enemies. Again, most of these attacks were directed at Bosniak spaces and symbols: 1,000–1,100 attacks on mosques, 350 attacks on Serbian Orthodox churches and monasteries, and 450 attacks on Croatian Catholic sites (Baker 2015: 65). In addition, during the Croat-Bosniak War, Croatian forces surrounded the Bosniak-occupied sections of the city of Mostar and destroyed the historic Stari Most bridge. The bridge was destroyed to isolate the Bosniaks and cut them off from any sources of aid, but the bridge also had cultural value and significance for the Bosniak people as it had been constructed in the sixteenth century for the Turkish Ottoman Empire. But even as ethnically defined national identities were used in these ways to attack one's enemies during the Yugoslav wars, ethno-nationalism was used more as an "instrument" rather than a "cause" of war (Baker 2015: 129).

Indeed, some feminist analysts have asserted that rather than ethnic "blood feuds," militarized hegemonic masculinity inspired the male Yugoslav leaders to make war and dominate their enemies. Serbian feminist Zarana Papic, for example, has argued that the eruption of violence across the Yugoslav region in the 1990s was a "male drama" that played out at a specific post–Cold War moment in European history:

> The wars in the ex-Yugoslavia were a result of the systematic cultural production of violent representations/narrations before and during the actual militarized violence. The social world in Serbia was constructed through a discourse of exclusion of the "other" which involved exteriorization of the "other"; erasure of empathy; denial of tolerance; and amnesia of a history of living together. In order to be effective, the overall practice of "otherness" and the tolerated destruction of the "other body" had to be prepared through a systematic (discursive, symbolic and iconic) cultural production. From the cultural production of various levels of identity, a consensus on fascist politics arose as a specific "culture of normality."
>
> PAPIC 2003: 47

Some feminist analysts have argued that "women" of all ethnic groups were more willing than "men" to reject nationalist or ethnic differences as causal factors in the war, and some have made their own essentialist claims that "women," in general, are more interested than men in peace building. Liberal feminist Swanee Hunt, US ambassador to Austria from 1993 to 1997 who was active in the region throughout the war and spoke with women from all warring nations, rejected the idea that the Bosnian War was the result long-festering ethnic hatreds. She laid blame for the war on Slobodan Milosevic, whose imperial ambitions exploited people's anger and fears caused by post–Cold War economic struggles. She has asserted that "the story of the Bosnian war is the story of an evil genius—one who seized a moment of uncertainty in a nascent democracy, disoriented by a political vacuum and the grueling economic transition to a free-market economy" (Hunt 2011: xxiv). Hunt offered a gender-essentialist and anti-nationalist message of postwar reconciliation. She has asserted that Yugoslav women have the capacity to cross ethnic divides, to meet with one another as "mothers" and as feminist social and political activists who share interests in restoring peace and human security and in rebuilding multiethnic communities (Hunt 2004, 2015).

Women and men in the former Yugoslav republics had similar experiences in terms of how their national leaders defined two-gender roles in ethno-nationalist wars, even if they rejected those roles in their own lives. Leaders across the region and the region's national presses generally promoted a "neo-traditional ideology of gender, blending representations of innocent and defenseless women with representations of the national landscape, while praising men's heroic fighting strength" (Baker 2015: 55). Since the end of the Cold War, women in the Yugoslav republics were increasingly marginalized in politics. After Communist Party ideology with its gender equality message was discredited, the Yugoslav states eliminated gender quotas for political representation and established ethno-national quotas. Not surprisingly, ethnic nationalism became a factor in politics, and many nationalistic politicians also voiced conservative ideas about women's traditional roles in society and maintained that politics was a male realm. These ideas were particularly powerful in Bosnia, where patriarchal values reasserted themselves and "respectable" women stayed out of politics. In fact, "women" were most often defined as "mothers" or "victims" of violence, not "citizens" but "mothers of citizens-to-be." In the first postwar elections for Bosnia's national assemblies, after Bosnian territory was divided into the Bosniak- and Croat-majority Federation of Bosnia-Herzegovina and the Serb-majority Republika Srpska in the 1995 peace agreement, women representatives made up less than 5 percent of those elected, and women have remained a distinct minority in elected political positions during the ensuing postwar decades (Björkdahl 2012: 297–303).

Gender, ethnic cleansing, and genocide

During the Bosnian War, Serbian soldiers and the Croatian community in Bosnia both adopted the strategy of "ethnic cleansing." In at least one episode, during the occupation of Srebrenica in 1995, the Serbian troops perpetrated an act of "genocide." IR scholar James Gow defines "ethnic cleansing" as "the strategic use of excessive violence against civilian population centers, demonstrative atrocity and mass murder in order to remove that population . . . to secure the territory in question" (Gow quoted in Baker 2013: 64–65). The 1948 UN Convention on the Prevention and Punishment of the Crime of Genocide, defines "genocide" as those acts that are committed "with intent to destroy, in whole or in part, a national, ethnical, racial, or religious group, as such" (UN Convention on Genocide 1948: 280).

Ethnic-cleansing campaigns took various forms during the Bosnian War including mass murder, detention in prison camps, forced displacement, destruction of cultural symbols and property, and rape. These forms of ethnic cleansing were all gendered in that they targeted men and women in different ways, and all impacted men and women in different ways. During the Bosnian War, the widespread and systematic use of rape as a weapon of war was used most often to attack and defile Bosniak women, with estimates of the total numbers of rape victims of all ethnicities range from 20,000 to 35,000, or more (Blanchard 2003: 1301). From the time the Bosnian War broke out in 1992, journalists and feminist activists in the West and in Yugoslav states were publishing reports about the Bosnian Serbian soldiers who violently attacked tens of thousands of Bosniak women and established "rape camps." Just as rape, enforced pregnancy, and other forms of sexual violence perpetrated against women was intended to defile and shame the victim women and their husbands and fathers who could not protect them, the media reports were intended to shame Western male government leaders so they would take actions to stop the atrocities. Government action was slow to materialize, although in December 1992, the UN Security Council passed Resolution 798 that condemned the wartime rapes taking place in the former Yugoslavia and defined them as "massive, organized, and systematic." In May 1993, UNSCR 827 established the ICTY, the first international war crimes tribunal established since the Nuremberg and Tokyo War Crimes Tribunals were convened at the end of the Second World War. The report that led to the establishment of the ICTY defined rape and forced prostitution as "crimes against humanity" (Copelon 1998: 63–68).

The media and activists' reports garnered widespread international sympathy for the women under attack and allowed feminists to challenge the "conventional wisdom" regarding wartime rape. These reports rejected notions that rape and other forms of violence against women in wartime were a soldier's "right" or a "natural" expression of violent, militarized masculinity. Directing global attention to the mass rapes taking place in Bosnia allowed feminists to redefine the rape as a "weapon" used to "humiliate, shame, degrade, and terrify an entire population" and to carry out ethnic cleansing and genocide (Carol Douglas quoted in Garner 2013: 82). These reports also resulted in widespread recognition that systematic rapes carried out in wartime were in fact a "crime against humanity." However, in a classic example of unintended consequences, the sometimes-sensationalized reporting also re-traumatized the rape victims, as Jelena Batinic explained:

For the first time, rape in war found its place on the international agenda and in legal human rights discourses; it was a crucial moment for feminists to try to make critical interventions into these discourses and to struggle for a feminist reconceptualization of violence against women. . . . But soon the media coverage became sensationalist. Graphic depictions of atrocities appeared in the media, exploiting the topic without caring about adverse consequences . . . showing women on television without protecting their identities, and asking them to talk about their horrible experiences.

BATINIC 2001: 8–9

To be sure, much of the media coverage was insensitive. It essentialized Bosnian women as "only" rape victims, rather than human beings who had also lost their homes, family members and communities. Nonetheless, the focus on sexual assaults and violations of women during the Bosnian War was also part of a successful feminist campaign to transform the political discourse and institutional policy regarding women's rights, within individual Western and non-Western nations, and at the United Nations (as Chapter 4 will explain further). Because of the gendered waging of the Bosnian War, "Bosnia was a turning point in international recognition of protection of women in conflict and in attempts by governments and aid workers to solve the wartime problems of women and girls" (Mertus 2000:19).

While many instances of ethnic cleansing that occurred during the Bosnian War were recorded, and some of those instances included "systematic" rape of women that international courts subsequently defined as "crimes against humanity," one episode occurred where an act of "genocide" was committed, and this gendered attack was directed at Bosniak men. In July 1995, the Bosnian Serb army under the command of Ratko Mladic committed a mass murder of an estimated 7,000 to 8,000 Bosniak men and boys in the city of Srebrenica. Most of those murdered were soldiers but several hundred elderly males and young boys were separated out from the group of 20,000 to 25,000 refugees housed in a camp established by UN peacekeepers. A UN peacekeeping force, an international military police force contributed by UN member states to maintain peace and security in specific assigned missions, was in charge of maintaining safe areas around several Bosnian cities, including Srebrenica. But, by mid-1995, Serbian forces overwhelmed them. In hearings investigating this incident in 2004, ICTY judges ruled that Serbian troops committed the mass murder with the intent to destroy an ethnic group, and the 1995 "Srebrenica massacre" constituted an act of genocide according to international law.

Following the Srebrenica massacre, UN peacekeepers requested aerial bombing support from the NATO alliance to weaken the Bosnian Serb army, while they attacked Serbian forces on the ground. An intensive NATO bombing campaign in August and September 1995 led to a ceasefire, and forced all warring parties, including Croatian president Tudman, Serbian president Milosevic, Bosnian Serb leader Radovan Karadzic, and Bosniak president Izetbegovic to join US arbitrators led by President Clinton to engage in peace talks in Dayton, Ohio. The talks led to a peace settlement in November. The Dayton Peace Accords would be enforced by a 60,000-strong NATO peacekeeping force that remained in place until 2004, when it was replaced by a much smaller military peacekeeping force deployed by the EU member states.

Gender and the ICTY

When the UN Security Council authorized the establishment of the ICTY in 1993, it defined the ICTY's mandate to "contribute to the restoration and maintenance of peace" in the war-torn Balkan region. This was to be achieved as the ICTY prosecutors gathered evidence to identify specific individuals—not states or institutions—who were responsible for perpetrating "grave breaches" of the Geneva Conventions including genocide and other crimes against humanity in the region, and by bringing those individuals to trial. The Criminal Tribunal, a formal mechanism for trying and punishing high-level war criminals based on international law, was established, rather than a less-formal "truth and reconciliation commission" that might have been a forum for communities to air grievances and share collective responsibility for war crimes. While male leaders in the UN Security Council established the ICTY, women's interventions influenced some of its prosecutorial decisions and were responsible for defining a portion of the ICTY's historical significance.

During the 1990s, women activists effectively directed international attention to massive wartime rape of women that was used as a gendered "weapon of war" to achieve "ethnic cleansing" of a population. Based on the activists' arguments, the "international community" (as it has previously been defined) and UN member states recognized the Bosnian War rapes as gross violations of human rights to be prosecuted as war crimes against humanity. Prior to the establishment of the ICTY, rape and other forms of sexual assault had been classified as "lesser crimes" under the Geneva Conventions, not as "grave breaches" of international law. In their report on "Women's Participation in the International Criminal Tribunal for the Former Yugoslavia" Julie Mertus and Olja Hocevar Van Wely asserted that:

> Women's involvement in the ICTY has led to a significant shift in the way international organizations and, specifically but not exclusively, international courts, think about: (a) the inclusion of women and gender expertise among tribunal staff; (b) the inclusion and valuing of women witnesses; (c) the treatment of wartime rape and sexual violence under international law; and (d) the participation of indigenous NGOs (and specifically local women's groups).

MERTUS AND VAN WELY 2004: 11

In terms of the inclusion of women, women were appointed to the ICTY as judges when it first formed in 1993, which was the first time "women" served in such an elite capacity in an international court. Two of the court's chief prosecutors were women, Canadian judge Louise Arbour (1996–99) and Swiss judge Carla del Ponte (1999–2007). In terms of incorporating "gender expertise" in the operations of the ICTY, the tribunal formally adopted the practice of "gender mainstreaming" (see Chapter 4) to include women and their supposed gendered perceptions among the appointees to all professional positions on the court. The tribunal also brought women forward as witnesses to testify against wartime leaders who were accused of ordering the systematic rapes and other ethnic-cleansing war crimes, and gave those women the protection and other supports they needed to feel safe when confronting their attackers. These were new practices in international justice arenas, as the ICTY was the first time an international court recognized wartime sexual violence and rape perpetrated against civilians constituted prosecutable "crimes against humanity."

Yugoslav women's organizations that sought retributive justice through holding their attackers accountable for their actions assisted the ICTY in gathering women's testimonies and in transforming international norms in regard to sexual violence. Among the most active of these women's organizations was the Association of Women Victims of War founded by Bosniak activist Bakira Hasečić in 2003. As a rape survivor, Hasečić talked to Yugoslav women, and to some men, of all ethnic backgrounds and collected their stories of sexual war crimes in order to present them to the ICTY and to Bosnian courts for prosecution (Helms 2013: 105–106; 211–13). Other Western women's organizations such as New York–based Equality Now, as well as other international human rights organizations, rallied political pressure on the ICTY to indict Radovan Karadzic and Ratko Mladic, commander of the Bosnian Serb army, in 1995. These elite leaders who ordered the rapes as part of their ethnic-cleansing strategy against the Bosniaks were not arrested and put on trial until 2008 and 2011, respectively. Nonetheless, their indictments were significant in building the feminist case that "systematic" rape was against civilian populations, "on national, political, ethnic, or racial grounds," and was a heinous war crime (Copelon 1995: 203). Moreover, feminists also pushed the ICTY to prosecute these cases in order for justice to be served:

> Nor is it enough for the Tribunal statute simply to recognize rape as a crime; those responsible for rape and related crimes must be charged and prosecuted in accordance with bias-free standards and recognized procedure. This is essential if the women of Bosnia are to be recognized as full subjects, as well as objects, of this terrible victimization, and if the international attention focused on Bosnia is to have meaning for women subjected to rape in other parts of the world.

COPELON 1995: 207

Other Yugoslav women's organizations, such as Medica Zenica a self-defined "feminist" and "anti-nationalist" organization that formed in 1993 to provide refuge and counseling for wartime victims of sexual violence, were more cautious about urging women to testify at the ICTY, without some serious qualifications. One of the Medica Zenica associates, Duska Andric-Ruzicic, acknowledged the "historic step forward" that the recognition of wartime rape as a crime against humanity by the ICTY represented. And she gave credit to the international group of feminists whose effective activism made this progress in furthering gender justice possible. But she also identified problems when the ICTY and local Bosnian courts prosecuted rape as a war crime: victims had to come forward to testify in public, facing justifiable fears of shame and social rejection, and putting themselves and their families in physical danger and at risk of revenge. She recalled the wrongs done to women by the media during the war as journalists and academics sought out "rape victims" to tell their stories and re-experience the traumas, in order to further their own agendas. According to Andric-Ruzicic, women's NGOs like Medica Zenica have recognized that: "The effects of sexual abuse are long-term, while the interests of the state are only short-term, lasting as long as the situation can be used to win political points and gain sympathy from the international community" (Andric-Ruzicic 2003: 109–13).

Gender, peace, and postwar reconciliation

The Peace Accords hammered out in Dayton, Ohio by the male heads of state and their military and mostly male diplomatic advisers created a postwar state that divided territory into Serbian-dominated Republika Srpska and Bosnian Muslim- and Croat-dominated Federation of Bosnia-Herzegovina. Twenty years after the 1995 Dayton Accords were negotiated and enforced by international peacekeepers with hopes that in time Bosnia-Herzegovina would evolve into a peaceful, multiethnic parliamentary democracy, the formal political realm remained deadlocked in conflict, corrupt governance, and recriminations; separate ethnicity-based bureaucracies and political divisions along ethnic lines remained entrenched. Women were nearly absent from the Dayton negotiations. There were a few exceptions from the arbitrating powers including British senior diplomat Pauline Neville-Jones and US ambassador to the United Nations Madeleine Albright, but their presence was not consequential, and the Dayton Accords are an example of what IR scholar Annika Björkdahl has termed a gendered "peace gap." The peace gap allowed men to set the terms of the postwar political and gender order as they had in past twentieth-century wars. In the case of the Bosnian War peace talks, the male peace negotiators strengthened nationalist narratives defining women as passive victims of their enemies' war violence. These narratives led to a conservative backlash against women in politics and reinforced conservative emphasis on women's traditional roles in Bosnia in the postwar period (Björkdahl 2012: 297–99).

What is necessary to achieve lasting "sustainable" peace and to achieve "reconciliation" among peoples who have engaged in bitter and bloody wars? Many peace studies focus on the *process* of achieving peace and reconciliation as one that requires that any transition phase must guarantee some measure of "justice" for those who have suffered human rights abuses or other profound losses. In defining "transitional justice" peace scholar Elizabeth Porter has argued that transitional justice strategies must "deal with the past in confronting the legacies of human rights abuses and human suffering, ensuring accountability for past injustices while maintaining peace, the rule of law, and democratic processes"; they must also include provisions "to move into the future, including fostering reconciliation," that is, "healing for communities that have been 'traumatized by violence.'" These goals should be achieved within an institutional framework for pursuing *legal* justice that includes criminal prosecution, and punishment for violations of human rights, that is, *retributive justice* that deters future violations. But to achieve "reconciliation," there must also be *restorative justice* measures that focus "on the well-being of the victim, *and* usually on reintegrating perpetrators of the abuse into community norms and events." Reconciliation measures should proceed with "compassion" in order to restore "some sort of empathetic connection to the other" (Porter 2015: 10–12, 76, 158).

Feminist and nonfeminist activists have put forward numerous proposals regarding what is necessary to achieve a lasting peace in Bosnia-Herzegovina that go beyond ICTY indictments and prosecutions of wartime leaders. Some feminist activists, such as Bakira Hasečić, have asserted that women raped in war *must* tell their stories at the ICTY, in courts in Bosnia, or in other community forums so that they may see retributive justice served in order to heal. Moreover, the Bosnian government must not ignore or forget the crimes that men and women suffered as some postwar politicians have called on them to "move on" from their status of "victim." In addition, Hasečić and other activists in women's groups such as Medica Zenica successfully lobbied Federation of Bosnia and Herzegovina government officials so that victims of wartime sexual violence could receive postwar pension payments, addressing their goals for postwar justice, but this law has not been enacted in Republika Srpska. Other women's activists have focused on more individualized and private approaches to providing counseling for war crimes victims and other social supports to promote recovery from war trauma. These proposals imply a broad definition of the peace-building process, as it might be achieved at the individual or micro level. At the macro level, other proposals have focused on transforming the political culture of male privilege that permeated Yugoslav politics during the war and since the war has ended.

There is a growing body of scholarship that documents links between gender equality and peaceful stable societies around the world (Caprioli and Boyer 2001; Regan and Paskeviciute 2003; Hudson, et al. 2012; O'Reilly, et al. 2015). According to these studies, a "gender-just" peace, in which women participate fully in the peace negotiations, would provide guarantees for women's rights and equitable participation in postwar societies and could thus transform male-over-female gender power relations that led to militarized violence. When a few women have participated in peace negotiations to settle interstate and intrastate conflicts in the twenty-first-century, they brought forth social and economic needs, raised human rights issues, and represented diverse community concerns that might not have been considered by the elite male leaders who traditionally negotiated peace settlements. In some instances, the women peace negotiators moved stalled peace negotiations forward by interjecting nontraditional ideas because they generally did not represent entrenched centers of power that often rejected compromise. These studies also provide evidence that women's "empowerment" through political participation, education, and enforcement of laws that prohibit gender-based discrimination and violence against women contributes to a society's overall economic development, which also lays the foundation for a sustainable peace.

Summing up

When the anti–Vietnam War organization "Another Mother for Peace" entered the gendered realms of war and peacemaking in the United States in 1967, its members and literature emphasized the contrasts between "human security" and state-defined "national security" with their popular slogan "War is not healthy for children and other living things." The organization's rhetoric and activist strategies called on the power of gender stereotypes to drive their anti-war message home. Their message resonated with large numbers of American men and women because it used familiar gendered political rhetoric, defining "women" as nurturing mothers whose concern with giving and preserving human life reinforced traditional "family values." As other historic women-led peace movements had done before them, they tried to subvert the state-sponsored and masculinized war policy with their own feminine version of gender power. Their movement is one more example added to the gendered histories of twentieth-century wars and the peace movements that have opposed them that have been recounted in this chapter.

As all these examples make clear, gender power has shaped the roles that men and women are socialized to play during wartimes and long into the postwar periods. These gendered roles may have originated in Western societies that dominated the international realm of politics in the twentieth century, but the gender stereotypes of the male "Just Warrior" and the female "Beautiful Soul" also resonate in non-Western societies at war, where male soldiers are constructed as "violent," "aggressive" protectors and women are constructed as "innocent," "passive" victims. Although militarized definitions of national security achieved through "power-over" state and nonstate rivals traditionally associated with masculine gender power have historically prevailed among the ranks of elite government war-policy makers, counterarguments that are traditionally associated with feminine gender power that advocate a more holistic state of human security and interdependent "power-with" outcomes have always been present to challenge war-policy makers. These counterarguments may be gaining strength in the twenty-first century as the most pressing global issues including accelerated globalization of the economy, global climate change, and mass migrations of war refugees demand more cooperative forms of conflict resolution.

References for further study

Cockburn, C. (2010), "Gender Relations as Causal in Militarization and War," *International Feminist Journal of Politics*, 12: 139–57.

Dean, R. D. (2001), *Imperial Brotherhood: Gender and the Making of Cold War Foreign Policy*, Amherst, MA: University of Massachusetts Press.

Enloe, C. (2000), *Maneuvers: The International Politics of Militarizing Women's Lives*, Berkeley, CA: University of California Press.

Mertus, J. (2000), *War's Offensive on Women: The Humanitarian Challenge in Bosnia, Kosovo, and Afghanistan*, West Hartford, CA: Kumarian Press, Inc.

Sjoberg, L. (2013), *Gendering Global Conflict: Toward a Feminist Theory of War*, New York, NY: Columbia University Press.

Web resources

"International War Crimes Tribunal for the Former Yugoslavia," United Nations. http://www.icty.org/ (Accessed July 28, 2017).

"Results on Women and Gender from the 'Broader Participation' and 'Civil Society and Peacebuilding Projects'," Graduate Institute, Geneva Centre on Conflict, Development and Peacebuilding, (2015). http://graduateinstitute.ch/files/live/sites/iheid/files/sites/ccdp/shared/Docs/Publications/briefingpaperwomen%20gender.pdf (Accessed July 28, 2017).

"Stockholm International Peace Research Institute." https://www.sipri.org/ (Accessed July 28, 2017).

"United Nations Peacekeeping." http://www.un.org/en/peacekeeping/ (Accessed July 28, 2017).

"Uppsala Conflict Data Program," Uppsala University Department of Peace and Conflict Research. http://ucdp.uu.se/?id=1 (Accessed July 28, 2017).

World War I Propaganda Posters. http://www.ww1propaganda.com/world-war-1-posters/american-ww1-propaganda-posters (Accessed July 28, 2017).

Bibliography

Addams, J. and Joslin, K. (1922/2002), *Peace and Bread in Time of War*, Urbana, IL: University of Illinois Press.

Albrinck, M. (2009), "Humanitarians and He-Men: Recruitment Posters and the Masculine Ideal," in P. James (ed.), *Picture This: World War I Posters and Visual Culture*, 312–36, Lincoln, NE: University of Nebraska Press.

Alison, M. (2007), "Wartime Sexual Violence: Women's Human Rights and Questions of Masculinity," *Review of International Studies*, 33: 75–90.

Anderson, B. S. and Zinsser, J. P. (2000), *A History of Their Own, Volume 2, Women in Europe from Prehistory to the Present*, revised ed., New York, NY: Oxford University Press.

Andric-Ruzicic, D. (2003), "War Rape and the Political Manipulation of Survivors," in W. Giles (ed.), *Feminists Under Fire: Exchanges Across War Zones*, 103–14, Toronto, CAN: Between the Lines.

Appy, C. G. (2000), *Cold War Constructions: The Political Culture of United States Imperialism, 1945–1966*, Amherst, MA: University of Massachusetts Press.

Ashworth, L. M. (2011), "Feminism, War and the Prospects for Peace," *International Feminist Journal of Politics*, 13: 25–43.

Baetens, F. (2010), "The Forgotten Peace Conference: the 1915 International Congress of Women," in Rüdiger Wolfrum (ed.), *Max Planck Encyclopedia of Public International Law*, New York, NY: Oxford University Press.

Bailey, B. and Farber, D. (1992), "Hotel Street: Prostitution and the Politics of War," *Radical History Review*, 52: 54–77.

Baker, C. (2015), *The Yugoslav Wars of the 1990s*, New York, NY: Palgrave MacMillan.

Batinic, J. (2001), "Feminism, Nationalism, and War: The 'Yugoslav Case' in Feminist Texts," *Journal of International Women's Studies*, 3: 1–23.

Bingham, M. W. and Gross, S. H. (1987), *Women in Japan*, St. Louis Park, MN: Glenhurst Publications, Inc.

Björkdahl, A. (2012), "A Gender-Just Peace? Exploring the Post-Dayton Peace Process in Bosnia," *Peace & Change*, 37: 286–317.

Blanchard, E. M. (2003), "Gender, International Relations and the Development of Feminist Security Theory," *Signs: Journal of Women in Culture and Society*, 28: 1289–1312.

Boxer, M. and Quataert, J. H. (2000), *Connecting Spheres: European Women in a Globalizing World, 1500 to the Present*, 2nd ed., Oxford, UK: Oxford University Press.

Caprioli, M. and Boyer, M. (2001), "Gender, Violence and International Crisis," *Journal of Conflict Resolution*, 45: 503–18.

Chinkin, C. and Kaldor, M. (2013), "Gender and New Wars," *Journal of International Affairs*, 67: 167–87.

Cockburn, C. (2015), "Militarism," in L. J. Shepherd (ed.), *Gender Matters in Global Politics: A Feminist Introduction to International Relations*, 110–19, New York, NY: Routledge.

Cohn, C. (2013), *Women & Wars*, Malden, MA: Polity Press.

Cooper, S. E. (2002), "Peace as a Human Right: The Invasion of Women into the World of High International Politics," *Journal of Women's History*, 14: 9–25.

Copelon, R. (1995), "Gendered War Crimes: Reconceptualizing Rape in Time of War," in J. P. Wolper (ed.), *Women's Rights, Human Rights: International Feminist Perspectives*, 197–214, New York, NY: Routledge.

Copelon, R. (1998), "Surfacing Gender: Reconceptualizing Crimes Against Women in Times of War," in L. A. Lorentzen and J. Turpin (eds.), *The Women and War Reader*, 63–79, New York, NY: New York University Press.

de Haan, F. (2010), "Continuing Cold War Paradigms in Western Historiography of Transnational Women's Organizations: The Case of the Women's International Democratic Federation," *Women's History Review*, 19: 547–73.

Diez, T., Bode, I., and Fernandes Da Costa, A. (2011), *Key Concepts in International Relations*, Thousand Oaks, CA: Sage Publications.

Dombrowski, N. A. (1999), *Women and War in the Twentieth Century: Enlisted Without Consent*, New York, NY: Garland Publishing.

Dower, J. W. (1986), *War Without Mercy: Race and Power in the Pacific War*, New York, NY: Pantheon Books.

Downes, A. (2006), "Desperate Times, Desperate Measures: The Causes of Civilian Victimization in War," *International Security*, 31: 152–95.

Duiker, W. and Spielvogel, J. J. (1998), *World History*, 2nd ed., Belmont, CA: Wadsworth Publishing Company.

Elshtain, J. B. (1987), *Women and War*, New York, NY: Basic Books.

Elshtain, J. B. and Tobias, S. (1990), *Women, Militarism and War*, Lanham, MD: Rowman & Littlefield Publishers, Inc.

Enloe, C. (1983), *Does Khaki Become You? The Militarization of Women's Lives*, Boston, MA: South End Press.

Enloe, C. (2013), "Foreward: Gender Analysis Isn't Easy," in C. Cohn (ed.), *Women & Wars*, xv–xvi, Malden, MA: Polity Press.

European Women's Lobby (c. 2009), Toward Human Security: Engendering Peace, Brussels, Belgium: European Women's Lobby.

Ferguson, T. and Rogers, J. (1987), *Right Turn: The Decline of the Democrats and the Future of American Politics*, New York, NY: Hill and Wang.

Findley, C. V. and Rothney, J. A. M. (2011), *Twentieth-Century World*, 7th ed., Belmont, CA: Wadsworth.

Fujimura-Fanselow, K. and Kameda, A. (1995), *Japanese Women: New Feminist Perspectives on the Past, Present, and Future*, New York, NY: The Feminist Press.

Gaddis, J. L. (1989), *A Long Peace: Inquiries into the History of the Cold War*, New York, NY: Oxford University Press.

Galtung, J. (2013), *Johan Galtung: Pioneer of Peace Research*, Berlin, Germany: Springer.

Garner, K. (2010), *Shaping a Global Women's Agenda: Women's NGOs and Global Governance.* Manchester, UK: Manchester University Press.

Garner, K. (2013), *Gender and Foreign Policy in the Clinton Administration*, Boulder, CO: First Forum Books, Lynne Rienner Publishers.

Ghada, M. (2008), "Gender Aspects of Human Security," *International Social Science Journal*, 59: 81–100.

Gilbert, S. M. (2000), "Soldier's Heart: Literary Men, Literary Women, and the Great War," in M. Boxer and J. B. Quataert (eds.), *Connecting Spheres: European Women in Globalizing World, 1500 to the Present*, 2nd ed., New York, NY: Oxford University Press.

Goldstein, J. S. (2001), *War and Gender: How Gender Shapes the War System and Vice Versa*, New York, NY: Cambridge University Press.

Grazel, S. R. (1999), *Women's Identities at War: Gender, Motherhood and Politics in Britain and France During the First World War*, Chapel Hill, NC: University of North Carolina Press.

Hanssen, F. (1935), "The Average American and the Next War," *Literary Digest*, 4–5.

Hartmann, F. H. and Wendzel, R. L. (1994), *America's Foreign Policy in a Chnaging World*, New York: NY: Harper Collins College Publishers.

Haslam, B. (1999), *From Suffrage to Internationalism: The Political Evolution of Three British Feminists, 1909–1939*, New York, NY: Peter Lang.

Helms, E. (2013), *Innocence and Victimhood: Gender, Nation, and Women's Activism in Postwar Bosnia-Herzegovina*, Madison, WI: University of Wisconsin Press.

Hopton, J. (2003), "The State and Military Masculinity," in P. R. Higate (ed.), *Military Masculinites: Identity and the State*, 111–23, Westport, CT: Praeger.

Hudson, V. M., Ballif-Spanvill, B., Caprioli, M., and Emmett, C. F. (2012). *Sex & World Peace*, New York, NY: Columbia University Press.

Hunt, M. H. (1996), *Crises in U.S. Foreign Policy: An International History Reader*, New Haven, CT: Yale University Press.

Hunt, S. (2004), *This Was Not Our War: Bosnian Women Reclaiming the Peace*, Durham, NC: Duke University Press.

Hunt, S. (2011), *Worlds Apart: Bosnian Lessons for Global Security*, Durham, NC: Duke University Press.

Hunt, S. (2015), "Twenty Years After the Srebrenica Massacre, Women are the Healers," *Boston Globe*. https://www.bostonglobe.com/opinion/2015/07/05/years-after-srebrenica-massacre-women-are-healers/BgGD5G6rz2jzmjGV9SwAiM/story.html (Accessed November 17, 2017).

Hunt, S. (2015), "20 Years After Bosnian Peace Accords Women Still Give Me Hope," Washington DC: Institute for Inclusive Security.

Ilic, M. (2011), "Soviet Women, Cultural Exchange and the Women's International Democratic Federation," in S. Autio-Sarasmo and K. Miklossy (eds.), *Reassessing Cold War Europe*, 157–74, New York, NY: Routledge.

James, P. (2009), *Picture This: World War I Visual Culture*, Lincoln, NE: University of Nebraska Press.

Jeffreys-Jones, R. (1995), *Changing Differences: Women and the Shaping of American Foreign Policy*, New Brunswick, NJ: Rutgers University Press.

Kaldor, M. (1999, 2012), *New and Old Wars: Organized Violence in a Global Era*, Cambridge, UK: Polity Press.

Kaplan, L. D. (1994), "Woman as Caretaker: An Archetype that Supports Patriarchal Militarism," *Hypatia*, 9: 123–33.

Kaplan, R. D. (1993), *Balkan Ghosts: A Journey Through History*, New York, NY: St. Martin's Press.

Keylor, W. (2011), *The Twentieth Century World and Beyond, An International History Since 1900*, 6th ed., New York, NY: Oxford University Press.

King, S. (2015), "Another Mother for Peace: Motherhood, Celebrities, and Antiwar Activism during the Vietnam War," Geneva, NY: Upstate New York Women's History Organization Conference.

Kovitz, M. (2003), "The Roots of Military Masculinity," in P. R. Higate (ed.), *Military Masculinities: Identity and the State*, 1–14, Westport, CT: Praeger.

LeFeber, W. (1989), *The American Age: United States Foreign Policy at Home and Abroad since 1750*, New York, NY: W. W. Norton.

Lorentzen, L. A. and Turpin, J. (1998), *The Women and War Reader*, New York, NY: New York University Press.

Managhan, T. (2012), *Gender, Agency and War: The Maternalized Body in US Foreign Policy*, New York, NY: Routledge.

Matsumura, J. (2007), "Unfaithful Wives and Dissolute Laborers: Moral Panic and the Mobilization of Women into the Japanese Workforce, 1931–45," *Gender & History*, 19: 78–100.

May, E. T. (1999), *Homeward Bound: American Families in the Cold War Era*, revised ed., New York, NY: Basic Books.

McEnaney, L. (2000), *Civil Defense Begins at Home: Militarization Meets Everyday Life in the Fifties*, Princeton, NJ: Princeton University Press.

Mertus, J. and Hocevar Van Wely, O. (2004), *Women's Participation in the International Criminal Court for the Former Yugoslavia: Transitional Justice for Bosnia and Herzegovina*, Cambridge, MA: Women Waging Peace Commission Hunt Alternative Funds.

Miyake, Y. (1991), "Doubling Expectations: Motherhood and Women's Factory Work Under State Management in Japan in the 1930s and 1940s," in G. L. Bernstein (ed.), *Recreating Japanese Women, 1600-1945*, 267–95, Berkeley, CA: University of California Press.

O'Reilly, M., Suilleabhain, A. O., and Paffenholz, T. (2015), *Reimagining Peacemaking: Women's Role in Peace Processes*, New York, NY: International Peace Institute.

Papic, Z. (2003), "Bosnian, Albanian, and Roma Women are Our Sisters," in W. Giles (ed.), *Feminists Under Fire: Exchanges Across War Zones*, 45–54, Toronto, CAN: Between the Lines.

Parashar, S. (2015), "War," in L. J. Shepherd (ed.), *Gender Matters in Global Politics: A Feminist Introduction to International Relations*, 2nd ed., 99–109, New York, NY: Routledge.

Paret, P., Irwin Lewis, B., and Paret, P. (1992), *Persuasive Images: Posters of War and Revolution from the Hoover Institution Archives*, Princeton, NJ: Princeton University Press.

Peterson, V. S. and Runyan, A. S. (2009), *Global Gender Issues in the New Millenium*, 3rd ed., Boulder, CO: Westview Press.

Pishchikova, K. (2011), *Promoting Democracy in Post Communist Ukraine: The Contradictory Ourcomes of U.S. Aid to Women's NGOs*, Boulder, CO: First Forum Press.

Porter, E. (2015), *Connecting Peace, Justice & Reconciliation*, Boulder, CO: Lynne Rienner Publishers.

Powaski, R. E. (1998), *The Cold War: The United States and the Soviet Union, 1917–1991*, New York, NY: Oxford University Press.

Ramusack, B. and Sievers, S. (1999), *Women in Asia: Restoring Women to History*, Bloomington, IN: Indiana University Press.

Reardon, B. (1996), *Sexism and the War System*, Syracuse, NY: Syracuse University Press.

Regan, P. M. and Paskeviciute, A. (2003), "Women's Access to Politics and Peaceful States," *Journal of Peace Research*, 40: 287–302.

Reid, S. E. (2009), "Communist Confort: Socialist Modernism and the Making of Cozy Homes in the Khrushchev Era," *Gender & History*, 21: 465–98.

Rupp, L. J. (1978), *Mobilizing Women for War: German and American Propaganda, 1939-1945*, Princeton, NJ: Princeton University Press.

Rupp, L. J. (1997), *Worlds of Women: The Making of an International Women's Movement*, Princeton, NJ: Princeton University Press.

Schmitz, D. F. (1999), *Thank God They're On Our Side: The United States and Right-Wing Dictatorships, 1921-1965*, Chapel Hill, NC: University of North Carolina Press.

Sjoberg, L. and Peet, J. L. (2011), "Targeting Civilians in War: Feminist Contributions," in J. A. Tickner and L. Sjoberg (eds.), *Feminism and International Relations: Conversations about the Past, Present and Future*, 171–80, New York, NY: Routledge.

Spence, J. D. (1990), *The Search for Modern China*, New York, NY: W. W. Norton & Company.

Stachowitsch, S. (2012), "Military Gender Integration and Foreign Policy in the United States: A Feminist International Relations Perspective," *Security Dialogue*, 43: 305–21.

Steans, J. (2013), *Gender and International Relations: Theory, Practice Policy*, 3rd ed., Cambridge, UK: Polity Press.

Steinson, B. J. (1980), "The Mother Half of Humanity: American Women in Peace Preparedness Movements in World War I," in C. R. Lovett (ed.), *Women, War and Revolution*, New York, NY: Holmes & Meier Publishing, 259–85.

Stienstra, D. (1994), *Women's Movements and International Organizations*, London, UK: St. Martin's Press.

Sundstrom, L. M. (2010), "Russian Women's Activism: Two Steps Forward, One Step Back," in A. Basu (ed.), *Women's Movements in the Global Era: The Power of Local Feminisms*, 229–54, Boulder, CO: Westview Press.

Swerdlow, A. (1993), *Women Strike for Peace: Traditional Motherhood and Radical Politics in the 1960s*, Chicago, IL: University of Chicago Press.

Tickner, J. A. (2001), *Gendering World Politics: Issues and Approaches in the Post-Cold War Era*, New York, NY: Columbia University Press.

Towns, A. E. (2010), *Women and States: Norms and Hierarchies in International Society*, Cambridge, UK: Cambridge University Press.

UN General Assembly (1948), *Convention on the Prevention and Punishment of the Crime of Genocide*, New York, NY: United Nations.

Westbrook, R. B. (December 1990), "I Want a Girl, Just Like the Girl, That Married Henry James: American Women and the Problem of Political Oblication in World War II," *American Quarterly*, 42: 587–614.

Williams, A. (2006), *Liberalism and War: The Victors and the Vanquished*, New York, NY: Routledge.

Williams, A. J., Hadfield, A., and Rofe, J. S. (2012), *International History and International Relations*, New York, NY: Routledge.

CHAPTER FOUR

Women, gender, and intergovernmental organizations

Foundational questions

How have the key intergovernmental bodies of the twentieth and twenty-first centuries founded in the aftermaths of the First and Second World Wars, the League of Nations and the United Nations Organization, incorporated Western-defined male-over-female gender-power relationships that have restricted global policy deliberations, contributed to world conflicts, and reduced their ability to solve global problems?

How have "women" fought for rights to participate as equals with men in these intergovernmental bodies and how have they transformed the patriarchal values and operations of these bodies?

Likewise, how have post–Second World War regional efforts to promote greater economic, social, and political cooperation among Western European nation-states, the major belligerent powers in the two world wars, resulted in the creation of the European Union, and how has the European Union included "women" and addressed the "problem" of "unequal" gender-power relations in its policies and operations?

Key concepts

Civil Society refers to "the people" who associate with one another in voluntary societies, religious groups, and churches, social movements, workers' unions, and other independently organized citizens' groups. The nature of civil society and its interests can be understood in contrast to government authorities or corporate business interests. Civil society creates a public sphere in which values-determining discourse, debates among competing interests, consensus-building, and organizing collective actions around local, national, or global public policy issues all take place. *Global civil society* asserts its necessary participation in democratic forms of global governance as well as in individual state governments' decision-making. Global civil society groups address public issues of worldwide relevance such as slavery and human trafficking, human rights, nuclear weapons proliferation, environmental protection, and the sustainable use of natural resources. *Transnational civil society* groups collaborate and organize public interest or issues campaigns across national borders.

Gender Mainstreaming is a deliberate methodology for determining bureaucratic and institutional policies and establishing government and other institutional programs that considers the differential gendered impacts of policies and programs on men and women. Gender mainstreaming recognizes that "gender equality" is a fundamental principle of democracy and that gender mainstreaming practices must be incorporated into *all* government or other institutions' operations to ensure the principle becomes a reality. Gender-mainstreaming practices involve men and women in relatively "equal" ways in all phases of an institution's policy and program development, including, for example, in the numbers of male and female participants, in terms of equal consideration and valuation of male and female needs and perspectives, or in terms of equal attention to outcomes that impact men's and women's lives. Gender mainstreaming also implies that government officers or other institutional personnel will be trained to understand and respect gender differences, formal guidelines will be established to implement gender-equality policies and programs, and policies and programs will be assessed to determine their effectiveness in reducing gender inequalities. In recent decades, the United Nations and the European Union have both committed through intergovernmental treaties to incorporate gender-mainstreaming practices to achieve gender equality in a wide range of their social, economic, development, and security policies.

Global Governance as opposed to global govern*ment*, refers to the collective activities of state governments, intergovernmental bodies, and their bureaucracies, NGOs, multinational corporations, and other civil society groups as they devise norms and establish agreements or institutional procedures to address problems that transcend national boundaries. A global govern*ment* would have centralized governing authority and legitimized use of coercive force over all world territories. In contrast, global govern*nance* consists of cooperative arrangements among various state and nonstate actors to deal with complex political, economic, and social problems that affect multiple states or regions of the world. Although the system of global governance that developed in the twentieth century and that exists currently relies on voluntary participation of all state and nonstate actors, the various participants in global governance are not all equal in power and influence within the system. Western-defined hegemonic masculine-gender-power relations have historically determined which states and entities have the *most* power and privilege to assert their will within global governance operations. Nonetheless, considerations of legitimacy, accountability, and moral authority limit even the most powerful states' actions. Moreover, growing awareness of the need to improve cooperative relationships among states and peoples on a global scale has accompanied the accelerated pace of globalization of the economy, global communications, and other systems integration, and global migration patterns and global social integration that have marked the end of the twentieth century and end of Cold War–era superpower relations. With growing numbers of nonstate actors participating in global arenas, some with benevolent and some with malevolent intentions, and with the recognition that new threats to human security have changed the nature of world politics, states and other global actors are recognizing the need for new, more effective forms of global governance.

Nongovernmental Organizations (**NGOs**) are voluntary associations that bring together members of social movements or other individuals within an organizational structure to pursue a common cause, that is often, but not always, in the service of the common good. NGOs that engage in the international realm of politics emerged in their modern form during the post–First World War era. Within international politics and global governance, NGOs represent their memberships and causes through advocacy with governments, intergovernmental organizations, and global agency bureaucracies. Their numbers and significance in global governance operations have increased exponentially with the acceleration of late-twentieth-century globalization processes. NGOs may provide research data and technical expertise for global policy makers as they strive to influence policy agendas and outcomes. At the international level, NGOs also increasingly act as service providers to implement governmental foreign aid or other global governance-mandated programs as NGOs have links to grassroots organizations and to local populations that are the recipients of aid or other targeted program goals. NGOs traditionally received funding through private donors but as their service provider activities increased during the twentieth and into the twenty-first centuries, so has funding from governments and intergovernmental bodies increased. In recent decades, networks of NGOs have come together through UN-sponsored and other global or regional forums to form *transnational advocacy networks* or TANs (Keck and Sikkink 1998). TANs share information and strategies and leverage their influence with global policy makers around complex problems such as expansion and protection of human rights, environmental degradation, and global violence against women.

Social Movements engage ordinary people who share common perspectives and conscious desires to challenge established policies or power structures over sustained periods of time. Social movements emerge when common causes or urgent demands for change to the status quo are deter-

mined that seem to have no state-sanctioned or authorized outlet for expression. All social movements bring together people who seek some sort of
transformational systemic change or form of justice. Some social movements
may engage in violent protests or may lead revolutions that overthrow the
established order; others may organize nonviolent collective actions, but
all seek to introduce new values and social practices and to leverage and
maximize the power of many individually disempowered people against the
power wielded by elite political, ideological, cultural, social, or economic
authorities.

Introduction

It is a fact which cannot be ignored that women are not only feminists in
a perpetual state of protest against restrictions and disabilities, they are
also, to an increasing extent, keen citizens, peace workers, reformers and
educators. The greatest freedom won by women is surely precisely this
equal right with men to effective interest in the whole of life.

MARGERY CORBETT ASHBY, PRESIDENT OF THE
INTERNATIONAL ALLIANCE OF WOMEN, 1928 QUOTED
IN KAREN OFFEN 2001: 244

International organizations—from the World Health Organization and
NATO to the International Red Cross and the International Labor
Organization—are as deeply gendered as a corporate law firm or an
Olympic gymnastics team. Sometimes, especially since the end of the
Cold War, all these agencies and their sponsors are clumped together
and referred to as "the international community." The founders, the
maintainers, and each international organization's chief constituencies—
those citizens who have a conscious stake in using them and influencing
their decisions—have particular ideas about what is "normal" for women
to do, what is "proper" for men to do, what is unsurprising when it
happens to women, what is expected when men do it. The politics of
each of these institutions . . . will only be fully understood when each is
subjected to feminist analysis.

CYNTHIA ENLOE 2000: 136

This chapter examines women's challenges to Western-defined two-gender-
power relations that have privileged elite male leaders within the key
intergovernmental organizations of the twentieth and twenty-first centuries:
the League of Nations (1919–45) and the United Nations Organization
(1945–to date). At the inception of the League of Nations, and due to the
intervention of a deputation of women from the victorious allied nations
who met with the League's founding commission, the League Charter

included Article 7 that declared "all positions under and in connection with the League, including the Secretariat, shall be open to men and women." Article 7, according to the women who pushed for it, represented "women's great charter," so that their presence would be assured and their interests would not be overlooked in global governance deliberations (Margery Corbett Ashby quoted in Northcroft 1923: 1). The UN Charter similarly included Article 8, opening all positions in UN bodies including the Secretariat equally to men and women. International women's organizations and women delegates representing UN founding member nation--states again were responsible for drafting Article 8, as well as for the gender-inclusive language in the Charter's preamble, asserting that "we the peoples of the United Nations, . . . reaffirm faith in fundamental human rights, in the dignity and worth of the human person, in the *equal rights of men and women*, and of nations large and small."

Despite these foundational pledges and myriad additional UN member states' agreements reasserting women's equality and pledging nondiscrimination based on sex, the levels of participation and status of women within these intergovernmental organizations have never been equal to that of men. This chapter includes feminist critiques of women's unequal status within these organizations. It explains how "women" made a difference in League and UN histories despite their fewer numbers and lower status, as they broadened the global policy-making agenda generally and expanded member states' understandings of human rights specifically. This chapter also exposes the unequal power relations between white, Western women and non-Western women as they engaged with each other and with member states in League of Nations and UN forums. These encounters illuminate some of the ways that women's relative positions of power and privilege within twentieth- and twenty-first-century Western-dominated racial and economic world orders have produced different perspectives among women regarding their "needs" and the strategies they employed to increase human security and promote social justice throughout the world.

In the 1920s and 1930s, women's international organizations that were founded in Western nations were led, for the most part, by white, privileged Western women. The few women who represented their nations as delegates to the League or who joined the League Secretariat professional staff, again, were mostly white Western European women. These women worked together in League of Nations forums and raised many gendered issues of wide concern, aiming to convince the mostly male League members that these issues were "problems" that the global governance body should address. A small number of women also served on various male-led League committees or commissions that sometimes recognized "women's" gendered needs, but more often ignored underlying gender-power relations. In 1932, women representing international NGOs and a few female government-appointed delegates were invited to bring their "feminine" perspectives to the League-sponsored Conference on the Reduction and Limitation of

Armaments. Although male leaders tried to define women's participation in state-centric disarmament negotiations in limited ways, women activists engaged in ongoing efforts to promote "peace" and support human rights in League forums throughout the critical interwar decade. At the time, they achieved few of the results they desired.

Nonetheless, new generations of women that included increasing numbers from non-Western nations pursued many of these goals through the United Nations Organization that was formed at the end of the Second World War. The UN Charter formalized advisory roles for NGOs and established the CSW. These institutional arrangements and an ever-expanding number of "social" concerns taken up by UN bureaus assured greater numbers of women would participate in the United Nations' global policy deliberations. Over time, more women of all nationalities and racial backgrounds joined UN bodies as government delegates, technical experts, and nongovernmental advisers, sometimes assuming leadership roles in those bodies. Their presence and contributions led to more democratic practices within UN forums and more expansive definitions of human rights among UN member states.

Although it was slow to happen, the years of women's feminist activism and persistent involvement in UN forums led to a series of UN-sponsored conferences that focused on the global status of women beginning in the 1970s. The first International Women's Year Conference held in 1975 focused on the themes of "equality, development, and peace." International Women's Year kicked off the United Nations' Decade for Women (1976–85) that included two more world women's conferences in 1980 and 1985, as well as a follow-up conference, the UN Fourth World Conference on Women, held in 1995. The "Platforms for Action" or government treaties that came out of these conferences established new gender-conscious research agencies and UN development funds devoted to the previously unacknowledged economic and social needs that were specific to women's populations; these changes will be discussed further in Chapter 5. The Platforms for Action also focused on defining women's human rights and raising awareness about the ways that gender inequalities undermined global security policies; this will be discussed later in this chapter. Additional treaties such as the Convention on the Elimination of All Forms of Discrimination Against Women or CEDAW, adopted by the UN General Assembly in 1979, and the Declaration on the Elimination of Violence Against Women or DEVAW, adopted by the United Nations in 1993, represented further progress toward transforming global gender consciousness regarding women's human rights and toward wider acceptance of gender-equality norms and their links to global human security. The UN Security Council adopted Resolution 1325 on Women, Peace and Security in 2000, another milestone that represented a new, higher level of recognition among the elite policy-making circles where males still dominated that "women" are necessary actors in determining and implementing effective global security policies and in creating the conditions for sustainable peace.

As these transformations in UN gender-equality policies were underway, Western European nations were concurrently focused on establishing more integration regarding economic policy, as well as more cooperative political relationships and greater agreement on social values and policy. The European Union, a regional intergovernmental body, is discussed in this chapter because from its earliest manifestation as the European Economic Commission (EEC) it has been at the forefront of efforts to establish gender-equality norms and to apply gender-mainstreaming practices to improve measures of gender equality in its institutional structure and operations, and among its member states.

The histories of "women's" involvement in the League of Nations, United Nations, and European Union illuminate how traditional gender-power relationships were reified when these intergovernmental organizations were formed. However, feminists who were "present at the creation" of these organizations have always challenged gender inequalities and antidemocratic institutional values, structures, and practices. Although these feminist challenges have at times been resisted by male-dominated power structures that continue to undergird international institutions and relationships, this chapter explains how new gender-equality norms and new respect for women's human rights among UN and EU member states emerged in the late-twentieth century and are gaining saliency in global governance settings.

Women, gender, and the League of Nations

Feminist women's suffrage advocates had long been active in Western European states and in other liberal democracies pushing for women's equal rights to participate in national politics, as well as challenging other gender barriers to women's social and economic equality imposed by the Western ideology of "separate spheres" for "active" men and "passive" women. The First World War, however, marked a turning point in the history of Western women's political status, as women had proved their "worth" to national leaders through war-support work and thus earned their full citizenship rights including the right to vote in national elections (Table 3.1). After the war, feminist activists aimed to enter the elite realm of international politics, as well. As Chapter 3 has recounted, at the outset of the First World War in 1915, 1,200 women from twelve nations organized a Peace Congress at The Hague. Together they formulated proposals to transform "traditional" male-dominated practices of international diplomacy that relied on threats of force and other forms of coercion with a peace policy that addressed global inequalities that caused violent conflict and that promoted social justice. The women's innovative ideas, the "Principles of a Permanent Peace," for ending the First World War and preventing the outbreak of future wars proposed "equal rights" for women, including rights to suffrage and equal representation in governments as *necessary* conditions for peace among nations, among ten other necessary conditions (Table 3.2). Representatives of the Women's Congress actively promoted these Principles of a Permanent Peace throughout the war even as they faced criticisms for failing to support their nations' war projects and for their "unrealistic" idealism. Nonetheless, many of the principles and values of a "new diplomacy" as outlined in the Principles of a Permanent Peace were echoed in US president Woodrow Wilson's proposed Fourteen Points to end the First World War—transparency and civic engagement in foreign policy making; multilateralism in treaty making; arbitration, disarmament and collective security measures to settle conflicts, and so forth (Table 3.3). These components of a "new diplomacy" were discussed at the male-led peace negotiations that determined the interstate peace settlement in Versailles at end of the war.

The peace treaty that came out of these negotiations in 1919, however, was drafted in secrecy and according to traditional values and established practices of nineteenth-century power politics, in violation of many of the principles and values that women's organizations articulated, including guarantees of women's rights. Yet one of the proposals that was put forth by the 1915 Women's Congress, as well as by President Wilson and other civil society groups during the war, was implemented: the Versailles Peace Treaty included provisions for a League of Nations. The League of Nations was to meet regularly in General Assembly to settle international disputes through new diplomatic practices, without resort to violence unless collective security measures against an aggressor state were agreed upon by member states. League members also agreed to a vaguely defined general disarmament of nation-states, starting with the defeated Central Powers. Women lobbied hard to carve out a space for women in the newly formed League of Nations. Because of their effective arguments the League Charter included Article 7, opening participation to men and women, equally. By the terms of its Charter, however, the League also established the supremacy of national sovereignty, and required unanimity among League members to engage in collective actions or to adopt guiding principles. Thus, the principles of "race equality" raised by Japanese government representatives and "gender equality" raised by feminist activists were not included in the League Charter. The League's framers, including its champion Woodrow Wilson, determined that racial and gender discrimination laws were "prerogative(s) of national self-determination and definitive of national sovereignty"; these points would be "insisted upon repeatedly in the working League" (Sluga 2013: 50–51). Spanish diplomat and frustrated advocate for an international disarmament treaty Salvador de Madariaga noted the irony of the League's experiment in "internationalism" when he observed in the late 1920s: "Nations meet and discuss in Geneva as nations, and thereby acquire a deeper sense of their existence, a greater sense of their importance" (Sluga 2013: 61).

Although President Wilson played an influential role in drafting the League Charter, the US government did not join the League of Nations that included forty-two founding member states, mostly drawn from the members of the Western Entente First World War alliance. Nonetheless, many activists and NGOs flocked to the League's Geneva headquarters, including well-known feminist activists such as American social reformer Jane Addams, British chair of the Women's International League for Peace and Freedom from 1915 to 1922 and journalist Helena Swanwick, Swedish writer Ellen Key, along with representatives of many Western-led women's international organizations with large global memberships. They enthusiastically supported the League and its potential for establishing a "rational" and cooperative "liberal" international order (Sluga 2013: 36–38). Together, twelve of these organizations formed a "Joint Standing Committee" (later expanded and renamed as a "Liaison Committee") and advocated collectively for "women's" concerns and for the appointment of women national delegates to the League's committees and commissions throughout the League's existence (Table 4.1; Miller 1994; Northcroft 1923). While these organizations represented large memberships drawn from Western and non-Western nations in many cases, they nonetheless expressed Western "middle-class values" in their approach to global issues, and the interests of nonwhite peoples were marginalized throughout the life of the League (Sluga 2013: 65–68).

In the 1920s, a governing League Council, comprising the four "permanent" leading member states, Great Britain, France, Italy, and Japan (1919–33), directed the League of Nations. Four other League member states also served as elected and rotating members on the League Council, drawn from the whole League General Assembly of member states. The League Secretariat performed bureaucratic tasks for the Council and the Assembly, as well as for the six permanent committees of the Assembly: The First Committee took up constitutional and legal questions; the Second Committee was concerned with technical organizations, international communications, transit, health, and epidemics; the Third Committee focused on disarmament; the Fourth Committee developed the League budget and directed internal administration; the Fifth Committee addressed social questions including those of international traffic in women and children, child welfare, protection of women and children in the Near East, opium traffic, intellectual cooperation, and refugees; and the Sixth Committee focused on political questions, abolishing slavery, protection of minorities, and admission of new member states.

In addition, the League also oversaw both permanent and temporary advisory commissions, among them a Permanent Mandates Commission "concerned with the well-being and development of peoples in territories formerly controlled by enemy countries and now assigned as mandatories to other nations" (Northcroft 1923: 16). Mandatory powers (Britain, France, South Africa, Australia, and New Zealand) governed over former German colonies and other colonial territories (in the Middle East, Southwest Africa, and in the Pacific). In 1920, women's organizations lobbied successfully

Table 4.1 Members of the Joint Standing Committee of Women's International Organizations, est. 1925

World's Women's Christian Temperance Union, est. 1883
International Council of Women, est. 1888
World Young Women's Christian Association, est. 1890
International Women's Suffrage Alliance, est. 1904
St. Joan's Political and Social Alliance, est. 1911
Women's International League for Peace and Freedom, est. 1915
World Union of Women for International Concord, est. 1915
International Federation of University Women, est. 1919
International Cooperative Women's Guild, est. 1921
American National Committee on the Cause and Cure of War, est. 1925
International Federation of Women Magistrates and Members of the Legal Profession, est. 1929
International Federation of Business and Professional Women, est. 1930
With a Name Change to the Liaison Committee of Women's International Organizations in 1931, the following organizations joined the established coalition in active engagement with the League of Nations
League of Jewish Women, est. 1920
World Organization of Jewish Women, est. 1920
League of Iberian and Latin American Women, est. 1921
European Federation of Soroptimist Clubs (International Soroptimist Clubs), est. 1924
League of Mothers and Educators for Peace, est. 1928
Equal Rights International, est. 1930

Source: (1945), *"An Experiment in Cooperation, 1925-1945; History of the Liaison Committee of Women's International Organizations."*

for the appointment of "at least one woman" to serve on the Permanent Mandates Commission. The women who served on the commission (one at a time in succession, and not concurrently), Anna Bugge-Wicksell, a Swedish feminist and social reformer who served until her death in 1928, and Valentine Dannevig, a Norwegian educator who served from 1928 to 1939, changed the nature of the Mandates Commission operations. These women envisioned themselves as part of their liberal democracies' civilizational "uplift" mission, but this sense of mission according to historian Susan Pedersen was a "feminized" mission. Therefore, the presence of women on the Mandates Commission implied that:

> Imperial rule . . . would henceforth be based on tutelage and not force; social progress guided by women's hands could justify the perpetuation of non-consensual alien rule. Social progress and imperialism could thus be reconciled, with the women Commissioners articulating standards of native uplift and betterment while joining their colleagues in repressing all claims to self-determination. Indeed, this "logic of the system" was so ingrained, so accepted, that few grasped the productive symbiosis between benevolence and autocracy that lay at its heart.
>
> PEDERSEN 2008: 192

The League also established an International Labor Organization (ILO) that was equally open to men and women members to collect data on industrial and other labor conditions throughout the world and to recommend common labor conventions to states' governments. A Permanent Court of International Justice seated at The Hague heard cases with international scope of concern. The International Institute of Intellectual Cooperation, the International Institute for the Codification of Private Law, and the International Educational Cinematographic Institute (concerned with censorship and propaganda) also formed intergovernmental entities within the League of Nations' global governance system. As this organizational structure suggests, international bureaucracy expanded in size and global information sharing increased in scope. Consequently, there was a growing need to educate popular opinion to support the League's operations that relied on technical knowledge experts and engaged with civil society organizations on a "semi-official" basis (Herren 2015: 183–84).

Women's political space and gender roles at the League of Nations

The League's expanded bureaucratic structure and educational mission increased opportunities for feminist activists in Western-led women's international organizations to participate in League operations, even as women's formal representation on committees and on government delegations remained minimal throughout the life of the League. Feminists and their organizations were not, however, mere conduits for sharing information between the League member states and the general population. Beginning in the 1920s and continuing throughout the League's operations, representatives of women's international organizations contributed their visions and technical knowledge to shape League efforts to abolish slavery and trafficking in women and children, to establish international aid and protection for migrants and refugees, to establish women's nationality rights, and to raise concerns for women's unequal status worldwide, among many other international issues. During the interwar decades, these organizations also worked through the new International Labor Office to establish universal workplace laws to protect the health and safety of women and children and to establish the principle of equal pay for equal work performed by men and women. Western-led women's organizations engaged in these collaborative policy advocacy efforts through their Liaison Committee, and through advisory committees they formed in conjunction with the League to focus on women's nationality rights and disarmament policy throughout the 1930s (Tables 4.2 and 4.3).

Women active in these organizations generally shared beliefs that "women" could bring a "unique sensitivity and empathy for others" to international politics, as "women" shared a "historical condition, as legally, economically and politically disadvantaged members of their respective societies." Nonetheless, there were fundamental differences regarding strategies to push for "women's equality" with no distinctions from men, or to recognize women's "difference," and emphasize their maternal roles or "pacifistic" natures to assert the need for women's participation in global politics. Some of these feminist activists were more "conservative" than others in their social outlooks, although even the most "progressive" feminist thinkers such as those who joined the Women's International League for Peace and Freedom at times demonstrated a "paternalistic" approach to "uplifting" non-Western peoples, as Anna Bugge-Wicksell and Valentine Dannevig demonstrated on the Permanent Mandates Commission. Some

Table 4.2 Members of the Women's Consultative Committee on Nationality, est. 1930

Equal Rights International
Inter-American Commission of Women
International Council of Women
International Federation of University Women
International Women's Suffrage Alliance
Union of Women for International Concord
Women's International League for Peace and Freedom

Source: Rupp, L. J. (1997), *Worlds of Women: The Making of an International Women's Movement*, Princeton, NJ: Princeton University Press.

Table 4.3 Members of the Peace and Disarmament Committee of Women's International Organizations, est. 1931

International Cooperative Women's Guild
International Council of Women
International Federation of Business and Professional Women
International Federation of University Women
International Soroptimist Clubs
International Women's Suffrage Alliance
League of Jewish Women
Women's International League for Peace and Freedom
World Union of Women for International Concord
World Women's Christian Temperance Union
World Young Women's Christian Association
Union of Women for International Concord
US National Committee on the Cause and Cure of War

Source: Rupp, L. J. (1997), *Worlds of Women: The Making of an International Women's Movement*, Princeton, NJ: Princeton University Press.

activists operating from nongovernmental roles outside the League focused on educating public opinion or supplying male government delegates with data to support their feminist positions, others pushed for women to enter the ranks of elite policy makers and to change the League global governance system from within (Beers 2016: 204–05).

During the League era, only a very few women were appointed to leading positions in the League's Secretariat; less than 1 percent of the top-tier positions were held by women during the life of the League (Sluga 2013: 69). The only female section head was British Dame Rachel Crowdy, for the Fifth Committee on Social Questions from 1919 to 1931, and she worked closely with the Western-led women's international organizations throughout the 1920s. She relied on these women's support for League initiatives and she also gave the women's organizations notice regarding League agenda items so that they could more effectively lobby government delegates to consider women's needs and concerns. When Crowdy retired from her post, Lithuanian Princess Gabriella Radziwill who worked in the League's information section became the women's organizations' chief source of inside information and informal adviser on League operations during the 1930s (Garner 2010: 31–32; Beers 2016: 206–07). Crowdy and Radziwill held two of the most senior positions among the women who worked with the Secretariat. Other professional women from Western and non-Western nations served in League offices in lower-ranking positions. Even though they were generally paid less than their male coworkers as Crowdy was paid less than other male section heads, "the League's Secretariat remained the most attractive employer for women in the international field" during the interwar decades (Herren 2015: 196). Throughout the life of the League, feminist activists continued to raise the issue of appointing women to higher-ranking positions of responsibility within the Secretariat, and they continued to press their governments to appoint women to national delegations and to the League committees.

Not surprisingly given the Western gender role expectations at the time, women appointed as delegates to their nation's missions or to League committees and commissions served most often in areas focused on humanitarian and social issues where it was assumed that their feminine

FIGURE 4.1 *Dame Rachel Crowdy, League of Nations Secretariat. C. 1925.*
Credit: United Nations Archives at Geneva

interests and talents most "naturally" coincided. For example, Marie Curie served on the Committee on Intellectual Cooperation and Avril de Sainte-Croix served on the Advisory Committee on the Traffic in Women, both appointed by the French government. British Liberal Party politician Eleanor Rathbone served the Child Welfare Committee (Pedersen 2008: 190). Apart from advisory bodies associated with the Fifth Committee on Social Questions where women tended to serve in more equal numbers with men, men dominated or populated exclusively other League committees that focused on political, financial, economic, or legal issues. Helena Swanwick, one of Britain's delegates to the League in 1924, complained that even though her expertise was in the field of disarmament and political issues, "I knew that, as a woman, I was predestined for the Fifth Committee." The Fifth Committee, as Swanwick described it in "unwomanly" terms, was "a sort of rag-bag of miseries and forlorn hopes. . . . A woman, it appeared, was assumed to be well-informed about Opium, Refugees, Protection of Children, Relief after Earthquakes, Prison Reform, Municipal Cooperation, Alcoholism, and Traffic in Women." Swanwick "often remarked that there was no such thing as a woman's point of view or a specific woman's role in international politics" (Swanwick quoted in Miller 1991: 68, 70). Swanwick was, however, in the distinct minority of opinion during the years of League operations.

It was generally assumed by men and women in Western societies that there was in fact a "woman's point of view" and a "specific role for women" in international politics. Following these gender assumptions, Western-led women's organizations most often intervened in League business by focusing on neglected areas of "women's concern," such as advocating for the legal guarantee that women could retain their independent nationality rights if they married men from other countries, at the Conference on the Codification of International Law held at The Hague in 1930. Although feminist activists did not achieve their goal of protected nationality rights for married women as part of the intergovernmental treaty negotiated in 1930, they achieved a significant concession. Following the conference, the League Council established a women's advisory committee to study the matter further and to report their findings to the League Assembly. The officially sanctioned "Women's Consultative Committee on Nationality" gained access to the Secretariat's informational resources and it opened the door for wider discussions of women's rights in League forums throughout the 1930s (Miller 1994: 232; Rupp 1997: 146–47).

The "League of Nations Inquiry on the Status of Women" formally launched in 1937 was one result of these wider discussions. Beginning in 1930 when feminist activists initiated their married women's nationality rights campaign, women's international organizations began collecting data on national laws regarding women's political and civil rights, as well as on labor laws that discriminated against women workers, in nations around the world. Women's organizations funneled their data documenting women's unequal rights and status to Gabriella Radziwill at the League Secretariat and to Marguerite Thibert, a staff member assigned to women's labor issues at the International Labor Office in Geneva. The data they collected prompted the League's First Committee on Legal Questions to launch an official "Inquiry on the Status of Women" and prompted a simultaneous ILO inquiry into the status of women workers. One of Sweden's delegates to the League, MP Kersten Hesselgren, was appointed as rapporteur to update the General Assembly on the progress of the inquiry. She had advocated for "some sort of survey on the legal position of women" at the League since 1932. Hesselgren was an important ally to the women's international organizations, as were the other distinguished Western legal experts, four women and three men, from Britain, France, Belgium, the United States, and Hungary who were appointed to conduct the inquiry (Linder 2001: 167). Women's organizations used their influence to widen the scope of the inquiry to include non-Western states, which was not part of the initial charge. They also publicized the ongoing work of the inquiry and touted its importance at a time when League member states' attentions were focused on the rise of the aggressive fascist powers. Progress on the inquiry stalled when the Second World War broke out in Europe in 1939, but US lawyer Dorothy Kenyon who had served as one of the legal experts on the Inquiry Committee preserved some of the committee's reports and they resurfaced when the UN global governance system formed in 1945–46. These reports informed some of the early work of the Commission on the Status of Women (Garner 2010: 101–03).

Women, gender, and League of Nations Disarmament Efforts

In addition to their campaign for women's nationality rights, feminist activists in the women's international organizations also intervened the League's efforts to negotiate a broad-ranging international disarmament treaty in the 1930s. At the time, both male and female government delegates and feminist peace activists identified a "special," although limited, role for women as maternal advocates for peace at the League-sponsored disarmament conferences that took place in London in 1930 and in Geneva beginning in 1932. Male diplomats who organized these conferences recognized that the women who were already engaged with League offices could mobilize pro-peace public opinion through their organizational structures and could use their feminine status as "mothers" to make "moral" demands for disarmament to put pressure on reluctant governments, supplementing the "legal" arguments that male diplomats would raise. Pro-disarmament male diplomats and government leaders, such as US president Herbert Hoover, British Labor Party prime minister Ramsay MacDonald, and his government's foreign minister Arthur Henderson were concerned about an escalating arms race in the late 1920s and early 1930s. They sought out female allies to support them in difficult disarmament negotiations. Feminist activists and their organizations were more than willing to comply. When Britain convened the London Naval Disarmament Conference in 1930, feminist peace activists collected nearly 200,000 signatures on petitions calling for global disarmament and formed a delegation calling themselves the Women's Peace Crusade. With the support of British Labor Party politicians, the Women's Peace Crusade presented their petitions to the assembled London Conference leaders. This was a symbolic gesture but it previewed the more substantive actions that women's international organizations would take to influence the outcome of the League Conference on the Reduction and Limitation of Armaments (or, the League Disarmament Conference) that convened in Geneva in 1932 (Bussey and Tims 1965: 91; Lynch 1999: 98).

A resolution presented to the League General Assembly in September 1931 by the leader of the Spanish delegation, Salvador de Madariaga, opened the way for women's involvement at the 1932 Disarmament Conference. De Madariaga called on the League Council to "consider the possibility of studying the means of associating feminine action and feminine feeling in the work of the League of Nations by effective and direct collaboration." In response, the Liaison Committee of Women's International Organizations reorganized their ongoing peace petition campaign and formed a sub-committee on "Peace and Disarmament" to direct women's energies toward ensuring the success of the upcoming Disarmament Conference ("Collaboration of Women in the Organization of Peace," League document A.10.1932). The Peace and Disarmament sub-committee (PDC) of the Liaison Committee of Women's International Organizations, was part of a broad-based, international, gender-mixed interwar peace movement that represented a wide spectrum of positions from liberal internationalists who supported the application of both political and economic sanctions to rein in aggressor states to absolute pacifists who rejected any use of coercive force (Lynch 1999: 28–30, 35).

Six women elected by Liaison Committee member organizations, Mary Dingman, Laura Dreyfus-Barney, Clara Guthrie d'Arcis, Laura Puffer Morgan, Kathleen Courtney, and Rosa Manus, led the PDC and performed the bulk of the committee's work in Geneva. These Western women, four Americans, one British, and one Dutch, cultivated connections to male leaders who were active in the interwar peace movement or who served in Western governments or in the League Secretariat. They drew on the male leaders' Western-defined two-gender expectations when they argued that "women" provided the necessary nurturing skills and humanitarian values to move militaristic and hypermasculine international relations toward more peaceful and cooperative directions. Laura Puffer Morgan also learned to talk the tough talk of power politics to capture male leaders' attention and be taken seriously, and to speak to their security concerns in disarmament debates as world conflicts escalated. These women mobilized and coordinated collective pro-peace actions of the Liaison Committee of Women's International Organizations' multimillion memberships at the Disarmament Conference and continued their educational mission through their publications and peace conferences in the Conference's aftermath, until the Second World War broke out in Europe in 1939 (Garner 2010: 35, 46–51).

Government members of the League of Nations, non-League member governments of the United States and the Soviet Union, and a variety of peace advocates and women's international organizations had all been working in earnest to convene a global Disarmament Conference since 1927. By 1931, a League conference preparatory commission had worked out the barest bones of a proposed international disarmament treaty to open conference debates. However, the draft treaty did not include any specifics in terms of armaments-reduction targets, or weapons to be abolished, or agreement regarding the establishment of a permanent disarmament commission, all of which were goals of various international peace and disarmament advocates. Since 1930, women's international organizations had been circulating petitions supporting a disarmament treaty to lay the foundation for lasting peace, as they had done at the London Naval Disarmament Conference. By early 1931, their petition campaign had become an international phenomenon, ultimately collecting over nine million petitions from fifty-six nations (Manus 1932). The women's Peace and Disarmament Committee that formed in September 1931 coordinated the international petition campaign and staged the presentation of the petitions at the opening of the government Disarmament Conference in February 1932. The presentation of the petitions to the delegates of the conference, the majority of whom were male, at the opening plenary session was a dramatic departure from traditional protocol at government meetings. Although some male diplomats objected, the women's organizations and their spokesperson, Mary Dingman, had the support of the conference president, Arthur Henderson, and the League secretary-general, Sir Eric Drummond, who continued to cultivate and appreciate the women's support throughout the life of the conference (Garner 2010: 55, 60–61).

A few prominent women also participated in the 1932 Disarmament Conference as official government delegates. Britain appointed Margery Corbett Ashby as an alternate delegate, the United States appointed Mary Woolley, Canada sent Winifred Kydd, Poland sent Anna Poradowska-Szelagowska, and Uruguay sent Dr. Pauline Luisi. These few women delegates banded together and took on the role of representing the "human element" during conference negotiations. They advocated for "moral disarmament," that is, for educational initiatives and cultural exchanges to develop common pacific values that would guide national and global politics (Garner 2010: 59–60). The women delegates' views regarding women's gendered contributions to peace making were mirrored and supported at every point by the PDC and Liaison Committee women's organizations worldwide. Much of the PDC's published literature and the committee officers' public statements referenced women's maternal roles and corresponding pacific nature. This strategy rallied support from men and women and it established a unique purpose for women, justifying their participation in male-dominated security politics. In the end, women's gendered moral arguments and the public pressure they exerted on diplomats did not persuade governments to reach concrete arms-reduction agreements, or agree to abolish various weapons of war, such as aerial bombs, or to establish a permanent disarmament commission. The conference failed to reach any substantive arms-reduction agreements.

Given the power politics that were playing out in Europe and East Asia in the 1930s, the reasons for the failure of the disarmament negotiations are clear. Chapter 3 has noted the fascist powers' increasingly violent drives to expand their territorial empires during the 1930s. The Japanese military occupation of Chinese Manchuria and bombing of civilian populations in Shanghai took place just as the Disarmament Conference was about to open. Japan's attacks on China abrogated international treaties its government had previously signed disavowing the use of force to settle international disputes: the League of Nations Covenant and the largely symbolic but nonetheless significant 1928 Kellogg-Briand Pact that "outlawed war" as an instrument of state foreign policy. The Japanese government exposed the sham of the League's collective security agreements, as it ignored diplomatic pressures to withdraw from Manchuria issued by League member nations and by the US government. Military "experts" testified at conference proceedings and their emphasis on military strength to achieve national security gained many government delegations' support, especially in light of Japan's actions. Moreover, the League's weak response to Japanese aggression emboldened Germany. Although German diplomats had participated in conference negotiations during the first year of meetings, in 1933, when Adolf Hitler and the Nazi Party came to power, Germany launched an aggressive rearmament program that violated the Versailles Peace Treaty terms and then formally withdrew from the conference. At that point, the United States for all practical purposes also withdrew from the conference and Franklin Roosevelt's administration temporarily gave way to the dominant mood of isolationism that directed the actions of US Congress during the 1930s. Considering the historical context, most scholars have agreed that reaching any international agreement on disarmament at the League Disarmament Conference was "almost impossible" (Northedge 1986: 136).

Despite the best efforts of disarmament advocates, the many men and women who joined peace organizations and those who served in the League Secretariat during the 1930s, government interest in hashing out a substantive disarmament treaty could not be revived. The League Conference ended public sessions in 1934, although some private government negotiations continued through 1935. By early 1936, the Disarmament Conference officially "suspended its labors" (League of Nations document A.64.1936 IX). Through early 1936, until the Disarmament Conference finally and officially adjourned, the women's PDC continued its international public education campaign focused on the purpose and work of the conference. The women's organizations also took principled stands on other international conflicts of the decade, issuing resolutions that called on governments to support India's bid for self-rule and condemning the Nazi persecution of the Eastern European Jews (Beers 2016: 211–12, 215). They also issued public condemnations of Italy's invasion of Ethiopia and the German bombing and Spanish Nationalist Army's slaughter of civilians in Guernica during the Spanish Civil War. Feminist activists representing the women's international organizations joined with male and female peace advocates and organized an International Peace Campaign that met in a World Congress in Brussels in 1936, gathering 40,000 people from thirty-five nations (Garner 2010: 88–98). Women activists remained engaged in international affairs throughout the 1930s. They remained vocal advocates for "liberal internationalism," that is international cooperation and effective collective security agreements, and they supported reformation of the League into a new, more democratic, and effective global governance system that would come into being after the Second World War.

Women, gender, and the United Nations, 1940s–60s

The United Nations Organization, like the League of Nations, was conceived during a world at war, and like the League of Nations, the original plan for its operations reflected the national security interests of the war's victorious "Great Powers." The elite male leaders of the Second World War "Big Three" allied powers, Great Britain, the Soviet Union, and the United States, came together in wartime conferences held at Dumbarton Oaks in Washington DC in 1944 and at Yalta in the Ukraine in 1945 to draft plans for a postwar global governance system that assured them and their Second World War allies, free France and nationalist China, a premier status in the United Nation's governing Security Council with the right to veto any decisions made by the new intergovernmental organization. The Big Three's original plans for the United Nations envisioned a weak and advisory body of member states, the General Assembly, with no formal roles for the participation of NGOs. When the UN draft Charter was released to the NGOs in advance of the organizational conference held in San Francisco from April 25 to June 26, 1945, concerned international NGOs that had supported the Western Allies' Second World War goals in many substantial ways successfully put forward their own plans for a more democratic international organization, one that would address social welfare and human rights as well as global security and regulation of the global economy.

Representatives of 250 NGOs attended the UN-organizing conference in San Francisco, along with delegates from fifty-one founding United Nations member nations (Sluga 2013: 88). Among them were five hundred twenty-one men and fourteen women (Linder 2001: 168). NGO representatives, including those from women's international NGOs that had been active throughout the League era, persuaded the government delegations that framed the UN Charter to add an Economic and Social Council (ECOSOC) as one of six "principal organs" of the new United Nations, along with the Security Council, General Assembly, Secretariat, International Court of Justice, and Trusteeship Council. The lobbying by NGOs in San Francisco also resulted in Article 71 of the UN Charter, whereby NGOs could apply for "consultative status" with ECOSOC Specialized Agencies (Weiss and Gordenker 1996: 21–22; Willetts 1996: 37–40). Within the first decade of the UN operations, twenty established women's international organizations representing 18 percent of all selected NGOs were granted consultative status to various ECOSOC agencies; among them were the International Council of Women, the International Alliance of Women, the Women's International League for Peace and Freedom, the International Federation of Business and Professional Women and the International Federation of University Women. They consulted on the work of ECOSOC agencies such as: the United Nations Educational, Scientific, and Cultural Organization (UNESCO); the Food and Agriculture Organization (FAO); the Children's Emergency Fund (UNICEF); the United Nations High Commission for Refugees (UNHCR); the World Health Organization (WHO); the ILO, among others, that drew on their "expertise" regarding "women's and children's" needs (Berkovitch 1999: 108).

Women's international NGOs also resolved to expand women's formal roles in the new United Nations based on their convictions that women's perspectives were needed to convince states to exhibit "respect for human rights and for fundamental freedoms for all without distinction as to race, sex, language or religion" as they persuaded the overwhelmingly male national delegates to the San Francisco conference to include in Article I Section 3 of the UN Charter, and to include an affirmation of human rights for all persons and equal rights for men and women in the Charter Preamble. To be sure, the human rights abuses perpetrated during the Second World War sensitized world leaders to the need to assert respect for human rights as a foundational principle of the new United Nations, but a few female national delegates played key roles in advocating for the inclusion of these human rights clauses in the UN Charter. Jessie Street from Australia, Bertha Lutz from Brazil, Minerva Bernardino from the Dominican Republic, Amalia Ledón from Mexico, and Isabela Urdaneta from Venezuela together led the campaign for human rights and gender-inclusive language in the UN Charter. These women were joined by a few other female national delegates and representatives of women's international NGOs who lobbied successfully for the establishment of the Sub-commission on the Status of Women at the inaugural session of the UN General Assembly that met in London in January and February 1946, which was soon awarded full "Commission" status. Danish delegate and feminist Bodil Begtrup chaired the first appointed CSW. Begtrup was active in international governance at the League of Nations during the 1930s and was a long-time member of the International Council of Women NGO (Linder 2001: 166). The CSW gathered data and made recommendations to the Economic and Social Council for proposed government treaties and UN policies and programs to promote women's human rights and gender equality in all fields of human enterprise (Reanda 1992: 269).

The CSW was initially the only UN body where female government-appointed delegates were in the clear majority and where women from non-Western nations played key leadership roles. The first CSW, for example, included Minerva Bernardino as its vice chair, as well as Angela Jurdak from Lebanon who became rapporteur, Hansa Mehta from India,

FIGURE 4.2 UN 224294 *At Hunter College, New York City, the Sub-Commission on the Status of Women meets. From left to right are: Mrs. Hansa Mehta, India; Mrs. Way Sung New, China; Miss Fryderyka Kalinowski, Poland; Miss Angela Jurdak, Lebanon; Miss Minerva Bernardino, Dominican Republic; Mrs. Marie Helene Lefaucheux, France; and Mrs. Bodgil Begtrup, Denmark and chairman of the committee. May 8, 1946. Credit: UN Photo*

and representatives from Chile, China, and the Soviet Union who joined delegates from Britain, France, and the United States. Nonetheless, some feminist scholars have argued that this almost-all-female body became a "ghetto" for "women's issues" without "sufficient funding, staff and political clout to carry out [its mission] fully" (Meyer and Prügl 1999: 7–8). In the six principal organs of the United Nations, women's "near invisibility" was the pattern. UN member states rarely appointed women to their nation's delegations except as support staff to their missions, and even more rarely appointed women as their ambassador, or "permanent representative," to head their nation's delegation. Moreover, following prevalent gender role stereotypes "women from national delegations tend to be elected or appointed to General Assembly committees and commissions perceived as gender appropriate or gender specific," such as the Social, Humanitarian and Cultural Committee of the 1950s or the Committee on the Elimination of Discrimination Against Women of the 1980s, for example (D'Amico 1999: 31–32, 36). Until recent decades, very few women were appointed as government delegates to the Security Council and no women served as judges on the International Court of Justice. Even regarding the Economic and Social Council, few governments overcame their societies' male-gender preferences as they appointed delegates to top diplomatic posts.

Early assertions of women's human rights

In the first few decades of the UN's existence as Cold War geopolitics imposed limits on international cooperation, the established Western-led women's international organizations pushed to realize some of their long-running goals to gain equal political and legal rights for women. Western women's organizations and Western government delegates to the CSW, such as Dorothy Kenyon who served as US delegate to the CSW until 1950, tried to revive interest in the League of Nation's Inquiry on the Status of Women and pushed for women's rights as individuals. Although non-Western socialist women and women from underdeveloped Third World nations pushed back with their own policy priorities including decolonization, the antinuclear peace movement, social welfare policies to benefit women and children, and economic-development initiatives, during the 1940s, 1950s, and early 1960s, the UN CSW displayed a distinct "Western orientation" (Reanda 1992: 276). As Indian scholar Devaki Jain wrote about the early years of UN and CSW operations, there was a "skewed distribution of power" that resulted in many non-Western nations' initiatives "being overlooked or dismissed" (Jain 2017: 66). India's CSW delegate, feminist Hansa Mehta appointed by Jawaharlal Nehru, for example, rarely got credit for her contributions. She lobbied the Human Rights Commission (and argued with the Commission's chairwoman, Eleanor Roosevelt, who initially disagreed) to assure that gender-inclusive language appeared in Article I of the

Universal Declaration of Human Rights adopted in 1948 (Jain 2005: 20). In the end, most of the voting nations agreed to gender-inclusive language, asserting: "*All human beings* are born free and equal in dignity and rights," and in Article II: "*Everyone* is entitled to all the rights and freedoms set forth in this Declaration, without distinction of any kind, such as race, color, sex, language, religion, political or other opinion, national or social origin, property, birth or other status." In its first decade of operation, the CSW also proposed several conventions pertaining specifically to protecting women's individual rights, as Western liberal democracies defined them. The UN General Assembly adopted the Convention on the Political Rights of Women (1952); the Convention on the Nationality of Married Women (1957), and the Convention on the Consent to Marriage, Minimum Age for Marriage, and Registration of Marriages (1962). A study cosponsored by the CSW and the ILO also resulted in the ILO Convention on Equal Remuneration for Men and Women for Work of Equal Value (1951).

As Chapter 3 has explained, Cold War–era "Eastern bloc" socialist and Soviet women, along with forty-one socialist women's international organizations, founded the WIDF in 1945. These women challenged Western liberal leadership of an emerging global women's movement. Some of those challenges were played out in UN CSW meetings. Moreover, non-Western women who represented many newly independent Third World nations also joined UN forums, including the CSW, representing their nations' governments as those nations formally became UN members during the 1950s and 1960s. These Third World women also engaged with the Non-Aligned Movement (NAM) of nations that declared their "neutrality," rather than align with the interests of one of the two major superpower rivals of the Cold War era. The NAM focused on eliminating global practices of racial discrimination and the overcoming problems associated with economic and political dependence on First World nations. These issues will be discussed further in Chapter 5.

In the early decades of UN operations Third World women made their presence felt at all UN forums. They organized new NGOs and rejected the Cold War politics that had shaped women's and men's participation at the United Nations. They sometimes allied with socialist women, as they did in 1963, when they joined Eastern European and Soviet CSW delegates in drafting a comprehensive resolution condemning all forms of discrimination against women. Their resolution became a formal Declaration on the Elimination of Discrimination Against Women (DEDAW), adopted by the UN General Assembly in 1967, and a formal CEDAW with monitoring mechanisms, which was adopted in 1979. The landmark women's human rights convention, the result of women's "diplomatic manoeuvres" in UN forums (Jain 2017: 72–73), "defined discrimination on the basis of sex internationally for the first time, giving women an important legal instrument" to assert their claims to equality of opportunity with men to participate in all realms of political, economic, social, cultural, and civic life (Tickner

2001: 114). In the 1970s and 1980s, Eastern, Western, and Third World women's NGOs all helped to define a UN-sponsored International Women's Year (IWY) in 1975, and directed male-led national delegations' attention to the Year's themes: "equality, development, and peace." Working with the UN CSW, the Secretariat and government delegates, women's NGOs organized a UN-sponsored IWY conference held in Mexico City in 1975, subsequent UN Decade for Women conferences held in Copenhagen in 1980 and in Nairobi in 1985, and a major appraisal of the progress toward women's equality at a UN Fourth World Conference on Women in Beijing in 1995.

Global support from governments and civil society for gender equality and women's human rights were transformed during the years of international feminist organizing that preceded and followed these conferences. Devaki Jain has explained the significance:

> It is difficult to find word to describe the experience of the UN Decade for Women . . . for women around the world. The Decade was life-changing for many, and a watermark in public policies and programs that would transform gender relations everywhere—despite the fact that most people will not be aware of the context in which many of these changes took place: from laws against discrimination against women to changes in men's roles in domestic life and increasing responsibility for housework and childcare, from the introduction of Women's Studies and other programs at universities to the increase of women's access to a range of academic and professional fields previously closed to them. The Decade linked academics and researchers, bureaucrats and activists in processes of policymaking that would change women's lives across continents of the South and the industrialized North. In the academy, it produced new understandings, knowledge and theories that challenged conventional wisdom.
>
> JAIN 2017: 73

The UN Conferences on Women 1975, 1980, 1985, and 1995

IWY

When the 1972 meeting of the UN CSW recommended to the General Assembly that 1975 be designated IWY, they acted on Romanian delegate Florica Andrei's proposal that Eastern, Western, and Third World women's NGOs be enthusiastically supported. The General Assembly soon accepted the CSW's recommendation and appointed British deputy director of the UN Branch for Promotion of Equality of Men and Women Margaret K. Bruce and Finnish delegate Helvi Sipilä to organize UN-sponsored IWY activities. Sipilä had previously chaired the UN General Assembly's Third Committee for Social, Humanitarian, and Cultural Affairs, which was referred to as the "Ladies' Committee" in the 1970s, indicating that Western-defined feminine-gender stereotypes were still shaping women's participation in global governance bodies (Jain 2005: 173, n. 67). Sipilä held the rank of assistant secretary-general for the Centre for Social Development and Humanitarian Affairs when she was tasked to organize IWY activities in 1972. In October 1974, the General Assembly voted to sponsor a world conference to commemorate IWY, which was scheduled to take place in Mexico City over the course of two weeks in late June and early July 1975. The CSW was not scheduled to meet again until spring 1976 and thus offered no formal assistance, and the United Nations had no budget allocated for the last-minute conference. Consequently, Helvi Sipliä, who was named conference secretary-general, assisted by Margaret Bruce, relied on volunteers from government delegations and representatives from the women's NGOs that had consultative status to aid them in drafting a conference treaty that would promote gender equality, and would recognize women's gendered security and development concerns. Government delegations would then debate, amend, and vote to adopt the treaty in Mexico City. With the help of women's NGOs, Bruce and Sipilä solicited funds from governments and private foundations to support the UN conference; most funding came from US-based foundations and Western governments (Olcott 2017: 14). They also relied on the women's NGOs to raise funds for a separate "NGO forum," that is, an independent meeting of NGOs to be held concurrently with the official government conference.

There were two broad and parallel perspectives that guided UN global conferences and summits from the 1970s onward: the governments' and the nongovernmental organizations' perspectives, although there was far from unitary agreement among governments or among NGOs regarding contentious global conference issues such as: maintaining sustainable population growth, promoting social and economic development, preserving the environment, promoting social justice, protecting human rights and women's rights and status, and so forth. In the case of the four UN-sponsored global conferences that focused on "women," UN government delegations, usually led by men, defined one set of priorities, and feminist women's NGOs defined another regarding which women's rights and concerns would be recognized as part of the global governance agenda for determining international law, policy making, and government-funded programming that would affect the lives of men and women throughout global civil society. During the late Cold War era, governments and women's NGOs hotly contested what constituted attention-worthy "women's issues," which made reaching a common consensus and negotiating the four international women's conference treaties especially difficult.

In the run-up to IWY in late 1974, a power struggle between two women's NGO organizing committees emerged, revealing, again, ideological and geopolitical divisions among "women." These NGO committees were established to plan IWY activities in two of the UN's capital cities. One committee, located at UN headquarters in New York City, was made up of mostly Western women from the United States, Canada, or Western European countries. These women assumed a leading role in organizing the 1975 IWY NGO forum, known as the IWY "Tribune," that took place in Mexico City before and during the official UN IWY government conference meetings. Another NGO organizing committee was led by women in WIDF chapters and other international NGOs that were based in Geneva. These women tried to assert their "non-Western" perspectives and priorities at the Tribune planning sessions, but came away frustrated by meeting locations and decision-making processes that prevented their full participation. Consequently, the WIDF organized an independent Women's Congress during the IWY that took place in East Berlin in October 1975. Despite these divisions that resulted in two separate IWY NGO meetings, women from Eastern, Western, and Third World nations came together and continued to debate "women's" policy priorities with one another at both gatherings. At the Mexico City Tribune, women's NGOs engaged with government delegates to the UN IWY conference, as well.

The Western-led organizing committee for the Mexico City NGO Tribune represented, for the most part, liberal feminist perspectives of the reformist rather than revolutionary variety. The Westerners designed an NGO Tribune agenda that consisted of twenty-five panel sessions focused on global women's roles and status as presented by "representative" women who presented case studies describing specific women and development, peace, and women's leadership projects that were operating in various parts of the world. The organizing committee also determined that the NGO Tribune would not issue any formal "political" statements to the UN conference delegates or to the media, since political statements would not represent the unanimous views of all who attended the Tribune. These arrangements angered many feminist activists who attended the Tribune, whether they came from the East, West, or the Third World, because the ban on political statements presumed that "women's issues" were somehow separate from geopolitical issues of the day. When statements were issued anyway, some women voiced their objections, resurfacing fundamental differences among "women of the world" based on race, class, geographical location, and ideological orientation; global media focused on these contentious controversies in their conference coverage.

The UN government-sponsored conference experienced related controversies as the NAM raised its objections to US-led Western powers that dominated the UN political and economic agendas and had retained their neocolonial relationships with Third World countries. In the 1960s, the NAM forged their own "Group of 77" (G-77) Third World nations to leverage their collective power to set UN policy-making agendas when they voted as a bloc in UN meetings. In 1973, the G-77 proposed the New International Economic Order (NIEO), calling for substantial revisions of the post–Second World War global economic order that the leading Western powers, the United States and Great Britain, had defined in the 1944 Bretton Woods Agreements to maintain their historic privileges in the global capitalist market economy (Jain 2017: 67–68). The NIEO outlined more equitable international trade policies regarding pricing, restoration of national controls over the sale of raw materials and commodities produced in developing nations, more liberal financing terms for economic development, and increased technology transfer from the developed Western nations to the underdeveloped Third World. Eastern bloc nations supported the NIEO throughout the decade of the 1970s, and the Third World–socialist world coalition was vocal at the IWY conference. They asserted that Western nations and international financial institutions must address worldwide economic inequities in the distribution of wealth before inequalities between men and women could be addressed effectively within nations (Popa 2009: 62–67). Third World nations also recognized and condemned systems of race and class oppression that encompassed and transcended men's use of gender power to dominate women, including South Africa's policy of racial *apartheid* and Israel's Palestinian policy, and Zionist ideology, which they defined as racism (Snyder 2004: 42). Most often, public debates among government delegates and demonstrations at the conference site, including a dramatic walkout staged by Asian and African nations when Lea Rabin, wife of the Israeli prime minister Yitzhak Rabin, rose to speak at the conference, focused on these geopolitical disputes rather than on expanding "women's equal power" vis-à-vis men, specifically (Garner 2010: 226–27).

The government treaty that came out of the conference, the "World Plan of Action for the Implementation of the Objectives of the International Women's Year," proposed government action to increase women's political participation, expand education for women and girls, train and employ women in the formal economy, improve levels of health and nutrition for women, implement programs to benefit families, develop gender-conscious population policies, improve housing, and addressed other social issues affecting women (UN Document E/conf.66/34). Governments also agreed to hold periodic reviews to evaluate progress on achieving World Plan of Action goals during the UN Decade for Women, 1976–85, and to establish two new UN offices: the International Research and Training Institute for the Advancement of Women (INSTRAW) and United Nations Development Fund for Women (UNIFEM) specifically targeting women and development projects (Snyder 2004: 44–46). In addition to the World Plan of Action, a second IWY conference document, the "Declaration of Mexico on the Equality of Women and Their Contribution to Development and Peace," specifically addressed unequal global power relationships of the Cold War era between the First and the Third Worlds that the Platform for Action avoided, including a call to "eliminate colonialism, neo-colonialism, imperialism, foreign domination and occupation, Zionism, *apartheid*, racial discrimination, the acquisition of land by force and the recognition of such acquisition, since such practices inflict incalculable suffering on women, men and children" (UN Document E/conf.66/34). Government delegates approved thirty statements of principle enumerated in the Declaration of Mexico by a vote that exposed Cold War–era divisions. The majority, eighty-nine Third World and Eastern bloc nations, voted in favor of the Declaration. The United States, Israel, and Denmark opposed the Declaration because Zionism was equated with racism and, by implication, the right of Israel to exist as a state was denied. Eighteen nations, most of them US allies in Western Europe, abstained from voting on the Declaration (Allan, Galey, and Persinger 1995: 35–39).

UN Decade for Women

Eastern bloc and Third World women energetically promoted their alternate feminist agendas throughout the UN Decade for Women and criticized "imperialistic" Western male-led governments and Western feminist-led women's organizations alike. Their criticisms gained momentum and shaped politics at the UN Women's Conferences held in Copenhagen in 1980 and in Nairobi in 1985 (Ghodsee 2010: 5–8). When the United Nations initiated the planning process for the Copenhagen Mid-Decade Conference, it named three additional conference sub-themes: "education, health, and employment," all related to the Decade theme of "global development" that particularly concerned Third World nations. The United Nations also named Lucille Mair from Jamaica as conference secretary-general. Lucille Mair held strong political convictions that were drawn from her life experiences growing up in a Third World nation and serving in several posts in Jamaican prime minister Michael Manley's democratic socialist government. In addition to other diplomatic posts she had held at the United Nations, Mair had served as Jamaica's delegate to the Mexico City IWY conference and had been a vocal member within the G-77 nonaligned nations that had proposed the NIEO. As conference secretary-general Mair included government discussions of the NIEO and the status of Palestinian women to be part of the official UN conference agenda. According to Devaki Jain, Mair "was in many ways as committed to Third World concerns as she was to those of women. She was able to link quite explicitly macro issues of imperialism and the 'violence of development' with the violence women face within more intimate spaces" (2005: 89). When she was interviewed by the *New York Times* after she was named secretary-general for the Mid-Decade Conference Mair openly acknowledged that she had been selected because she was a black woman from a developing nation. She had accepted the post because she had a political agenda that she hoped to further. Mair told

FIGURE 4.3   UN 66204 *Lucille Mair, secretary-general of the 1980 World Conference for the UN Decade for Women. April 10, 1979. Credit: UN Photo/ Milton Grant*

The Times reporter that "Third World women are acutely conscious of their condition. There comes a time when we need to put the problem in a global context. This is it" (Fraser 1987: 71).

As in Mexico City, the government conference delegates focused on geopolitical conflicts, including the Israeli-Palestinian territorial and sovereignty disputes, global government recognition of the Palestinian Liberation Organization (PLO), and widespread objections to South Africa's *apartheid* policy. Cold War politics influenced government debates as well as women's NGO interactions at the concurrent NGO forum. When the mid-decade conference treaty, the Copenhagen Program of Action, officially recognized the legitimacy of the PLO's opposition to the Israeli occupation and state security policies and explicitly named Zionism as a form of racism as the IWY Declaration of Mexico had done, the United States, Australia, Canada, and Israel rejected the treaty and twenty-two US-allied nations abstained from adopting the treaty, which, nevertheless, most governments approved (UN Document A/conf.94/35). Eastern bloc nations considered the approval of the conference treaty to be a triumph, not only because the treaty challenged their Cold War rivals' foreign policy but also because it included language that celebrated the status of women in socialist countries.

The conference treaty asserted that women in socialist states "actively participated in social and economic development and in all other fields of public life of their countries, including in the active struggle for peace, disarmament, détente, and international cooperation," and consequently they experienced "a high level of employment, health, education and political participation" (Ghodsee 2010: 7).

Both the long-established Eastern- and Western-bloc NGOs and the more recently formed Third World women's NGOs expanded their influence in planning for the UN's End-of-Decade Women's Conference held in Nairobi, Kenya. At this conference, the CSW was named official UN conference planning body. The CSW, now chaired by Nigeria's delegate Olajumoke Oladayo Obafemi, called a special session to meet in Vienna in February 1983 to start the planning process. Leticia Ramos Shahani from the Philippines, then serving as assistant secretary-general in charge of the Vienna-based Centre for Social Development and Humanitarian Affairs, worked closely with the CSW over the next two years to plan the 1985 Nairobi Conference and was named conference secretary-general. The CSW and Shahani welcomed the input of women's NGOs into the government conference planning process. The UN General Assembly formalized the NGO's expanded role with a special invitation to NGOs to join government conference preparatory meetings. As they had done at past UN Women's Conferences, women's NGOs planned and funded a concurrent NGO forum. A New York–based NGO committee and a local Kenya-based NGO forum organizing committee worked together, opening hundreds of forum sessions to a record attendance of 14,000 women who expressed many differing global perspectives on women's needs and women's rights.

Political controversies that had played out over the UN Decade for Women were again evident in Nairobi. The Israeli-Palestinian conflict, South African *apartheid* policy, and global social and economic inequities all caused heated debates among the government delegates. Nonetheless, the final conference document, the Forward Looking Strategies for the Advancement of Women to the Year 2000, was adopted by consensus (UN Document A/conf.116/28). Government delegates agreed to compromise in the much-debated conference document. More widely acceptable language denouncing "all forms of racism and racial discrimination" replaced condemnations of Zionism. The final document also "emphasized action over intention" and defined specific actions that governments should take to achieve women's equality and to recognize women's central roles in furthering national development and in achieving international peace (Zinsser 2002: 158–64). As the UN Decade for Women ended, contemporary feminist observers identified an "emergent global feminism" that resulted from the three world women's conferences and NGO forums and especially from the Nairobi meetings, which had helped to move the government delegations beyond Cold War-era geopolitical debates to produce the Nairobi Conference treaty, which was "an international working agenda for women" (O'Barr 1986: 585).

UN Fourth World Conference on Women

The bipolar East-West power struggle that had started during the Cold War came to an end during the late 1980s, and this transformed global politics. This was evident in UN forums when governments and NGOs began to define the new conflicts that emerged as threats to "human security," a concept defined as more encompassing than "national security." When the Soviet Union dissolved, its ability to direct foreign aid to its Eastern Europe and Third World allies broke down. Without the compulsion to "contain" the socialist world that was no longer backed by a formidable Soviet rival, US foreign aid priorities shifted, as well. Without Cold War levels of foreign aid to sustain them, some states' governments failed to provide "order" and stability, and various nonstate actors jumped in to address unmet physical security, social organization, spiritual, and sustenance needs among global populations. Some progressive civil society groups and NGOs promoted peaceful methods of demilitarization and social reconciliation in response to the profusion of violent conflicts. Other progressives advocated for "protection" of the human rights of various populations of women, children, workers, and people with lesbian, gay, bisexual, and transgender (LGBT) sexual orientations who were targets of the violence or who disproportionately experienced the negative consequences of the "new wars," global neoliberal economic policies, or environmental degradation. At the same time, "reactionary" fundamentalist religious groups and politically conservative movements and organizations opposed globalizing forces that challenged traditional social orders and their autonomy. Some groups took up arms against weakened or ineffective states, and others sought to liberalize and democratize state governments to make them more responsive to peoples' needs. Pro-democracy groups sometimes used the global forums provided by the United Nations to advance their causes, hoping to expand the scope of international law and international cooperation to improve human security. Many women's international NGOs from First and Third World nations took this route to during the decade of the 1990s. These activist women's NGOs and their academic, government, and UN Secretariat allies aimed to redefine global norms regarding respect for women's human rights and support for gender equality, linking these goals to advancing democracy and human security in all parts of the world. To achieve their goals, they engaged with governments and UN agencies to shape global treaties at several key UN conferences and summits that took place in the 1990s (Cohen and Rai 2000).

For example, women's NGOs and their allies were instrumental in directing governments' attention to the gendered impacts of environmental degradation on women's health and livelihoods in preparation for their interventions at the 1992 UN Conference on the Environment and Development (UNCED), held in Rio de Janeiro. Women's organizations including the Women's Environment and Development Organization (WEDO), Development

Alternatives with Women for a New Era (DAWN), and the International Women's Health Coalition (IWHC), among others, convened the "Women's Congress for a Healthy Planet" attended by 1,500 activists in Miami in 1991. The Congress drafted a "women's agenda" for environmental standards and protections that would address environmental impacts of various economic-development practices on women's health, to counter the male-led-government-determined "Agenda 21" treaty that was proposed at the UNCED to establish global environmental protection standards into the twenty-first century. Through interventions at the government conference and at the concurrent NGO forum, women's organizations persuaded governments to incorporate provisions acknowledging women's equal rights to participate in environmental policy making and addressing women's gendered development and population policy concerns into the final conference treaty (UN Document A/conf.151/26).

In 1993, women's NGOs led by the Center for Women's Global Leadership (CWGL), along with Amnesty International and Human Rights Action Watch and their allies in the UNIFEM played key roles at the UN Conference on Human Rights held in Vienna. With world attention focused on violence against women perpetrated during the Bosnian, Somali, and Rwandan Wars, women's organizations articulated the concept of "women's human rights" for male-led governments, explaining that it was a human right to be free from gender violence at all times, but especially when violence against women escalated during times of war. Feminist activists organized a "Global Tribunal on Violations of Women's Human Rights" held at the NGO forum prior to the opening of the government conference that many government delegates attended. Women testified before an international panel of judges about the specific gendered forms of violence they had experienced and brought their concerns into the open. Ultimately, the Vienna Declaration and Program of Action treaty that 171 governments signed agreed to the normative statement that "women's human rights" are "an inalienable, integral, and indivisible part of universal human rights" (UN Document A/conf.157/23). Government delegates also agreed to support the UN DEVAW that held governments responsible for identifying and eliminating violence against women, whether it was perpetrated by public or state authorities or by private entities, and did not to accept cultural or religious traditions as license to commit gender violence with impunity (UN Document A/RES/ 48/104). The UN member governments adopted the Declaration at the General Assembly held in September 1993, and appointed a special rapporteur to investigate the underlying causes of violence against women, as well as to investigate specific complaints citing violations of DEVAW that came to her office (Joachim 1999: 149–50).

At the International Conference on Population and Development (ICPD) held in Cairo in 1994, WEDO and IWHC and other women's NGOs that had gained experience in organizing effective caucuses and lobbying government delegates in 1992 and 1993, came together again. At the ICPD, women's organizations advocated for women's "reproductive rights" that included maternal-health provisions and decision-making power regarding the timing of pregnancies and the number of children they would bear, and, more generally, calls for expanded women's health research and access to care. At the conference, the contentious issue of women's right to abortion was the subject of bitter government debates waged by the Vatican and Catholic-majority nations on one side, and other governments that accepted women's rights to obtain abortions in nations where abortion was "legal" and "safe" on the other side. These disputes dominated global press coverage of the ICPD (Danguilin 1997: 85). Yet other measures that women's organizations sought were included in the conference treaty: the ICPD Program of Action committed the 181 governments that signed the treaty to fund UN programs supporting women's reproductive health, expanding educational opportunities for women and girls, and to raise women's legal, social, and economic status to levels that were equal to those of men (UN Document A/conf.171/13).

In March 1995, 186 UN member nations came together for a World Summit on Social Development in Copenhagen. Again, a women's NGO caucus led by WEDO, DAWN, CWGL, and others joined with UNICEF and UN Development Program (UNDP) allies and organized and directed government attention to the negative gendered impacts of neoliberal economic policies on women in all global locations. In roundtables and at a public "Hearing on Economic Justice and Women's Rights" held at the Summit's NGO forum, women's NGOs criticized international financial institutions and Western governments that imposed onerous debt repayment schedules on impoverished Third World nations. These NGOs continued their campaigns to transform neoliberal economic policies followed by the World Bank at the Beijing Fourth World Women's Conference. They also criticized the negative impacts of US foreign policies on nations in militarized regions of the world that experienced high incidences of trafficking in women and forced prostitution, and they condemned the general lack of First World aid for social welfare and development programs that would benefit the poorest populations in countries around the world (Runyan 1999: 218–19; Fried 1995). In the end, the Summit Report included more norm-setting language proposed by the women's NGO caucus: "We acknowledge that social and economic development cannot be secured in a sustainable way without the full participation of women and that equality and equity between women and men is a priority for the international community and as such must be at the centre of economic and social development" (UN Document A/conf.166/9). The Dutch and Norwegian governments also amended their development funding formulas and the US government made a one-time pledge of $100 million to increase education initiatives for women and girls. As US feminist Bella Abzug, who had spearheaded WEDO campaigns for women's equality at the series of UN conferences during the 1990s, pronounced at the end of the World Summit, "especially for women the world over, Copenhagen was a small but decisive step forward in the Sisyphean struggle for equity and equality" (Abzug 1995).

These conferences of the early 1990s developed the women's agenda that was the focus of feminist women's NGO activism at the UN Fourth World Conference held in Beijing in September 1995. Women's international NGOs, including those of long-standing such as the Women's International League for Peace and Freedom (WILPF) and those of more recent origins such as DAWN, WEDO, and CWGL, had worked with one another and crossed national and regional borders to negotiate some common "women's interests" and global policy goals. They established working relationships with academics and UN agencies that researched issues and drafted conference agreements for UN member states to consider, and they made alliances with government delegates who attended the UN conferences to promote their women's rights agendas. As a result, women's NGOs achieved concessions in the government treaties negotiated at the 1990s conferences acknowledging many women's rights as essential treaty objectives. Women's NGOs set their goals for the Beijing Women's Conference to maintain the progress they had made since IWY, and to establish concrete government commitments in regard to procedures for implementation, with established timelines and benchmarks, to hold governments accountable for fulfilling their past treaty pledges made in the CEDAW, the Nairobi Forward Looking Strategies, and the Rio, Vienna, Cairo, and Copenhagen conference treaties.

The lengthy and detailed treaty finalized in Beijing, the Platform for Action, outlined a blueprint for government action to remove legal and social obstacles to women's full equality within their societies. To achieve these goals, the Platform for Action established the procedural method of "gender mainstreaming" for government and global governance policy making. In brief: "Gender mainstreaming systematically assesses the implications of any planned action to ensure that all policies contribute to gender equality. Starting with the policy-planning stage and proceeding through the policy cycle, the aim is to evaluate policy effects in all policy areas by using a gender perspective" (Woodward 2012: 98). Gender mainstreaming "became the directive for system-wide policy development in the UN" beginning in 1997. The ILO also "officially prioritized" gender-mainstreaming practices in the late 1990s and the World Bank adopted gender-mainstreaming practices for its institutional policy making in 2001. Regional intergovernmental bodies, such as the European Union and the Asia Pacific Economic Corporation, also established gender mainstreaming as "institutional norms" directing policy-making processes in the late 1990s (True and Parisi 2013: 37–38). The Beijing Platform for Action identified "twelve areas of concern" or objectives for governments and global governance bodies to strive for, including ending violence against women, promoting women's access and participation in social and economic development, and poverty eradication programs, protecting women's reproductive rights, and establishing women's equal access to education and health care and to economic resources such as land, credit, and technology. An additional policy objective focused on "women and armed conflict," which asserted the need for women's full participation in conflict resolution, disarmament initiatives, and peace building around the world (UN Beijing Declaration and Platform for Action). Holding the 189 governments that signed the Platform for Action accountable to their commitments to reach these objectives in national and global governance settings directed feminist NGOs' activism in the years following the Beijing Conference. Regarding the concern for "women and armed conflict" feminists successfully focused government attention on protecting women's human rights in security sector policies in the late 1990s, leading to the adoption of UNSCR 1325 on Women, Peace, and Security (WPS) in October 2000 and the further WPS Security Council Resolutions, which will be discussed below.

Women, gender, and the European Union

During the past sixty years as the process of European integration evolved, beginning with the 1957 Rome Treaty that established the European Economic Community of six Western European member nations to the current iteration of the European Union of twenty-eight member nations, men have dominated the European Union's governing and policy-making bodies. The leadership of the governing European Council has been made up of European countries' national leaders, predominantly men. And the EU parliament has only slowly included more female representatives, who have been elected in growing numbers since 1979, when the EU parliament introduced direct universal elections. As recently as 2008, Margot Wallström, then European commissioner for Institutional Relations Communications Strategy, remarked that the European Union's governing bodies were still dominated by "the reign of old men" (Abels and Mushaben 2012: 4). Nonetheless, over the decades within this male-dominated regional governance body, the European Union has adopted gender-equality norms and put gender-equality laws into place. Gender-equality policy was initially confined to directives to ensure equal pay and equal opportunities for women's employment, as Article 119 of the 1957 Rome Treaty stipulated. By 2009 and the establishment of the Lisbon Treaty on the Functioning of the European Union, however, EU member nations agreed that "the Union is founded on the values of respect for human dignity, freedom, democracy, equality, the rule of law and respect for human rights, including the rights of persons belonging to minorities. These values are common to Member States in a society in which pluralism, non-discrimination, tolerance, justice, solidarity and equality between men and women prevail" (Article 2). EU members pledged to "combat social exclusion and discrimination, and shall promote . . . equality between women and men" (Article 3). EU members also extended their pledge to all EU operations: "In all its activities, the Union shall aim to eliminate inequalities and to promote equality, between men and women" (Article 8).

Much of the credit for the expansion of gender-equality norms and laws has been due to collaborations of government and nongovernment women who were active in European feminist movements since the 1970s (Abels and Mushaben 2012: 4–5, 7). These feminist movements drew reform energy and developed effective norming strategies out of networks and collaborations forged during the IWY, UN Decade for Women conferences, and NGO forums, including the effective strategy of reporting out on women's status and rights in international forums to expose gender inequalities to public scrutiny (Woodward 2012: 91–92). Activists working inside the European Community (EC) governance structures established a standing Committee on Women's Rights and Gender Equality (FEMM) in the European parliament in 1984. These EC "insiders" encouraged the establishment of the "outsider" nongovernmental European Women's Lobby to advocate for further actions to advance women's equality in 1990. Working together, feminist networks established "symbolic and political" spaces in EU governance and used those spaces to influence governments to address women's equality issues (Rossilli 2000: 7, 11). As the European Community evolved into a more integrated European Union following the signing of the Maastricht Treaty in 1992, the European Union expanded the scope of its efforts to achieve gender equality into a wide range of intergovernmental offices and programs. In 1997, the Amsterdam Treaty prohibited discriminations based on gender, race, religion, nationality, and sexual orientation. And, beginning in 2009 with the signing of the Lisbon Treaty, gender equality has been defined as a "fundamental principle" of EU bodies and operations, as noted above.

The European Union has adopted three different methods to achieve gender equality in its operations and in member states that have been applied in a roughly chronological sequence: advocating for "equal treatment" of men and women, primarily through integrating women as workers into the marketplace and social security systems during the 1960s and 1970s; pushing for adoption of "positive actions" such as encouraging businesses and institutions to implement affirmative action vis-à-vis hiring and promotion policies, flexible work schedules, and to provide more childcare support for working mothers and more support for women to exercise their full political and citizenship rights, including establishment of gender quotas in electoral politics during the 1980s and 1990s; and supporting "gender mainstreaming" practices by the late 1990s (Rossilli 2000: 18–19; Woodward 2012: 88–89). Although the gender-mainstreaming approach has its feminist critics mainly because it has failed to achieve its ultimate objective: gender equality, the methodology has been adopted widely in EU governance bodies. Beginning in 1996 after EU member governments signed the Beijing Platform for Action treaty, the European Union has been at the forefront of global efforts to apply gender-mainstreaming practices when formulating and implementing EU governance policies. Gender mainstreaming was codified in the Amsterdam Treaty and reaffirmed in the Lisbon Treaty. In the European Union, gender mainstreaming applied gender-equality norms to policies focused on the common market and employment, as well as to migration, research, and technology, justice, development, and foreign and security policies.

Proponents of gender mainstreaming recognized that EU officials and government members needed to be educated to understand the need for and benefits of gender mainstreaming in their institutions to become invested in these practices. Officials also needed to be trained in gender-mainstreaming methods to apply them consistently and effectively in all government operations. This recognition among feminist theorists and activists inspired the establishment of the European Institute for Gender Equality in 2010. The Institute, an autonomous body of the European Union, has provided research, data, and "gender expertise" that supported gender-mainstreaming practices in EU governance operations, in member states and in "pre-accession" countries as they applied for EU membership. Its mission is "to become the European knowledge centre on gender equality" and its work is directed at projects requested by the EU parliament and its governing council. For example, it monitors progress toward achieving Beijing Platform for Action gender-equality targets in the realms of work, access to financial resources and women's economic status, women's health, and women's relative decision-making "power" and leadership, and publishes its findings. These are available on its institute's website, along with databases, maps, graphs, and statistics, all freely available to researchers (http://eige.europa.eu/). The institute also focuses its education and advocacy on monitoring the widespread problem of gender-based violence toward women. It offers tools and best practices for agencies and governments combating gender-based violence, and resources for victims of violence to access support services.

At this current point in the unfolding of EU gender-equality efforts, most analysts describe a mixed record of successes and shortcomings. There are many reasons that the goal of gender equality has not been fully realized across Europe, and the diversity among European nations even in an "integrated" European Union is one major factor, among others. As Alison Woodward concluded in her 2012 assessment of the European Union's gender-equality policy experiments:

> Our understanding of what equality can and should mean in Europe has evolved thanks to women's activism, advances in gender theory, European enlargement, better statistics and more critical analysis. There is still much to be done: the goals of bodily integrity, of being able to profit from meaningful work, and of enjoying complete social and political equality have not yet been attained for many of Europe's women. European gender realities cover the spectrum from Malta in the South to Finland in the North, from Romania in the East to Ireland in the West. European

integration provides a living laboratory for how cultures, policy and activism can redefine and alter gender relations. Thanks to this learning laboratory, European Union experiences can provide ammunition for other countries that still have a longer way to go in changing gender relations, while raising new questions about the right way to proceed in Europe itself.

WOODWARD 2012: 102

Women, gender, and UNSCR 1325

During the 1990s, historical developments at the end of the Cold War era seemed to open opportunities that would allow the United Nations to play a new, expanded role in global affairs. Without the gridlock that the Cold War "inter-bloc rivalry" between the East and West had imposed on the UN development and human rights agendas, on security and peacekeeping and on other divisive global issues for over forty years, UN secretary-general Boutros Boutros-Ghali and other UN leaders proposed an expanded field of operations for global cooperation, particularly in the realms of peacekeeping, human rights, and environmental protection (Rushton 2008: 95–96). These new directions coincided with the concerns and policy goals put forward by feminist NGOs in the 1990s.

When Secretary-General Boutros Boutros-Ghali began his term of service in January 1992, an increasing number of "new wars" of the post–Cold War era prompted the UN Security Council to request a report outlining new roles that the United Nations could play in establishing and maintaining global peace and security. Secretary-General Boutros-Ghali presented "An Agenda for Peace" to the Security Council in June 1992. In the report, Boutros-Ghali identified broad issues relating to human security and structural violence that created conditions of inequality and that led to new wars between nation-states, and, more frequently, to violent intrastate armed conflicts. These destabilizing conditions, Boutros-Ghali suggested, could be addressed through UN interventions that were supported by greater government cooperation, or through "preventative diplomacy." In the Secretary-General's view, expanding democratic governing practices in nations around the world was key to creating conditions for "peace" and social and economic development; his goal was to develop a new global norm supporting "democratic governance." Boutros-Ghali repeated his assertions that "peace, development, and democracy" were linked, conceptually and practically, throughout his term as Secretary-General in a series of reports to the General Assembly: "An Agenda for Peace" followed by "An Agenda for Development" (1994), and "An Agenda for Democratization" (1996).

In repeating these key phrases, Boutros-Ghali was norming democratic governance as the "duty" of nation-states, and the most efficacious route to achieving international peace and security and supporting human rights and international development. This was a controversial norming campaign because it implied both military and nonmilitary interventions in nondemocratic but sovereign states. In fact, as the norm of democratic governance gained saliency among civil society groups and others, it led to a growing number of UN peacekeeping missions, wherein armed UN peacekeepers entered active conflict zones, sometimes without the consent of the warring parties. Between 1948 and 1988, only sixteen UN peacekeeping missions had been deployed compared to more than forty UN peacekeeping operations that were undertaken between 1989 and 2010 (Harrington 2011: 566). Establishing a global norm or expectation that "legitimate" states would adopt democratic forms of government led to much greater UN involvement in "organizing and monitoring electoral processes, promoting respect for human rights, assisting in reforming security services and judiciaries, and supporting the development of civil society," all activities that the UN Secretariat had avoided in the interests of maintaining "impartiality" during the Cold War era of the United States–Soviet Union superpower rivalry (Rushton 2008: 107).

These same post–Cold War global realignments also transformed the United Nation's agenda in terms of recognizing and protecting "women's human rights." Feminist NGOs advocated for these changes in UN forums and media campaigns, and gained widespread state and nonstate support as gender and sexual violence against women escalated during the new wars fought in the 1990s. Feminist NGO networks involved powerful governments, such as the United States and its Western European allies, in interventions to criminalize wartime sexual violence through the temporary International War Crimes Tribunals and at the permanent International Criminal Court, and in "policing" the states and nonstate militias that perpetrated the violence. These "police actions," however, also had some negative and anti-feminist impacts. For one, an expansion of states' mostly male-military interventions and UN peacekeeping's mostly male-military missions increased the incidences of male violence against women in war zones for the reasons discussed in Chapter 3. For another, states' militaries and UN peacekeeping missions narrowed the wide-ranging global governance conversation surrounding "women's human rights" that feminist NGOs had started in the early 1990s down to a conversation focused on protecting women's bodies from gender and sexual violence in wartime. As political scientist Carol Harrington has explained, the ways that state governments and global governance bodies began to define the "problem" of women's human rights in the 1990s was shaped by their concerns about how to establish peace and security in new war zones where combatants deliberately targeted female civilian populations: "In the new wars discourse, the notion of 'women's human rights' typically refers to women's bodily integrity, rather than broader notions of social or economic rights. Thus, in post–Cold War security discourse the term 'human rights violations' typically means bodily violation and signifies a lack of democracy" (2011: 566).

As UN secretary-general Boutros Boutros-Ghali and his successor, Secretary-General Kofi Annan, promoted the linkages between democratic governance, peace, and global development, Western governments added the link to capitalist neoliberal economic development as a necessary element in their promotion of democratic governance, peace, and development. Feminist women's NGOs advocated for links to women's human rights *and* gender equality as additional and *necessary* conditions to achieve democracy, peace, and development in a humane and just world. After the Beijing Platform for Action identified "women and armed conflicts" as one of its twelve objectives, feminist advocates for gender equality called for women's equal participation in the United Nations and government peace and security initiatives, as well as attention to the gendered impacts of war on women, especially gender and sexual violence toward women that violated women's human rights.

During the 1998 meeting of the UN CSW, a caucus of women's NGOs formed to focus on the topic of "women, peace, and security" in preparation for the 5-year review of governments' progress toward meeting their Beijing Platform for Action commitments that was scheduled to take place in June 2000. In early March 2000, a landmark International Women's Day address by UN Security Council president Anwarul Chowdhury called on the Security Council to examine the links between "gender, peace, and security." This address opened the door for the establishment of the women's NGO WPS at the subsequent March 2000 meeting of the UN CSW. The Women's Working Group, founded by representatives of six NGOs including the historic WILPF, began drafting a UNSCR on women, peace, and security to present to Security Council members for consideration and adoption:

> Reaffirming the important role of women in the prevention and resolution of conflicts in peace-building, and stressing the importance of their equal participation and full involvement in all efforts for the maintenance and promotion of peace and security, and the need to increase their role in decision-making with regard to prevention and resolution. . . .
>
> Urges Member States to ensure increased representation of women at all decision-making levels in national, regional and international institutions and mechanisms for the prevention, management, and resolution of conflict. (UN Document S/RES/1325)

UNSCR 1325, "the only Security Council resolution for which the groundwork, the diplomacy and lobbying, the drafting and redrafting was almost entirely the work of civil society," illuminated states' obligations to protect women and girls in conflict zones and to ensure that women were involved in all aspects of conflict prevention, conflict resolution, and post-conflict peace building (UN Women report 2015: 30). Although the drafting and adoption of UNSCR 1325 took place over a relatively brief period, it involved an intense level of work and a "sophisticated strategy" on the part of the NGO Working Group that met with Security Council members and key government and UN staff members, providing legal foundations for the resolution in previous UN treaties, educating them with data, and bringing in women from conflict zones to share their first-hand experiences of war with elite policy makers. As feminist IR scholar Carol Cohn explained the successful advocacy strategy: "Generally, the Working Group self-consciously decided to position themselves as 'helpers' to the Council, rather than confrontational adversaries" (Cohn 2008: 187–88).

While the campaign to persuade the UN Security Council to adopt resolution 1325 was successful, the implementation of UNSCR 1325 relied on the individual UN member states to make changes in their security operations. UNSCR 1325 "has been translated into over 80 languages and has become a key reference point for women's organizations around the world," however, the problem is "the pace of implementation has been lamentably slow" (von Braunmühl 2013: 164–65). A Human Rights Watch Report issued in 2015 noted that only eighteen of the peace agreements signed between 1998 and 2008 "addressed any aspect of women's rights and concerns" in their final documents (Human Rights Watch 2015: 9). In 2015, only fifty-four nations had adopted National Action Plans to implement UNSCR 1325.

Subsequent WPS Security Council Resolutions 1820, 1888, 1889, 1960, 2106, and 2122 were deemed necessary to address ongoing problems that women face during wartimes. These Security Council Resolutions clarify states' obligations, address the sexist culture and abuse of women and girls perpetrated by UN peacekeepers, and establish international monitoring and reporting regimes to promote states' compliance. Together these resolutions provide a "WPS agenda," that is based on three "pillars": "protection" from gender-based and sexualized violence; "prevention" of gender-based and sexualized violence that compromise human rights; and necessary "participation" of women in all conflict prevention, peacemaking, and peace-building activities undertaken by states and the United Nations. Critics of the implementation of UNSCR such as IR scholar Claudia von Braunmühl have argued that from 2000 to 2008, the focus of the WPS agenda shifted from women's equal participation in peacemaking processes and operations to a focus on protecting women from gender and sexual violence during conflicts. With the shift in focus of the WPS agenda to protection of women, women have been "re-victimized" and "the old social construct of the male protector" has been "reanimated." As Claudia von Braunmühl explains the significance of this shifting focus, "the logic of patriarchal protection [assures that] women's subordination is reinstalled" (2013: 168–69). This is the opposite effect that feminist activists who lobbied for UNSCR 1325 desired as they sought to further women's human rights *and* to advance gender equality. Feminists will need to develop more effective strategies to

Table 4.4 **UNSCR** on Women, Peace, and Security

UNSCR 1325 (adopted 2000) recognized the important role that women play in the prevention and resolution of armed conflicts and in peace building, and urged states to ensure the full and equal participation of women at all levels of decision-making within regional, national, and international institutions established to prevent, manage, and resolve armed conflicts.

UNSCR 1820 (adopted 2008) linked wartime rape and sexual violence that targeted civilian populations to prolonged and intensified armed conflicts, and called on states and on UN peacekeeping forces to prohibit, and prevent or shut down all acts of sexual violence against civilians during conflicts that are classified as war crimes or crimes against humanity.

UNSCR 1888 (adopted 2009) reaffirmed and strengthened UNSCR 1820, mandated that UN peacekeeping missions protect women and children from sexual violence during armed conflict, and called on the UN secretary-general to appoint a special representative on Sexual Violence in Armed Conflict who would monitor and report on states' militaries and UN peacekeepers' violations to ensure that investigations and disciplinary measures would be enforced.

UNSCR 1889 (adopted 2009) reaffirmed the need for women's full and equal participation in all stages of peace processes, and called on states and UN peacekeeping missions to include women in peace negotiations and conflict resolution, postwar reconstruction, and peace-building activities, as well as in political and economic decision-making and leadership roles, and urged states to develop national action plans to carry out the mandates of previous women, peace, and security resolutions.

UNSCR 1960 (adopted 2010) reaffirmed prohibitions against sexual violence against civilian populations during armed conflicts, and called on the UN secretary-general to establish monitoring, analyzing, and reporting protocols to determine patterns of wartime rape and other forms of sexual violence, to coordinate efforts of the UN special representatives on Children and Armed Conflict and on Sexual Violence in Conflict to ensure concrete and specific commitments to combat sexual violence, and to hold violators accountable for their crimes.

UNSCR 2106 (adopted 2013) reaffirmed the need for more systematic monitoring and attention to sexual violence in armed conflict and post-conflict states and for women's full participation in all peace processes, and called for further deployment of women protection advisers with UN peacekeeping missions and of gender advisers to ensure that gender perspectives are mainstreamed in all peacekeeping policies and missions and in all disarmament, demobilization, and reintegration processes.

UNSCR 2122 (adopted 2013) reaffirmed women's and girls' empowerment and gender equality as necessary components of international peace and security, reaffirmed the UN commitments to protect civilian populations from sexual violence during armed conflicts and in post-conflict states, and pledged to monitor and strengthen specific measures to implement the Women, Peace, and Security resolutions.

Source: "Women, Peace and Security," United Nations Peacekeeping Issues www.un.org/en/peacekeeping/issues/women/wps.shtml (Accessed August 4, 2017)

FIGURE 4.4 **UN 453079** *Hillary Rodham Clinton, secretary of state of the United States of America, addresses a meeting of the Security Council marking the tenth anniversary of landmark Council Resolution 1325 on Women, Peace, and Security. October 26, 2010. Credit: UN Photo/Paulo Filgueiras*

achieve gender equality in their societies, which might alleviate some of the need to "protect" women from gender violence. As Claudia von Braunmühl explains, "sexual violence against women as an instrument of war would not be possible without women being objectified, denigrated and suppressed in civil life" (2013: 174).

Just as they had played an important role in lobbying the UN Security Council to adopt the WPS agenda, feminist women's NGOs have taken the leading role in disseminating information about these resolutions in nations around the world to improve the poor record of implementation. Various NGO networks such as the European Women's Lobby conduct independent studies regarding progress on states' implementation of the resolutions. They also publish reports for governments and nongovernmental agencies, offer gender-specific trainings for governments and nongovernmental entities, and lobby the UN General Assembly to appropriate funds for programs that implement gender mainstreaming in peace operations and that employ personnel with gender expertise in UN security agencies and in the UN peacekeeping mission fields. These NGO activities keep the WPS agenda in the minds of UN Secretariat officials and government diplomats and present "women" as legitimate political actors with rights to participate in global peace and security operations.

Summing up

Women were rarely appointed as formal government delegates to the League of Nations Assembly or its committees and commissions and rarely attained positions of leadership within the League of Nations Secretariat. Nonetheless, the few women delegates and their feminist allies in women's nongovernmental organizations made their presence and their gender-specific concerns known to elite male policy makers throughout the life of the League. They added missing dimensions to male-led intergovernmental conversations regarding human rights, social justice, and disarmament and conflict resolution. After 1945, a growing number of women delegates, UN Secretariat staff and feminist NGOs continued to interject their gender-specific concerns into global governance forums at the United Nations. These women achieved increasing success in norming women's human rights and in persuading member state governments to recognize and protect women's rights within national borders and in conflict zones. Due to feminist interventions, UN organizational policies and practices have changed and incorporated new international norms regarding women's human rights and links to global peace and security, democratic governance, and to economic and social development. Although women's participation in high-level decision-making roles within global governance bodies has never been equal to that of men's participation, feminist activism has been responsible for interjecting the language of gender quality into global policy rhetoric and for including measures that recognize and address women's gender needs through gender-mainstreaming practices in some global governance programs and operations. Progress toward achieving social, economic and political gender-equality goals has been significant and would not have occurred without feminist-inspired activist campaigns in these important twentieth- and twenty-first-century global governance forums; nonetheless, these goals are yet to be reached.

References for further study

Calgar, G., Prügl, E., and Zwingel, S. (2013), *Feminist Strategies in International Governance*, New York, NY: Routledge.

Shepherd, L. J. (2011), "Sex, Security and Superhero(in)es: From 1325 to 1820 and Beyond," *International Feminist Journal of Politics*, 13: 504–21.

Web resources

The Covenant of the League of Nations (Yale Law School Avalon Project *Documents in Law, History and Diplomacy*). http://avalon.law.yale.edu/20th_century/leagcov.asp (Accessed August 4, 2017).

Convention on the Elimination of all forms of Discrimination Against Women, United Nations Human Rights Office of the High Commissioner. http://www. ohchr.org/EN/ProfessionalInterest/Pages/CEDAW.aspx (Accessed August 4, 2017).

European Institute for Gender Equality. http://eige.europa.eu/ (Accessed August 4, 2017).

"Peace Women," website of the Women's International League for Peace and Freedom. http://www.peacewomen.org/ (Accessed August 4, 2017).

United Nations Charter (Yale Law School Avalon Project *Documents in Law, History and Diplomacy*). http://avalon.law.yale.edu/20th_century/unchart.asp (Accessed August 4, 2017).

United States Institute of Peace. "What is UN Security Council Resolution 1325 and Why is it so Critical Today?" Washington, DC n.d. http://www.usip.org/ gender_peacebuilding/about_UNSCR_1325 (Accessed August 4, 2017).

UN Women. "The Four Global Women's Conferences." http://www.un.org/ womenwatch/daw/followup/session/presskit/hist.htm (Accessed August 4, 2017).

Bibliography

Abels, G. and Mushaben, J. M. (2012), *Gendering the European Union: New Approaches to Old Democratic Deficit*, New York, NY: Palgrave MacMillan.

Abzug, B. (1995), "The Glass Half-Full: Looking at some of the Courageous Initiatives," *Earth Times*: 15–31.

Allan, V., Galey M., and Persinger, M. (1995), "World Conference of International Women's Year," in A. Winslow (ed.), *Women, Politics and the United Nations*, 29–44, Westport, CT: Greenwood Press.

Ashworth, G. and Bonnerjea, L. (1985), *The Invisible Decade: UK Women and the UN Decade for Women, 1976–1985*, London, UK: Gower Publishing Co., Ltd.

Baldez, L. (2014), *Defying Convention: U.S. Resistance to the UN Treaty on Women's Rights*, New York, NY: Cambridge University Press.

Beers, L. (2016), "Advocating for a Feminist Internationalism Between the Wars," in G. Sluga and C. James (eds.), *Women, Diplomacy and International Politics*, 202–21, New York, NY: Routledge.

Bendinger, E. (1975), *No Time for Angels: The Tragicomic History of the League of Nations*, New York, NY: Alfred A. Knopf.

Berkovitch, N. (1999), *From Motherhood to Citizenship: Women's Rights and International Organizations*, Baltimore, MD: Johns Hopkins University Press.

Birn, D. S. (1981), *The League of Nations Union, 1918–1945*, Oxford, UK: Clarendon Press.

Bussey, G. and Tims, M. (1965), *Women's International League for Peace and Freedom 1915-1965, A Record of Fifty Years' Work*, London, UK: George Allen & Unwin, Ltd.

Cohen, R. and Rai, S. M. (2000), *Global Social Movements*, London, UK: Continuum.

Cohn, C. (2008), "Mainstreaming Gender in UN Security Policy: A Path to Political Transformation?," in S. M. Rai and G. Waylen (eds.), *Global Governance: Feminist Perspectives*, 185–206, New York, NY: Palgrave MacMillan.

Connors, J. (1996), "NGOs and the Human Rights of Women at the United Nations," in P. Willetts (ed.), *"The Conscience of the World": The Infuence of Nongovernmental Organizations in the UN System*, 147–80, London, UK: Hurst & Company.

D'Amico, F. (1999), "Women Workers in the United Nations: From Margin to Mainstream?" in E. Prügl and M. K. Meyer (eds.), *Gender Politics in Global Governance*, 19–40, Lanham, MD: Rowman and Littlefield Publishers, Inc.

Danguilan, M. (1997), *Women in Brackets: A Chronicle of Vatican Control*, Manila, Philippines: The Philippine Center for Investigative Journalism.

de Haan, F. (September 2010), "Continuing Cold War Paradigms in Western Historiography of Transnantional Women's Organizations: The Case of the Women's International Democratic Federation," *Women's History Review*, 19: 547–73.

de Haan, F. (2011), "The Women's International Democratic Federation (WIDF): History, Main Agenda, and Contributions, 1945-1991," in K. Kish Sklar and T. Dublin (eds.), *Women and Social Movements International, 1840 to the Present*, New York City: Alexander Street Press.

Enloe, C. (2000), *Maneuvers: The International Politics of Militarizing Women's Lives*, Berkeley, CA: University of California Press.

European Women's Lobby (2008), *Toward Human Security: Engendering Peace*, Brussels, Belgium: European Women's Lobby.

Fraser, A. S. (1987), *The UN Decade for Women: Documents and Dialogue*, Boulder, CO: Westview Press.

Fried, S. T. (August 1995), "Women's Human Rights at the World Summit for Social Development," *AWID News*, 9.

Garner, K. (2010), *Shaping a Global Women's Agenda: Women's NGOs and Global Governance*, Manchester, UK: Manchester University Press.

Garner, K. (2013), *Gender and Foreign Policy in the Clinton Administration*, Boulder, CO: Lynne Rienner Publishers, First Forum Books.

Ghodsee, K. (2010), "Revisiting the United Nations Decade for Women: Brief Reflections on Feminism, Capitalism, and Cold War Politics in the Early Years of the International Women's Movement," *Women's Studies International Forum*, 33: 3–12.

Ghodsee, K. (2012), "Rethinking Socialist Mass Women's Organizations: The Committee of the Bulgarian Women's Movement and the United Nations Decade for Women, 1975–85," *Journal of Women's History*, 24: 49–73.

Harrington, C. (2011), "Resolution 1325 and Post-Cold War Feminist Politics," *International Feminist Journal of Politics*, 13: 557–75.

Hawkesworth, M. E. (2006), *Globalization and Feminist Activism*, Lanham, MD: Rowman & Littlefield Publishers.

Herren, M. (2015), "Gender and International Relations through the Lens of the League of Nations, 1919-1945," in G. Sluga and C. James (eds.), *Women, Diplomacy and Politics Since 1500*, Florence, KY: Taylor and Francis.

Hoskyns, C. (1999), "Gender and Transnational Democracy: The Case of the European Union," in E. Prügl and M. K. Meyer (eds.), *Gender Politics in Global Governance*, 72–87, Lanham, MD: Rowman and Littlefield Publishers, Inc.

Human Rights Watch (2015), *Our Rights Are Fundamental to Peace: Slow Implementation of UN Security Council Resolution 1325 (2000) Denies the Rights of Women and Girls in Armed Conflict*, New York, NY: Human Rights Watch.

Ilic, M. (2011), "Soviet Women, Cultural Exchange, and the Women's International Democratic Federation," in S. Autio-Sarasmo and K. Miklossy (eds.), *Reassessing Cold War Europe*, 157–74, New York, NY: Routledge.

Jain, D. (2005), *Women, Development and the UN: A Sixty year Quest for Equality and Justice*, 65–80, Bloomington, IN: Indiana University Press.

Jain, D. (2017), "Women of the South: Engaging with the UN as a Diplomatic Manoeuvre," in J. A. Cassidy (ed.), *Gender and Diplomacy*, New York, NY: Routledge.

Joachim, J. (1999), "Shaping the Human Rights Agenda: The Case of Violence against Women," in E. Prügl and M. K. Meyer (eds.), *Gender Politics in Global Governance*, 142–60, Lanham, MD: Rowman and Littlefield Publishers.

Krook, M. L. and Childs, S. (2010), *Women, Gender and Politics: A Reader*, Oxford, UK: Oxford University Press.

Laville, H. (2002), *Cold War Women: The International Activities of American Women's Organizations*, New York, NY: Palgrave.

Linder, D. H. (2001), "Equality for Women: The Contribution of Scandinavian Women to the United Nations, 1946-66," *Scandinavian Studies*, 73: 165–208.

Lynch, C. (1999), *Beyond Appeasement: Interpreting Interwar Peace Movements in World Politics*, Ithaca, NY: Cornell University Press.

Manus, R. (April 1932), "Disarmament," *The International Women's News*, 70.

McCarthy, H. (2011), *British People and the League of Nations: Democracy, Citizenship and Internationalism, c. 1918-45*, Manchester, UK: Manchester University Press.

Miller, C. (1991), "Women in International Relations? The Debate in Interwar Britain," in R. Grant and K. Newland (eds.), *Gender and International Relations*, Bloomington, IN: Indiana University Press.

Miller, C. (1994), "Geneva–the Key to Equality: Interwar Feminists and the League of Nations" *Women's History Review*, 3: 219–45.

Mlambo-Ngcuka, P. (2017), "Becoming UN Women: A Journey in Realizing Rights and Gaining Global Recognition," in J. A. Cassidy (ed.), *Gender and Diplomacy*, 170–86, New York, NY: Routledge.

Noel-Baker, P. (1979), *The First World Disarmament Conference, 1932-33, and Why it Failed*, Oxford, UK: Pergamon Press.

Northcroft, D. M. (1923), *Women at Work in the League of Nations*, London, UK: Page and Pratt, Ltd.

Northedge, F. S. (1986), *The League of Nations, Its Life and Times, 1920-1946*, London, UK: Page and Pratt, Ltd.

O'Barr, J. (1986), "Reflections on Forum '85 in Nairobi, Kenya: Voices from the International Women's Studies Community," *Signs: Journal of Women in Culture and Society*, 11: 584–86.

Offen, K. (2001), "Women's Rights or Human Rights? International Feminism Between the Wars," in K. Holmes, M. Lake and P. Grimshaw (eds.), *Women's Rights and Human Rights*, 243–53, New York, NY: Palgrave.

Olcott, J. (2017), *International Women's Year: The Greatest Consciousness-raising Event in History*, New York, NY: Oxford University Press.

Parisi, L. and True, J. (2013), "Gender mainstreaming Strategies in International Governance," in E. Prügl, S. Zwingel, and G. Calgar (eds.), *Feminist Strategies in International Governance*, 37–56, New York, NY: Routledge.

Pedersen, S. (2008), "Metaphors of the Schoolroom: Women Working the Mandates System of the League of Nations," *History Workshop Journal*, 66: 188–207.

Peterson, V. S. and Runyan, A. S. (2009), *Global Gender Issues in the New Millennium*, 3rd ed., Boulder, CO: Westview Press.

Popa, R. M. (2009), "Translating Equality between Men and Women across Cold War Divides: Women Activists from Hungary and Romania and the Creation of International Women's Year," in S. Penn and J. Massino (eds.), *Gender Politics and Everyday Life in State Socialist Eastern and Central Europe*, 59–74, New York, NY: Palgrave.

Prügl, E. (2009), "Does Gender Mainstreaming Work? Feminist Engagements with the German Agricultural State," *International Feminist Journal of Politics*, 11: 174–95.

Reanda, L. (1992), "The Commission on the Status of Women," in P. Alston (ed.), *The United Nations and Human Rights: A Critical Appraisal*, 265–303, Oxford, UK: Oxford University Press.

Rossilli, M. (2000), "The European Union's Gender Policies," in M. Rossilli (ed.), *Gender Politics in the European Union*, 1–23, New York, NY: Peter Lang.

Runyan, A. S. (1999), "Women in the NeoLiberal Frame," in E. Prügl and M. K. Meyer (eds.), *Gender Politics in Global Governance*, 210–20, Lanham, MD: Rowman and Littlefield Publishers, Inc.

Rupp, L. J. (1997), *Worlds of Women: The Making of an International Women's Movement*, Princeton, NJ: Princeton University Press.

Rushton, S. (2008), "The UN Secretary-General and Norm Entrepreneurship: Boutros Boutros-Ghali and Democracy Promotion," *Global Governance*, 14: 95–110.

Shepherd, L. J. (2015), *Gender Matters in Global Politics: A Feminist Introduction to International Relations*, 2nd ed., New York, NY: Routledge.

Sluga, G. (2013), *Internationalism in the Age of Nationalism*, Philadelphia, PA: University of Pennsylvania Press.

Snyder, C. J. (2003), "The Influence of Transnational Peace Groups on U.S. Foreign Policy Decision-Makers during the 1930s: Incorporating NGOs into the UN," *Diplomatic History*, 27: 377–404.

Snyder, M. (2004), "Walking My Own Road: How a Sabbatical Year Led to a United Nations Career," in A. Fraser and I. Tinker (eds.), *Developing Power: How Women Transformed International Development*, 38–49, New York, NY: The Feminist Press.

Steans, J. (2013), *Gender and International Relations: Theory, Practice, Policy*, 3rd ed., Cambridge, UK: Polity Press.

"The United Nations Decade for Women, 1976-1985" (1985), *Soviet Women's World*, Moscow: Novosti House Press Agency.

Tickner, J. A. (2001), *Gendering World Politics: Issues and Approaches in the Post-Cold War Era*, New York, NY: Columbia University Press.

Towns, A. E. (2010), *Women and States: Norms and Hierarchies in International Society*, Cambridge, UK: Cambridge University Press.

UN Women, (2015), *Preventing Conflict, Transforming Justice, Securing the Peace: A Global Study on the Implementation of the United Nations Security Council Resolution 1325*, New York, NY: UN Women.

Von Braunmühl, C. (2013), "A Feminist Analysis of UN Security Council Resolutions on Women, Peace and Security," in E. Prügl, S. Zwingel, and

G. Calgar (eds.), *Feminist Strategies in International Governance*, 163–80, New York, NY: Routledge.

Walters, F. P. (1952), *A History of the League of Nations*, New York, NY: Oxford University Press.

Weiss, T. G. and Gordenker, L. (1996), *NGOs, the UN and Global Governance*, Boulder, CO: Lynne Rienner Publishers.

Willetts, P. (1996), "Consultative Status for NGOs at the United Nations," in P. Willetts (ed.), *"The Conscience of the World": The Influence of Nongovernmental Organization in the UN Systems*, 31–62, London, UK: Hurst & Company.

Woodward, A. E. (2012), "From Equal Treatment to Gender Mainstreaming and Diversity Management," in G. Abels and J. M. Mushaben (eds.), *Gendering the European Union: New Approaches to Old Democratic Deficits*, 85–102, New York, NY: Palgrave.

Zinsser, J. (2002), "From Mexico to Copenhagen to Nairobi: The United Nations Decade for Women," *Journal of World History*, 13: 139–68.

CHAPTER FIVE

Women, gender, and global development

Foundational questions

How have mid-twentieth-century modernization and development theories and post-1970s neoliberal economic policies that were designed to promote global economic and social development reflected and reinforced male-over-female gender power relations associated with Western-defined hegemonic masculinity?

How have feminists, speaking from many different global locations, developed theories to reveal the positive connections between gender equality and global development, human security, and peace and stability among nations?

How successfully have feminists devised strategies and programs to undermine the male-defined status quo global power relations embedded in mid-century development and neoliberal economic theories, policies, and programs?

Key concepts

Dependency Theory recognizes the persistent and stifling socioeconomic effects and debilitating psychological legacies imposed by the European powers that colonized vast regions of the non-European world beginning in the 1500s, on the social and economic development of those former colonies today. Independence movements and decolonization processes have dismantled formal colonial governing systems over the last seventy years, following the Second World War. Nonetheless, most people living in these newly independent nations have generally struggled to regain control of their lands and natural resources that continue to be owned by First

World investors, multinational corporations, or a small native elite class. Governments in these new nations also struggled to educate and improve the health of their impoverished populations. With their disadvantaged positions in the geopolitical power structure established during the colonial era, former European colonies may have gained nominal independence and state sovereignty, but many retain a "neocolonial" or "dependent" status in terms of economic relations with international financial institutions and multinational corporations, and in terms of political relations with First World nations.

Dependency theories are based on Marxist critiques of exploitative capitalist economic relations. Dependent developing Third World nations buy higher-priced manufactured goods, borrow capital from, and sell their lower-priced raw materials to, multinational corporations and other investors based in First World nations. Through these arrangements they accumulate large national debts and deplete their natural resources. Their less-educated and often-times impoverished populations may work for multinational corporations in their home countries, or may be migrant, temporary workers employed in First World nations, laboring at reduced wages compared to some more-educated and elite workers in First World nations. Dependency theorists assert that these circumstances are responsible for slow social and economic development in Third World nations.

Dependency theorists argue that Third World nations are stuck in a cycle of perpetual dependency, a cycle that may be broken (or not) through a Marxist-inspired class revolution. Dependency theories also have gender power implications, privileging the masculine, in that revolutionary leadership is associated with "heroic," usually male leadership of autonomous individuals, who often elevate the importance of science and technology in liberating Third World states from their subordinate positions in the world economy and global power structure (Scott 1996: 5–13; Kaufman 2013: 23).

The Feminization of Poverty refers to the growing share of the world's female population living below the poverty line, that is, living on less than $1.25 per day, as the United Nations Development Program has determined the measurement. The feminization of poverty, where the percentages of women and girls living in extreme poverty were greater and grew faster than the percentages of men and boys living in extreme poverty, was first recognized as a global phenomenon in the 1980s. It was a consequence of the combined adverse effects of gender discrimination and neoliberal economic policies and the globalization of the labor market. Even as the global capitalist workforce employed more women than at any time previously in world history, women faced more barriers than men to "lifting themselves" out of poverty (Moghadam 2005: 39). Gendered divisions of labor persisted, that is, "men's work" is constructed as paid, productive, independent work that provides the primary income for the family; "women's work" is constructed as unpaid, reproductive, dependent, and supplementary to the family income. Consequently, more often than men, women worldwide were employed as part-time, temporary, or casual labor, which allowed global capitalist employers to pay women lower wages to minimize labor costs and maximize profits. Moreover, women worldwide continued to serve as the primary, and unpaid, household laborers and caregivers for children and the elderly within their families. The observed consequences of neoliberal economic policies also inspired economists to coin the phrase "the feminization of labor" to describe the devaluation and disempowerment of the global labor market that also began in 1980s and disadvantaged all but the most elite workers, male and female. Neoliberal economic policies reduced government support for labor unions and government oversight of private business practices. Without union or government support for labor interests, businesses have reduced the number of full-time salaried positions with pensions, health insurance, and other employment benefits attached to them and have kept wages low, generally degrading and feminizing labor conditions (Runyan and Peterson 2014: 181–82; Rai 2011: 19–20).

First, Second, and Third Worlds are distinctions that were first made in the 1950s to differentiate the relative levels of national wealth, market capitalist economic development, and industrialization as measured by such indexes as gross domestic product (GDP) that also signified the relative power of nations in international affairs. First World "masculinized," wealthy, and empowered countries are also referred to as "developed" or "highly developed" nations; Third World "feminized," often impoverished, and disempowered countries are also referred to as "developing" or "underdeveloped" nations. During the Cold War era, Second World countries referred to those governed by Communist Party rule and centrally planned socialist economies.

As most First World nations were the former colonial powers of Western Europe and the neocolonial United States located in the Northern Hemisphere, beginning in the 1980s they have been referred to collectively as the "global North." Developing or underdeveloped Third World nations were often former colonized regions located in the Southern Hemisphere and have been referred to collectively as the "global South" or the "economic South."

First World nations control a disproportionate share of the world's wealth and provide most development aid and program funding. Therefore, they have shaped global development strategies promoting Western-style representative democratic governments and capitalist market economies. First World donor nations may send aid directly to individual recipient countries. Or, they may funnel aid through UN development agencies and funds, the World Bank or various regional development banks, or through the Organization for Economic Cooperation and Development (OECD) and its Development Assistance Committee (DAC), or through NGOs (Connelly et al. 2000).

Globalization, as it has occurred in the twentieth and twenty-first centuries, refers to processes that have integrated the local, national, and regional economies, cultures, politics, social institutions, and so forth.

Globalization has accelerated in recent decades due to new technologies and new forms of communication, militarization of societies, forced and voluntary migrations, expansion of global capitalist markets and trade relations, expansion of global governance operations, and the adoption of new global-norming treaties and policies, expansion of global social movements, and more. Globalization is not a gender-neutral or race-neutral or economically benign process in any of these realms. Globalization processes are "gendered masculine" in that they perpetuate male-over-female gender power hierarchies and other manifestations of Western-defined hegemonic masculine power hierarchies such as those based on race, class, nationality, and sexual orientation, among others, that affect people's lives on an individual level as well as institutions and state-to-state relationships on a global level. Globalization disrupts traditional social, economic, and political relationships and cultural values at the local level. But even though these disruptions may diminish some men's power, the negative impact of economic, political, and social restructuring is greater on women because local men may react to reductions in their power by exerting their patriarchal privilege over women in the private sphere, or through public-sphere movements that resurrect religious fundamentalism or ethnic nationalism to recover their masculine autonomy and control.

Modernization Theory or developmentalist theory, postulates an evolutionary advance of human societies from a state of "traditional" social organization to one of mature and "modern" social relations. "Tradition" is associated with rural, nonindustrialized or "tribal" societies, and with familial, affectionate, or private relationships, where economic development is defined as "stagnant." As feminist scholars have noted, "tradition" is stereotypically associated with the feminine gender. "Modernity" is associated with urbanized, industrialized, and technologized societies, where autonomous, self-reliant, and entrepreneurial relationships thrive in a public masculine realm, and where expansive economic growth as the result of participation in a capitalist marketplace is the norm (Tickner 2001: 88).

Modernization theories relying on capitalist economic development trajectories are contrasted with dependency theories that rely on Marxist criticisms of colonialism and capitalism, but both theories are based on gender stereotypes that associate the traditional, private, and disempowered spheres of society with the feminine, and the modern, public, and privileged spheres with the masculine.

Neoliberal Economic Policies have focused on balancing government budgets and reducing the national debts that crippled the economies of Third World nations. As post–Second World War decolonization processes solidified dependent economic relationships between the First and Third Worlds, Third World nations accumulated large debts owed to First World lenders that reduced their ability to repay debts and purchase more goods from First World manufacturers. Consequently, excessive Third World debt slowed the growth of the global capitalist market economy and threatened First World economies. Beginning in the late 1970s, global lenders such as the World Bank and International Monetary Fund (IMF) led by First World donor nations initiated neoliberal structural adjustment policies (SAPs), or "austerity" programs that restricted access to credit and the amount of money in circulation within Third World nations. SAPs forced developing nations that received Western loans and aid to reduce foreign trade barriers, lift government restrictions on private foreign investment, privatize previously state-run services to lower government operating costs, cut social spending to stimulate the growth of the globalized business sector, and reduce government dependence on development aid and other loans. Neoliberal economic policies have been gendered in several ways. Neoliberal economics privilege rationalized economic activity, technocratic solutions, and abstract global models that disregard human development and favor capital accumulation for elite business owners and corporate shareholders. Neoliberal economics do not take into account the needs of individual states' economies. The negative consequences of these masculine-gendered neoliberal economic policies also disproportionately disadvantaged women around the world as these policies decreased public sector jobs and public funds for social services, especially those related to health care and child care, increased competition for scarce private sector jobs, reduced trade union protections that lowered wages in the public and private sector labor market, and increased structural violence and instability in developing nations (Runyan and Peterson 2014: 191–96).

Sustainable Development as a construct and development strategy grew out of criticisms of nineteenth- and twentieth-century modernization/developmentalist theories of "unlimited" growth and progress that economists, environmental scientists, activists, and public officials began to voice in the late 1960s. These criticisms gained currency as environmental and conservation movements grew in numbers and influence in the 1970s and 1980s. A seminal report published by the UN World Commission on Environment and Development in 1987, *Our Common Future*, shifted the conversation from recognition of the planet's finite resources to strategies for "sustainable development." Sustainable development, as defined in *Our Common Future*, "meets the needs of the present without compromising the ability of future generations to meet their own needs. [It acknowledges] not absolute limits but limitations imposed by the present state of technology and social organization on environmental resources and by the ability of the biosphere to absorb the effects of human activities" (quoted in Mitcham 1995: 317). The "Agenda 21" global development goals that the 1992 UN Conference on the Environment and Development produced incorporated the concept of sustainable development for future environmental, population, and development policies looking forward to the twenty-first century. Sustainable development has been at the center of UN development discourse and development targets ever since that time: recognizing limits on resources, but developing political agreements and social structures to manage a steady rate of economic growth.

Introduction

Conventional IPE [International Political Economy] has typically focused on issues such as the economic behavior of the most powerful states, hegemony, and the potential for building international institutions in an anarchic system populated by self-interested actors; within a shared state-centric framework, neorealists and neoliberals debate the possibilities and limitations of cooperation using the notion of absolute versus relative gains. Feminists more often focus on economic inequality, marginalized populations, the growing feminization of poverty and economic justice, particularly in the context of North/South relations. Whereas IR has generally taken a "top down" approach focused on the Great Powers, feminist IR often begins its analysis at the local level, with individuals embedded in social structures. While IR has been concerned with explaining the behavior and interaction of states and markets in an anarchic international environment, feminist IR, with its intellectual roots in feminist theory more generally, is seeking to understand the various ways in which unequal gender structures constrain women's, as well as some men's, life chances and to prescribe ways in which these hierarchical social relations might be eliminated.

J. ANN TICKNER (2001: 4)

We want to underscore that many of the issues we discuss . . . are universal to women all over the world; access to education, stable employment, adequate political representation, and physical and mental wellbeing are important goals that all women share, in all countries. Yet a variety of problems—colonial legacies, weak governments, endemic poverty, and some traditional cultural values—ensure that many women in the developing world have a fundamentally different experience from Western women in achieving these goals.

SARAH L. HENDERSON AND ALANA S. JEYDEL (2014: 223–24)

This chapter examines global development theories and practices that emerged in the post–Second World War decades, and introduces feminist critiques of the gendered aspects of those theories and practices that, in general, have privileged males and disadvantaged female populations. Governments and international agencies have defined "development" in generally positive ways as modifications of the environment and applications of the earth's living and nonliving resources to satisfy human needs and improve the quality of human life (Mitcham 1995: 315). Indeed, most people, whether living in "developed" or "developing" regions of the world would define "development" as a self-evident goal. However, various development strategies that equated improving the quality of human life with the achievement of high levels of mass consumption have in fact served the needs and benefited selected human populations, usually those living in First World nations, while they have constrained the lives of others, usually those living in Third World nations. Moreover, many of those mid-twentieth-century development strategies have jeopardized the health of the earth's biosphere. Dominant postwar Western modernization theories and development practices that focused on science- and technology-driven industrialization and rationalization of production processes, fueled by the exploitation of natural resources, geared toward accumulation of capital and profit, and that posited an undifferentiated and unlimited growth, have since been recognized to be "unsustainable" in supporting life as we know it on earth. These modernization theories and practices are gendered, as feminist IR scholars Anne Sisson Runyan and V. Spike Peterson have explained, in that they perpetuate "gendered inequalities and intesif[y] a polarization of (masculinized) haves and (feminized) have nots, manifested . . . in the masculinized North dumping its disproportionate waste on the feminized South. These stark economic inequalities constitute structural violence and global insecurities, including the insecurity of environmental conditions upon which all else depends" (2014: 184).

Following the Second World War, Western-sponsored and Soviet-socialist-sponsored development or "modernization" projects most often focused on large-scale, technologically complex capital construction projects that took place in the public sphere. Modernization projects, while perhaps intended to develop infrastructure and grow economies in aid-recipient nations, in fact enriched already-developed donor nations, as Marxist dependency theorists documented and described. By the 1970s, Western governments and development agencies responded to some of the criticisms that dependency theorists voiced. At that time, Western donors redirected some development funding to address unmet "basic needs" of impoverished human populations in Third World nations. At the same time, global distributions of power and privilege remained in place and were strengthened by neoliberal economic austerity policies that Western nations and global financial institutions such as the World Bank, IMF, and regional development banks adopted to regulate Third World governments' spending and reduce Third World debt. Moreover, as global populations migrated to Western developed nations, whether lured by the promise of economic opportunity or driven from their homes by wars, and as Western nations restricted social spending within their own borders, impoverished populations in First World nations increased in size, as well. Thus, borders demarcating the "developed" and "developing" worlds have blurred in the late twentieth and early twenty-first centuries.

During the 1970s and 1980s, feminists also raised criticisms regarding the gendered aspects of both modernization and dependency theories that devalued "traditional," unindustrialized societies and social relationships, and associated "tradition" with feminine, particularized, and emotional social relations while valorizing "modern," masculine, independent, rational, and self-reliant social relations. Feminists asserted that male-defined development theories and strategies generally ignored women's reproductive work and contributions to small-scale family farming and community-management work, leaving "women" out of the gender-blind development equation even though "women" were disproportionately represented among the world's poor. These feminist criticisms produced various "women in development" (WID) theories that directed Western governments' and intergovernmental agencies' attention to women's needs. Beginning in the 1970s, various WID programs transferred some Western aid to woman-focused development projects administered by women development officers, adopting what was known as "women and development" (WAD) strategies. These transformations corresponded with a new stage in the expansion of global capitalism and with a revitalized wave of global feminist activism that emerged during the second United Nations Development Decade (1971–80), and that continued during the four UN Conferences for Women (1975, 1980, 1985, 1995).

In the 1980s and 1990s, criticisms from feminist and nonfeminist sources regarding the global social, economic, and environmental consequences of neoliberal economic policies produced new "sustainable development" and "gender and development" (GAD) theories and development projects. GAD theories focused on problems of how to "empower" women in terms of their social relations with men and how to address the interlinked unequal power relations based on class, race, ethnicity, nationality, and sexuality of other disempowered populations in environmentally sustainable ways, in the public and private spheres of society. New feminist development theories, many originated by multicultural feminists working in feminist NGOs such as DAWN and located in Third World nations, addressed the implicit and explicit Western biases in WID liberal development theories that had focused on women's "equal" participation in the global market economy, rather than on developing alternatives to global market capitalism to improve the quality of life for all disempowered groups.

In recent decades, the UN Millennium Development Goals, established in 2000, as well as the Agenda 2030 Sustainable Development Goals, established in 2015, were set by UN member states. These broad-based but "top-down" development goals reveal the extent of feminist influence on UN development agency rhetoric and resource allocation to benefit disadvantaged populations. These government-determined global development agreements have defined various goals to address global needs for economic development, environmental sustainability, and social inclusion, including promotion of women's "equal access" to social and economic resources. The competing interests inherent in addressing all these development needs have not always been acknowledged, nor have they been resolved, by UN member states.

This chapter explains how feminist scholars and activists formulated new, gender-sensitive development theories, some liberal and some radical, and how these theories were operationalized by government and nongovernment women, "insiders" and "outsiders," who worked in or with development programs established by the United Nations and Western government aid bureaucracies. As this chapter will argue, feminist insider-outsider collaborations have been responsible for initiating the practice of collecting gender-disaggregated development data, and for incorporating the data and gender-conscious analyses into global donors' development projects. These interventions have helped to transform the understanding of such concepts as "development," "modernization," and "progress" as elite global policy makers defined them in the twentieth and twenty-first centuries, and have linked these new understandings to "sustainable" and "just" development policy goals that aim to reduce levels of structural violence worldwide and thus to promote peace.

Women, gender, and development in the League of Nations era

From the early decades of the twentieth century and throughout the League of Nations era, Western women-led NGOs worked to improve the lives of "underprivileged" women in their nations' "underdeveloped" colonies, even though these efforts often proceeded according to Western women's own cultural biases and Western definitions of what was necessary to achieve gender equality and economic opportunity (Chaudhuri and Strobel 1992). As Chapter 4 has explained, when the League of Nations global governance system was developed, Western-led women's organizations sought to leverage their power within the male-led system to achieve gender-equality goals. Elite, educated Western women collaborated with elite, educated women in non-Western countries and with the few elite, educated women employed in official capacities at the League of Nations to marshal support for international women's suffrage campaigns, married women's nationality rights, and to expand educational opportunities for women and girls. Feminist women's international organizations asserted "women's" rights to work and working women's rights to equal pay for equal work, as they worked in conjunction with women officials employed at the ILO (Thébaud 2014: 169–71). League-era women's organizations led campaigns against prostitution and against cross-border trafficking in women and children, and they established social-welfare programs for women who were refugees of war. These campaigns were linked to their gendered efforts to promote peace and disarmament (Rupp 1997; Garner 2010). These campaigns addressed women's practical gender needs, that is, their immediate socioeconomic needs, as well as women's longer-term strategic gender interests to gain a greater measure of equality with men in their respective societies. During the 1920s and 1930s, liberal feminist Western-led women's organizations established relationships of mutual regard to bring the "benefits" of the "modern" world, as they defined them, to women in non-Western, nonindustrialized nations. These efforts were sometimes welcomed, and non-Western, elite, educated women sometimes worked together with Western women to provide social welfare and assert the human rights of the impoverished women in their nations.

Western government members at the League of Nations also established several bureaus that provided development assistance to needy populations. Among these, the "Permanent Mandates Commission" addressed the needs of peoples living in Germany's and the Ottoman Empire's former colonies and occupied territories. The Commission designated these territories as "more developed," "less developed," or "non-developed." All were judged to need Western democratic governing tutelage provided by the commission that included two female members, Anna Bugge-Wicksell and Valentine Dannevig, as Chapter 4 has explained. League members also established a Refugee Commission, whose first high commissioner, Fridtjof Nansen, established the commission's founding humanitarian principles and various cooperative practices for repatriation and international protection of war refugees. In addition, the League's Health Organization provided technical assistance that focused on intergovernmental cooperative efforts to provide nutritious food and housing for impoverished populations, and to offer "modernizing" agricultural-sector support to increase food production through the introduction of new crops and mechanized farming methods, as well as support for transportation and infrastructure development in nonindustrialized regions of the world. These early efforts on the part of the League Secretariat's offices linked development and international socioeconomic and cultural cooperation with efforts to promote peace. In 1939, a report requested by the League secretary-general Joseph Louis Avenol titled "The Development of International Cooperation in Economic and Social Affairs," was compiled by Australian diplomat Stanley Bruce. The resulting "Bruce Report" took stock of the League's two-decades of social, economic, and humanitarian work and proposed significant future expansion of the League's development activities. The outbreak of the Second World War delayed the implementation of the holistic development vision that the Bruce Report articulated, but the United Nations Economic and Social Council (ECOSOC) incorporated many of the report's proposals during the postwar decades (Frey et al. 2014: 5–7).

Women, gender, and post–Second World War modernization, 1945–60s

Development and postwar reconstruction: Japan, Germany, and the Marshall Plan

In 1944, leaders of the anti-fascist Allied Nations, most prominently the United States, Great Britain, and Canada, laid the first plans for the postwar resumption of global trade and for postwar global security in two wartime conferences held in Bretton Woods in New Hampshire and at the Dumbarton Oaks mansion in the Georgetown neighborhood of Washington DC. The Bretton Woods Conference established the IMF, funded by contributing member states, to lend money or to arrange other credit for poorer "developing" nations, with conditions set for repayment. Lending decisions made by weighted votes assured that the states that contributed the most to the IMF (such as the United States, the largest contributor), had the most power to determine loan conditions. The Bretton Woods Conference attendees also established the International Bank for Reconstruction and Development, or the World Bank, that was also originally funded by member states. The development aid provided by the IMF and World Bank in the early Cold War era had two goals: to expand the capitalist economic order into new markets and to form strong political alliances against the Soviet Union, the West's Cold War rival (Rai 2011: 15). Initially, the World Bank lent money to Western European nations so that they could restore and expand their capitalist economies and increase global trade relationships. The United States, as the world's wealthiest economic power, also established a unilateral foreign aid program, the European Recovery Program or the Marshall Plan, to restore the capitalist economies of its Western European trade partners and thus ensure that their US-friendly democratic governments would remain in power and European citizens would resist the appeal of the Soviet Union's central-planning economic model and communist ideology. Likewise, the multilateral foreign aid provided by the Bretton Woods financial institutions and by the US-led postwar reconstruction programs established in the occupied zones of Japan and Germany, the defeated fascist powers, were designed to promote capitalist economic interdependence and anti-communist political alliances. As Third World nations gained their independence from colonial rule in the 1950s and 1960s, these developing nations also borrowed from the World Bank and IMF and received development aid from Western states to establish capitalist market economies and to win political allegiances from nonaligned nations.

Liberal feminist Western-led women's organizations, including many of the organizations that had joined the Liaison Committee of Women's

International Organizations in the 1930s (Table 4.1) continued to be active in the postwar period in their Western national politics and in international politics at the United Nations. They were joined by many liberal feminist US women's organizations such as the League of Women Voters, the Federation of Business and Professional Women, and the American Association of University Women, and generally supported Cold War–era anti-communist foreign aid and capitalist economic reconstruction projects, as they had supported their nation's anti-fascist war projects. In addition to supporting their nations' economic and security goals, these liberal feminist organizations advocated for the extension of individual rights guaranteed by liberal democratic states to women living in the former-fascist empires and in the newly independent Third World states. They promoted the principle of gender equality in all nations of the world, including their own. They believed that women's active participation in democratic governments, as well as all other public realms of society, would "earn" men's recognition of women's equal worth and support for women's equal political and human rights, as participation in the world wars had earned them voting rights and "rights to work" in previously male-only professions (Laville 2002).

The victorious Allied Powers, or the Supreme Command of Allied Powers (SCAP), that was dominated by the US military and State Department officials, led the postwar occupation and reconstruction of defeated Japan. Some historians have described the US-led Japanese occupation as "benevolent and constructive" (McWilliams, Piotrowski 2014: 48). Others, such as historian John Dower, have criticized the blatantly "neo-colonial" aspects of the occupation. As evidence, Dower has pointed to the "messianic fervor" of the Supreme Commander, US general Douglas MacArthur, and his anti-communist, evangelical Christian mission to remake Japan in the West's image, and to the US-written Japanese constitution that imposed Western cultural values on the defeated Japanese people, at least in the short term. Dower's analysis reveals the Western-defined hegemonic masculine power relations that provided the ideological foundations for the US occupation of postwar Japan (1945–52):

> There was no historical precedent for this sort of [occupation] relationship, nor anything truly comparable elsewhere in the wake of the war. Responsibility for Germany, Japan's former Axis partner, divided as it was among the United States, England, France and the Soviet Union lacked the focused intensity that came with America's unilateral control over Japan. Germany also escaped the messianic fervor of General Douglas MacArthur, the post-surrender potentate in Tokyo. For the victors, occupying defeated Germany had none of the exoticism of what took place in Japan: the total control over a pagan, "Oriental" society by white men who were (unequivocally in General MacArthur's view) engaged in a Christian mission. The occupation of Japan was

the last immodest exercise in the colonial conceit known as the "white man's burden."

DOWER 1999: 23–24

The US-written constitution that Japan adopted in 1947 included Article 9 that outlawed war as an instrument of Japan's foreign policy and prohibited the formation of a national military force capable of attacking other states. This in effect ensured that Japan would require the "protection" of the US nuclear weapons "umbrella" and a continuing US military presence on Japanese soil to maintain a base of operations in Southeast Asia. The 1947 constitution also contained Article 14, that has been referred to as the Japanese women's Equal Rights Amendment, that outlawed all forms of discrimination based on race, creed, social status, family origin, *or sex*, and Article 24, that extended women's equality into the private sphere by guaranteeing women's rights to choose their own spouse, divorce, and to inherit or own property in their own names. The United States' own national constitution did not so-explicitly guarantee equal rights for American women, but in the 1940s US government representatives, male and female, recognized the benefits of including these provisions in Japan's constitution with the hope of winning Japanese women's support for the West's democratization project by elevating women's status (Sirota Gordon 1997). Generally, the US officials believed that Japanese women had not been responsible for Japan's war policy, therefore, Japanese women were defined as potential allies for the Western occupation forces (Koikari 2008: 17–20). Western women's NGOs and American women serving in SCAP forces repeated these gender stereotypes in their interactions with male government and military leaders—that Japanese women were victimized by their nation's war makers and were not responsible for the imperialist war policy. Liberal feminist Japanese women's organizations also asserted these gender stereotypes to advocate for more opportunities for women to formally participate in the public sphere, one of their long-term goals that had been diverted during the Second World War (Garner 2010: 163–65).

In addition, there were Japanese women who adopted a Western-defined "internationalist identity" and displayed *akogare*, an expression that anthropologist Karen Kelsky has defined as a "longing, desire, or idealization" of the West and that implicated Japanese women in "eroticized Western agendas of modernity and universalism and [in] the emergence of a global cosmopolitan class that contains its own hierarchies of race, gender, and capital." During the occupation era, Japanese women who adopted this internationalist identity participated in "a discourse of women's 'deliverance' at the hands of the United States from what women insisted were the odious and intolerable oppressions of the patriarchal Japanese family system." American men in the SCAP forces began to imagine themselves as Japanese women's saviors, "not only . . . generous father figures to young Japanese children, but 'loving, supportive, democratic' husbands to Japanese women whom they had freed from a medieval patriarchal system" (Kelsky 2001: 25–26, 68). Nonetheless, Japan's patriarchal social order remained fundamentally intact during the Cold War era. SCAP occupation forces may have temporarily emasculated Japanese men to punish them for waging the imperialist war but the occupation did not seriously undercut Japanese male power. Japanese women may have gained formal guarantees of equal rights in the new constitution, but they did not participate as equals in Japan's public sphere of politics or the paid workforce, during, or in the years following, the occupation (Garner 2010: 167).

When Germany was defeated in 1945, the Big Four anti-fascist Allied Powers, the United States, Great Britain, France, and the Soviet Union, together formed an Allied Council that divided Germany into zones of occupation where each occupying power was responsible for "denazification" and "democratization," as well as for collecting war reparations. Dividing Germany was the practical solution to move postwar reconstruction projects forward, given the apparently irreconcilable views on war reparations and governing models held by the rival Western Powers and the Soviet Union.

Within its occupation zone, the Soviet Union created an anti-fascist government led by Communist Party officials that followed the socialist central-planning model, enacted land reform policies and collectivized farming, and collected war reparations by transporting East Germany's industrial infrastructure back to the Soviet Union. The Soviet Union recognized, as the Western Powers recognized, the important role that women would play in Germany's reconstruction. Given the fact that in the immediate postwar period German women outnumbered men by a ratio of three to two in the age range of twenty-five to forty years, women's full participation in the productive labor force and in politics was necessary, for practical and ideological reasons. Consequently, East German women entered the public sphere in large numbers after the war, even without much state-sponsored childcare or other social-welfare supports throughout most of the 1950s (Rueschemeyer and Schissler 1990: 72–74).

The United States established the Office of the Military Government of the US (OMGUS) to administer its occupation zone in West Germany. Although its leader, General Lucius Clay who directed the US occupation, tried to persuade Britain and France, who also administered occupation zones in West Germany, and the Soviet Union to coordinate a unified economic policy to achieve economic recovery, his efforts were rebuffed (Schwartz 1991: 30). Allied occupation efforts remained stalemated and the German economic recovery stalled until the US State Department proposed a massive and coordinated European Recovery Program known as the Marshall Plan, named after the US secretary of state who introduced the plan in June 1947, George C. Marshall. The Soviet Union refused to participate in the Marshall Plan, rejecting what it perceived to be an attempt to weaken Soviet influence in East Germany and to increase East Germany's economic dependence on the West, as a supplier of raw materials to industrialized Western Europe. The Marshall Plan proposed a significant investment of capital into Western Europe, eventually totaling $12.4 billion, in the form of loans, grants, and technical assistance, or US development "missions" that visited European countries with proposals to modernize industrial and agricultural production and to integrate local production into the global capitalist market. While Europeans did not accept US economic plans without question or adopt modernization projects without modifications, the Marshall Plan funding jumpstarted Western Europe's postwar economic recovery. Marshall Plan interventions also served as an anti-communist propaganda tool and a pro-consumption propaganda tool, which defused the appeal of socialist-leaning worker's unions and socialist political parties and led to rising expectations for an American-style standard of living among populations in European nations (Cull et al. 2003). The Organization for European Economic Cooperation (OEEC), which was founded to distribute Marshall Plan aid and to promote capitalist market development in Europe in 1948, also became active in development aid programs in Europe's former colonies as Western European states' economies stabilized and grew, beginning in the 1950s (Schmelzer 2014: 173).

The Cold War rivalry between the Soviet Union and the West intensified as the Marshall Plan went forward, and especially after the United States and the Western European powers formed the NATO, a collective security military alliance in 1949, and military aid quickly superseded the development aid flowing into Western Europe. The Soviet Union responded to the Marshall Plan with its own comprehensive plan to develop the Eastern European socialist state economies in 1949, administered by the Council of Mutual Economic Aid. When West Germany was admitted to NATO in 1955, the Soviet Union established its own Eastern European military alliance, the Warsaw Treaty Organization, known as the Warsaw Pact. Eastern European countries' membership in the Warsaw Pact was compulsory, enforced by the Soviet Army, as Hungary discovered when it tried to withdraw and assert its "neutrality" in the Cold War in 1956 (McWilliams and Piotrowski 2014:78).

As part of the Marshall Plan aid package the US government maintained an occupation force in West Germany until a formal Second World War peace treaty was signed with West Germany in 1952. General Clay's Office of the Military Government continued to supervise German government operations in the Western occupation zone and initiated programs to build Western-oriented democratic institutions. The Allies lifted a postwar ban on political parties soon after they established their authority within the Western occupation zones. The Cultural, Educational, and Information Divisions of the Allied governing councils also promoted democratic values in their realms of activity (Hiscocks 1954: 496–97). In 1948, the OMGUS established a Women's Affairs Division to persuade German women to participate in the West's denazification and democratization projects. After 1949, the American, British, and French occupation zones were consolidated into the Federal Republic of Germany and a new constitution established women's equality and banned discrimination against women. The American women who ran the Women's Affairs Division programs, Lorena Hahn and Ruth Woodsmall, provided tutoring and guidance for German women to promote their social and political engagement, which was presented as a "responsibility" of all citizens in a democratic state. Once again, American women and men assumed that German women were politically naïve and innocent of war crimes. In fact, according to historian Helen Laville, German women were war-weary, "drained and apathetic to anyone offering political solutions" (2002: 74). By 1950, the American women who ran the Women's Division also succumbed to Cold War–era propagandizing, refuting the Soviet Union's assertions that women in socialist countries were liberated and equal in rights and status to men and proclaiming that women in Western liberal democracies experienced greater political and social benefits.

Western and Soviet development models in the early Cold War era

As the United Nations defined its development activities in the late 1940s, 1950s, and 1960s, development theorists and practitioners were focused on two competing development models: the Western capitalist free-market development model and the Soviet socialist central-planning development model. Both these models conceptualized strategies to promote "development" in masculinized terms, focusing on optimal economic organization that would follow a linear and progressive path to reach a highly industrialized, technologically advanced, and "modern" state of society. Both development models focused on mechanizing agricultural production and developing large-scale transportation systems and other infrastructure to move raw materials and finished goods to markets. While fundamental differences in political ideology separated these competing development models and their rationalizing discourses, both concentrated power in the hands of the male government policy-making leaders and scientific and technological social-scientist elites. Many Third World women and other colonized populations remained at a disadvantage (Rai 2011: 16–18). These two development models, and the Cold War–era adversarial Western and Soviet governments that promoted them, competed for the allegiances of Third World nations, newly independent from colonial rule.

The United States was the geographic center of theorizing and foreign aid support for the Western model of capitalist free-market modernization. Walt W. Rostow, an economic historian from the Massachusetts Institute of Technology, articulated the most well-known version of Western modernization theory that explained economic growth in Western states in the modern era in his treatise *The Stages of Economic Growth: A Non-Communist Manifesto* (1960). The five stages of economic growth outlined by Rostow provided a "universal" model for Third World nations to follow, and for Western development aid donors to promote. Rostow envisioned a "natural" economic development progression of societies, advancing from "primitive," unindustrialized, subsistence-agricultural societies that would evolve through the incorporation of scientific and technological innovations, spurred on by capitalist free-market competition, into "modern," fully developed, high-production, and high-consumption nation-states. Rostow theorized that already-modernized states, such as the United States, would have to intervene to promote the Western development model in Third World nations. They would have to fund the industrial transformation of developing economies by investing in infrastructure projects and integrate the developing states into the global capitalist economy by purchasing their raw materials exports. The modernized states would also tutor Third World leaders in developing states in liberal democratic forms of government—and help them suppress communist party–led revolutions that advocated the rival socialist development model (Nashell 2000: 134–40).

The OEEC and its successor, the OECD established in 1961, adopted the Western modernization development model within Europe and when aiding former European colonies through its "Overseas Territories Committee." Within Europe, the "poorer" member countries of Southern Europe (Italy, Greece, Turkey, and Spain) received aid funds from the United States, administered through the OEEC, and were recipients of "the newest" United States' productivity-enhancing techniques and methods applied to agriculture and manufacturing, to integrate the European national economies and cement anti-socialist political alliances. When Marshall Plan aid from the United States ended in 1951, the former colonial powers of Belgium, France, Great Britain, the Netherlands, and Portugal funneled development aid to Third World countries, following an export-oriented development model for Third World raw materials, and an import model for Western European- and US-produced and -manufactured goods (Schmelzer 2014: 173–75). Beginning in 1960, the United States, Canada, and West Germany joined the OEEC Western European aid donors to form the Development Assistance Group (DAG), which was later renamed Development Assistance Committee (DAC) with additional Northern aid donor members added. The DAG and DAC also focused on building alliances with Third World nations, following a not-so-subtle Cold War–era political agenda articulated by the US representative George W. Ball:

Without substantial outside help there is small chance that most less-developed countries (LDCs) will achieve rapid economic growth in freedom. Only by the hope and reality of achieving an adequate level of [economic] growth will they be able to turn their energies toward constructive purposes. If they are frustrated in this—if progress proves a delusion—then their energies will be diverted to purposes which are not only self-destructive, but destructive of our whole Free Society.

QUOTED IN SCHMELZER 2014: 178

Cold War–era politics also inspired the US government's "covert" use of development aid to promote its foreign-policy objectives. During the 1950s and 1960s, the Central Intelligence Agency (CIA) funneled development aid through purportedly "independent" NGOs, such as the Committee of Correspondence. The Committee of Correspondence was founded by elite US women who were ideologically opposed to communism and fervently supported the US foreign policy of "containment" of communist party–led states. The women, Cold War liberals who joined the Committee of Correspondence, were well-connected to women's NGOs in the First and Third Worlds, and used these connections to spread their own gendered form of anti-communist propaganda and democracy-promotion campaigns. Through "anonymous donations" that were in fact donations from the CIA, the Committee of Correspondence funded international women's conferences and cultivated anti-communist women's networks in Third World regions where the US government considered communist expansion to be national security threats. The Committee of Correspondence worked with the United States Information Agency (USIA), created in 1953 to oversee various cultural programs and information outlets (such as the Voice of America, US libraries abroad, the US Information Service) to promote the "American way of life" in developing countries. They also worked with the US Agency for International Development (USAID) when it was created in 1961. In the 1960s, the USIA's and USAID's Women's Affairs offices encouraged the Committee of Correspondence to develop contacts with women leaders in South Vietnam and other Southeast Asian countries where the US military was engaged in anti-communist conflicts, to establish the women's political allegiance to Western democracies. The USAID also urged the Committee to develop NGO networks to promote anti-communist/pro-Western women's programming in Latin America, and to host democratic leadership training seminars for Latin American women in New York and Washington DC. African women leaders in newly independent states also received leadership training and other educational programming devised by the Committee through its "field worker," Sarale Owens, who was sent to work with African women's organizations in Nigeria, Uganda, Tanganyika, Northern Rhodesia, Southern Rhodesia, and Kenya from 1961 to 1963. When the Committee's CIA sponsorship was exposed in 1967, the "scandal" led to the Committee's dissolution a year later (Laville 2002: 171–96; Women Organizing Transnationally: The Committee of Correspondence, 1952–69).

Countering the United States' efforts to use development aid as propaganda, the Soviet Union's political leaders and social scientists launched their own "economic offensive" to appeal to newly independent Third World nations in the 1950s and 1960s (Schmelzer 2014: 177). The Soviet Republic promoted the "Stalinist" socialist development model that called for state-controlled and centralized planning focused on heavy industrial production that was funded by profits from a collectivized agricultural sector. According to the socialist development model, production targets emanated from central planners, who also distributed resources and kept workers' wages and consumption artificially low. State planning and rationalization of the agricultural and industrial production processes was supposed to produce rapid economic growth and thus accelerate state modernization. According to Soviet development theorists, the socialist model would give developing states a greater measure of economic self-sufficiency, and would free them from economic dependency on their former colonial rulers and from entanglements in an exploitative world capitalist marketplace. For Third World leaders, such as Jawaharlal Nehru, India's first prime minister and a leader in the NAM, rapid industrialization would help to reduce national poverty, which the Soviet development model promised, and which was Nehru's ultimate aim. Nehru "maintained a wary distance from Soviet political positions" according to historian David Engerman. "Nehru's promotion of neutralism was about economic and political self-determination, not a desire to create people's republics across the third world" (Engerman 2004: 34–35). Nonetheless, the Soviet Republic sent aid to India through the 1960s, even as India also received an increasing amount of Cold War–inspired aid from Western Europe and the United States.

Women and gender and The United Nations "technical assistance" aid programs

As Chapter 4 has explained, when the United Nations Organization was founded in 1945, NGOs played a critical role in assuring that the UN global governance offices would engage in programs to promote social development and to expand and protect human rights, as well as to regulate the global economy and maintain global security. Article 55 of the UN Charter spelled out the "conditions of stability and well-being" necessary for achieving peace and protecting human rights, and thus defined a role for the United Nations in promoting international cooperation to address global migration and population problems, social and economic development, and global health, education, and cultural affairs. NGOs lobbied government delegates and collaborated with sympathetic UN Secretariat officials to ensure that the ECOSOC, with an expansive mandate of operations as had been proposed in the 1939 Bruce Report, would be established as a "principle organ" within the UN global governance system. From its humbler beginnings in 1946, the ECOSOC's development activities have greatly expanded, and it currently acts as a coordinator and mediator, overseeing a wide range of functional and regional commissions associated with development and human well-being, such as the Social Development Council, the Population and Development Commission, the CSW, to name a few examples. It oversees various development-focused funds and programs such as the UN Development Program (UNDP), the UN Environment Program (UNEP), and the UN Population Fund (UNFPA), among others. It also oversees an array of specialized agencies such as the World Bank Group of regional development banks, the Food and Agriculture Organization (FAO), the World Health Organization (WHO), the UN Industrial Development Organization (UNIDO), and the UN Educational, Scientific, and Cultural Organization (UNESCO), to name just a few of the key development agencies. In addition to commissioning data collection and status reports from these offices and agencies, ECOSOC reports out to the UN General Assembly on the offices' and agencies' activities. ECOSOC staff and officials act as intermediaries between the UN General Assembly and the NGOs that have great interests in all of ECOSOC's humanitarian and social- and economic development offices and agency functions. Many NGOs, including many women's international NGOs headquartered in the First and Third Worlds, add their knowledge expertise and advice to UN development policy debates and currently run many of the programs that implement the UN development policies and are funded by UN member states.

In the early Cold War era, development initiatives at the United Nations proceeded under the programming terminology of "technical assistance" (TA). UN TA, nominally nonpolitical, provided social science–based, "rational," social and economic planning on an international scale through the UN Department of Social Welfare and through ECOSOC specialized agencies such as FAO and UNESCO. UN TA programs aimed at raising standards of living, standards of health, education levels, and so forth in developing regions of the Third World. They were also politically oriented to the Western development agenda and were founded on an interventionist, modernizing, and liberal democracy "nation-building" philosophy. Between 1950 and 1956, the Technical Assistance Committee of ECOSOC and the Technical Assistance Board of various UN agencies spent nearly $150 million, dispatched more than five thousand technical development "experts" to developing countries and awarded eight thousand training fellowships to Third World recipients (Sluga 2013: 112). Individuals, such as the Swedish feminist and political activist Alva Myrdal, led the UN TA programs. The liberal Western development agenda inspired Myrdal, but she also incorporated a social-justice and gender-justice mission into her work at the United Nations (Sluga 2014: 46–49).

Alva Myrdal worked at the United Nations for seven years, and during that time she was appointed "top-ranking" director of Social Sciences at UNESCO from 1950 to 1955, "the only woman to scale the heights of the UN and UNESCO during these years" (Sluga 2013: 111, 114). Like many Western development specialists at the time, Myrdal advocated for research-

FIGURE 5.1 **UN 144312** *Alva Myrdal, principal director of UN Department of Social Affairs and Dr. Jose Correa, of Ecuador, chairman of the Social Commission. April 4, 1950. Credit: UN Photo*

based social planning and for population control, or "family planning" initiatives, which she believed gave women in developing countries greater freedom of choice to work outside the home. She had coauthored a 1934 study with her husband, Gunnar Myrdal, *Crisis in the Population Question,* and had been a long-standing member of the International Business and Professional Women's NGO. Those experiences shaped her elite Western perspective on women's reproductive and economic needs. The issue of "family planning," or the use of contraceptives to limit the number or timing of children a woman gave birth to, was a contentious one in the 1950s and 1960s. It has since been criticized by Third World feminists and national leaders as Western-centric, that is, family planning has been interpreted as a way to limit population growth in Third World nations without regard for cultural traditions or religious beliefs (Hussein 2004: 6; Jaquette 2004: 192). Nonetheless, Myrdal was one of the first women who brought questions about family and women's and children's welfare into UN development discussions. Her reports and office correspondence from the years she worked for UNESCO demonstrated she understood that economic parity for women and women's ability to make decisions about their own bodies and lives was linked to women's human rights and to peaceful social relations. At the time Myrdal worked at the United Nations in the 1950s, and when she joined Sweden's diplomatic corps in the 1960s, women's concerns were generally not represented in elite development theory or practice discussions (Sluga 2014: 64–66; Linder 2001: 180–82).

The UN development decades: The 1960s and 1970s

The post–Second World War decolonization process and the emergence of modernization theory and Western and socialist development models in the 1950s inspired the UN General Assembly to name the 1960s as the "Development Decade" (1961–70). Later, when the United Nations continued its focus on development onto the 1970s, the 1960s was known as the "First Development Decade." In 1961, US president John F. Kennedy proposed the Development Decade to the UN General Assembly in New York City with the declaration: "To those peoples in the huts and villages of half the globe struggling to break the bonds of mass misery, we pledge our best efforts to help them help themselves." Inspired by Walt Rostow's modernization model for linear, progressive economic growth, the already-developed UN member nations took on the challenge and set a goal to reach 5 percent growth per annum in underdeveloped countries by 1970. The UN General Assembly urged developed First World nations to contribute more foreign aid and investment in developing nations, to reach 1 percent of the combined national incomes of the developed nations of the world. With seventeen countries in Africa gaining their political independence from colonial rule in 1960 alone, UN members set optimistic and ambitious goals to accelerate the pace of development and alleviate the conditions of poverty that many of those new nations faced. The United Nations had already established a special voluntary fund to support technical assistance and development activities in the Third World in 1957 that became the UNDP. During the Development Decade other UN agencies, including UNICEF, UNESCO, FAO, and WHO also provided "humanitarian aid" to needy populations and set ambitious development goals. For example, the UNESCO set goals to expand literacy education in newly independent developing nations. The WHO set goals to eradicate small pox worldwide within the Decade. Following the Western development model's prescriptions for economic growth, UN agencies emphasized scientific and technological solutions to the problems of underdevelopment (UNICEF; The UN and Development Policies; Engerman 2004: 39–40).

Although many of the development goals set in the 1960s were not met at that time, newly independent and nonaligned Third World nations also began to organize to define and assert their own development needs, needs that Western-led development theories and practices had ignored or dismissed. As Chapter 4 has explained, nations in the NAM formed the G-77 developing nations to gain political leverage in the UN General Assembly in 1964. The G-77 nations sought social justice and a more equitable global economic order that would allow them to be truly independent, challenging global "economic arrangements that privileged the already privileged." These goals, for social justice and equality, as Indian feminist economist Devaki Jain has pointed out, "are similar to those that women around the world have made at various times" (Jain 2017: 67–68). The G-77 kept the United Nations focused on development throughout a Second Development Decade (1971–80) through their campaign for a NIEO. The NIEO linked issues such as debt relief, fairer global commodity pricing, regulating multinational corporations' business practices, improving technology transfer agreements and improving terms of trade for developing nations (Karns, Mingst, Stiles 2015: 429).

Women's role in development had not been a conscious focus of UN development efforts through most of the First Development Decade, but as Third World nations pushed for a greater role in development program agenda setting at the United Nations, the Western development model of top-down, science and technology-driven, infrastructure-building development was revised, and women's needs and contributions began to command some attention from development experts and program administrators. The Second Development Decade shifted emphasis away from infrastructure-building and capital-intensive development projects and toward "meeting basic needs." "Basic needs" were defined as food, shelter, clothing and a minimum income set for each family to purchase those goods, earned through some form of employment or participation in food production. The UN agencies in conjunction with national governments were to provide basic literacy education, safe drinking water, sanitary conditions, access to medical care to achieve a basic standard of health, and opportunities for people to participate in governing decisions that affected their lives. Economic growth was still the overall development goal, but redistributing the benefits of economic growth so that all members of society received some benefits in order to meet their basic needs also became part of the development goals set by UN planners and by the World Bank under its new president, Robert McNamara, during the 1970s (Rai 2011: 30). Women's NGOs pushed UN development agencies and governments to address women's gender-specific basic needs, based on their reproductive and productive roles in society, in their programs as well.

Women, gender, and development, 1970s–80s

Beginning in the 1960s and accelerating in the 1970s and 1980s, feminist NGO activism that focused on development issues at the United Nations took place within the context of a general expansion of NGOs' influence within the UN global governance system. The NGOs built on their "consultative status" with various UN ECOSOC development agencies and commissions to assist the UN Secretariat and government delegates in defining the development "problems" that their offices would address, and then provided data based on research and experience operating in Third World nations to propose development programs or other educational or health initiatives to meet women's needs. These NGO interventions took place at public agency meetings or commission sessions, at UN world conferences that were organized to focus on development-related topics, and through relationships built with UN Secretariat officials or with government delegates, such as Aziza Hussein who served as Egypt's delegate to the UN CSW during the Development Decades, Helvi Sipilä who served as Finland's delegate to the UN CSW, and Inga Thorsson, a Swedish MP who persuaded her government to provide some funding dedicated to women in its foreign aid programs in the mid-1960s. These women, along with other national delegates to the United Nations from developing nations focused on "women and development" issues and brought them to the attention of male government representatives and UN development officials (Garner 2010: 199–205; Jain 2017: 73–75).

For example, these insider–outsider coalitions of feminist activists introduced consideration of women's reproductive roles into UN conversations about population growth and economic development strategies for Third World nations. By the 1960s and 1970s improvements in food production and nutrition in Third World nations had led to rapid population growth. Although there was near-universal acknowledgment among First and Third World governments that population growth and economic development were linked, distinct differences existed in the ways that governments and financial institutions in First World nations identified the cause and effects of those relationships, compared to Third World developing nations. In general, First World aid donor nations and lenders argued that slowing down population growth in Third World nations would reduce "drains" on national resources and would allow for faster economic growth. Consequently, they advocated for state-sponsored population controls, such as state-distributed contraceptives, to slow population growth. Third World aid-recipient developing nations generally pushed for further economic development before introducing population controls. They argued that economic development would lead to reduced fertility rates as soon as families realize that they could limit their numbers of working children and still meet their basic needs (Fraser and Tinker 2004: 21).

Taking up a conversation that had stalled when Alva Myrdal raised the subject in the 1950s, the UN CSW introduced discussions of "family planning," which included promotion of contraceptives from a woman's perspective, into discussions of Third World development by the late 1960s. These discussions began to forge conceptual links between women's status and economic development in Third World nations during the First Development Decade. In the 1960s, family planning discussions were still considered radical and the links between raising women's status and improving development outcomes were asserted but not yet proved. Nonetheless, women delegates to the UN CSW and feminist NGOs persisted in making connections between lowering fertility rates, raising women's status, and supporting Third World development that eventually migrated into UN member states' deliberations at the 1974 World Population Conference (Hussein 2004: 6, 12). Helvi Sipilä, named as chair of the UN General Assembly's Third Committee on Social Affairs in 1971, also challenged UN members to include women in their delegations to the World Population Conference and to consider women's perspectives and proposals when drafting conference documents. According to her contemporaries at the United Nations in the 1970s, Sipilä played a "pivotal" role in energizing the "women and development" conversation (Jain 2005: 60–61).

Ester Boserup and WID strategies

Ester Boserup, a Danish economist, was another key figure who documented the important roles women played in supporting their nation's economic development. Boserup's research enabled feminist advocates for gender equality to make their case with social science research-based evidence that the United Nations' and First World's development experts could not ignore. Prior to the publication of Ester Boserup's seminal study *Woman's Role in Economic Development* (1970), male development experts rarely considered women's contributions to their nation's economic development to be a significant factor in the achievement of development goals. Western development theorists and program administrators generally defined women as "homemakers" and men as the "breadwinners" who worked outside the home, earned the family's income, and provided the family's sustenance. When they did consider women's needs, development policy makers focused on women as mothers, and sometimes incorporated development provisions that addressed women's maternal health or children's health needs. Theorists and development planners did not collect data on women's work within Third World societies to learn about the economic activities that women were involved in, nor did they try to determine the impact of their modernization and development policies and programs on women's lives. Some Western modernization theorists, such as Walt Rostow, considered women to be a drag on economic development as they represented the traditional values and practices that kept primitive societies from engaging in the progressive development/modernization trajectory that they believed should be universally adopted (Henderson and Jeydel 2014: 236). Ester Boserup challenged these male assumptions when she documented women's necessary contributions to national productivity, redefined women as human and economic development resources (not only as "mothers"), and mapped women's inequality and their lack of access to national and international development funds in her comprehensive global survey.

Boserup's research demonstrated that women's contributions to their nation's agricultural production had not only been underestimated, they had sometimes been diminished by Western modernization strategies that were based on a sexual division of labor that assumed women's work was only performed "in the home." Rather than encouraging women to work in the productive sphere and contribute to their nations' economic development, these assumptions discouraged women's contributions, and thus retarded economic growth. Western development strategies to modernize the agricultural sector had focused on aid and investments that supported the production of cash export crops and, again, pushed women out of the small-farm food production they had traditionally performed and that had been valued in their communities. Boserup criticized the Western development model with its colonialist and masculinist assumptions that contributed to the deterioration of women's status in the former African colonies, and by extension, in other formerly colonized regions of the world. Her research identified male bias as the "problem" in Western modernization and development theories and practices. Her research also prompted liberal feminists to propose "solutions" as they sought to raise women's status *and* to promote economic development within developing societies, thus "powerfully combin[ing] an argument for equality with one for efficiency" (Rai 2011: 29). These liberal feminist solutions became known as the "Women in Development" or WID approach, that is, the insistence that women's activities must be considered when designing development projects so that women could contribute their productive labor and be fully integrated into the economic development process (Henderson and Jeydel 2014; Sisson and Runyan 2014: 185–86).

Boserup's work inspired much more scholarship and activism on the part of liberal feminist scholars and women's rights advocates throughout the 1970s and 1980s as they fought for women's "equality of opportunity" with men. It was among the inspirations for the UN-sponsored IWY Conference in 1975 and subsequent Decade for Women Conferences in 1980 and 1985, that focused UN member states' and UN agencies' attention on three policy and programming themes: (1) the achievement of women's equality, (2) recognition of women's necessary contributions to peace building, and (3) the integration of women into social and economic development initiatives. Both the UNIFEM and the INSTRAW were founded in the late 1970s because WID scholars and activists who organized at the IWY Conference and NGO Tribune in Mexico City exerted pressure on government delegates. Boserup's study was also the inspiration for the establishment of WID offices within Western government international aid agencies, such as the WID office at the USAID, founded in 1974, for WID offices that formed in Canada, the Netherlands, and in the Nordic countries, for women's studies programs established at universities in the global North and South, and for the founding of many WID-focused feminist NGOs. These initiatives led to the hiring of WID "experts" and feminist staff to lead UN and government WID offices. The WID experts created new knowledge through research and teaching at universities, devised new development programs that directed resources to

Table 5.1 "The Responsibility of Europeans" by Ester Boserup

European settlers, colonial administrators and technical advisers are largely
responsible for the deterioration in the status of women in the agricultural sectors
of developing countries. It was they who neglected the female agricultural labor
force when they helped to introduce modern commercial agriculture to the
overseas world and promoted the productivity of male labor.

It has already been mentioned that the Europeans showed little sympathy for
the female farming systems which they found in many of their colonies and in
those independent countries where they settled. Their European acceptance
that cultivation is naturally a job for men persuaded them to believe that men
could become far better farmers than women, if only they would abandon
their customary "laziness." They wanted proof of their belief, and they found
it. Baumann noted that cultivation with the hoe was very superficial when
undertaken by women, and that the intensity of hoe culture increased in
proportion to the men's share in it. Also Daryll Forde noted that a higher standard
of yam cultivation was achieved where men worked with women and supervised
them.

How to explain the higher intensity of cultivation and better yields where men help
the women is an open question. One possible explanation could be found in the
superior physical strength of the men; but it may just as well be contended that
the higher productivity simply reflects the fact, . . . that men take part in cultivation
where population is dense and where, therefore, relatively intensive methods
are needed, while women work alone where fertile land is abundant and there
is no need to apply labor-intensive methods. In any case, virtually all Europeans
shared the opinion that men are superior to women in the art of farming; and it
then seemed to follow that for the development of agriculture male farming ought
to be promoted to replace female farming. Many Europeans did all they could to
achieve this.

In Uganda women began the cultivation of cotton, yet in 1923 the European director
of agriculture in the territory had stated that "cotton growing could not be left to
the women and old people," and one decade later most of the men were growing
cotton and coffee, and importing hired labor from other tribes to do most of the
work.

In those parts of Uganda where cultivation continued to be done mainly by women,
the Europeans neglected to instruct the female cultivators when they introduced
new agricultural methods, teaching only the men in an agricultural setting of
traditional female farming, with particularly unfortunate results in regions with
large male emigration, as observed by A. W. Southall: "Now that new agricultural
rules are being introduced for contouring, strip cropping, weed bunding, etc.,
the wife with husband away will be at a worse disadvantage or rather it is in her
fields that such rules will not be observed, for all these new tasks fall mainly
within the men's province, and only men are subjected to the propaganda in
their favour."

(Continued)

Table 5.1 Continued

This warning against teaching modern farming techniques to men but not to women dates back to 1952. Many more recent warnings against the neglect of women cultivators by the extension services could be quoted. One of the studies from the Central African Republic, . . . has this to say: "Although women play such an important role in agricultural production, the extension services never approach her, but always her husband or brother. The education of the women, even as regards labour productivity, must be done immediately."

In spite of these warnings, nearly all technical advisers further the policy of promoting male work as initiated by the colonial administrators. And this is true not only of European and American experts. In Senegal, West Africa, Chinese instructors (from Taiwan) failed in their efforts to introduce better techniques in paddy production because they taught only the men, who took no notice since their wives were the cultivators and the wives being untaught, continued, of course, in the old way, subdividing the carefully improved fields into small traditional plots.

As a result of the attitudes of the extension services, the gap between labor productivity of men and women continues to widen. Men are taught to apply modern methods in the cultivation of a given crop, while women continue to use the traditional methods in the cultivation of the same crop, thus getting much less out of their efforts than the men. The inevitable result is that women are discouraged from participating in agriculture, and are glad to abandon cultivation whenever the increase in their husband's income makes it possible.

And this is not all. The tendency towards a widening gap in labor productivity and income of the two sexes is exacerbated by the fact that it is the cash crops that the men are taught to cultivate by modern methods. These crops are gradually being improved by means of systematic research and other government investment, while the cultivation of the women's food crops is favoured by no government support or research activities, at least not until recently. Moreover, men can use part of their earnings from cash crops to invest in the improvement of their production, while women who produce food crops for family use have no cash income for improving their farming techniques. Farming improvements are thus concentrated in the male sector, while the female sector continued with traditional low-productivity methods.

Such a development has the unavoidable effect of enhancing the prestige of men and of lowering the status of women. It is the men who do the modern things. They handle industrial inputs while women perform the degrading manual jobs; men often have the task of spreading fertilizer in the fields, while women spread manure; men ride the bicycle and drive the lorry, while women carry headloads, as did their grandmothers. In short, men represent modern farming in the village, women represent the old drudgery.

Source: Boserup, E., Tan, S. F., and Toulmin, C. (2013), *Woman's Role in Economic Development*, London, UK: Routledge, 41–44.

meet the needs of women in the developing world and challenged gender stereotypes and masculine-gendered development theories. These experts also generated support for gender-equality norms more broadly within the UN global governance system and in many national government bureaucracies (Jain 2017: 73–75; Tickner 2001: 89).

From WID to gender and development

The WID approach was the starting point for feminist engagement in development theorizing and practice. It gained some support from male-run government- and UN-development agencies because it did not challenge the concept of "modernization" as a laudable goal, or the progressive trajectory of modernization inevitably leading to social improvement and economic expansion. It also ignored other "significant problems" such as: "the devaluation of feminized labor, the structural privilege of men and masculinity, or the increasing pressure on women to work a triple shift (in familial, informal and formal activities) to ensure family survival during economic crises," and thus did not undermine male-over-female gender power relations (Peterson and Runyan 2014: 186). The WID approach sought to increase economic opportunities and educational opportunities for women so that they could better compete with men in the paid workforce. It promoted women's participation in the formal economy to achieve Third World development more effectively and efficiently, based on the assumption that the economic and social benefits of development would trickle down to all members of society, male and female. Yet the incorporation of women into the paid workforce in the First and Third Worlds, which did occur, did not result in women's social or economic equality. Nor did the benefits of development trickle down to society's poorest members. Women entered the paid workforce, but not at the same levels as men because women continued to perform more care work and other unpaid work in support of the household economy which was not counted as part of national income. Moreover, women's wages were consistently lower than men's in nearly all labor markets, and women owned fewer resources, such as farm land, than men owned, and thus constituted a greater share of the world's population living in poverty than men. These circumstances, feminist critics have asserted, resulted in the "feminization of poverty" over the decades of the late twentieth century (Chant 2011: 174).

By the 1980s, some feminists were criticizing the WID approach, arguing that integration of women into existing modernization and development strategies merely perpetuated women's subordination. They proposed "women only" development projects that funded women in ways that protected them from patriarchal male domination. These WAD advocates lobbied for development projects that would draw on "women's knowledge" of agricultural production, for example, would value women's productive *and* reproductive work, and would proceed according to women-defined development goals. Rather than marginalizing women's gendered needs or the work that women performed, WAD projects placed women at the center of planning and activities. Nonetheless, WAD projects sometimes had the opposite results than those the project advocates sought: WAD projects perpetuated the marginalization of women's development projects *because* they operated separately from the "mainstream" development programs. In many cases, WAD projects did not receive adequate funding and remained small in scope and impact (Connelly et al. 2000: 60–61).

Other feminist critics of the WID approach focused on "gender power relations" as a means of explaining women's continuing low status in societies around the world. By the 1980s, feminist theories had begun to analyze the "social construction of gender" and the unequal power relationship between male and female genders. Feminists focused on the understanding that male-over-female or "patriarchal" gender power relationships were not fixed and immutable, but were fluid and were interlinked with historical and cultural contexts, race and class relations, and national positions within the international political order. Because of their feminist analyses, GAD proposals began to gain saliency in UN development agencies. These proposals were one aspect of the "gender mainstreaming" strategy discussed in Chapter 4 that UN agencies and EU regional governance agencies were applying more generally to their policy and program development by the mid-1990s. The GAD analyses focused on raising awareness of the consequences of patriarchal gender power relationships within the home as well as in the public spheres of society. These analyses also took note of women's "agency" in certain circumstances, when women acted rather than always reacting to shape development processes, and shaped those processes in ways that served women's interests even as they continued to occupy a subordinated status vis-à-vis men in their societies. Nonetheless, GAD analyses advocated for "gender equality" through a women's "empowerment" approach as the goal of feminist social development and political activism. In this context, "empowerment" did not mean women using power-over-men, but redefining gender power relationships to achieve "power with" men, and using power to achieve societal transformations. GAD analyses distinguished between women's empowerment projects that would meet women's immediate, practical needs for adequate food, shelter, education, health care, and so forth, and those development projects that would address women's long-term, strategic interests to gain gender equality and a greater measure of social justice for all, through analyzing and challenging the power structures defined by gender, race, class, sexuality, and so on, that led to their subordination. In other words, GAD analyses recognized that "women's" status in society was determined by the material conditions of their lives or their specific socioeconomic class positions, and that those material conditions were often determined by the specific patriarchal gender power structures that existed within their particular societies (Connelly et al. 2000: 62–63).

GAD analyses also emerged as women researchers from the Third World questioned the relevance of First World feminists' research in identifying Third World–specific problems. Along with the questioning of Western modernization models and liberal feminist WID models that called for "adding women" to existing economic structures, nonwhite minority scholars living in Western nations and feminists living in Third World nations scrutinized and criticized the notion of a "global sisterhood" that Western feminist scholarship and activism in the 1970s had espoused (Wilson 2011: 99–101). To compare their circumstances, women in African, Latin American, and Asian nations formed regional feminist scholarship and activist networks such as the Association for African Women for Research and Development (AAWORD), Comité Latinoamericano de Defensa de los Derechos de la Mujer (CLADEM), and DAWN. Feminists in these organizations produced research, analyses, and development proposals that better met their self-identified and region- or society-specific development needs.

The emergence of "sustainable development" and "ecofeminist" development

Other development "experts," some feminist and some not, also began to question the logic and viability of Western development models in the 1970s. Until then, economic growth had been the raison d'etre of global development policies and programs with the goal being a high level of technologized mass consumption for all human populations. Perceived "crises" in rapid population growth, environmental "disasters," a global economic recession and a Third World "debt crisis," however, began to transform global development theories, if not practices. Economist and industrialist Aurelio Peccei published his critical development analyses *The Limits of Growth* (1970) and *Mankind at the Turning Point* (1974) and formed an association of like-minded critics, the "Club of Rome." These economists were among the first to criticize the notion of unlimited resources and "undifferentiated" growth (Mitcham 1995: 314). A 1972 UN Conference on the Human Environment held in Stockholm issued a declaration that reflected a continuing androcentric perspective regarding the use of natural resources, but that also recognized the "harm" being done to the planet by current development practices. The conference and its Declaration enumerated twenty-five "principles" for more environmentally responsible development strategies that recognized the needs of developing nations and proposed fairer use of environmental resources, but the conference issued no "binding" treaty pledges (UNEP 2002: 3). Instead, environmental advocates hoped to build support for states' "cooperation" in setting global environmental policy and longer-term conservation strategies.

Following the Stockholm Conference, the United Nations formed a new agency, the UNEP, and "major environmental laws" were passed in numerous countries, many European members of the OECD included. Other nations, 110 in number by 1982, formed environmental protection ministries (UNEP 2002: 4–5). Further rethinking of development goals and strategies at the 1974 UNEP/UN Commission on Trade and Development (UNCTAD) joint summit held in Cocoyoc, Mexico foreshadowed the concept of sustainable development that emerged in the 1980s. The Cocoyoc Declaration articulated new attitudes among development "experts" that began to link responsible—and more equitable—use of the earth's resources to "human rights." The Declaration ended with the following words:

> The road forward does not lie through the despair of doomwatching or through the easy optimism of successive technological fixes. It lies through a careful and dispassionate assessment of the "outer limits," through cooperative search for ways to achieve the "inner limits" of fundamental human rights, through the building of social structures to express those rights, and through all the patient work of devising techniques and styles of development which enhance and preserve our planetary inheritance.

> UNEP 2002: 7

In 1983, yet another UN commission was formed, the World Commission on Environment and Development (WCED).

By the mid-1980s, a growing number of economists, population experts, and development theorists from the First and Third Worlds were voicing environmental cautions. Scholars and activists began proposing development alternatives, many that fell under the umbrella of a new concept christened "sustainable development," that was popularized in the final report of the UN WCED. The 1987 WCED report, "Our Common Future," also named the "Brundtland Report" after the commission's director Norwegian prime minister Gro Harlem Brundtland, responded to a growing environmental movement that criticized development practices that had destroyed natural habitats and decimated natural resources (UN Document A/42/427). The Brundtland Report called for "sustainable development" that "meets the needs of the present without compromising the ability of future generations to meet their own needs" (A/42/427 1987: 43). In other words, natural resources would be consumed to satisfy basic human needs, by integrating conservation goals with development goals, by maintaining the ecological integrity of the natural environments, *and* by incorporating considerations of equity, social justice, national self-determination, and respect for cultural diversity into development schemes. Although "sustainable development" recognized that some of the earth's natural resources were "finite" and not "renewable," according to sustainable development advocates, the goals of global development projects and strategies should be to distribute available resources more equitably and to spread the benefits of development more widely to improve the quality of life for all. At the time, new grassroots organizations and researchers were studying environmental changes, including global warming, ozone depletion, deforestation, and desertification of agricultural lands. Rhetoric was changing in UN agencies and in the academic and scientific communities, but these changes were not yet transforming development practices. Implementation of "sustainable development" practices evolved slowly, in the 1990s (UNEP 2002: 10–11).

By the mid-1980s, feminist theorists and activists were proposing a "feminist version" of sustainable development, which also included broader goals for societal transformation of male-over-female gender power relations. "Ecofeminist" was a term first used by French feminist Françoise d'Eaubonne in 1974 to alert Western feminists to the global economic practices that led to environmental destruction and that impacted women globally, but especially rural women and those living in the Third World (Johnson 1999: 222). Disastrous environmental "accidents" of the 1970s and 1980s (e.g., Three Mile Island, Pennsylvania; Bhopal, India; Chernobyl, the Soviet Union) as well as "natural" disasters including famines, typhoons, and monsoons of increasing severity, raised Western women's consciousness to threats to human health, and especially to women's reproductive systems. Grassroots women's movements also emerged in various regions of the Third World where women saw firsthand the destruction of their natural

FIGURE 5.2 UN 149071 *Gro Harlem Brundtland, prime minister of Norway, addressing the General Assembly on Environment and Development. October 19, 1987. Credit: UN Photo*

environments that also destroyed their communities. The South Asian Indian women's Chipko "tree-hugging" movement revived traditional and sustainable uses of forest plants for fuel, fertilizer, medicine, and so on, and the Kenyan Women's Greenbelt Movement rehabilitated deforested areas and restored local water sources for local uses. Both these ecofeminist movements, and others originating in First and Third World regions, challenged development policies that destroyed the planet in the name of "economic growth" (Merchant 1995: 20–21).

"Ecofeminists" reacting to global environmental degradation were rethinking the relationship between humans and nature, where "nature," associated with the feminine, was always in a subordinate position of service to "humanity/mankind," associated with the needs of the masculine/male human being. They were making connections between sustainable development and the principle of "subsistence," rather than production of surplus to be sold for profit, and women's necessary and equal involvement in shaping environmentally conscious development and conservation policies to protect the health and well-being of all people on earth (Merchant 1995: 3–26; Shiva 2010: 1–13).

In 1984, a coalition of feminist economists and activists living in New Delhi, India, formed the NGO DAWN and criticized top-down modernization and development policies of the 1960s and 1970s. DAWN welcomed the new emphasis on ecofeminist approaches to development, and incorporated indigenous women's knowledge and attention to local conditions into alternative development strategies. DAWN advocates redefined the central goal of development projects to focus on meeting the needs of the nation's poorest members, often women and their children, and asserted that poor women must be involved in defining and planning specific development projects. The development theorizing of DAWN proceeded from its "ground up" research, examining specific communities of women and the multiple challenges they faced at the microeconomic level to feed and sustain their families and the natural environment around them. These scholars attempted to formulate development models by "scaling-up" from what was working for women in these local situations, drawing on the environmental knowledge of poor women who had direct experiences with sustainable development practices, to inform the more generally applicable regional or global development practices (Jain 2017: 75–76).

At the UN Women's End-of-Decade Conference held in Nairobi in 1985, these connections were made explicitly and ecofeminist values were incorporated in the Conference Treaty, the Forward Looking Strategies for the Advancement of Women, in a chapter focused on "Development" (UN Document A/conf.116/28). The Forward Looking Strategies (FLS) noted the impact of natural disasters and human practices that had led to environmental degradation had also deprived women who worked in the agricultural sectors, particularly poor women in developing countries, of their traditional means of livelihood and their access to natural resources.

The FLS also noted the lack of sex-disaggregated data regarding the impact of modernizing macro-development policies on the health of local, and especially women's reproductive health, and placed value on indigenous/local women's knowledge about preservation of the natural world and their holistic understanding that all human activities should take the health of the planet into consideration (FLS, Paragraphs 23–28).

Globalization, neoliberalism, and structural adjustment policies

In spite of the widespread discussion of new "women in development," "gender and development," "sustainable," and "ecofeminist" development theories in global and regional governance forums during the 1970s and 1980s, the globalization of the world capitalist economy proceeded according to Western neoliberal economic theories. Neoliberal economics touted the benefits of reducing "nationalist" or "protectionist" trade barriers to expand global trade and the free flow of global investment capital. Neoliberalism promoted balanced government budgets rather than deficit spending to reduce the scope of government operations. Neoliberal economic policies included strict credit practices that reduced the amount of money in circulation and curbed social-welfare spending, and reduced government protections for trade unions that resulted in lower wages for workers in both the public and private sectors. Neoliberal economic theories, in effect, supported "austerity" policies implemented by governments and global financiers, and it was these theories that transformed development assistance during the decade of the 1980s—not WID, GAD, sustainable development, or ecofeminist theories.

Neoliberal SAPs were imposed on the economic operations of developed and developing nations that had borrowed money from the IMF and World Bank and other First World lenders during the 1980s, but they emerged because of the globalization of commodity markets that had been underway since the 1960s. Global capitalist supply-and-demand market forces dictated commodity pricing, and the Third World nations that sold those commodities experienced a severe drop in revenues in the 1970s as prices for their exports dropped. Consequently, Third World debt to First World lenders spiked. Demand for manufactured goods produced in the First World also dropped, and First World economies likewise experienced economic downturns. Third World requests for additional loan money from First World lenders were answered with loans that came with strict repayment conditions that further curtailed Third World social spending. Third World and First World governments cut back on funding for public sector jobs, usually in education and healthcare fields. They cut subsidies to certain economic sectors such as the agricultural sector and slashed social-welfare programs to meet the demands for austerity from global lenders.

Public services were contracted out to private sector businesses, regulations on those businesses were reduced, and price controls were lifted. These practices benefited First World corporate businesses that took advantage of the increased capitalist market-driven business opportunities and lack of government regulations and oversight of business practices.

The negative consequences of these neoliberal economic policies all disadvantaged women more than men (Hirschmann 1993). They also represented a form of structural violence, applied by a new manifestation of Western-defined hegemonic masculinity that emerged in the 1980s and 1990s, one that "elevate[d] global capitalist development to the most manly pursuit, even over war, to which all men and many countries should aspire." Those who were concerned with the negative effects of neoliberal capitalist economic globalization on disadvantaged workers, or on women or the environment, "were seen as anachronistic (feminine) and thus should be brushed aside as being unready for the brave new world of the 'new economy'" (Peterson and Runyan 2014: 28). Neoliberal austerity policies led to the feminization of poverty and to the feminization of labor, with implications for preserving the status quo of male-over-female gender power relations, as discussed above.

Women, gender, and development, 1990s–2000s

Democratic transitions and global capitalist expansion in the post–Cold War era

As previous chapters have discussed, with the end of the Cold War era and the reformation of the Soviet Union into a new "Commonwealth of Independent States" that were no longer governed by single communist parties and that no longer posed existential political, economic, or ideological threats to Western democracies, the bipolar East-West geopolitical structure that had dominated international politics since 1945 was transformed. Nonetheless, Western government leaders, including the US presidential administrations led by Republican George H. W. Bush (1989–93) and the first term of Democrat William Jefferson Clinton (1993–97), were slow to react to the new world order. These US presidential administrations and their Western European allies offered weak and ineffective responses to the "new" intrastate wars of the 1990s. They also continued to follow the neoliberal economic policies of the 1980s, now applied on a near-global scale as socialist economic alternatives disappeared. With the Soviet threat diminished, promoting the transitions of democratic governments and civil societies and expanding the reach of the world capitalist economy became priority US national security interests. The US foreign-policy makers promoted "democratization" and provided aid to the countries of the former Soviet Union and Eastern Europe as they completed their "transitions" from single-party, centralized-planning states to pluralistic, multiparty democratic states and integrated into the competitive global capitalist market economy. The expectation expressed by the Bush administration foreign aid programs, such as the Support for Eastern European Democracy (SEED) Act of 1989, and the Freedom for Russia and Emerging Eurasian Democracies and Open Markets (FREEDOM) Support Act of 1992, was that democratic transitions and capitalist market development would proceed together (Pishchikova 2011: 40; 78–79). Third World countries that had received aid when they represented strategic interests during the Cold War consequently lost out on some aid money. Therefore, according to UN secretary-general Boutros Boutros-Ghali, they "[sank] into economic underdevelopment, or [foundered] in political disorder" (Boutros-Ghali 1996: 10).

As many feminist scholars and activists have argued, the expansion of the global capitalist market economy in the neoliberal framework of the 1980s and 1990s disproportionately penalized already-disadvantaged women in all regions of the world, including the former socialist states. In the words of Valentine Moghadam, women became the "shock absorbers of neoliberal economic policies" as "the gender as well as class biases of structural adjustment were clear" (2005: 39). At the same time, a concurrent global rise in religious fundamentalism also responded to the destabilizing economic, social, and political effects associated with the global application of neoliberal economic policies. Fundamentalist religious movements worldwide sought to impose strict controls on women's public and private behaviors, aiming "to recuperate traditional norms and codes, including patriarchal laws and family roles for women" (Moghadam 2005: 7). These pressures inspired a revitalized global feminist movement as well, that pushed back against the cuts in social supports and aid for women, and against the resurgence of restrictive gender roles that kept women out of the public sphere and out of government policy making (Antrobus 2004: 99–100). The series of UN conferences and the accompanying global NGO forums that were held in the 1990s and that were discussed in Chapter 4 provided arenas and organizational platforms for the revitalized global feminist movement.

The 1992 United Nations Conference on the Environment and Development and the "human" component in development

The 1992 UN Conference on the Environment and Development (UNCED) was particularly significant for feminists focused on the links between gender equality and sustainable development and socially responsible environmental policies. Their analyses and proposals were incorporated into the UNCED conference treaty, the subsequent the UN Millennium Development Goals drafted in 2000, as well as the recently articulated UN Sustainable Development Goals set in 2015. The UNCED held in Rio de Janeiro, Brazil, in June 1992, was organized to devise a global "sustainable development" plan that would guide the United Nation's and national governments' environmental-conservation efforts, renewable energy development, and population-planning commitments into the twenty-first century. Sustainable development treaty provisions included measures to protect biodiversity and the fast-disappearing forests, reduce human consumption of natural resources, and reduce human causes of global warming, such as the burning of fossil fuels that emitted carbon dioxide and trapped heat in the earth's atmosphere.

At UNCED preparatory meetings held in New York in March 1992, the Conference secretary-general Maurice Strong sought increased public and private sector contributions to UN environment and development funds, increased green technology transfers from First World to Third World nations and debt reductions for developing countries to counteract some of the most harmful effects of neoliberal SAP. Strong also welcomed the participation of NGOs focused on environmental concerns at the UNCED and at the NGO forum that ran concurrently with the government conference in Rio de Janeiro.

The US government, led by the Bush administration, rejected many of the proposals put forward by Maurice Strong, environmentalist NGOs, and Third World nations, as it had consistently promoted neoliberal capitalist free-market solutions as the most efficient approach to tackling world problems. From the Bush administration's perspective, high consumption in First World nations was not the major "problem" that global development policy makers needed to fix, the major problem was "over population" in the Third World where fertility rates were considerably higher than those in First World countries. The administration resisted setting targets to reduce global carbon dioxide emissions, as it vetoed the proposal that First World nations should agree to resource conservation and energy consumption reduction targets independently of agreements that bound Third World developing nations to the same targets, and as it generally rejected technology transfers to the Third World. The draft UNCED treaty also articulated a "right to development" for all nations in its proposed Principle 3. This had been determined in the 1986 UN Declaration on the Right to Development that asserted the right of "every human person and all peoples . . . to participate in, contribute to and enjoy economic, social, cultural and political development, in which all human rights and fundamental freedoms can be fully realized." The Bush administration would not sign on to Principle 3 without reservations and qualifications. All these stances put the US government at odds with most environmental activists, and with many UN member states.

As UNCED treaty negotiations began, most UN environment and development agencies, and most national government delegations including the US delegation initially ignored feminists' development concerns. In the early 1990s, male policy makers often did not recognize that global warming of the earth's atmosphere that caused more violent storms, rising sea levels, flooding of farmland, and so on, had different gendered effects on male and female populations. Natural and manmade environmental disasters disproportionately affected the world's poor, causing more injuries and mortalities among these vulnerable populations, and women made up a disproportionately large segment of the world's poor. Other environmental degradation, such as deforestation or droughts affected women whose livelihoods were dependent on farming, or whose responsibilities included obtaining water and food for their families. These factors also affected women's health generally and their reproductive health in particular, as women often sacrificed their own well-being to meet the needs of their families. Moreover, when families were forced to migrate from lands that were no longer habitable, women's abilities to keep their families secure and fed were further compromised. With these concerns in mind, feminist activists organized to get their voices heard by male government leaders at UNCED (Merchant 1995: 209–10).

Former US Congresswomen Bella Abzug and the organization she led, WEDO, became key advocates of ecofeminist positions at UN conferences during the 1990s, beginning with UNCED. At two November 1991 meetings convened in Miami, Florida, WEDO organized a global feminist coalition to formulate an alternative "women's agenda" for sustainable development policies that would address the gendered impacts of global environmental decline that UNCED government delegations ignored. The first meeting of academics, the Global Assembly of Women and the Environment—Partners in Life, compiled environmental research and case studies. The second meeting, the World Women's Congress for a Healthy Planet, gathered over 1,500 activists from eighty-three countries. There, the case studies were presented, and a "Women's Action Agenda 21" was forged by consensus. It asserted the necessity of establishing gender equality in any sustainable development projects and strategies to be worked out at the upcoming Rio Conference. This agenda was taken to UNCED, and presented to a Women's Caucus that met at the NGO forum site in Rio. The Women's Caucus adopted the Women's Agenda as its "Global Women's Treaty for NGOs Seeking a Just and Healthy Planet." At UNCED, the Women's Caucus successfully lobbied to incorporate their Treaty into Chapter 24 of the UNCED government treaty, titled "Global Action for Women Toward Sustainable and Equitable Development" (UN Document A/conf.151/26, Vol. III). Their contributions included recommendations for women's participation as policy decision makers, and proposals to promote women's equality in all aspects of society. They recommended prohibitions against gender violence, provisions for women's health care, fair labor practices, and advocated for gender research on differential impacts of environment and development policies and environmental technologies on women in collaboration with INSTRAW and UNIFEM agencies. In addition, the UNCED treaty's Declaration of Principles included agreement that women had a "vital role" to play in environmental management and development, and asserted women's "full participation" was "essential to achieve sustainable development" (UN Document A/conf.151/26 Vol. I).

The UNCED took place in the context of another shift in focus of UN-sponsored development projects to emphasize "human development," as opposed to economic development. As the UN agencies put "people at the center of development," they were harkening back to pledges made in the Preamble of the UN Charter: to protect the dignity and worth of the human being, to assert the equality of men and women, and to promote social welfare and progress. These pledges had not been fully realized in UN development policies and programs since 1945, even when the UN development agencies focused on meeting "basic needs" of human communities in the late 1970s and early 1980s. By the 1990s, UN agencies were recognizing that neoliberal economic policies were having devastating effects on the livelihoods, health, and welfare of many global populations, leading to a new programming focus on "human development." In 1990, the lead UNDP released the first of its annual Human Development Reports that noted the ill-effects of neoliberal economic policies as they perpetuated race, class, and gender inequalities, dismissed cultural differences, and violated human rights. The UNDP defined human development as "a process of enlarging people's choices" by devoting funds to improve health and education and working conditions and to expand political and civil rights (UN and Human Development Briefing Note 8). Individual countries followed the UNDP's lead and many subsequently produced their own Human Development Reports.

To construct these global reports, the UNDP had developed a measurement tool, the Human Development Index (HDI), to measure and compare national life expectancies, access to education and literacy rates, and income per capita among nations worldwide. Additional measurement tools such as the Gender-related Development Index (GDI) that measured women's economic contributions and documented inequalities between men and women in UN member states, and the Gender Empowerment Measure (GEM) that measured opportunities for men and women to participate in politics and other decision-making bodies in their nations, were formulated in 1995. These new gender data-collection tools were devised to follow up on the UNDP's report on "Gender and Human Development" introduced at the 1995 UN Fourth World Women's Conference in Beijing, and again were consequences of UN institutional commitments to adopt gender-mainstreaming strategies to promote gender equality. A Human Poverty Index (HPI) was also developed to measure the proportions of people living in poverty without access to economic resources and illiteracy rates in individual nations. In recent years, development economists have also tried to measure people's overall satisfaction with their lives, or their "Gross National Happiness" (GNH), based on their nation's record of "sustainable development, preservation and promotion of cultural values, conservation of the natural environment, and good governance" (Campanella 2016). A Gender Inequality Index (GII) introduced by UNDP in 2010 also measured gaps in education, political, and workforce participation for men and women within societies. These more-holistic development measures—some more subjective than others—have revealed the limits of the historic standalone gross domestic product (GDP) measurement that ignored human dimensions of nations' wealth and relative levels of development. The UNDP's reports and measures exposed persistent gender and other inequalities that have destabilized societies and jeopardized world peace. These shortfalls led to the general acknowledgment that development policies and programs needed to be reconceptualized. But the reports also can be used as tools to promote human development worldwide: global comparisons could lead to shared strategies between nations to achieve higher levels of race-, gender-, and social-equality and justice, leading to more opportunities for all populations to improve their lives (Runyan and Peterson 2014: 126–27).

The Millennium Development Goals

The UN Millennium Development Summit held in September 2000 brought together government leaders, UN representatives, NGO representatives, OECD representatives, and First World financial lenders at the World Bank and IMF to develop new international development strategies and an implementation agreement. At the summit, government leaders from 147 nations agreed to pursue eight interlinked Millennium Development Goals (MDGs) and they established a timeframe with pledges to achieve these goals by 2015. Goals 3 and 5 specifically focused on expanding women's and girls' equality and improving women's maternal health. These goals and other gender-equality objectives related to the remaining MDGs represented wide recognition among governments of the necessity to improve women's lives and opportunities in order to achieve the overall success of development initiatives, particularly because women played such important roles in securing the well-being of their families and communities (Henderson and Jeydel 2014: 227).

In terms of Goal 1 to "Eradicate Extreme Poverty and Hunger," reductions have been made, but according to UNIFEM's 2008–09 report, "poor women in the global South [still] have the highest rates of poverty, hunger, maternal mortality, poor maternal health, HIV/AIDS, and their children are most subject to high child mortality rates" (Sisson and Runyan 2014: 230). The MDGs also focus on women's "maternal" health, assuming most women will become mothers, but they do not address the growing numbers of women who do not have access to contraceptives or safe terminations of pregnancies with any corrective measures. Women's continuing lack "power" to make decisions about their bodies is also reflected in higher rates of contraction HIV/AIDS "attributed to a combination of poverty, high rates of sexual assault in war and peace that lead to infections, a relative lack of information and treatment services provided to poor women, a greater stigma attached to having HIV/AIDS for women, and a relative lack of information and treatment services provided to poor women," as UNIFEM and UN Women have reported (Runyan and Peterson 2014: 231).

Although the MDGs achieved some results as outlined in Table 5.2, the prevalent neoliberal economic philosophy that has relied on market efficiency

Table 5.2 The UN Millennium Goals Report 2015, results achieved as of 2015

Goal 1: Eradicate Extreme Poverty and Hunger

- Proportion of developing world's population living on less than $1.25 per day in 1990 was nearly 50% (1.9 billion), by 2015 the proportion dropped to 14% (836 million)
- Proportion of undernourished people among the world's developing nations reduced from 23.3 % in 1990–92, to 12.9% in 2014–16

Goal 2: Achieve Universal Primary Education

- Primary school enrollment in the world's developing nations has reached 91% in 2015, up from 83% in 2000
- The literacy rate among youth, aged 14–24, has also risen from 83% to 91%, and literacy gap between men and women has narrowed

---

Goal 3: Promote Gender Equality and Empower Women

- More girls are enrolled in primary school in world's developing nations, with significant gains in Southeast Asia
- More women entering the paid workforce outside the agricultural sector in the developing world, increasing from 35% in 1990 to 41% in 2015
- More women serving in parliaments in nearly 90% of the 174 countries reporting data

---

Goal 4: Reduce Child Mortality

- The global under-five mortality rate declined from 90 to 43 deaths per 1,000 live births, from 1990 to 2015, with significant reductions in under-five mortality in Sub-Saharan Africa in the 2005–13 period
- Measles vaccinations have prevented over 15 million deaths between 2000 and 2013, and reduced globally reported cases of measles by 67% between 2000 and 2013

Goal 5: Improve Maternal Health

- Since 1990, the maternal mortality rate has declined by 45% globally, by 64% in Southeast Asia, and by 49% in Sub-Saharan Africa
- Worldwide, more than 71% of births were assisted by skilled medical personnel in 2014, an increase of 59% from 1990
- Worldwide, married women's access and use of contraceptives increased from 55% in 1990 to 64% in 2015

Goal 6: Combat HIV/AIDS, Malaria and Other Diseases

- New HIV infections fell by approximately 40% between 2000 and 2013
- By June 2014, 13.4 million people with HIV received antiretroviral therapy (ART), compared to 800,000 who received ART in 2003. ART averted 7.6 million deaths from HIV between 1995 and 2013
- Globally, the malaria incidence rate has been reduced by an estimated 37%, and mortality rates from malaria reduced by an estimated 58%, between 2000 and 2015
- Globally, the mortality rate from tuberculosis fell by 45% between 1995 and 2013

Goal 7: Ensure Environmental Sustainability

- Ozone-depleting substances have been virtually eliminated since 1990, and the ozone layer of the earth's atmosphere is expected to recover by mid-twenty-first century
- Terrestrial and marine-protected areas have increased in many regions of the world since 1990
- The percentage of people worldwide with access to improved drinking water has increased
- Globally, 2.1 billion people have improved access to sanitation since 1990
- The proportion of urban populations living in slums in developing countries fell from 39.4 % in 2000 to 29.7 % in 2014

Goal 8: Develop a Global Partnership for Development

- Official development assistance (ODA) from developed countries increased by 66% in real terms, reaching $135.2 billion
- In 2014, 79% of imports from developing to developed countries were admitted duty free, up from 65% in 2000
- The proportion of external debt service to export revenue in developing countries fell from 12% in 2000 to 3% in 2013
- Mobile cellular signal coverage has increased to cover 95 % of the world's population; internet coverage has also increased to link 3.2 billion people in a global network of web access

Source: *The Millennium Development Goals Report* (2015). http://www.un.org/millenniumgoals/2015_MDG_Report/pdf/MDG%202015%20rev%20(July%201).pdf (Accessed August 16, 2017).

to govern economic transactions, that has lifted government regulations on business operations, and that has rejected economic redistribution projects, has continued into the twenty-first century as well. The global economic crisis of 2007–09 was the result of lax regulation of the banking and financial industries and their speculative manipulations of money markets. The ensuing economic recession set back progress on achieving the MDGs. During the recession, there was a rise in global hunger and malnutrition rates as poor populations in First World and Third World countries could not afford food, and there was a general rise global poverty rates. Again, women in all regions of the world and racial minorities in First World nations were disproportionately affected as they made up a larger portion of the world's malnourished and poor populations. Cutbacks in social services and education funding and losses of paid wage work also disproportionately penalized racial minorities, women, and girls who were subject to ongoing gender discriminations (Runyan and Peterson 2014: 232–33).

Summing up

Historically, male international development experts have not considered gender power relationships when devising development theories, designing development projects, or dispersing development funds. These considerations have come into global governance development policy deliberations in the latter half of the twentieth century, due to the intervention of feminist scholars and activists from the First and Third Worlds. Feminist scholars have documented the ways that women's subordinate social, economic, and political status vis-à-vis men in most societies around the world has reduced women's and girls' opportunities to realize their full potential as human beings. Feminist activists working with local populations of women and girls have documented their unequal access to food and other necessities of life, to education, to health care, to economic resources, and to healthy environments, when compared to men's access. They have also documented how First World- and government-funded development projects have privileged males, harming women and girls and creating even greater gender inequalities in some communities. Mid-twentieth-century modernization theories and development projects and later-twentieth-century neoliberal economic policies have most explicitly served the economic and political interests of elite male leaders in First World nations, but socialist development models, dependency theories, and "basic needs" development strategies of the 1970s and 1980s also incorporated a male bias.

First World feminists' initial efforts to reduce gender inequality in development policies and programs through the WID approach of the 1970s and 1980s, brought attention to the continuing problems of global poverty and underdevelopment caused by the exclusion of women's ideas and lack of participation in male-led development planning and programs. Their liberal feminist analyses and development proposals raised women's visibility in international forums and government development agencies, but they did not effectively challenge global inequalities based on race, class, sexuality, or nationality that were linked to gender inequalities. Moreover, they did not always consider women's reproductive or social roles, focused as they were on involving women in productive labor and increasing their participation in the paid workforce. Feminist theorists and activists from the Third World, whose lives made them susceptible to global power distributions along all these axes of difference, raised these issues and more at UN World Women's Conferences in 1975, 1980, 1985, and 1995, and at other UN conferences focused on development, population, and the environment during these decades. They proposed various approaches to address women's gender-specific development needs through WAD, GAD and ecofeminist theories and projects. These approaches illuminated the multiple gendered effects of an unregulated, globalized, capitalist marketplace that perpetuated colonial relationships between First and Third World nations and damaged the global environment. They revealed gendered divisions of labor, gendered divisions of resources, and gendered distributions of power that reinforced and perpetuated Western-defined hegemonic masculine power and hindered development for all.

Nonetheless, the series of development approaches and projects that have been implemented by UN agencies and supported by UN member states chart a history of changing global norms regarding the need to promote gender equality in future development programs, to ensure their successful results. Among the world's financial leaders, such as those at the World Bank, the WID approach still represents the most popular argument in favor of gender equality, that is, involving women in the formal economy as paid workers can improve overall social and economic development levels. As the World Bank's 2012 report on "Gender Equality and Development" asserted: "Gender equality is smart economics: it can enhance economic efficiency and improve other development outcomes." These outcomes include greater productivity among societies that include women's labor; improvements in the health and well-being of communities because women pass on benefits that they receive to their families; and more inclusive and democratic societies that draw on the talents of all to improve governing institutions and development policies. The UNDP's new Sustainable Development Goals, seventeen goals adopted by the UN General Assembly in 2015 to be achieved by 2030, enumerate broad, far-reaching goals as they also set specific objectives regarding what is needed to achieve gender equality, human rights, and a peaceful planet that can sustain human life and promote human progress. Goal 5, to "Achieve Gender Equality and Empower All Women and Girls," has laid out an impressive list of targets that reflect many of the issues that feminist scholars and activists have raised throughout the twentieth and into the twenty-first centuries, as they

Table 5.3 Sustainable Development Goals for 2030, Goal Five: Achieve Gender Equality and Empower All Women and Girls

End all forms of discrimination against all women and girls everywhere
Eliminate all forms of violence against all women and girls in the public and private spheres, including trafficking and sexual and other types of exploitation
Eliminate all harmful practices, such as child, early, and forced marriages and female genital mutilation
Recognize and value unpaid care and domestic work through the provision of public services, infrastructure, and social protection policies and the promotion of shared responsibility within the household and the family as nationally appropriate
Ensure women's full and effective participation and equal opportunities for leadership at all levels of decision-making in political, economic, and public life
Ensure universal access to sexual and reproductive health and reproductive rights as agreed in accordance with the Programme of Action of the International Conference on Population and Development and the Beijing Platform for Action and the outcome documents of their review conferences
Undertake reforms to give women equal rights to economic resources, as well as access to ownership and control over land and other forms of property, financial services, inheritance, and natural resources, in accordance with national laws
Enhance the use of enabling technology, in particular information and communications technology, to promote the empowerment of women
Adopt and strengthen sound policies and enforceable legislation for the promotion of gender equality and the empowerment of all women and girls at all levels

Source: UN Sustainable Development Goals. Goal 5: Achieve Gender Equality and Empower all women and Girls. Targets. http://www.un.org/sustainabledevelopment/gender-equality/ (Accessed August 16, 2017).

articulate women's needs and reflect women's growing influence in global development policy making. Rhetorically, "women's equality" has arrived in global governance policy language, as it has in many nations' formal policy language. Now language must inform practice. As the current UN under-secretary and executive director of UN Women Phumzil Mlambo-Ngcuka has put it, "marginal progress will not suffice" (Mlambo-Ngcuka 2017: 185).

References for further study

Fraser, A. S. and Tinker, I. (2004), *Developing Power: How Women Transformed International Development*, New York: The Feminist Press.

Scott, C. V. (1996), *Gender and Development: Rethinking Modernization and Dependency Theory*, Boulder, CO: Lynne Rienner Publishers.

Visivanathan, N., Duggan, L., Wiegersma, N., and Nisonoff, L. (2011), *The Women, Gender and Development Reader*, 2nd ed., London, UK: Zed Books.

Web resources

The Association for Women's Rights in Development (AWID). https://www.awid.org/ (Accessed August 16, 2017).

Development Alternatives with Women for a New Era (DAWN). http://www.dawnnet.org/feminist-resources/ (Accessed August 16, 2017)].

Gender Statistics Manual. United Nations Statistics. http://unstats.un.org/unsd/genderstatmanual/Default.aspx (Accessed August 16, 2017).

United Nations Development Program. Human Development Reports: Gender Inequality Index. http://hdr.undp.org/en/content/gender-inequality-index-gii (Accessed August 16, 2017).

United Nations Sustainable Development Goals (for 2030): Seventeen Goals to transform Our World. http://www.un.org/sustainabledevelopment/sustainable-development-goals/ (Accessed August 16, 2017).

Women's Environment and Development Organization (WEDO). http://wedo.org/ (Accessed August 16, 2017).

Bibliography

Antrobus, P. (2004), *The Global Women's Movement: Origins, Issues and Strategies*, London, UK: Zed Books.

Boserup, E., Tan, S. F., and Toulmin, C. (2013), *Woman's Role in Economic Development*. London, UK: Routledge.

Boutros-Ghali, B. (1996), "Foreward," in T. G. Weiss and L. Gordenker (eds.), *NGOs, the UN, and Global Governance*, 7–12, Boulder, CO: Lynne Rienner Publishers.

Campanella, E. (November 4, 2016), "Is it Time to Abandon the GDP?," *Project Syndicate*.

Chant, S. (2011), "The 'Feminization of Poverty' and the 'Feminization' of Anti-Poverty Programs: Room for Revision?" in N. Visivanathan, L. Duggan, N. Wiegersma, and L. Nisonoff (eds.), *The Women, Gender and Development Reader*, 2nd ed., 174–94, London, UK: Zed Books.

Chaudhuri, N. and Strobel, M. (1992), *Western Women and Imperialism*, Bloomington, IN: Indiana University Press.

Connelly, M. P., Li, T. M., MacDonald, M., and Parpart. J. L. (2000), "Feminism and Development: Theoretical Perspectives," in M. P. Connelly, V. E. Barriteau, and J. L. Parpart (eds.), *Theoretical Perspectives on Gender and Development*, 51–160, Ottawa, CAN: International Development Research Centre.

Cull, N. J., Culbert, D. H., and Welch, D. (2003), "Marshall Plan, 1947-1951." in *Propaganda and Mass Persuasion: A Historical Encyclopedia*, 238, Santa Barbara, CA: ABC-CLIO Books.

Dower, J. (1999), *Embracing Defeat: Japan in the Wake of World War II*, New York, NY: W. W. Norton & Co.

Engerman, D. C. (2004), "The Romance of Economic Development and the New Histories of the Cold War," *Diplomatic History*, 28: 23–54.

Fasulo, L. (2004), *An Insider's Guide to the UN*, New Haven, CT: Yale University Press.

Frey, M., Kunkel, S., and Unger, C. R. (2014), *International Organizations and Development, 1945-1990*, New York, NY: Palgrave MacMillan.

Garner, K. (2010), *Shaping a Global Women's Agenda: Women's NGOs and Global Governance, 1925-85*, Manchester, UK: Manchester University Press.

Garner, K. (2013), *Gender and Foreign Policy in the Clinton Administration*, Boulder, CO: Lynne Rienner Publishers, First Forum Books.

Goldstein, J. S. and Pevehouse, J. C. (2006), *International Relations*, 7th ed., New York, NY: Pearson Longman.

Henderson, S. L. and Jeydel, A. S. (2014), *Women and Politics in a Global World*, 3rd ed., New York, NY: Oxford University Press.

Hirschmann, D. (1993), *Democracy and Gender: A Practical Gide to USAID Programs*. Washington DC: The GENYSYS Project, The Futures Group, Prepared for the Office of Women in Development, Bureau for Research and Development, USAID.

Hiscocks, C. R. (1954), "The Development of Democracy in Western Germany Since the Second World War," *Canadian Journal of Economics and Political Science*, 20: 493–503.

Hussein, A. (2004), "Crossroads for Women at the UN," in A. S. Fraser and I. Tinker (eds.), *Developing Power: How International Women Transformed Development*, 3–13, New York, NY: The Feminist Press.

Jain, D. (2005), *Women, Development and the UN: A Sixty year Quest for Equality and Justice*, Bloomington, IN: Indiana University Press.

Jain, D. (2017), "Women of the South: Engaging with the UN as a Diplomatic Maneuver," in J. A. Cassidy (ed.), *Gender and Diplomacy*, 65–80, New York, NY: Routledge.

Jaquette, J. (2004), "Crossing the Line: From Academia to the WID Office at USAID," in A. S. Fraser and I. Tinker (eds.), *Developing Power: How Women Transformed International Development*, 189–99, New York, NY: The Feminist Press.

Johnson, S. H. (1999), "An Ecofeminist Critique of the International Economic Structure," in E. Prügl and M. K. Meyer (eds.), *Gender Politics in Global Governance*, 221–29, Lanham, MD: Rowman and Littlefield Publishers, Inc.

Karns, M. P., Mingst, K. A., and Stiles, K. W. (2015), *International Organizations: the Politics and Processes of Global Governance*, 3rd ed., Boulder, CO: Lynne Rienner Publishers.

Kaufman, J. (2013), *Introduction to International Relations: Theory and Practice*, Lanham, MD: Rowman and Littlefield Publishers, Inc.

Kelsky, K. (2001), *Women on the Verge: Japanese Women, Western Dreams*, Durham, NC: Duke University Press.

Koikari, M. (2008), *Pedagogy of Democracy: Feminism and the Cold War in the U.S. Occupation of Japan*, Philadelphia, PA: Temple University Press.

Laville, H. (2002), *Cold War Women: The International Activities of American Women's Organizations*, New York, NY: Palgrave MacMillan.

Linder, D. H. (2001), "Equality for Women: The Contribution of Scandinavian Women to the United Nations, 1946-66," *Scandinavian Studies*, 63: 165–208.

McWilliams, W. G. and Piotrowski, H. (2014), *The World Since 1945: A History of International Relations*, Boulder, CO: Lynne Rienner Publishers.

Merchant, C. (1995), *Earthcare: Women and the Environment*, New York, NY: Routledge.

Mitcham, C. (1995), "The Concept of Sustainable Development: Its Origins and Ambivalence," *Technology in Society*, 17: 311–26.

Mlambo-Ngcuka, P. (2017), "Becoming UN Women: A Journey in Realizing Rights and Gaining Global Recognition," in J. A. Cassidy (ed.), *Gender and Diplomacy*, 170–86, New York, NY: Routledge.

Moghadam, V. (2005), *Globalizing Women: Transnational feminist Networks*, Baltimore, MD: Johns Hopkins University Press.

Nashell, J. (2000), "The Road to Vietnam: Modernization Theory in Fact and Fiction," in C. G. Appy (ed.), *Cold War Constructions: The Political Culture of United States Imperialism, 1945-1966*, 132–54, Amherst, MA: University of Massachusetts Press.

Northup, C. C. (2013), "Foreign Aid," in Cynthia Clark Northrup and Jerry H. Bentley (eds.), *Encyclopedia of World Trade: From Ancient Times to the Present*, Armonk, NY: Sharpe Reference.

Paxton, P. and Hughes, M. M. (2007), *Women, Politics and Power: A Global Perspective*, Los Angeles, CA: Pine Forge Press.

Peterson, V. S. (2014), "International Global Political Economy," in L. J. Shepherd (ed.), *Gender Matters in Global Politics: A Feminist Introduction to International Relations*, 2nd ed., 173–85, New York, NY: Routledge.

Pishchikova, K. (2011), *Promoting Democracy in Postcommunist Ukraine: The Contradictory Outcomes of US Aid to Women's NGOs*, Boulder, CO: Lynne Rienner Publishers, First Forum Books.

Rai, S. (2011), "Gender and Development: Theoretical Perspectives," in N. Visvanathan, L. Duggan, N. Wiergersma, and L. Nisonoff (eds.), *The Women, Gender and Development Reader*, 2nd ed., 28–37, London, UK: Zed Books.

Rai, S. (2011), "The History of International Development: Concepts and Contexts," in N. Visvanathan, L. Duggan, N. Wiergersma, and L. Nisonoff (eds.), *The Women, Gender and Development Reader*, 2nd ed., 14–21, London, UK: Zed Books.

Rostow, W. W. (1960), *The States of Economic Growth: A Non-Communist Manifesto*, Cambridge, UK: Cambridge University Press.

Rueschemeyer, M. and Schissler, H. (1990), "Women in the Two Germanys," *German Studies Review*, 13: 71–85.

Runyan, A. S and Peterson, V. S. (2014), *Global Gender Issues in the New Millennium*, 4th ed., Boulder, CO: Westview Press.

Rupp, L. J. (1997), *Worlds of Women: The Making of an International Women's Movement*, Princeton, NJ: Princeton University Press.

Schmelzer, M. (2014), "A Club of the Rich to Help the Poor?," in M. Frey, S. Kunkel, and C. R. Unger (eds.), *International Organizations and Development, 1945-1990*, 171–95, New York, NY: Palgrave MacMillan.

Schwartz, T. A. (1991), *America's Germany: John J. McCloy and the Federal Republic of Germany*, Cambridge, MA: Harvard University Press.

Shepherd, L. J. (2015), *Gender Matters in Global Politics: A Feminist Introduction to International Relations*, 2nd ed., New York, NY: Routledge.

Shiva, V. (1988, 2010), *Staying Alive: Women, Ecology and Development*, Brooklyn, NY: South End Press.

Sirota Gordon, B. (1997), *The Only Woman in the Room: A Memoir*, New York, NY: Kodansha International.

Sluga, G. (2013), *Internationalism in the Age of Nationalism*, Philadelphia, PA: University of Pennsylvania Press.

Sluga, G. (2014), "The Human Story of Development: Alva Myrdal at the UN, 1949-1955," in M. Frey, S. Kunkel, and C. R. Unger (eds.), *International Organizations and Development, 1945-1990*, 46–74, New York, NY: Palgrave MacMillan.

Steans, J. (2013), *Gender and International Relations: Theory, Practice, Policy*, 3rd ed., Cambridge, UK: Polity Press.

Thébaud, F. (2014), "What is a Transnational Life? Some Thoughts About Marguerite Thibert's Career and Life (1886-1982)," in O. Janz and D. Schonpflug (eds.), *Gender History in a Transnational Perspective*, 162–83, New York, NY: Berghan Books.

Tickner, J. A. (2001), *Gendering World Politics: Issues and Approaches in the Post-Cold War Era*, New York, NY: Columbia University Press.

Towns, A. E. (2010), *Women and States: Norms and Hierarchies in International Society*, Cambridge, UK: Cambridge University Press.

UN Environmental Program, (2002), *Integrating Environment and Development: 1972-2002*. New York, NY: UNEP.

UN Intellectual History Project, (2009), *The UN and Human Development, Briefing Note 8*. New York, NY: United Nations.

UNICEF, n.d. "The 1960s: Decade of Development," New York, NY, UNICEF.

United Nations High Commission for Refugees, (2016), "About Fridtjof Nansen," Geneva, Switzerland: UNHCR.

Wilson, K. (2011), "From Missionaries to Microcredit? 'Race,' Gender and Agency in Neoliberal Development," in N. Visvanathan, L. Duggan, N. Wiergersma, and L. Nisonoff (eds.), *The Women, Gender and Development Reader*, 2nd ed., 99–101, London, UK: Zed Books.

(n.d.), *Women Organizing Transnationally: The Committee of Correspondence, 1952-1969*, Gale Group, A Cengage Company.

CHAPTER SIX

Women, gender, and government leadership

Foundational questions

Why are women underrepresented in elite global leadership positions that is, in executive positions as heads of state or heads of government, who direct their nations' foreign policies and interact with other world leaders in intergovernmental forums, historically and currently, throughout the world?

Why does women's underrepresentation in these elite executive leadership roles matter?

When women attain executive leadership positions, do they govern differently than men?

What impact have female heads of state and gendered notions of leadership had on the course of international history and the conduct of international relations in the twentieth and twenty-first centuries?

Key concepts

Critical Mass is an organizational behavior concept that is often cited in relation to women's participation within political systems. Feminist theorists have asserted that female politicians will only begin to make a difference in terms of interjecting "women's issues" into public policy making or "feminist values" into political systems when the numbers of females involved reaches a specific threshold, usually defined as 30 percent, within political systems. The feminist objective to reach a critical mass of women leaders in governing positions is based on democratic principles of equality and gender justice and on essentialist claims that "women" experience the world in distinctly different ways than "men" do, and therefore have different political concerns and understand and use power differently than men. When the proportion of women elected in a political body or system reaches the threshold of critical mass, feminist theorists assert that these women will be able to leverage the power of their collective gendered "voice" to impact policy-making agendas and revise political practices.

Leadership is demonstrated by the ability to define and articulate a vision or a goal that goes beyond an individual context and into the collective realm of experience, and then to inspire and motivate a group to take up that vision or goal as their own and act to bring it to fruition. Leadership theories focus on typology of leaders, styles of leadership, ascension to positions of power and uses of power, and on the historical, or situational, or institutional context in which leaders emerge.

Feminist theorists focus on gendered differences in leadership visions, uses of power, and styles of political leadership. According to gendered leadership theories, in general, male leaders more often display the characteristics and traits associated with Western-defined hegemonic masculinity, using greater strength of will, assertiveness, and a more autocratic or directive style to exercise power *over* weaker, less-powerful members of a group. In general, female leaders more often display collaborative, participatory, or inclusive styles of leadership, to exercise empowerment *with* other members of a group. Feminist theorists also argue that "feminist values," identified as compassionate concerns for the welfare of others and commitments to social justice, equality, freedom, and human security, are values that all leaders, male or female, should aspire to exhibit, especially if they aim to be transformational leaders who seek to bring progressive changes to world political systems.

Quotas are used in democratic electoral political systems by political parties to diversify slates of political candidates and/or by government legislatures to increase the numbers of elected participants of underrepresented groups in the public-policy-making process. Quotas are established with the values of fairness, diversity of perspective, and government legitimacy in mind. Quota practices recognize that some underrepresented groups, such as those that are outside the hegemonic masculine or other privileged in-groups, have faced formal or informal barriers to power that privileged groups do not face. Quotas are a form of *affirmative action* used to overcome those barriers.

Regarding the adoption of *gender quotas* to bring women into political systems, feminists argue that they are necessary because, in the modern world, men have designed political systems, their masculine values pervade political systems, and, therefore, these systems advantage male participants. In the contemporary world, women may not face de jure or legal restrictions that prevent them from participating in their nation's political electoral processes, but many women who live under democratic political systems in nations around the world experience de facto discriminations against women in leadership positions that prevent them from participating in numbers that would reflect their proportion of the general electorate.

To address this inherent male bias, some governments in democratic nations and some political parties within those nations have adopted gender quotas, to ensure that women have at least minimal *descriptive* or numerical representation in political systems. For groups to achieve *substantive* representation, that is, so that their specific group interests impact policy formulation and their values affect governing practices, feminists argue that quotas can ensure that a critical mass of marginalized groups will enter political systems.

Introduction

Woman President's Manifesto

If I'm ever made President
The corridors of power, packed with intoxicated men
Will quake at my every Prada-shod step.
With compassion over dominion,
The age of absolute power will be over.
If I'm ever made President
Maternity leave shall be compulsory and fully paid
No mother will have to go out to work
Because she has to.
If I'm ever made President
War will be redundant, nuclear stations for energy only
Soldiers put to work fighting poverty
To build and not destroy.
If I'm ever made President
Elections will be free and fair, I'll lose with grace, concede with ease
Put on Jimmy Choo shoes and dance the night away
At the next inaugural ball.

NOMATHEMBA DZINOTYIWEI, SOUTH AFRICAN POET

Women cannot lead without men, but men have, to this day, considered themselves capable of leading without women. Women would always take men into consideration. That's the difference.

VIGDIS FINNBOGADÓTTIR, FORMER PRESIDENT OF ICELAND, QUOTED IN LISWOOD 1996: 75

There are clearly reasons to continue to treat states as masculinized coercive institutions. But this is not the only thing states have been and are presently made to be. There are also reasons to argue that adding women has disrupted some of the prior masculinist foundations of the state by inserting presumably feminine traits. . . .

States have taken on roles and practices expressly seen as female and mired in gendered metaphors, such as caring for children, the elderly and the infirm. And not only have women been central in reconfiguring the gender of states, but the feminization of states has simultaneously prompted the inclusion of women as "female expertise.". . .

Female traits are sometimes elevated in international politics; used to exalt rather than to diminish the standing of a state.

ANN TOWNS 2010: 200–01

Although most twentieth- and twenty-first-century national governments have been disproportionately dominated by male leaders and power structures that have institutionalized elite male privilege, a small but growing number of women have become heads of state or heads of government, or have held leading posts in their nation's executive cabinet ministries, especially since the 1990s (Jalalzai 2016: 3). These elite female leaders have participated in state-to-state relations as they have traditionally operated in male-defined political systems and some of these female leaders have challenged male-over-female gender power relationships and other hierarchical power relationships that have privileged hegemonic masculinity. This chapter examines the gendered nature of executive political positions and institutions. It also examines the characteristics and policy priorities of female leaders who have held executive governing positions and compares them with characteristics and policy priorities of male leaders, in theory and in practice.

In recent decades, the numbers of women filling national leadership positions have been rising so that, as of 2017, globally women occupied 7.2 percent of the positions as heads of state, 11 out of 152 states worldwide and 5.7 percent as heads of government, 11 out of 193 states worldwide.[1] As of 2016, women occupied 16.9 percent of the leading positions in their nation's foreign ministries, that is, thirty-three women foreign ministers out of 195 countries of the world.[2] This chapter addresses the slow but steady rise in the numbers of women assuming these leading international policy-making positions with the goal of determining the reasons for the pace and the direction of change. Feminist IR scholars have defined disproportional male dominance in government leadership positions as a "problem" in purportedly democratic governing systems that should be corrected to achieve more just and peaceful international relationships and a greater measure of human security in the world. They have also identified the formal and informal barriers that women have faced in ascending to national and international leadership positions, and their findings will be related here. Feminist scholars and activists have also developed strategies to overcome both formal and informal barriers to women's leadership and to transform institutional values and practices to address women's needs and interests. To the extent that these strategies have been implemented, their effectiveness will also be evaluated here.

In order to move from the general discussion of women's leadership to the specific, this chapter also profiles a few selected women who have led their states or governments over the last half of the twentieth century and into the twenty-first century. These leaders have been selected because they exhibited a range of leadership styles and governing philosophies, some "feminist" and some not. They represent nations from the global North and South with varied political traditions, as well as different generations of leaders. This chapter examines the leadership, foreign policies, and international relationships cultivated by Indira Gandhi (India) and Margaret Thatcher (Great Britain), as compared to Ellen Johnson Sirleaf (Liberia), Michelle Bachelet (Chile), and Angela Merkel (Germany). Comparing these leaders illuminates some of the ways that modern era, Western-defined gender power and colonial power relationships have been reified in specific foreign policies of the governments led by these exemplary women, and, therefore, how these women leaders have perpetuated the gender status quo in world politics. But it also reveals how these women leaders were involved in defining international relationships that challenged traditional gender power and colonial power relations and how their presence and some of their actions have instigated ongoing and transformative changes in world politics. By examining the leadership records of these women, we can evaluate, in a preliminary way, whether the norms that govern the conduct of elite government leadership are, in fact, changing, and whether feminist challenges to male-over-female gender power relations are starting to have an impact on international relations.

Small numbers of women in elite leadership

Feminist scholars and activists have long-argued that (feminist) women should occupy leadership positions in governing bodies, and in the workforce and in other social institutions, in numbers that are roughly equal to those of men. In democratic political systems, democratic theory makes the strongest argument in support of electing more women leaders based on principles of equality and fairness; in other words, "democratically elected bodies should look something like the larger society they represent" (Han 2010: 2). Moreover, some scholars have pointed out that since women make up half of humanity, it is "unnatural" that they do not make up half the elected leaders, and if they did, governments would be more "legitimate" (Nanivadekar 2010: 293).

To be sure, over the last several decades, the numbers of women leading their nations have been slowly rising. Consider these figures: in the 1960s, only three women occupied the highest executive office in their countries; in the 1970s, the number of women leaders rose to six; in the 1980s, the number rose to seven; in the 1990s, twenty-six women served as president or prime minister of their countries; and in the first decade of the 2000s, twenty-nine women led their nations (Bauer and Tremblay 2011: 1). Indeed, the 2016 ascension of Theresa May as Britain's prime minister, along with other female Western European heads of government who were also in power at the time, including Scotland's first minister Nicola Sturgeon and Germany's chancellor Angela Merkel, led political commentators to proclaim that a new form of government, a *"femocracy,"* was emerging, supplanting male-defined Western European democracies (Adley and Connolly 2016; McDonagh 2016). Although the more "feared" triumvirate, the possibility that three women would occupy the top executive governing positions of the world's leading First World democracies—Great Britain, Germany, and the United States—did not occur following the defeat of Democratic Party nominee Hillary Clinton in November 2016 US presidential election, women who represent a wide spectrum of political orientations are moving into positions of power and international leadership, in all types of political systems, and in all regions of the world (Timsit 2016). Yet within the governments of nation-states around the world, and at the leading intergovernmental body of the United Nations, women are far from reaching parity with men in terms of the numbers of women occupying the most elite political leadership positions, that is, in terms of their descriptive representation. This "matters," according to feminist critics, because descriptive representation also impacts substantive representation of "women's interests" in government and intergovernmental policy making, however broadly those women's interests or "women-friendly policy agendas" must be defined within specific political, cultural, national, and historical contexts (Jalalzai 2016: 12). Male-dominated environments, as they have been observed many times, "are not conducive to promotion of gender equality" (Hannan 2013: 86).

Laura Liswood, who has studied and advocated for women's leadership at the executive level of governing power for more than two decades, has answered the question of why women leaders are necessary at all levels of political power. She has asserted that the answer is "simple and basic: women have different points of view, values, experiences, priorities, interests and conditions of life. Theirs are not necessarily better, more noble, more important [than men's], but they are theirs. . . . Men and women can walk in each other's shoes only partially—the rest is imagined or not considered at all" (Liswood 1995: 131).

Bearing out Laura Liswood's assertions, male-dominated governing institutions have historically excluded women from political participation, and from property ownership, from working for wages outside the home, from obtaining certain types of education, from practicing certain professions, and from attaining physical and economic independence from their male protectors (Lowndes 2014: 687). Historically, male-dominated governing institutions have determined "how and what resources are distributed and who gets to do the distributing" (Chappell and Waylen 2013: 602). Those in power determine policy agendas. Those in power speak for others and may represent the interests of those others fairly and faithfully, or they may not. Feminists argue that if only one gender, the hegemonic male gender that privileges one race, or class, or sexual orientation, and so forth, monopolizes the offices of power, their gendered perspective on defining governing problems and on solving those problems will prevail, and existing power hierarchies will continue. This "crisis of representation" was recognized in societies governed by liberal democratic political systems in the nineteenth and twentieth centuries and it led to a slow expansion of voting rights in democratic nations, and to greater diversity among elected representatives. To date, however, the dominant Western-defined male gender, race, and class hierarchies continue to control government and intergovernmental policy-making bodies (Peterson and Runyan 2009: 105).

Feminist scholars have also provided data and evidence to demonstrate that less-powerful groups are more vulnerable to physical violence and other forms of exploitation perpetrated by those in power. Previous chapters have highlighted some of the scholarship that establishes a historic record of instances when gender-based violence and other forms of structural violence targeted and disadvantaged female populations over the last 100 years. Unequal access to power in the public sphere both reflects and perpetuates unequal and sometimes abusive gender power relationships in the private sphere (Nanivadekar 2010: 302). Nonetheless, feminists and some women leaders have mounted significant challenges to male-dominated political institutions and public policy making that will be discussed further below. These feminist challenges have not always focused on elevating more women to leadership positions or specifically on gaining political parity for women, although those transformations are part of the goal to reject the hegemonic male-gendered hierarchies that have determined power and privilege in the modern world, and to institute progressive, more inclusive, and more humane forms of organizing and using power to govern societies.

Gender and elite leadership

For millennia women have dedicated themselves almost exclusively to the task of nurturing, protecting and caring for the young and old, striving for conditions of peace that favor life as a whole. . . . It is time to apply in the arena of the world the wisdom and experience that women have gained.

AUNG SAN SUU KYI, 1995 UN FOURTH WORLD CONFERENCE ON
WOMEN (QUOTED IN ADLER 1996: 155)

Aung San Suu Kyi, an opposition leader who protested Myanmar's ruling military government for over two decades beginning in 1988, expressed some widely held gender stereotypes when she spoke before world leaders at the UN Fourth World Conference on Women in Beijing in 1995, with the hope of interjecting "feminine" knowledge and values into the practice of world politics. The stereotypes she articulated carry over into expectations about how men and women will act once they attain leadership positions. Many cultures in the modern world have adopted Western-defined gender stereotypes regarding expected masculine and feminine behaviors and understand the two genders as binary opposites. Hegemonic masculinity, as noted in Chapter 2, defines "ideal" male characteristics as: rational thinkers, autonomous, independent beings, who display physical and mental strength, (sexual) aggressiveness, and exert power over others. These male characteristics have historically, at least since the nineteenth century, been associated with elite political leadership in the public sphere, in Western and non-Western nation-states. "Ideal" female characteristics are defined in opposition to male characteristics. Ideal females are emotional nurturers, connected to others, and are weak, passive, vulnerable, and peaceful beings who belong in the private sphere, *not* in elite government leadership roles. These "entrenched" Western-defined gender stereotypes, although not native to all world cultures at all points in their histories, now operate and resonate with cultures in all regions of the world. Moreover, these gender stereotypes tend to be "sticky," as they are taught in formal and informal ways and are reinforced throughout our lives through personal relationships and through social, economic and political institutions. Men or women whose behaviors challenge these gender stereotypes "have often been treated as 'deviants' and punished through acts of censure, ridicule, or harassment" (Chappell and Waylen 2013: 602–03).

Masculine versus feminine leadership

Although a study of global women political leaders by Nancy Adler published in 1996 observed that with so few women attaining elite governing positions in the twentieth century it was hard to make strong, evidence-based arguments for distinct sex differences in men's and women's leadership styles, in the studies of women's leadership that she surveyed, some of the gender stereotypes noted above seemed to be repeated. Many studies found that men exhibited a "more autocratic or directive style" and women exhibited a "more democratic" or "people-centered" style of leadership (Adler 1996: 151; see also: Eagley and Carli 2003: 813; Han 2010: 8). Researchers who have conducted leadership studies in corporate as well as political realms have also noted that male leaders more often than females exhibit a "hard" leadership style, stressing "hierarchy, dominance, and order." In contrast, women more often than men exhibit "soft" leadership styles, relying on "cooperation, influence, and empowerment" to achieve their governing visions or policy goals (Liswood 1995: 77). Other studies note the impact of women's supposed pacific natures, making them less likely to support wars or defense spending, and more likely to support compromises to avoid war and to favor social spending (Jaquette 1997: 35; Henderson and Jeydel 2014: 6). These studies generally did not factor in differences other than male-female gender distinctions, differences such as race or ethnicity, economic class, sexual orientation, or age, for example, that would also influence how particular groups of men and women might be socialized to lead in certain gender stereotypical ways, or would not be socialized to lead at all.

Feminist activists and scholars also highlight distinctions between *women's leadership* and *feminist leadership* in regard to transforming unequal interstate relations that cause instability and to transforming the confrontational nature of world politics. According to many feminist critics, most women who have attained elite levels of leadership "owe their position to their conformity with male models of leadership and their acceptance of the *status quo*" (Antrobus 2004: 164). While their visibility *as women* cannot be denied, and many women leaders have used the symbolism of female roles as "mothers" or "grandmothers" of the nation to solidify their claims to governing power or to disarm their critics, not all women leaders will support the issues that most women in their nations find most important. Nor will they challenge male privilege, beyond their mere presence in the male-dominated halls of power (Adler 1996: 149–50).

In contrast to women's leadership, feminist leadership seeks to transform political systems by challenging hegemonic masculinity and its monopoly of governing power, as well as by opposing other forms of oppression based on race, ethnicity, religion, class, or sexuality and by promoting social justice. These feminist commitments to challenge unequal power relations and unjust systems inspire leaders to advocate for alternative ways of exercising power or distributing resources, such as those "feminist foreign policies" described in Chapter 2.

What would feminist public policies look like? UN Women, the UN Entity for Gender Equality and the Empowerment of Women, drafts an annual "Progress of the World's Women" report. The report for 2015–16 identified the following recommendations for public-policy makers, the "Ten Priorities for Public Action," that addressed changes needed to achieve gender equality throughout societies. These priorities:

> span the imperatives to create decent work, implement gender-responsive social policies and adopt a rights-based macroeconomic

policy framework. They highlight the need for resource mobilization, an enabling global environment, support for women's organizing and an expanded evidence base on women's economic and social rights, in order to achieve substantive equality. They should be deliberated and finetuned through open dialogue involving the active participation of civil society organizations representing the interests of women and girls, especially the most disadvantaged.[3]

Feminist leaders tend to emerge from or support the goals of feminist women's movements (Antrobus 2004: 166–70). Some women who are political leaders or social activists, especially those from non-Western countries or underprivileged groups within Western societies, may reject the "feminist label" because they feel it does not adequately describe their social-justice goals that must address all forms of oppression with understanding and specificity, and not just sexist forms of oppression. Yet feminist leaders will always be conscious of unequal power relationships and will "embrace" the diversity and complexity of the most broadly-conceptualized human rights movements. They will be passionate about pursuing progressive social change and they will be strategic in making alliances with other leaders or movements and in adopting methods to keep moving toward their progressive, egalitarian, and inclusive power-sharing goals (Wilson 2005: 228–29).

Formal and informal barriers to women's leadership

There are multiple gender barriers, both formal and informal, that prevent women from attaining political leadership positions in numbers that accurately represent their proportion of their nations' populations. These barriers are especially difficult to overcome at the highest, most-privileged masculine levels of national leadership. In many modern liberal democratic nations, the formal barriers to women's political participation have been eliminated as women attained the constitutional rights to vote and to stand for office in electoral political systems in the mid-twentieth century. Chapter 3 has revealed just how recently women's suffrage laws were adopted in many countries around the world, with many of those suffrage laws enacted by male legislators as a reward for women's patriotic national service during the twentieth-century world wars (Table 3.1). Having entered the competition for leadership in electoral systems after men had already established those systems and asserted male primacy within them, however, has kept women at a disadvantage. The legacy of exclusion continues to have an impact on the electorate's voting behavior. It also impacts the amount of material resources and other relevant but less-tangible resources such as homosocial

Table 6.1 Ten Priorities for Public Action

Create more and better jobs for women
Reduce occupational segregation and gender pay gaps
Strengthen women's security throughout the life cycle
Recognize, reduce, and redistribute unpaid care and domestic work
Invest in gender-responsive social services
Maximize resources for the achievement of substantive equality
Support women's organizations to claim rights and shape policy agendas at all levels
Create an enabling global environment for the realization of women's rights
Use human rights standards to shape policies and catalyze change
Generate evidence to assess progress on women's economic and social rights

Source: UN Women, Progress of the World's Women: 2015–16, Summary, "Transforming Economies, Realizing Rights."

bonds that have privileged males who have been long-time participants in political systems have been able to accumulate, versus the resources that women or other formerly excluded groups who are also relative newcomers to electoral systems have been able to accumulate. Moreover, some countries retain discriminatory laws that limit women's options to run for office.

Gender stereotypes, as discussed throughout this text, have also historically sent men and women messages about who "belongs" in the public realm of society, and whose gendered behaviors are most appropriate for leading nations or other political and public-sphere institutions. Those gender stereotypes also contribute to women's unequal status in societies around the world. Because of gender stereotypes that enable gender inequality, women, historically, have been excluded from higher-paying jobs, from educational opportunities, and from highly trained professions that might give them the financial resources and allow them to form the personal and professional relationships that might promote their success in electoral contests. Women may not have equal access to health care, which limits their life opportunities. Or, they may have gendered familial obligations to care for others in the domestic sphere that reduces the amount of time they have available to pursue political office in the public sphere (UN Women, Women's Leadership, and Political Participation).

Women also internalize gender stereotypes and their internal doubts may prevent them from entering public-sphere politics. Some women reject the male-gendered competitiveness of electoral politics, or they reject the perceived lack of morality in the operations of many political systems that would "taint" them by association if they joined the system. Women may not enter the masculine realm of politics because they fear it compromises their femininity. Some women lack the self-assurance to enter competitive politics. They may see themselves as "too soft" for the tough political world, or they may devalue their own experiences and qualifications, even when their credentials match or exceed those of male politicians. Men can be gatekeepers for political parties and may discourage women from entering politics, but women may also exclude themselves from running for political office or entering political leadership positions in other ways (Hunt 2007: 109–20; McDonagh 1999: 65).

Studies that consider how gender stereotypes can erect barriers to women's political leadership do not always take into account more specific historical or cultural differences that also erect barriers for different populations of women. Later in this chapter Ellen Johnson Sirleaf's leadership in Liberia will be discussed in more detail, but studies such as those published by Gretchen Bauer and Manon Tremblay also describe some historical and regional differences that can impact women's rise to governing power within their societies, such as those that have impacted African women. They note that in the history of the twentieth and twenty-first centuries, "only a handful of women have . . . served in top executive positions in Africa" (Bauer and Tremblay 2011: 85). Although women ruled in ancient Egyptian civilization and in some African tribal societies prior to European colonization of Africa, in the modern era, colonization imposed more rigid and differentiated Western gender roles on African men and women, stripping women of public governing power, destroying many traditional female institutions and relegating disempowered women to the private realm of society. Even after African states attained their independence from colonial rule in the mid-twentieth century, the male-led governments that came to power often did so through military coups. The military governments that held onto power were generally led by strongmen, who exercised dictatorial rule and excluded women from formal political participation. Nonetheless, in many African nations after independence, women formed NGOs. During the Cold War era, these voluntary women's associations sometimes formed alliances with Eastern or Western bloc women's organizations or with other women's organizations from the global South through the United Nations and other international forums, and they exercised significant informal power in the civil society realm within their own nations. But it has only been in recent decades that women leaders have emerged from these nongovernmental movements to enter the formal political realm as some nations, like Liberia, have transitioned to more democratic forms of government (Bauer and Tremblay 2011: 88–90). This example reveals how formal and informal gender barriers to women's ascension to political leadership roles are present in many societies in different regions of the world, but different cultural, historical, and geopolitical contexts modify these barriers.

Feminist institutionalism

Recent feminist scholarship also focuses attention on studying the formal and informal gender rules and norms that are infused throughout all institutions, and especially political institutions. Scholars of feminist institutionalism (FI) study the "gendered organization of political life" through conducting case studies of specific political institutions such as parties, government bureaus, presidential cabinets, executive offices, legislative bodies, intergovernmental secretariats, and so forth, to uncover "the complex ways in which gender plays out in different institutional sites" (Kenny 2014: 681). These case studies are focused on understanding gender rules in specific sites, in terms of how they are constructed and how they are communicated and perpetrated, with the goal of building theory to predict gender-biased behaviors and to challenge gender-biased practices that privilege males and disadvantage females in political systems. Institutional gender rules may be "hidden" behind seemingly neutral rules or practices, such as when and where political meetings are held. These rules do not acknowledge the ongoing gendered divisions of labor that determine men's and women's work in the private sphere that impacts their availability for work in the public sphere. Additionally, institutions may value and follow their long-standing "traditions," such as "masculine" dress codes that are a legacy of male-only political chambers. Or, institutions may employ aggressive, masculine styles of debate or gendered military rhetoric in ways that disadvantage female politicians (Chappell and Waylen 2013: 599–601). Making the hidden rules visible "draws our attention to the asymmetry of institutional power relations" (Chappell and Waylen 2013: 602).

As FI scholars seek out ways to transform gender power relations in political systems they argue that "if institutions are gendered, there is also the possibility that they can be 're-gendered' through ongoing processes of political contestation, opening up possibilities for reform at a later point in time" (Kenny 2014: 683). Individual political actors can challenge the gender regimes in historic institutions. New institutions, such as the recently established women's policy offices discussed below, can reject gender norms that reinforce male privilege in their missions and operations. Most FI research to date has studied legislative bodies and formal and informal gender rules that determine women's representation within those bodies, but some studies have been focused on the executive branch of government as well, such as the recently published collection of essays edited by Georgina Waylen, *Gender, Institutions, and Change in Bachelet's Chile* and Farida Jalalzai's study of *Women Presidents of Latin America: Beyond Family Ties?* Waylen notes that FI scholars who have focused on "gendering the executive" study how women have been recruited to executive leadership roles. Or, they have compared women executives in terms of their leadership styles and whether they have adopted a "gender agenda" for their policy making. Or, these studies have sought to examine the formal and informal gender rules that govern the executive offices of the president or prime minister or the composition of executive cabinets (Waylen 2016: 21).

Some of these studies have focused on women's "pathways to power." In recent years, as the sample size of women who have attained the highest political leadership positions in countries around the world has increased, these studies have revealed some patterns in women's elite leadership. Four distinct pathways to power for elite women leaders have been identified. These include the "family path," that is, when women leaders are drawn from dynastic political families that have dominated national leadership positions, and women within these families may have been raised to rule. A second path to power occurs when women are drawn into leadership roles as "surrogates" because they are the daughters or sisters or wives of political leaders, who assumed a leadership role when their fathers or brothers or husbands died while holding office. These women leaders can wield power but they often serve as "placeholders" until a male leader returns to power. A third path that women leaders follow is to enter politics through a political party and to work their way up into the party leadership ranks, coming to power through their "insider" connections. A fourth path, in contrast, is when women enter politics as "outsiders." Outsiders criticize the status quo or bring some new element to national politics that inspires support from the electorate and brings them to power through popular mandate (Henderson and Jeydel 2014: 20–21). Women following these various paths to power may still face barriers to attaining elite leadership positions, just as some of these paths may enable their ascension. Nonetheless, as "women" they must overcome institutional barriers that privilege males once they enter high office in order to carry out their governing agendas. Some women leaders adopt hypermasculine styles of leadership to overcome objections to their presence emanating from their male critics. However, feminists often reject this strategy because it does not disrupt male-over-female gender power relations in political or social realms (Peterson and Runyan 2009: 121). Instead, feminist theorists and activists have developed strategies that women leaders may employ to overcome gender barriers, attain positions of political power, and realize their policy goals.

Feminist strategies to overcome barriers

As Chapters 4 and 5 have explained, feminist scholars and activists and their NGOs have been key advocates supporting women's human rights and broadly applied gender-equality measures. Feminists have documented male bias and pressured governments and intergovernmental organizations to enact gender-equality laws and to make other institutional changes to challenge male privilege throughout the twentieth and twenty-first centuries.

Since the 1970s and the UN Decade for Women conferences and related activities, many nation-states have established women's policy offices or ministries that created new formal government institutions, layered onto the established male-dominated government institutions, just as the United Nations established multiple gender-equality offices beginning with the CSW established in 1946–47 and culminating with the establishment of UN Women in 2010. These national government and global women's policy offices were formed because feminist scholars and activists gathered data and made persuasive arguments that women's inequality was a "problem" that was linked to unrealized global social and economic development and human security goals, and that needed to be addressed by male-led governments. The feminist women who ran these women's policy offices or who held political office and served inside government agencies, the so-called "femocrats," often sponsored gender studies and worked together with feminist scholars and activists outside of government to challenge male privilege and to support women's equality measures from within established governments (Towns 2010: 122–24). Regarding feminist studies that focused on women's leadership, studies documented that when women held national leadership positions, the nation's economic performance and levels of social stability improved. Studies also showed that women leaders generally displayed more participatory and democratic styles of leadership and were better at working through complex governing problems because they were more willing to compromise to overcome partisan political divides. Additional studies revealed that women leaders were perceived to be "more trustworthy and public-spirited" than men leaders (Towns 2010: 170–72; see also Hunt 2007).

These national and global women's policy offices gave women's issues and a few women leaders greater visibility within formal governing systems. With that visibility came some power to influence national and global policy agendas, thus women's policy offices have proven to be important instruments for breaking down formal institutional and informal or hidden barriers to women's political leadership. These offices also have been responsible for monitoring discrimination against women in countries that have signed on to the Convention on the Elimination of All Forms of Discrimination Against Women (CEDAW) treaty and that adopted the Women, Peace, and Security UNSCR discussed in Chapter 4, and for advocating for the inclusion of gender equality as integral components of the UNMDG and the 2030 Sustainable Development Goals discussed in Chapter 5. National and global women's policy offices also initiated gender-equality measurements that have been tracked in nations over time, such as the GDI and the GEM. All these offices and practices have contributed to "institutionalizing global gender equality" as they interjected feminist concerns into national and global political systems (Peterson and Runyan 2009: 124, 137).

Feminists have also studied how the design of political institutions in nation-states can advantage or disadvantage underrepresented groups.

They have documented how nation-states that employ proportional representation in their electoral political systems are much more likely to include underrepresented groups in party candidate slates than majoritarian systems where the "winner-takes-all." In proportional representation systems, women or other underrepresented groups may be included in party-supported slates of candidates in efforts to broaden the appeal of those parties, with less risk of losing all political power in individual electoral contests that pit a male against a female candidate (Henderson and Jeydel 2014: 13–14). Likewise, at the highest levels of leadership, women are more likely to be elected to the position of prime minister in a proportional representation system, than to the position of president in a majoritarian system. In recent decades, most female national leaders have been elected in "dual executive" systems that divide power between a president and a prime minister. However, in these dual executive systems, if the prime minister position wields more actual governing power, men are more likely to occupy the prime ministerial role, and women more likely to occupy the less-powerful presidential role (Jalalzai and Krook 2010: 9).

Gender quotas

Another feminist strategy to achieve a greater measure of gender equality in political representation has been the increasing use of gender quotas by political parties and by national legislatures, especially since the 1995 Beijing Platform for Action at the UN Fourth World Conference on Women defined one of its goals to increase women's participation in government and political leadership (Sacchet 2008: 370). Employing gender quotas that require a specific proportion of candidates within a political party's slate, or a specific number of seats in national legislatures to be reserved for women representatives, is a strategy that is used to achieve a "critical mass" of representation by women, who will then be empowered to promote public-policy agendas that are important to women in their societies (Nanivadekar 2010: 295). Beginning in the 1990s, and led by countries in Latin America, South Asia, and in South Africa, gender quotas have been used to increase the numbers of women elected to high political office. Their use has spread so that, "as of 2006, around 40 countries have introduced gender quotas in elections to national parliaments, either by means of constitutional amendment or by changing the electoral laws (legal quotas). In more than 50 countries major political parties have voluntarily set out quota provisions in their own statutes (party quotas)" (The Quota Project). These gender quotas are more likely to be in place in countries where proportional representation systems operate. Nonetheless, women are still underrepresented in national legislatures around the world, and are especially scarce at the highest level of national leadership (Jalalzai and Krook 2010: 16).

In a recent study on the efficacy of gender quotas as applied to increase women's representation in political systems and in corporate settings that was conducted for the 2012 UN World Development Report, Rohini Pande and Deanna Ford brought forward three important conclusions. They asserted that:

[1] To the extent that equitable representation in policy-making is desirable, quotas are a good policy tool to achieve it. [2] In politics, there is no evidence that such representation has come at a cost of efficiency. . . . [3] That said, we do find evidence that groups that are affected adversely— male incumbents, party leaders, and firm owners—respond strategically in order to reduce the impact of gender on leadership outcomes.

PANDE AND FORD 2012: 3

In other words, gender quotas increase women's representation in political bodies, but male politicians (or corporate leaders) will still resist women-friendly public policies (or women-friendly corporate practices) that women leaders might advocate for when they attain power. Although male leadership may resist change, the attitudes of voters in countries that apply gender quotas in political systems, however, seem to be changing and growing more accepting of women leaders as more women occupy political leadership positions and prove their value once they are in office (Pande and Ford 2012: 26). Feminist activists also continue to support the expanded use of gender quotas at the national and international levels of politics to increase the number of women in leadership positions. For example, in 2000, the NGO WEDO launched a global campaign promoting "gender balance" in political systems, the "50/50" campaign to "Get the Gender Balance Right" (Towns 2010: 158). In 2008, the European Women's Lobby launched a similar "50/50" campaign to promote gender equality in European democracies. These public-relations campaigns publicize gender equality and promote support for democratic principles of "fairness" and "justice," and they put pressure on governments and global governance agencies to include more women among their ranks, through application of gender quotas or other affirmative-action methods.

While gender quotas can and do increase the numbers of women elected to political offices, feminist scholars point to the limits of their effectiveness in transforming gender power relations as they study specific national and cultural contexts. Teresa Sacchet, for example, has studied the application of gender quota laws in political systems in Latin America. Drawing most of her data and conclusions from a case study of Brazil in the late 1990s and early 2000s, a national setting where political institutional rules and social biases worked against women entering politics, quotas did "create real political opportunities" for women and brought a few women into the political system. Because quotas provoke "strong debate" within societies, that is, they are vocally supported or vocally contested by different segments within a population, they can raise public consciousness regarding continuing gender inequalities. As Sacchet concluded, "quotas are worthwhile, then, even when the number of women elected is not increased as a result. The Brazilian case provides an example of this. Although the implementation of the quota law in Brazil has not yet worked to produce a 'critical mass' of women in political positions, it has helped to set in motion a series of legislative and social changes" (Sacchet 2008: 381).

Petra Meier studied gender quotas as applied in Belgium during the same period as Sacchet's study. Meier asked the question: "Does the adoption of gender quotas equal *recognition* that gender inequality is a problem?" To answer her question she studied attitudinal survey responses from male and female members of Belgian parliament (Meier 2008: 332). Survey results revealed a clear gender split in responses from women versus responses from men, indicating to her that gender quotas had not transformed elite male attitudes regarding the necessity of equal gender representation in Belgium's democratic system:

> The majority of women think that the democratic system functions badly and that quotas correct this bias. Quotas are considered to be legitimate because they promote equality and justice. A majority of women also think that quotas fit into the prevailing conceptualization of political representation and do not clash with the principles underlying a fair, democratic electoral process. Nor do quotas affect voters' freedom to vote for a candidate of their choice, or an equitable selection of candidates. Finally, a majority of women argue quotas do not overemphasize differences between the sexes, an argument often used against quotas, stemming from a fear of essentialism.
>
> Men think the opposite of their female colleagues. Quotas are unacceptable because they undermine the basic principles of the Belgian democratic order. They undermine the principle of non-discrimination. Nor are men convinced that quotas would promote equality or justice. This fits in with the conviction that quotas would not correct the poor functioning of democracy. Furthermore, men consider that quotas do not fit into the dominant conceptualization of representation, but lead to an unfair selection of candidates and deprive the voters of the right to vote for a candidate of their choice. Finally, a majority of men are convinced that quotas emphasize differences between the sexes.

MEIER 2008: 335

Meier's study reinforces a conclusion that most feminist advocates would agree with: multiple strategies are needed to promote gender equality in the political sphere. As significant as women's policy offices and gender quotas have been to increasing women's numbers and visibility in politics over the last several decades, patriarchal attitudes prevail in political systems.

Women in elite leadership positions

Feminist scholars V. Spike Peterson and Anne Sisson Runyan have observed that in most media coverage and in many academic studies, the women whose political leadership is recognized and studied are of two types, those who "are perceived as . . . traditional women" or those that are in fact "invisible women," because they act "like men." Neither of these two types of women leaders disrupt gender expectations. Peterson and Runyan assert that, "by appearing as traditional women or honorary men, female politicians do not challenge the categorical distinction between femininity and masculinity and do not politicize this gender dichotomy" (2009: 121).

Yet these two generalized types of women leaders do not do justice to the complexity of the individual women leaders discussed here. The actions of Indira Gandhi, Margaret Thatcher, Ellen Johnson Sirleaf, Michelle Bachelet, and Angela Merkel demonstrate that in their responses to specific historical circumstances, in their relations with other world leaders, and in their ways of navigating their elite leadership roles as women in an international system that historically and currently privileges masculine leadership, they were living up to *and* rejecting *and* transcending female gender stereotypes. To be sure, by identifying a few exemplary political leaders to discuss in this textbook, this text is also vulnerable to criticisms that, like most accounts in the media or in academic studies, it presents a very limited account of women's elite political leadership. In efforts to address these limits, there have been some significant broader-based comparative studies of women who have led their nations in the twentieth and twenty-first centuries, and an emerging body of feminist scholarship that focuses on how gender power operates in political institutions rather than focusing on individual women leaders. A sample of these studies is given in the references for further study at the close of this chapter. Here, these few brief profiles of women leaders are included as examples of how gender rules have impacted the highest level of government offices and how a few women leaders have challenged those gender rules—or, at least have made them visible.

Indira Gandhi, prime minister of India, 1966–77, 1980–84 (assassinated in 1984)

India's independence and Indira Gandhi's political education

Born in 1917, Indira Gandhi grew up in British colonial India, the daughter of Jawaharlal Nehru, leader of the Indian National Congress Party who along with Mohandas (Mahatma) Gandhi demanded India's independence from Great Britain. During Indira Gandhi's childhood and young adulthood, her parents and other family members and close associates in the Quit India campaign to eject British colonial rulers during and after the Second World War, were all jailed by the British at different times. But the instability of the times made her strong and her parents' anti-colonialist politics became Indira's politics. When India achieved its independence in 1947 and Indira's father became India's first prime minister as leader of the majority Congress Party, Indira joined the Congress Party. Although she had married Feroze Gandhi and had two sons, she became her widowed father's de facto first lady, the "daughter of the nation" that stood by her father's side at political rallies, in government, and on state visits to world capitals. These political obligations strained her marriage and after her husband died in 1960, she never remarried. When her father died in 1964, she was already deeply involved in Congress Party politics. After the interim prime minister, Lal Bahadur Shastri, who held power for brief two years, also died in office, the Congress Party asked her to step in as prime minister (Fallaci 1976: 154–56). Gandhi's family background and her father's popularity worked to her advantage over other Congress Party candidates for the prime minister's post. Moreover, "being a woman, Mrs. Gandhi could be expected to be more pliable and dependent on the [party] president, K. Kamaraj" (Steinberg 2008: 25). This expectation, however, was not fulfilled. Gandhi ruled over India with a "masculine" strength of will, even to the point of seizing absolute power over India's government for twenty-one months in 1975–77, when she declared a state of national Emergency to hold onto her leadership position. One analysis of her "path to power, agenda, style of leadership and overall performance" as India's governing leader holds that Gandhi's tenure in power was "shaped by a patriarchal political system in which women in power are there on men's terms and for their survival they have to forget they are women, and that as women they are unequal" (Manushi Collective, quoted in Everett 2013: 168). Gandhi's first term as India's prime minister began in 1966.

When Britain very reluctantly granted India its independence in 1947, it also inflamed religious, ethnic, and caste divisions among the formerly colonized Hindus, Muslims, and Sikhs, and of the elite Brahmin and lower social castes by giving in to the demands of the Muslim League that advocated for the partition of India, as a Hindu majority nation-state, and Pakistan, as a Muslim-majority state. Although the elite Hindu leaders of the Congress Party disagreed with the partition of one nation into two, that also separated East Pakistan from West Pakistan by over a thousand miles of Indian territory, the last British viceroy of colonial India, Lord Louis Mountbatten, gave in to Muslim League pressures. Religious and ethnic violence followed partition as Hindus, Muslims, and Sikhs brutally attacked each other to establish their claims to territory and governing power. A million people were killed in the violence and an estimated ten to fifteen million displaced persons fled their homes, migrating to ethnic- and religious-majority territories. Mahatma Gandhi, a lifelong advocate of nonviolent resistance and India's foremost independence movement leader, was assassinated by a Hindu extremist following the partition in 1948 (McWilliams and Piotrowski 2014: 105–106). Jawaharlal Nehru, who had also opposed partition, was left to lead the new Indian nation to peace. Independent India also had to establish a viable economy to feed the population of 350 million people, as the population grew at an annual rate of 3 percent throughout his tenure in office, from 1947 to 1964.

Prime Minister Indira Gandhi and India's foreign relations

Nehru followed both liberal capitalist and democratic socialist policies as a pragmatic prime minister, maintaining a "neutral" or nonaligned position in relations with the US-led Western democracies and the Soviet Union during the early Cold War era. When he adopted the mantle of leadership of the Third World NAM and implemented Soviet-style five-year development plans following a centralized-planning model to increase agricultural and industrial production, he earned the deep distrust of the US government (Everett 2013: 146). His daughter Indira Gandhi inherited that distrust. When Gandhi became prime minister, she initially took steps to improve relations with the United States. On a state visit to the White House in March 1966, she agreed to President Lyndon Johnson's proposals to devalue the Indian rupee, lowering prices for Indian commodities on the world market, and to establish an Indo-American Educational Foundation that would give the United States more influence on India's higher education system and on its advanced research agenda (and presumably to monitor India's nuclear and other weapons technology developments). In exchange, President Johnson promised development loans from the World Bank and IMF and food aid for India's impoverished population. Indian nationalists denounced these agreements, and when the US food aid did not arrive immediately, this had "a powerful and lasting effect on Gandhi and her style of leadership. Distrust and a deep sense of insecurity had been ingrained in her character since early childhood. Now these became more pre-eminent. . . . These developments stimulated her need for greater control to avoid further betrayals" (Steinberg 2008: 27). She also visited the Soviet Union in 1966 and began to negotiate for weapons purchases and development aid from the Soviets. She also hosted a Non-Aligned Summit for other Cold War–era "neutral" leaders, Presidents Tito and Nasser. In 1967, Gandhi's government pulled out of the planned Indo-American Education Foundation (Everett 2013: 157).

Gandhi regained her popularity over the next several years as her government moved to the "left" rhetorically, and as India developed its agricultural sector with aid from the East and West. Western aid focused on mechanizing India's agricultural production, introducing new strains of seeds, and applying heavy doses of chemical fertilizers and heavy irrigation

FIGURE 6.1 **UN 85279** *Indira Gandhi, prime minister of India and UN secretary-general U. Thant, outside the General Assembly Hall. At left is Sinan A. Korle, chief of protocol of the United Nations. At right are C.V. Narasimhan, under-secretary-general for General Assembly Affairs and Chef de Cabinet, and B.R. Bhagat (far right), minister of state in the Ministry of External Affairs of India. October 14, 1968. Credit: UN Photo/Yutaka Nagata*

that produced a high yield of crops. Improvements in India's agricultural output due to the "Green Revolution" instigated by the adoption of these Western agricultural practices benefited some members of Indian society who owned land and had the resources to adopt the expensive production techniques. Although India was feeding its population by the 1970s, widespread poverty still existed among the disadvantaged lower castes. As these economic developments unfolded, Gandhi also established her personal power and popularity by adopting some socialist economic strategies, such as nationalizing some banks and exerting controls over private business practices to curb the excesses of capitalist profiteering. And, she stood up to the United States when she led India into a war with the US ally, Western Pakistan, led by a military government headed by General Yahya Khan.

India's war with Pakistan and India Gandhi's leadership

In 1970–71, the geographically divided nation-state of Pakistan was undergoing its own national crisis, as the less-populated Western Pakistan that dominated the policy-making power and material resources within the national government confronted demands for secession from the more-populous Eastern Pakistan that occupied the Bengal region of South Asia. As Eastern Pakistan secessionists launched a campaign of civil disobedience against the Western-dominated government, the government sent its army to forcibly suppress the Bengalis of East Pakistan, killing three million civilians. The bloody suppression campaign led to waves of an estimated ten million refugees from East Pakistan who fled into India. The US consul in East Pakistan sent cables back to Washington DC, chronicling the "genocide" perpetrated by the West Pakistan army. Nonetheless, the US government's reaction, determined by President Richard Nixon and his national security adviser Henry Kissinger, supported the Pakistan army and opposed Eastern Pakistan's secession (McWilliams and Piotrowski 2014: 358–60).

During the crisis, Indira Gandhi followed a sophisticated diplomatic strategy. The Western Pakistan government, supported and supplied with military weaponry from the United States, had previously attacked India following Nehru's death back in 1964, but had been defeated by India following a short war. In 1971, following the West Pakistan army's attack on East Pakistan, Gandhi persuaded her generals and government to hold off from an immediate military response. Gandhi signed a treaty of friendship with the Soviet Union in August 1971, and gained assurances from the Soviets that they would support India's position if war with Pakistan occurred. As the numbers of refugees coming across India's borders mounted in the fall of 1971, Gandhi also appealed to the leaders of Western Europe, British prime minister Edward Heath, French president Georges Pompidou, and West Germany's chancellor Willy Brandt, as well as to US president Richard Nixon, to understand that India's position was untenable and that war between India and Pakistan was inevitable if West Pakistan did not change its position and accept the secession of East Pakistan, and the new independent state of Bangladesh. Gandhi recounted the story of her appeals to the Western leaders in an interview with Italian journalist Oriana Fallaci, conducted in 1972:

The truth is that I spoke clearly to Mr. Nixon. I told him what I had already told Mr. Heath, Mr. Pompidou, Mr. Brandt. I told him without mincing words that we couldn't go on with ten million refugees on our backs, we couldn't tolerate the fuse of such an explosive situation any longer. Well, Mr. Heath, Mr. Pompidou, and Mr. Brandt understood that very well. But not Mr. Nixon. The fact is that when others understand one thing, Mr. Nixon understands another. I suspect he was very pro-Pakistan. Or rather I knew that the Americans had always been in favor of Pakistan—not so much because they were in favor of Pakistan, but because they were against India.

My visit to Nixon did anything but avert the war. It was useful only to me. The experience taught me that when people do something against you, that something always turns out in your favor. At least you can use it to your advantage. . . . And do you know why I won this war? Because my army was able to do it, yes, but also because the Americans were on the side of Pakistan.

FALLACI 1976: 161

Other accounts of US-India relations during the Pakistan civil war bore out Gandhi's analysis of the situation. President Nixon "despised the 'devious' Indians" and referred to Indira Gandhi as the "old witch" (Nixon, quoted in McWilliams and Piotrowski 2014: 357). Nixon and his chief foreign-policy adviser Henry Kissinger were focused on "geostrategic concerns" of the Cold War era during the Pakistan crisis. They defined India as a "Soviet stooge" in the Cold War rivalry with the Soviet Union. They supported West Pakistan as an ally against India, and opposed the independent state of East Pakistan, renamed Bangladesh. They sent the US Seventh Fleet into the Bay of Bengal as a show of US military strength in the region, sending a message to India and to the North Vietnamese communists who were waging war against another US ally in South Vietnam. They urged the People's Republic of China, whose leaders worried about regional instability, to intervene on behalf of West Pakistan when India went to war to support Bangladesh in December 1971 (McWilliams and Piotrowski 2014: 360). China did not agree to intervene, thus averting a regional war when Pakistan's air force bombed Indian bases along the border with East Pakistan, and India launched a counterattack. The brief Indo-Pakistan war lasted 14 days, with India claiming a quick military victory and formally recognizing the independent state of Bangladesh. With the quick victory, Gandhi thwarted US plans to intervene on Pakistan's behalf at the United Nations. "Pakistan had lost its Eastern wing, and India was now clearly the predominant power in South Asia" (Everett 2013: 159). According to an Indian journalist, Kuldip Nayar, Indira Gandhi "won the war and appeared to have also won the peace. She was the undisputed leader of the country; the cynicism of the intellectuals had given way to admiration; the masses even more worshipful. . . . She was hailed as the greatest leader India ever had" (Steinberg 2008: 36).

Indira Gandhi's mixed legacy as a national leader

Gandhi's popularity did not hold as India experienced severe economic problems in the early 1970s. High rates of inflation and the rising price of oil led to factory closures, high unemployment, and social unrest. The Congress Party and Gandhi personally were accused of corruption and shady campaign financing practices that fixed the 1971 elections. Gandhi was found guilty of corruption in an Indian court of law in June 1975, but rather than resign she pledged to stay in power. Her critics accused her of establishing a fascist dictatorship, and in response she declared a state of national Emergency and did, in fact, establish a dictatorship that lasted twenty-one months. When Gandhi restored democracy and the country held elections in 1977, the Congress Party was voted out of office. But in January 1980, after the opposition party collapsed and after Gandhi successfully campaigned on a Congress Party platform to restore stability, law, and order around the country, the Congress Party regained majority power and Gandhi was reelected prime minister once again. Nonetheless, she continued to rule with little democratic consultation with others, keeping those who supported her close to her in her cabinet, and dismissing her critics as pawns of the US government or the Soviet government (Steinberg 2008: 39–40). After she resumed power, following through on campaign pledges to restore national stability, Gandhi ordered the suppression of ethnic violence emanating from the Sikh minority who were pushing to establish an autonomous Sikh state in India's Punjab region. A particularly bloody "botched" Indian army raid on the Sikh Golden Temple at Amritsar in June 1984 cost the lives of hundreds of Indian troops and a thousand Sikh pilgrims. Several months later, in October 1984, two of her Sikh bodyguards shot Indira Gandhi dead at close range. After she died, ethnic violence escalated across the country again and Gandhi's son Rajiv was named the new prime minister (Steinberg 2008: 44–45).

Indira Gandhi was a polarizing figure, who experienced many sexist reactions to her aggressive leadership style. Nevertheless, she did not identify with feminism, support contemporary global women's movements, or appoint women to her ruling cabinets. Nor did she advance any specific policies to meet the needs of India's large, impoverished, and underprivileged female population beyond supporting "family planning" to curb India's rapid population growth through a controversial practice of sterilizing lower caste males (Everett 2013: 168). In an interview with Oriana Fallaci, Gandhi explained how she justified the unpopular and chauvinistic practice:

> We must protect families, we must protect children, who have inalienable rights and should be loved, should be taken care of physically and mentally, and should not be brought into the world to suffer. . . . The sterilization of men is one method of birth control. The surest, most radical method. . . . I see nothing wrong in sterilizing a man who has already brought eight or ten children into the world. Especially if it helps those eight or ten children to live better.

> GANDHI, QUOTED IN FALLACI 1976: 170

Regarding her views on feminism, Indira Gandhi believed that for some women, such as her mother who had been denied the right to live as she chose and was kept in involuntary seclusion, a women's rights movement made sense. For Gandhi herself, who had "always been able to do what I wanted," feminism seemed unnecessary (Gandhi, quoted in Fallaci 1976: 170). As independent and strong as she was, Gandhi also stressed her role as a mother who adored her sons, and defined herself as "Mother India," the "mother of her country." In the words of Blema Steinberg, Gandhi "used gender imagery in a purposeful manner," dressing in feminine saris and associating herself with Hindu goddess imagery, such as Durga, the goddess of motherhood who was also known as "the invincible one," after India's victory in the 1971 war with Pakistan (Steinberg 2008: 10). She symbolized and she was, in fact, a "powerful" woman, and this inspired some women to assert themselves too. Ela Bhatt, a grassroots women's labor organizer who founded the Self-Employed Women's Association in India in 1972, asserted that "consciously or unconsciously, every woman, I think, feels that if Indira Gandhi could be prime minister of this country, then we all have opportunities" (quoted in Everett 2013: 171) The mixture of feminine and masculine traits Gandhi exhibited as a national leader of India defies easy gender stereotyping, but they did not transform gender power relations within world politics.

Margaret Thatcher, prime minister of the UK, 1979–90

Margaret Thatcher and gendered leadership stereotypes

Margaret Thatcher, too, has been described as using "a variety of different approaches to her female gender as circumstances dictated," presenting herself to different constituencies, or at different times, as a "devoted wife and mother [of twins Mark and Carol], . . . mother to the nation, firm nanny, wartime dominatrix, and . . . androgynous leader" (Steinberg 2008: 11). Michael Genovese in a recent biography notes that "Thatcher was very adept at sexual style flexing, using a variety of different approaches to her femaleness as circumstances dictated." He also notes that she, like Indira Gandhi, was "governing in a 'man's world' of politics . . . [that] forced her to jettison [at times] all aspects of femininity and 'act like a man'" (Genovese 2013: 299–300). She confounded her male colleagues because her behavior was "perceived as traditionally 'female' and, at the same time, clearly 'male'." Critics and admirers called her, variously, "the best man in the country," "not a real woman," the "Iron Lady," "Her Malignancy," "That Bloody Woman." French president François Mitterrand described Thatcher as having "the eyes of Caligula and the mouth of Marilyn Monroe" (Skard 2014: 85, 94). She disappointed feminists who had fought for opportunities for women to rise to national leadership roles as Thatcher had done, because Thatcher did not, in turn, use her power as a national leader to advance a so-called women's policy agenda or to challenge the male-gendered politics-as-usual international environment by paving the way for more women leaders to follow her into the elite chambers of power. "Practically no one on her staff or in her cabinet was female, and she spent her time in the company of men" (Genovese 2013: 299). One explanation for this is that Thatcher thought of herself as a "politician first," and, at the time she was in power in the 1970s and 1980s, politicians were male. She was quoted by British newspaper the *Daily Mirror* in 1980 asserting: "I don't notice that I'm a woman. I regard myself as 'Prime Minister'" (Thatcher, quoted in Wilson and Irwin 2015: 22). Moreover, although Margaret Thatcher engaged in a high-powered public career when she was also a wife and mother, she encouraged other British women to "stay at home, raise families and assume traditional roles" (Skard 2014: 95). John Wilson and Anthea Irwin have noted that "Thatcher didn't 'hide' her gender as such, but she certainly compartmentalized it and disregarded it in her political life" (2015: 38). In addition, under Thatcher's leadership, British Conservative (Tory) Party economic policies followed what some have termed an "anti-feminist" neoliberal agenda that reduced government regulations on the operations of the capitalist marketplace, reduced corporate taxes, dismantled government social services that working- and middle-class women and children (and men) relied upon, and promoted instead the privatization of government services that brought profits to a small sector of business owners (see Chapter 5).

Britain's Cold War–era economy and the rise of Margaret Thatcher and neoliberalism

These neoliberal economic policies brought the Conservative Party and its leader, Margaret Thatcher, who had risen through the party ranks and held a succession of ministerial posts as elected Tory MP from 1959, through the 1960s and 1970s, to power in the 1979 national elections. In large part, the Conservative Party came to power and Margaret Thatcher became Britain's first female prime minister because voters rejected the failed economic policies of the Labour Party and the economic "consensus" that had come to "utterly dominate British politics" through the 1950s and 1960s (Genovese 2013 271–72). Throughout the post–Second World War period, the Labour Party that dominated the British government had followed Keynesian economic policies that accumulated large government debts through deficit spending, subsidized labor to maintain full employment, and created an "inefficient" and costly welfare state requiring high taxes and that was "not friendly" to business interests. Thatcher's Conservative Party government denounced these economic practices and gained voters' support following the economic recession of the 1970s as global oil prices rose in the wake of the oil embargoes led by the Organization of the Petroleum Exporting Countries (OPEC) and when long-running manufacturing industries closed in First World countries as they relocated to Third World countries with "cheaper" labor costs. Over the course of its decade in power, Thatcher's government broke down the influence of worker's unions over government policies as unions tried to maintain high wages in a losing battle with global capitalist market forces. Thatcher's government gave primacy to private business interests, breaking the postwar "consensus" as it "radically transformed" Britain's political culture. Throughout the 1980s, Thatcher's government put neoliberal economic policies into place, led by Thatcher's vision of "nineteenth-century economic liberalism [and] a free market economy" (Genovese 2013: 279). Thatcher's leadership over the Conservative Party and her commanding influence on public-policy making reigned supreme until the consequences of radical neoliberalism caught up with the party in 1990. At that time, the state of the nation suffered as government expenditures for unemployment benefits rose to "unprecedented" levels as many workers in formerly unionized industries were laid off and it became clear that private business profits only benefited the few corporate business owners. Conservative Party leaders who had dissented from Thatcher's policies had been silenced or disempowered (Findley and Rothney 2011: 282–83).

Margaret Thatcher and Britain's foreign relations

Studies of Margaret Thatcher's tenure as prime minister often focus on her autocratic style of leadership and the importance of her forceful personality in leading Great Britain's domestic politics, as well as in determining her interactions with international leaders and her reactions to foreign-policy crises. Global relationships were changing in 1979, and Margaret Thatcher came to power within a global context of expanding neoliberal economic practices throughout the world capitalist system, the beginning of economic market reforms in the People's Republic of China, the rise of the Solidarity labor movement in Poland, and the onset of a costly war in Afghanistan that would both weaken the Soviet Union's Communist Party government, the Iranian Revolution, and the takeover of the US Embassy in Teheran that would have long-term repercussions for US power relations in the Middle East, and the rising influence of religious fundamentalist movements on national politics in various regions of the world (McWilliams and Piotrowski 2014: 383–84). All these complex macro-level changes were underway as Thatcher came to power, but in many ways Thatcher's foreign (and domestic) policy decisions were guided by her dichotomous way of thinking about the world in "black and white" categories. Stephen Benedict Dyson has asserted the importance of factoring in Thatcher's "lower-level cognitive style" to understand her leadership record regarding Britain's relationships with US and Soviet leaders, president Ronald Reagan and Communist Party general secretary Mikhail Gorbachev, Britain's response to the Argentinian invasion of the Falkland Islands, and Thatcher's opposition to German reunification, which she rejected as a restoration of German power in Europe that could threaten Britain's security in the future as it had during the twentieth-century world wars (Dyson 2009: 33–48). Michael Genovese has described her style in dealing with foreign-policy issues as "resolute, unyielding, nationalistic, rigid" (2013: 285).

When Thatcher was elected leader of the Conservative Party in the mid-1970s, she had little experience with foreign policy making. To expand her international education and meet foreign leaders, Thatcher began a series of international visits. Among those visits, meeting India's prime minister Indira Gandhi particularly impressed Thatcher. She "sat at Mrs. Gandhi's feet and wanted to know: how had she made it to the top, and how had she stayed there? The newly elected British leader seemed to gain confidence witnessing another woman successfully wielding power" (Skard 2014: 90; Steinberg 2008: 216). Although she may have seen herself as willing to learn from Indira Gandhi, in her relationships with Ronald Reagan and Mikhail Gorbachev, the two male leaders of the world's Cold War–era superpowers, Thatcher more often saw herself playing the role of mentor to the male leaders. By most accounts, Thatcher's relationship with Ronald Reagan was very close as they shared a faith in neoliberal economics and a conservative outlook on social policy as the bedrock of their governing philosophies. Their shared beliefs in the inherent dangers of communist ideology and their certainty that the Soviet Union was a hostile power also cemented their enduring "personal alliance" (Steinberg 2008: 221). Nonetheless, at times Thatcher had to press Reagan to maintain a hardline against Soviet power in arms-reduction talks, and to maintain pressure on Soviet leaders to enact modernizing reforms and retreat from military engagements (Steinberg 2008: 11). She also privately disparaged Reagan's intellectual abilities: "Poor dear," she once said. "there's not much between his ears" (Genovese 2013: 286). Thatcher's relationship with Mikhail Gorbachev also seemed to have been based on a quick assessment of his character made during Gorbachev's visit to London in 1984, an assessment that never wavered. When she met Gorbachev and he expressed his determination "to reform an outdated, failing socialist order," Thatcher recalled that "I immediately hit it off with him and that's when I coined the phrase 'we can do business with him'" (Thatcher, quoted in Dyson 2009: 43). With these "special relationships" forged with Reagan and Gorbachev, Thatcher acted as "an interlocutor between the superpowers, particularly in negotiations on arms control, a position she relished" (Steinberg 2008: 226).

While playing this influential role in Cold War geopolitics reaffirmed Thatcher's leadership on the world stage, she established global prominence when she led Britain into a brief war with Argentina and symbolically reasserted Britain's historic imperial power (Genovese 2013: 287). The Falkland Islands, located off the coast of Argentina in the South Atlantic,

FIGURE 6.2 **UN 116911** *Prime minister of the UK, Margaret Thatcher, official visit to the United Nations to address the Second Special Session of the General Assembly on Disarmament, with Secretary-General Javier Perez de Cuellar. June 22, 1982. Credit: UN Photo/Yutaka Nagata*

had been claimed by Britain as a Crown colony since 1841. The islands were inhabited by a few thousand British-descendant sheepherders who identified as British subjects. In 1982, the unpopular military government in Argentina, facing an economic recession and crippling national debt, decided to assert Argentina's historic claims to the islands and launched an invasion. Although prior to the invasion the British Parliament had considered negotiating territorial claims with Argentina, Thatcher and her Conservative Party colleagues adamantly opposed "giving the Falklands away." Nonetheless, the British Navy did nothing to strengthen the islands' defenses, and Argentina attacked and occupied the islands in April 1982. In response, a British submarine attack on an Argentine battleship in May cost nearly 400 Argentine sailors their lives. Argentina retaliated and sunk a British naval destroyer, taking British lives and strengthening further Thatcher's resolve to win a decisive victory and solidify British rule over the islands. After British troops landed on the islands in late May, the Argentine army was routed and forced to retreat by mid-June. With victory, Thatcher's personal popularity in Britain soared and she was pronounced a national hero and a "warrior queen" (Skard 2014: 91–92). The Conservative Party overcame opposition to its neoliberal economic policies and kept the governing majority in the national elections held in 1983. Thatcher's triumphant victory speech proclaimed: "We have ceased to be a nation in retreat. We have instead a new-found confidence, born in the economic battles at home and tested and found true 8,000 miles away" (Thatcher, quoted in Steinberg 2008: 225).

Popular support for Thatcher and her government did not last, and she was criticized for controversial economic and anti-organized labor policies, for not opposing the white supremacist government in South Africa as anti-apartheid protests gathered global support during the 1980s, and for her "overbearing and imperious" leadership style (Skard 2014: 92–93). Thatcher had showed the world that female leaders could be as tough and ruthless as the most hypermasculine male leaders, but these qualities did not lead immediately to greater numbers of women elected to British Parliament. As of 2015, women held 22 percent of seats in the House of Commons and 20 percent of seats in the House of Lords (Wilson and Boxer 2015: 2). Nor did Margaret Thatcher interject feminist values in the realm of international leadership to address gender or other social and economic inequalities, or to transform the masculine conduct of world politics (Skard 2014: 95). To be sure, these were not Thatcher's intentions. They were, however, the intentions of Ellen Johnson Sirleaf and Michelle Bachelet, whose leadership records will be discussed in the following sections.

Ellen Johnson Sirleaf, president of Liberia, 2006–17

Liberia's historical context

Previously in this chapter, some generalized comments about gendered resistance to women holding formal political leadership roles in African nations during the colonial and postcolonial periods were included. In relation to the African state of Liberia, its nineteenth- and twentieth-century history is unique in some respects, although not in regard to the primacy of patriarchal power. In 1820, formerly enslaved African-Americans returned to Africa to form the nation they named "Liberia" to commemorate their liberation. Thereafter, a succession of "Americo-Liberians," all men, governed the nation. Liberian women received the right to vote in 1946. The Americo-Liberians, although a small minority of the total population, dominated Liberia's political, economic, and social order. They ruled over the majority "indigenous" Liberians who were not the descendants of former US slaves, and thus created class and "race" divisions among the population. A 1980 military coup led by indigenous Liberian Samuel Doe overthrew and executed the elected civilian president William Tolbert. Following Doe's takeover, Liberia erupted in civil war. The civil war continued until 2003, through a succession of governments, led first by Doe and then by Charles

Taylor, both of whom claimed the title of "president" of Liberia following elections held after they seized power by force. In 2003, President Charles Taylor, who had brutally suppressed opposition in order to hold onto power, was finally deposed, and exiled to Nigeria. While he held power, from 1997 to 2003, Taylor's military forces committed violent atrocities that killed over 300,000 Liberians, internally displaced over 500,000, and forced many more Liberians to flee their country. The civil war destroyed Liberia's physical infrastructure and in 2003, the nation was mired in international debt, and the people impoverished. For two years following Taylor's ouster, from 2003 to 2005, a National Transition Government brought formerly warring forces and civil society representatives together to forge a comprehensive peace treaty. In 2005, national elections were held, monitored by 15,000 UN peacekeepers. After a hard-fought political contest between the two front-running candidates who emerged out of an initial field of twenty-two presidential office-seekers, national soccer star George Weah and elite, educated, political leader and civil servant Ellen Johnson Sirleaf, Sirleaf was elected. She became the first woman elected to lead a modern-era African nation (Bauer and Tremblay 2011: 91–92; Jones 2015: 316).

Ellen Sirleaf's circuitous path to the presidency

Sirleaf's educational and political background had certainly prepared her for an elite leadership position, although as a woman her path to leadership was obstructed by global and national gender power relations. Born in 1938, she grew up in the nation's capital city, Monrovia, was married at age 17, and had four sons. In 1962, Sirleaf and her husband went to the United States, where Sirleaf worked and completed a business degree. After returning to Monrovia she worked for Liberia's Treasury Department for a few years, then was awarded a scholarship to Harvard University. Back in the United States, she completed a master's degree in public administration at Harvard, and then returned again to Monrovia to serve as state secretary in the Ministry of Finance in President William Tolbert's administration. Critical of the government's financial operations, she left her position and moved to Washington DC where she worked for the World Bank. With this experience and despite her critical stance, Tolbert appointed her minister of finance in 1979.

When Samuel Doe seized power from Tolbert in 1980, Sirleaf briefly worked for his administration, but then returned to Washington, secured a position with Citicorp, and led the private bank's regional office in Nairobi, Kenya, until 1985. National elections brought her back to Liberia in 1985, but Doe's government arrested her as she opposed his leadership. Sirleaf narrowly escaped rape and murder because a prison guard came to her defense and kept her would-be attackers at bay (Skard 2014: 306). Following her release from prison, she returned to the United States and worked again for the World Bank and for regional development banks. In 1992 she was appointed director for African development at the UNDP, a position she held until 1997. In the early 1990s, Sirleaf briefly supported Charles Taylor who seized power from Samuel Doe. Her support for Taylor was short-lived, but it was a political position she would be condemned for after she became Liberia's president. In 1997, Sirleaf ran against Taylor in the presidential elections. Taylor's victory in 1997 forced Sirleaf to leave the country again. She moved to the neighboring Ivory Coast and remained involved in African and Liberian peace initiatives, returning to Liberia after Taylor's exile to run for the office of the president in 2005 (Skard 2014: 308).

The first round of elections for the office of Liberian president in 2005 winnowed down the field to the top two vote-getters: Ellen Johnson Sirleaf and George Weah. Sirleaf represented the Unity Party and mobilized active support from peace advocates and women in Liberia. She also had international allies in the United States, Western Europe, and in UN agencies who rooted for her victory. As an older woman, a member of the educated elite, and a veteran of Liberia's contentious political contests, Sirleaf somewhat transcended her female gender in a male-dominated society during her campaign for national leadership in 2005. Her supporters adopted the slogan "Ellen, she's our man." Her opponents, the supporters of George Weah, threatened violence if their candidate was not elected, with their slogan "No Weah, no peace." Liberian supporters and opponents alike referred to her as "Old Ma" or "Ma Ellen" and the "Iron Lady." Analyzing the discourse of the election campaign that continued into Sirleaf's presidency, Lennie Jones has explained that "through the strategic application of stereotypically masculine and stereotypically feminine discourse, Sirleaf managed to walk a political tightrope during her presidential campaign and elections. . . . [Sirleaf] incorporated deliberately gendered and deliberately non-gendered language, [and] evolved a 'dual' persona of matriarch and staunch political leader" (Jones 2015: 318). She won 60 percent of the vote to defeat George Weah, whom the international media grouped with male African leaders who were commonly labeled as "militants" and "warlords." Liberian women cast many of the votes that secured Sirleaf's victory, and she gained international notoriety for the unprecedented accomplishment of being an African woman voted directly to the presidency, on her own, without family connections or political patronage to smooth the way. Her presidency raised gender expectations in Liberia and around the world regarding what governing problems Sirleaf would focus on, and what leadership qualities she would demonstrate to address those problems. Sirlef's inaugural address acknowledged the debt she owed to Liberian women voters and voiced the commitments she made to improving women's lives:

> My Administration shall empower Liberian women in all areas of our national life. We will support and increase the writ of laws that restore dignity and deal drastically with crimes that dehumanize them. We will

enforce without fear or favor the law against rape recently passed by the National Transitional Legislature. We shall encourage families to educate all children, particularly the girl child. We will also try to provide economic programs that enable Liberian women—particularly our market women—to assume their proper place in our economic process.

SIRLEAF QUOTED IN JALALZAI 2013B: 203

Ellen Sirleaf and Liberia's postwar reconstruction

In her first year in office, 2006, Sirleaf took steps to demilitarize Liberian society and to demobilize the former warring factions to try to stabilize the still-fragile peace. While she had to address economic reconstruction to provide peacetime employment for the former soldiers, she also established a national Truth and Reconciliation Commission (TRC), modeled after the South African TRC, to bring a measure of justice to the people who had suffered through violent traumas in the twenty years of civil war (Skard 2014: 310). TRCs that have been established to build peaceful societies in the aftermath of brutal "new wars" of the late twentieth century were designed to bring together victims and perpetrators of violence in less-formal ways than a formal war crimes tribunal would allow, and to encourage the healing process that cathartic truth-telling could, theoretically, provide. The goal of dealing openly with the deep wounds caused by civil conflict was to promote social reconciliation that would lay the foundations for long-term peace (Jacobson 2013: 236–37; Porter 2015: 88–89). Yet in the final report issued by Liberia's TRC in 2009, Sirleaf was named along with fifty other Liberian nationals, on a list of those to be banned from holding political office for thirty years because of past associations with warring factions. Sirleaf had contributed funds to Charles Taylor in the early 1990s, when he was fighting against Samuel Doe. With an apology to the nation and the legislature, and a Supreme Court ruling that the TRC's ban on office holding violated the named individuals' rights to due process and was therefore unconstitutional, Sirleaf remained in office. She was reelected to a second presidential term in 2011 (Wild and Brown 2013: 191).

The other immediate problem facing her as she entered the presidency was Liberia's failing economy and rampant corruption among government officials. With the country physically torn apart by the war and many of its educated elite still in exile, Sirleaf had to restore a sense of national unity and rebuild the nation. She undertook a campaign of appealing to international banks and development aid donor countries to reduce or forgive Liberia's crippling multibillion-dollar debt with plans to institute new economic policies and reign in corruption, drawing on her international connections to US, EU, World Bank, and IMF officials. She succeeded in negotiating debt reductions from the US government and from the G-8 nations that partially paid Liberia's debt to the IMF, a reported debt forgiveness of

$4.6 billion (Jalalzai 2013b: 213). In taking on the problem of reducing corruption among government officials, she won international praise for appointing women to head key cabinet ministries of finance, agriculture, commerce, foreign affairs, justice, gender and development, and youth and sports. She took on the challenges of rebuilding infrastructure, schools, and health services. As a result, conditions in Monrovia and a few other cities improved somewhat over the course of her first term in office although the country has remained poor and underdeveloped in rural areas (Cooper 2010: 43–44). Foreign investments, including over $13 billion from China, led to improvements in the economy after mines were reopened and infrastructure was rebuilt after 2007; but an outbreak of the Ebola virus in 2014 reduced foreign investment and the economy and public health have since declined. Nonetheless, Sirleaf has received support and encouragement from the international community. She was awarded the Medal of Freedom by US President George W. Bush in 2007, the UN MDG Award for progress toward promoting gender equity and national development in 2010, and she shared the Nobel Peace Prize with female peace activists Leymah Gbowee (Liberia) and Tawakkol Karman (Yemen) in 2011. The Peace Prize citation lauded the three women for "their nonviolent struggle for the safety of women and for women's rights to full participation in peace building work" (The Nobel Peace Prize 2011).

Ellen Sirleaf and advocacy for gender equality

Liberian women's organizations, many that advocated for peace and an end to Liberia's destructive civil war, were a key constituency responsible for electing President Sirleaf in 2005, and one that she has credited for her electoral victory, calling the women voters her "secret weapon" (Bauer and Tremblay 2011: 98). Liberian women's peace and other organizations that supported Sirleaf's candidacy in 2005 had grown in number and in political influence over the years since the UN-sponsored women's conferences had been held in 1975, 1980, 1985, and 1995. As the civil war ended in 2003, these civil society groups advocated for women's equality during the National Transition Government and for a gender quota provision in the new electoral laws. Although they did not succeed in achieving a gender quota law, when Sirleaf entered office and in acknowledgment of women's votes that secured her victory she pledged "to give Liberian women prominence in all affairs of our country" (Sirleaf, quoted in Bauer and Tremblay 2011: 100). She appointed women to head cabinet ministries, referred to by the media as a "bevy of Iron Ladies," and adopted a policy of gender mainstreaming in all government agencies (Jones 2015: 341). In cross-cultural studies, women have been perceived as more sensitive and compassionate and less corrupt than men when they hold political office. These views, and Sirleaf's "vocal assurance of peace . . . couched in terms

FIGURE 6.3 **UN 624737** *Ellen Johnson Sirleaf, president of Liberia addresses the High-level Thematic Debate on Advancing Gender Equality and Empowerment of Women in the Post-2015 Development Agenda. March 6, 2015. Credit: UN Photo/ Mark Garten*

of women's protection, resonated with the general population of men and women alike," helped bring Sirleaf to power in Liberia and were values that voters prized after years of civil war (Jones 2015: 319). Farida Jalalzai, who published a profile of Ellen Johnson Sirleaf in 2013, asserted that "overall, Johnson Sirleaf appears to further women's descriptive, substantive, and symbolic representation and complicates traditional notions of women executive's leadership styles." She has taken steps to combat gender violence against women and girls, dedicated education funds for women and girls, and focused attention on women's contributions to rebuilding Liberia's economy (2013b: 204; 219–20).

Politics, however, remains a male-dominated realm in Liberia, with women representatives making up only 11 percent of the national legislature in 2016 (The Quota Project). Yet Sirleaf's example and influence have spread to other African countries, with African women entering political office in higher numbers than prior to Sirleaf taking office. Moreover, in countries such as Rwanda that have adopted gender quota laws, the numbers of female officeholders are much higher. Sirleaf has recognized her role in transforming gender expectations regarding women's involvement in political life: "I know I represent the aspirations of women. . . . It's an unbelievable responsibility because I'm always under the microscope. . . . [But] because of me the doors are open. Women are running for political office all over the continent" (Sirleaf, quoted in Cooper 2010: 48). Indeed, in 2006, in another region of the world, Michelle Bachelet, who had a similar outsider status as that of Sirleaf, was elected president in Chile, a country where politics were similarly male-dominated.

Michelle Bachelet Jeria, president of Chile 2006–10, first director of UN Women 2010–13; president of Chile 2014–present

Chile's Cold War–Era political history and Michelle Bachelet's family history

Michelle Bachelet was born in 1951, into a nation ruled by a democratically elected government, but also a nation whose capitalist economy and Cold War–era international affairs were dominated by US business interests and the US government's anti-communist foreign policies. By the 1950s, US corporations owned most of Chile's copper mines and other export industries. Corporate interests backed by US governments put pressure on conservative governments in Chile to suppress all left-leaning and communist social movements. When Salvador Allende, a Marxist, won the popular vote in the 1970 presidential election and came to power leading a leftist coalition government against the established US-allied powerholders, he planned to institute a peaceful transition to socialism. Allende nationalized the major industries and the banks, put price controls into place, and raised workers' wages, alarming conservative elites in Chile as well as US business interests and government leaders. US president Richard Nixon and his national security adviser Henry Kissinger opposed Allende's government from the start. Kissinger expressed the US administration's view when he noted: "I don't see why we have to let a country go Marxist just because its people are irresponsible" (Kissinger quoted in McWilliams and Piotrowski 2014: 304).

A downward spiral in the global economy and international copper prices after 1970 deeply affected Chile's economy and Allende's government lost its middle-class support. Conservative Chilean leaders, backed by the US government funding ($8 million was funneled to Allende's opponents) and CIA-sponsored subversion, actively plotted against Allende's government. The CIA enlisted Chilean Army chief of staff Augusto Pinochet, trained at the US Army School for the Americas, to lead a coup against Allende. In September 1973, Pinochet's forces bombed the presidential palace. Rather than being captured by the rebel forces, Allende committed suicide. Pinochet became Chile's dictator, and "swiftly carried out a relentless campaign against leftists and anyone suspected of being associated with Allende" (McWilliams and Pitrowski 2014: 305–06). Michelle Bachelet's father, Alberto Bachelet Martinez, a general in the Chilean Air Force under Allende's government, was arrested, imprisoned, and tortured; he died of cardiac arrest as a result of the torture in 1974. In 1975, the Pinochet regime also arrested and tortured Michelle Bachelet, at the time a university student, and her mother, Angela Jeria Gómez. When they were released from prison, they left the country and lived in exile, first in Australia and then in East Germany. Bachelet met and married her husband, Jorge Davalos, in East Germany and had two children. She returned to Chile in 1979, resumed her university studies, and became a medical doctor. During the 1980s, she separated from her husband.

Michelle Bachelet was active in socialist politics throughout the 1970s and into the 1980s. By the late 1980s, popular leftist protests against Pinochet's military dictatorship were mounting. Women's organizations in Chile played an active role in the opposition to Pinochet. Inspired by regional and global women's activism following the 1975 UN IWY Conference held in Mexico City, and at regular regional women's conferences held throughout Latin America in the 1980s, a Chilean women's movement grew, supporting democratization, women's health, and education (Skard 2014: 208–09). In 1990, giving way to the popular demands, Pinochet allowed a nationwide referendum to take place to determine Chile's future. Overwhelming popular support for restoring democratic rule forced Pinochet out of his leadership role in the government, although he retained his control over the Chilean Army until 1998.

Chile's democratic transition and Michelle Bachelet's entrance into public service

During the 1990s, however, Chile underwent a peaceful transition to democratic rule, governed by a succession of governments representing the center–left political coalition known as Concertación, formed by liberals, Christian democrats, and socialists. Bachelet, now a physician, worked for Chile's Ministry of Health, the WHO, and other health agencies. In the early-1990s, she had an affair and gave birth to her third child, all the while continuing her socialist political activism. She also pursued her interests in military strategy during the decade, and studied at the Chilean National Academy of Political and Strategic Studies and at the Inter-American Defense College in Washington DC. Back in Chile in the mid-1990s, she completed a master's degree in Military Science at the Chilean Army War Academy.

In 2000, Concertación's candidate Richard Lagos won the presidential election. Lagos appointed Bachelet to two important cabinet posts during his administration: first to lead the Ministry of Health from 2000 to 2002, then to lead the Defense Ministry from 2002 to 2005. Bachelet was the first woman to lead a defense ministry in a Latin American country. She gained popular support by voicing her own support and faith in the Chilean Army, even as she brought Pinochet's generals to justice. These cabinet posts, and Bachelet's support from women's organizations in Chile, as well as a perception that Bachelet was a political outsider who would govern with more integrity and less bias than career politicians, led the Socialist Party to select her as their presidential candidate in the 2005 presidential campaign. In a race against two other rightists, Sebastian Piñera and Joaquin Lanvin in the elections, she was one of the top two vote-getters. She prevailed over the center-right candidate Sebastian Piñera in the run-off election, winning over 53 percent of the popular vote.

Gwynn Thomas who studied the 2005 campaign focused on the gendered strategies followed by the three candidates. Thomas noted that Bachelet succeeded in "regendering beliefs about political power and leadership" and in valorizing *liderazgo femenino,* that is, feminine leadership, over the more traditionally valued stereotypical masculine leadership style (2011: 64–65). While Lavin and Piñera both "emphasized a type of political leadership that depended on specific understandings of men, masculinity and politics to simultaneously present their qualifications and to critique Bachelet's," their strategies backfired. They presented themselves as strong, authoritarian, paternalistic men who would "take charge" of Chile's government. They also emphasized their conservative, Catholic family values, implicitly criticizing Bachelet's personal character and life choices. Among many other analysts of this "unprecedented" campaign that brought Michelle Bachelet to power, Torild Skard has noted the various barriers to Bachelet's candidacy that Bachelet's male opponents believed should have prevented her victory:

> It was not just that she was a woman and the first woman elected president of a Latin American country without being a widow or a relative of a prominent male politician. It was about one of the region's most powerful positions as president, and Bachelet was agnostic, a socialist and a divorced mother of three children by two different fathers in a country strongly marked by the Catholic Church. "As the old saying goes, I have all the sins together," Michelle Bachelet commented.

> SKARD 2014: 224

Bachelet used stereotypical gender expectations to win the presidency. She ran on a platform of honesty, incorruptibility, and feminine values, noting that "I can do politics differently because I am a woman. People expect women to be more ethical and caring than men. Because I was the victim of hate, I have consecrated my life to turning hate into understanding, tolerance, and why not say it—love" (Bachelet quoted in Skard 2014: 228). In the run-off election, Piñera's slogan was "Piñera, More President," which meant, Gwynn Thomas explained, that "Piñera was more presidential that Bachelet," that is more masculine, and "that with Piñera as president, more was possible for Chile" (2011: 73). Bachelet turned Piñera's criticisms into positive attributes. She emphasized her *less* authoritarian and elitist style of leading, promising a more open and participatory, consensus-building political leadership, that is, a more feminine style of government that resonated with many Chileans, especially with women (Thomas 2011: 75–78).

President Michelle Bachelet: "I am here as a woman"

Once in office, she did not call herself a feminist although other observers have used this label to describe her, but she governed with a distinct gender consciousness (Waylen 2016: 202). In her first annual address to Congress, she noted that "I am here as a woman, representing the defeat of the exclusion which we have objected to for so long" (Bachelet quoted in Rios Tobar 2008: 509). Women activists in Chile claimed Bachelet's victory as their own and they held "massive street marches" following her election, "demonstrating that her candidacy and victory resonated strongly with their aspirations for equality" (Tobar 2008: 518). Once in office, Bachelet promoted gender quotas for political parties and for the national legislature. Although no gender quota laws were passed, several political parties voluntarily adopted gender quotas for slates of candidates after 2006. Bachelet also supported gender balance in political positions, and her first presidential cabinet appointed in January 2006 comprised 50 percent men and 50 percent women cabinet ministers. She also supported education, funding to improve children's nutrition, and gender equality in the workplace: issues that were important to her female voting constituency. Moreover, during her first term in office, government-sponsored health centers began to distribute contraceptives, although the Catholic Church opposed this and continues to oppose legalization of abortion. As a candidate and as an office holder, Bachelet's political speech promoted gender equality as well. But gender equality was presented as part of a holistic program of promoting the collective welfare and social justice for all Chilean people, rather than as an assertion of individual rights (Cortes-Conde and Boxer 2015: 44).

When Bachelet's first term ended in 2009, she was barred from running for immediate reelection by Chile's constitution. As she left office, she was soon appointed to serve as the founding executive director of UN Women. In that role, she provided leadership for UN women's agencies and advocated for global policies and programs that addressed women's role in promoting global security, global economic development, and gender equality with world leaders. UN secretary general Ban Ki-moon praised her leadership of the new UN agency, however, she resigned her post in 2013 to return to Chile to run for president again when she was legally allowed to stand for office. Again, she defeated her more conservative male opponent, brought

FIGURE 6.4 **UN 645743** *Michelle Bachelet Jeria, president of Chile, addresses the general debate of the UN General Assembly's seventieth session. September 28, 2015. Credit: UN Photo/Amanda Voisard*

the Concertación coalition back to power, and won the presidency with 62 percent of the popular vote.

Chilean women and political power: an Assessment of Michelle Bachelet's influence

In spite of Bachelet's personal popularity as a female leader, Chilean women did not dramatically increase their percentage of seats in the national legislature. In 2015, in the Chamber of Deputies, the lower house, women occupied 16 percent of the seats, and in the Senate, women held 18 percent of the seats. Bachelet's second-term cabinet included 39 percent women; that is, nine out of twenty-three cabinet ministers.

In Chile, as in other Latin American countries in general, women entered politics advocating for social policies and issues that were important to them as wives and mothers. During contentious transitions to democracy, women organized collective actions to demand that oppressive military governments release information about their husbands and sons who were killed or imprisoned or "disappeared" in dramatic and public protests. Latin American women's movements more often advocated for "practical gender interests" as opposed to "strategic gender interests" (Cortes-Conde and Boxer 2015: 46–47). In other words, these women's movements focused on what women needed *as women and mothers*, to feed and support their families' needs, to keep their households intact and secure from violence, rather than fighting for inalienable women's rights as independent and autonomous individuals (Henderson and Jeydel 2014: 83). Latin American women participated in revolutionary movements, but to overcome male resistance to their presence in the male-dominated world of Latin American politics, where *machismo* values governed male politicians' behaviors, they drew on predominant cultural stereotypes that idealized women as good wives and mothers, the so-called *marianismo* values. Women made the arguments that they were compelled to enter the public political realm to fight against the oppressive regimes that destroyed their families (Paxton and Hughes 2007: 233–35).

Bachelet, too, used her gender identity and *marianismo* values to win political support. She has emphasized her inclusiveness, her selflessness in seeking the office of the presidency to serve others, and to bring about a new, more egalitarian era in Chile's history. These messages have resonated with men as well as women (Cortes-Conde and Boxer 2015: 54–55). She has spoken out in international forums about the need to empower women to participate in their nation's economic development to reduce global poverty. She has also advocated for women's necessary and equal participation in negotiating peace agreements to achieve global human security (Bachelet, Remarks at Woodrow Wilson Center 2016). Nonetheless, as Florencia Cortes-Conde and Diane Boxer have argued, although Bachelet has broken through the glass ceiling in Chilean politics, she has not broken down the patriarchal order that controls gender power relations in Chile, in Latin America, or in the international realm of politics. They assert: "To eliminate the glass ceiling completely will take much more than women reaching the highest office" (Cortes-Conde and Boxer 2015: 65).

Angela Merkel, Chancellor of Germany, 2005–present

Angela Merkel, child of Germany's Cold War

When she was born in 1954, the oldest child of Horst and Herlind Kasner, Angela Merkel's family was living in a Germany divided into Eastern Soviet–dominated territory and Western US– and European-occupied territory. Divided by a militarized border into Eastern and Western zones after the Second World War, East and West Germany would follow two different historical, political, and economic developmental trajectories until 1989.

Born and raised in East Germany, Angela Merkel's education and formative experiences occurred within Cold War–era constraints. Her father was a Lutheran pastor in a Communist Party–led state that tolerated, within strict limits, religious expression. Her mother was trained as an

English teacher, a language that was not offered to students growing up in classrooms where Russian was the officially sanctioned second-language. The family lived in Templin, East Germany, 50 miles from Berlin, a city that was within East German territory, but that was also politically partitioned into Eastern and Western zones, with those zones physically divided by a wall built and guarded by the East German Army under Soviet directives in 1961. Crossing from Eastern to Western territory was forbidden, and the East German people's political allegiance to their German Democratic Republic (GDR) Communist Party government and international allegiance to the Soviet Union were monitored and enforced by the GDR's secret police, the Stasi. Raised in this restricted environment, Angela Merkel nonetheless displayed intellectual abilities. She studied quantum chemistry at Leipzig University and earned a PhD. Merkel was working in her field and living in East Berlin in 1989, when the German people seized on signals coming from Soviet Communist Party general secretary Mikhail Gorbachev that the Soviet Army would no longer force the Eastern European satellite states to follow Soviet foreign- or domestic-policy directives. East German dissidents began to cross German borders into Hungary and Czechoslovakia, the two most "liberalized" Eastern European satellites in the late summer and fall of 1989, without violent repercussions from the GDR army. As other Eastern European dissidents who also opposed their Communist Party governments demonstrated throughout the fall, East Berlin dissidents took to the streets. In November 1989, they gathered at the wall dividing the German city and demanded that the guards open the gates and open the checkpoints to allow free access to West Berlin, and into West German Federal Republic.

Angela Merkel's political career

Angela Merkel entered politics in 1989 after the "fall" of the Berlin Wall, as the GDR began to democratize and allow for multiple parties to compete in free elections. The breakdown of political, economic, and psychological borders between the East and West was a "life-changing" event, and most certainly a career-changing event, and one that signaled a new "freedom" for Merkel (Steckenrider 2013: 231) She joined what would become the Christian Democratic Union Party (CDU), a center-right coalition party that sought German reunification, a popular cause that all major parties in East and West Germany endorsed by mid-1990, and entered the world of politics. Against many odds, "serendipity" and Merkel's abilities to learn quickly and approach problems pragmatically allowed her to rise quickly in this new world (Steckenrider 2013: 235).

After the breach of the Berlin Wall, negotiations between the West German government led by Chancellor Helmut Kohl, West Germany's NATO partners, and the Soviet government led by Mikhail Gorbachev resulted in formal reunification of the German state in October 1990. Within the pro-unification CDU party, Angela Merkel was unique: she was East German in a party led by West Germans; she was female in a male-dominated political world; she was Protestant, divorced, and living with the man who would become her second husband in a Catholic-dominated and socially conservative party. Nonetheless, she rose quickly within the CDU party ranks because she consistently proved herself, making "a success of every position along her path" (Steckenrider 2013: 235). Merkel was elected to the lower house of German parliament, the *Bundestag,* in the early 1990s and soon after Chancellor Kohl appointed her to lead the Ministry of Women and Youth, and then to lead the Ministry of Environment, Protection of Nature, and Reactor Safety. In 1998, the CDU lost control over parliament to the Social Democrats led by Gerhard Schröder, who became German chancellor, following a campaign financing scandal. Merkel was not implicated and distanced herself from Helmut Kohl, her former mentor. Kohl subsequently lost his leadership role in CDU, and Merkel's "clean" political record enabled her assumption of party leadership. Then, following Germany's 2005 national elections, neither the CDU nor the incumbent Social Democrats won a clear majority. Governing coalitions formed and party insider negotiations began. Angela Merkel, who was then the CDU's secretary general, was elected chancellor, the first woman and the youngest government leader to hold power since the Second World War (Keylor 2011: 455–58; Vick and Shuster 2015: 56–70). Merkel has retained the chancellorship since 2005 and was elected to a fourth term in September 2017.

Angela Merkel and women's political power in Germany

During the Cold War era, the seven Eastern European socialist states, including East Germany, had all committed to gender-equality principles in their post–Second World War constitutions, and had ratified the CEDAW after the UN General Assembly adopted the convention in 1979. By the 1980s, within the Eastern European and Soviet socialist states, women had attained formal political equality, higher educational levels, and higher levels of workplace participation than in Western democracies. Nonetheless, women in socialist states had not reached equality in Communist Party or government leadership positions (Skard 2014: 326). When the GDR democratized its political arena after 1989, East German women lost a number of seats they had held in parliament, but in unified Germany, women have since recovered those losses in national government seats. In part, this was because German political parties on the left began to introduce gender quotas for their slates of candidates, mandating between 40 and 50 percent female party candidates run for each election. Even the more socially conservative CDU set a target, or a "soft quota," of 33 percent female candidates in 1996. Consequently, the percentage of women holding seats in the *Bundestag* rose from 8.5 percent in 1980 to 37 percent in 2016 (Bauer and Tremblay 2011: 148;

Interparliamentary Union, IPU.org). The current German cabinet formed by Angela Merkel in consultation with other party coalition leaders includes five women ministers in a twelve-member cabinet. Merkel has supported female cabinet appointees throughout her three terms as chancellor (Bauer and Tremblay 2011: 149). Merkel's biographer Janie Steckenrider notes that Merkel has "built a 'Girls Club' of talented and experienced women whom she draws on for trusted advice," who occupy positions in German ministries, in the *Bundestag* and on her personal staff (2013: 251)

Steckenrider also notes that when a woman becomes a leader of a country "the question is always raised whether gender matters in how she governs," although the question is rarely posed regarding male leaders (2013: 248–49). In Merkel's case, observers note gender contradictions. She is most often noted for her calm, reserved, and unflappable demeanor, and sometimes described as cold, reserved, or aloof, and these are not stereotypically identified as feminine gender traits; however, she is also referred to affectionately in Germany as "Mommy," or *Mutti*. And, like many other female leaders from the twentieth century onward, she has also been referred to as the "Iron Frau" when she stood up to her political critics (Vick and Shuster 2015: 70; Steckenrider 2013: 243, 249, 252).

In her position as cabinet minister for women and youth in the early 1990s, Angela Merkel focused her efforts on policy issues important to women. Whether this was because she was interested in those issues or because she wanted to excel in her post, she promoted family-friendly workplace laws and practices and she supported women's education and preservation of East Germany's extensive childcare institutions and women's abortion rights (Skard 2014: 416). In her earliest cabinet posts, she became known as a practical problem solver and that reputation has been confirmed in her subsequent elite leadership positions. Merkel does not call herself a feminist, however, observers note that "her appointments, allies and policies slant toward feminism." She "quietly" advocated for gender equality during her long tenure as Germany's head of government. She has been named *Time* magazine's Person of the Year in 2015, and has led *Forbes'* List of the World's Most Powerful Women for a record ten years since 2006. She is considered "a role model for women worldwide" (Skard 2014: 420–22).

Angela Merkel and Germany's twenty-first-century role in international politics

When Merkel was elected chancellor in 2005, unified Germany's economy was still struggling through East Germany's democratic and capitalist economic transition to catch up to Western levels of production and wage scales. Nonetheless, during her tenure in office she has led the nation to economic prosperity and has elevated Germany's global status in world governance arenas. Although Merkel's strict prescriptions for economic austerity to

FIGURE 6.5 **UN 678657** *Secretary-General Ban Ki-moon (fourth from left, front) chairs a High-level Leaders' Roundtable on "Political Leadership to Prevent and End Conflicts" during the World Humanitarian Summit, taking place on 23–24 May in Istanbul, Turkey. Pictured on Mr. Ban's right: Recep Tayyip Erdogan, president of Turkey; Angela Merkel, chancellor of Germany. May 23, 2016. Credit: UN Photo/Eskinder Debebe*

address the financial crisis in Greece garnered only very reluctant support from the Eurozone countries that were experiencing economic recession and high unemployment themselves, she prevented Greece's economic collapse by organizing aid from Germany and the other G8 countries. She chaired the G8 annual meetings in 2007 and 2015, only the second woman to do so, following Britain's prime minister Margaret Thatcher.

Merkel has consistently advocated for strengthening economic alliances and trade with the United States and for further integrating the EU economy throughout her chancellorship. Merkel's leadership of the European Union in both economic and political matters led to close relationships with US presidents George W. Bush and Barack Obama. With Great Britain's June 2016 vote to leave the European Union and its rejection of further economic and political integration with continental European countries, however, and with the November 2016 election of US President Donald Trump who campaigned for office on an "America First" platform and threatened to retreat from global trade and collective security alliances, Angela Merkel has gained recognition as the premier leader of Western liberal democracies, or the so-called "free world" (Smale and Erlanger, November 12, 2016).

One clear demonstration of her commitment to liberal democratic values and greater world cooperation has been evident in Angela Merkel's response to the hundreds of thousands of Muslim refugees who have fled from violent civil and regional wars in the Middle East, and have sought asylum in Western European countries. European nationalists and xenophobic political factions have rejected the increasingly large numbers of Muslim refugees seeking resettlement in Europe. They have expressed fears that more fundamentalist-Islamic-inspired terrorist attacks on European populations will be launched, and they mourn the loss of Western Europe's Christian- and white-majority identity as Muslims of other races who hold Islamic religious beliefs enter their societies. Rejecting xenophobic fears, Angela Merkel stood up to anti-Muslim nationalists in Germany and throughout Europe. In September 2015, Hungary shut down its borders with Serbia and Croatia and refused to allow Middle Eastern refugees passage through Hungarian territory. The Hungarian government led by Victor Orban shocked Europeans when it rebuilt a razor-wire border fence patrolled by armed soldiers and revived buried symbols of oppression. At the same time, a photograph of the body of a three-year-old Syrian refugee, who had drowned and been washed ashore on a Turkish beach, circulated throughout the global media. The memories of Cold War–era East-West divisions and the desperation of Syrian families that were victims of civil war raised raw emotions among many Germans, including Angela Merkel.

Chancellor Merkel announced that Germany would accept all refugees, hundreds of thousands, with the assertion that "Germany is a strong country, we will manage." She has also pledged up to $1 billion in refugee relief from Germany to the UN Central Emergency Response Fund. She called on Germans and all Europeans to remember their humanitarian concern for others "If Europe fails on the question of refugees, then it won't be the Europe we wished for" (Merkel quoted in Ridley, September 1, 2015). A former colleague in Helmut Kohl's cabinet, Matthias Wissmann, told *Time* magazine in December 2015:

[Angela Merkel] has one principle—an emotional belief, I think—as one who in her younger years was not able to travel around the world. . . . She does not want to see people surrounded by walls. I think she has an instinctive reaction if someone asks for a wall. I know her well. If you ask me what is her main principle belief, it's around this issue: Let us be free. From the station of a person, up to the free trade of a nation.

VICK AND SHUSTER 2015: 88

Merkel has led world leaders in calling for a principled and humanitarian response to the Middle East refugee crisis at the UN-sponsored World Humanitarian Summit held in Istanbul, Turkey, in May 2016. She linked a cooperative and collective European effort to help negotiate a peaceful settlement of the ongoing Middle Eastern civil wars to stem the tidal wave of refugees, and to achieve the far-reaching 2030 Sustainable Development Goals that world leaders had just pledged to support. While her calls for compassion and liberal embrace of diversity have not been answered by other European government leaders whose concerns about increased numbers of violent radical Islamic attacks on their countries predominate, Merkel has continued to issue appeals to European people's better nature, asserting that "the heart and soul of Europe is tolerance" (Merkel quoted in Vick and Shuster 2015: 91). International agencies supporting refugee relief and international cooperation have praised Merkel's courage and resolve to come to the aid of those who are suffering (Smale and Erlanger, November 12, 2016). In her empathy, elevation of concerns to protect human rights and *human security*, regardless of nation or race or class or religion, over more traditional and individualistic concerns for *national security*, Merkel has expressed the values that are the hallmarks of feminist leaders and feminist public policy making, as feminist theorists and activists have defined them.

Summing up

When women occupy leadership positions the mere fact that they are women does not challenge male-over-female gender power relations, although it makes those gender power relations undeniably visible. However, when feminist women occupy elite leadership positions and they bring forward feminist values of inclusion and gender equality and policy agendas that focus on meeting the needs of all disadvantaged populations, then male-over-female gender power relations and related hierarchies of race, ethnicity, class, sexuality, and so forth, that privilege only a small masculine elite in world politics can be transformed. While the numbers of feminist women occupying positions at the elite level of national and international leadership is admittedly very small, they are building an historical record that is taking the impact of feminist leadership out of the strictly theoretical realm and into the realm of "real world" politics. As those feminist leaders pave the way for more feminists to follow them into the ranks of power, the impact of their transformational agendas will become more widespread, more evident, and more popular. And the goals of those who advocate for more peaceful and just global relationships will be realized.

Notes

1 "Women in Politics: 2017" Map, Interparliamentary Union and UN Women, http://www.ipu.org/pdf/publications/wmnmap17-en.pdf (Accessed August 18, 2017).
2 "Worldwide Guide to Women in Leadership: Chronological List of Female Foreign Ministers," http://www.guide2womenleaders.com/Foreign_Ministers_

Chronological.htm (Accessed August 18, 2017). At the same time, UN Women has reported that in 2015, eight countries of the world had no women serving in any capacity in their governments. Annabelle Timsit (July 30, 2016), "Women in Charge: A New Record?" *Politico Magazine*, http://www.politico.com/magazine/story/2016/07/hillary-clinton-2016-theresa-may-angela-merkel-women-leaders-214100 (Accessed August 18, 2017).

3   UN Women, Progress of the World's Women: 2015–16, Summary, "Transforming Economies, Realizing Rights," http://progress.unwomen.org/en/2015/pdf/SUMMARY.pdf (Accessed August 18, 2017).

References for further study

Bauer, G. and Tremblay, M. (2011), *Women in Executive Power: A Global Overview*. New York, NY, Routledge.

Chappell, L. and Waylen, G. (2013), "Gender and the Hidden Life of Institutions," *Public Administration*, 91: 599–615.

Genovese, M. A. and Steckenrider, J. S. (2013), *Women as Political Leaders*, New York, NY: Routledge.

Skard, T. (2014), *Women of Power: Half a Century of Female Presidents and Prime Ministers Worldwide*. Bristol, UK: Policy Press.

Web resources

"Council of Women World Leaders," The United Nations Foundation. http://www.unfoundation.org/features/cwwl.html (Accessed August 18, 2017).

"Global Women's Leadership Initiative," Woodrow Wilson International Center for Scholars. https://www.wilsoncenter.org/program/global-womens-leadership-initiative (Accessed August 18, 2017).

"Speech by Federal Chancellor Angela Merkel speech during the plenary of the World Humanitarian Summit, 23 May 2016, in Istanbul, Turkey" https://www.bundesregierung.de/Content/EN/Reden/2016/2016-05-24-bkin-rede-whs.html (Accessed August 18, 2017).

"The Quota Project: Global Database of Quotas for Women," International IDEA, Inter-Parliamentary Union, and Stockholm University. http://www.quotaproject.org/ (Accessed August 18, 2017).

"Women in Politics: 2017" Interactive Map, Interparliamentary Union, UN Women. http://www.ipu.org/pdf/publications/wmnmap17-en.pdf (Accessed August 18, 2017).

"Women in Politics," Interparliamentary Union. http://www.ipu.org/iss-e/women.htm (Accessed August 18, 2017).

Bibliography

Adler, N. (1996), "Global Women Political Leaders: An Invisible History, An Increasingly Important Future," *Leadership Quarterly* 7: 133–61.

Adley, E. and Connolly, K. (July 5, 2016), "May, Sturgeon, Merkel: Women Rising from the Political Ashes of Men," *The Guardian.*

Antrobus, P. (2004), *The Global Women's Movement: Origins, Issues and Strategies,* London, UK: Zed Books.

Bachelet, M. (September 22, 2016), "Talk Given at the Woodrow Wilson Center," Washington DC: Woodrow Wilson International Center for Scholars.

Chappell, L. and Waylen, G. (2013), "Gender and the Hidden Life of Institutions," *Public Administration* 91: 599–615.

Cooper, H. (2010), "Iron Lady: The Promise of Liberia's Ellen Johnson Sirleaf," *World Affairs,* 173: 43–50.

Cortes-Conde, F. and Boxer, D. (2015), "Breaking the Glass and Keeping the Ceiling: Women Presidents' Discursive Practices in Latin America," in J. Wilson and D. Boxer (eds.), *Discourse, Politics and Women as Global Leaders*, 43–66, Philadelphia, PA: John Benjamins Publishing.

Dyson, S. B. (2009), "Cognitive Style and Foreign Policy: Margaret Thatcher's Black and White Thinking," *International Political Science Review* 30: 33–48.

Eagley, A. and Carli, L. (2003), "The Female Leadership Advantage: An Evaluation of Evidence," *The Leadership Quarterly* 14: 807–34.

Enloe, C. (2010), *Nimo's War, Emma's War: Making Feminist Sense of the Iraq War*, Berkeley, CA: University of California Press.

Everett, J. (2013), "Indira Gandhi and the Exercise of Power," in M. A. Genovese and J. S. Steckenrider (eds.), *Women as Political Leaders*, 144–75, New York, NY: Routledge.

Fallaci, O. (1976), *Interview With History*, New York, NY: Liveright Publishing Corporation.

Findley, C. V. and Rothney, J. A. M. (2011), *Twentieth-Century World*, 7th ed., Belmont, CA: Wadsworth, Cengage Learning.

Genovese, M. A. (2013), "Margaret Thatcher and the Politics of Conviction Leadership," in M. A. Genovese and J. S. Steckenrider (eds.), *Women as Political Leaders*, 270–305, New York, NY: Routledge.

George, R. A. (October 14, 2015), "Where Are All the Women in World Politics?" *Huffington Post.*

Han, L. C. (2010), *Women and US Politics: The Spectrum of Political Leadership*, 2nd ed., Boulder, CO: Lynne Rienner Publishers.

Hannan, C. (2013), "Feminist Strategies in the UN Context," in G. Calgar, E. Prügl, and S. Zwingel (eds.), *Feminist Strategies in International Governance*, 74–91, New York, NY: Routledge.

Henderson, S. L. and Jeydel, A. S. (2014), *Women and Politics in a Global World*, 3rd ed., New York, NY: Oxford University Press.

Hunt, S. (2007), "Let Women Rule," *Foreign Affairs* 86: 109–20.

Jacobson, R. (2013), "Women After Wars," in C. Cohn (ed.), *Women & Wars*, 215–40, Malden, MA: Polity Press.

Jalalzai, F. (2013), "Ma Ellen: The Iron Lady of Liberia," in M. A. Genovese and J. S. Steckenrider (eds.), *Women as Political Leaders*, 203–25, New York, NY: Routledge.

Jalalzai, F. (2016), *Women Presidents of Latin America: Beyond Family Ties?*, New York, NY: Routledge.

Jalalzai, F. and Krook, M. L. (2010), "Beyond Hillary and Benazir: Women's Political Leadership Worldwide," *International Political Science Review* 31: 5–21.

Jaquette, J. S. (1997), "Women in Power: From Tokenism to Critical Mass," *Foreign Policy* 108: 23–37.

Jones, L. M. (2015), "Media's 'Ma Ellen' or the 'Iron Lady' of West Africa? Textual Discourse and the Brand of a Leader," in J. Wilson and D. Boxer (eds.), *Discourse, Politics and Women as Global Leaders*, 315–44, Philadelphia, PA: John Benjamins Publishing Company.

Kenny, M. (2014), "A Feminist Institutionalist Approach," *Politics & Gender* 10: 679–84.

Keylor, W. (2011), *The Twentieth Century World and Beyond, An International History Since 1900*, 6th ed., New York, NY: Oxford University Press.

Liswood, L. A. (1995), *Women World Leaders: Fifteen Great Politicians Tell Their Stories*, London, UK: Pandora.

Lowndes, V. (2014), "How Are Things Done Around Here? Uncovering Institutional Rules and their Gendered Effects," *Politics & Gender* 10: 691–785.

McDonagh, E. (1999), "Assimilated Leaders: Democratization, Political Inclusion, and Female Leaders," *Harvard International Review* 21: 64–69.

McDonagh, M. (July 3, 2016), "Femocracy—Welcome to the Benign World of Female Governance," *The Spectator*.

McWilliams, W. C. and Piotrowski, H. (2014), *The World Since 1945: A History of International Relations*, 8th ed., Boulder, CO: Lynne Rienner Publishers.

Meier, P. (2008), "A Gender Gap Not Closed by Quotas," *International Feminist Journal of Politics* 10: 329–47.

Nanivadekar, M. (2010), "Overview: Women's Leadership in the Global Context," in K. O'Connor (ed.), *Gender and Women's Leadership: Reference Encyclopedia*, 293–303, Los Angeles, CA: Sage Reference Publications.

Pande, R. and Ford, D. (2012), *Gender Quotas and Female Leadership, World Development Report*, Gender, Equality and Development Background Paper, UN Development Program.

Paxton, P. and Hughes, M. M. (2007), *Women, Politics and Power: A Global Perspective*, Los Angeles, CA: Pine Forge Press.

Peterson, V. S. and Runyan, A. S. (2009), *Global Gender Issues in the New Millennium*, 3rd ed., Boulder, CO: Westview Press.

Phillips, A. (2010), "Quotas for Women," in M. L. Krook and S. Childs (eds.), *Women, Gender and Politics: A Reader*, 185–91, New York, NY: Oxford University Press.

Porter, E. (2015), *Connecting Peace, Justice & Reconciliation*, Boulder, CO: Lynne Rienner Publishers.

Ridley, L. (September 1, 2015), "Angela Merkel's Immigration Quotes Show Germany's Response to Refugees is Wildly Different to Britain's," *Huffington Post*.

Sacchet, T. (2008), "Beyond Numbers: The Impact of Gender Quotas in Latin America," *International Feminist Journal of Politics,* 10: 369–86.

Smale, A. and Erlanger, S. (2016), "Donald Trump's Election Leaves Angela Merkel as the Liberal West's Last Defender," *New York Times*, November 13, Late edition, page A8.

Steckenrider, J. S. (2013), "Angela Merkel: From Serendipity to Global Success," in M. A. Genovese and J. S. Steckenrider (eds.), *Women as Political Leaders*, 226–55, New York, NY: Routledge.

Steinberg, B. S. (2008), *Women in Power: The Personalities and Leadership Styles of Indira Gandhi, Golda Meir, and Margaret Thatcher*, Montreal, CAN: McGill-Queens University Press.

Thomas, G. (2011), "Michelle Bachelet's 'Liderazgo Femenino' (Feminine Leadership): Redefining Political Leadership in Chile's 2005 Presidential Campaign," *International Feminist Journal of Politics*, 13: 63–82.

Timsit, A. (July 30, 2016), "Women in Charge: A New Record?" *Politico Magazine*. https://www.politico.com/magazine/story/2016/07/hillary-clinton-2016-theresa-may-angela-merkel-women-leaders-214100 (Accessed November 15, 2017).

Tobar, M. R. (2008), "Seizing a Window of Opportunity: The Election of President Bachelet in Chile," *Politics & Gender*, 4: 509–19.

Towns, A. E. (2010), *Women and States: Norms and Hierarchies in International Society.* Cambridge, UK: Cambridge University Press.

UN Women, (2011), Women's Political Leadership and Political Participation, http://www.unwomen.org/~/media/headquarters/attachments/sections/library/publications/2013/12/un%20womenlgthembriefuswebrev2%20pdf.ashx (Accessed August 19, 2017).

Vick, K., Shuster, F. and Calabresi, M. (December 21, 2015), "Chancellor of the free World," *Time Magazine*, 186: 52–99.

Waylen, G. (2016), *Gender, Institutions and Change in Bachelet's Chile*, New York, NY: Palgrave MacMillan.

Wild, L. and Brown, C. B. (2013), Evaluation of UN Women's Contribution to Increasing Women's Leadership and Participation in Peace and Security and Humanitarian Response: Liberia Case Study, New York, NY: UN Women.

Wilson, J. and Irwin, A. (2015), "Margaret Thatcher and the Discourse of Leadership," in J. Wilson and D. Boxer (eds.), *Discourse, Politics and Women as Global Leaders*, 21–42, Philadelphia, PA: John Benjamins Publishing Company.

Wilson, S. (2005), "Feminist Leadership for Feminist Futures," in A. Sengupta, K. Evans, and S. Wilson (eds.), *Defending Our Dreams: Global Feminist Voices for a New Generation*, 224–39, London, UK: Zed Books.

CHAPTER SEVEN

Women, gender, and diplomacy

Foundational questions

What cultural and gender barriers have "women" faced that have prevented or limited their participation in the traditional, Western-defined nineteenth- and twentieth-century practices of international diplomacy?

How might a greater gender balance among diplomats in states' foreign ministries and in intergovernmental bodies transform the conduct of diplomatic relations? Will the inclusion of more women among the ranks of their nations' diplomatic corps achieve a greater measure of human security and a more peaceful world in the twenty-first century?

Key concepts

Diplomacy as referred to in this text, is defined as the institutions, principles, conventions, and protocols practiced within an international sovereign state system as an instrument of foreign policy to resolve conflicts among states. "Modern" Western European nation-states established diplomatic conventions at the 1814–15 Congress of Vienna. These conventions defined a style of diplomacy that persisted well into the twentieth century: international affairs would be settled through multilateral agreements, international treaties and "soft laws," were often negotiated at international gatherings where balance-of-power politics and the interests of the most powerful nations prevailed. Persuasion was the principal diplomatic tool, backed by implied use of force.

Diplomats sought to resolve conflicts with other states' diplomats in ways that maximized their national interests. The "classical diplomatic model" emphasized rank and ceremonial behaviors among state powers and their diplomatic emissaries. Formal diplomacy was "an exclusive and specialist pursuit" practiced by a state-sanctioned aristocratic diplomatic corps who represented their nations' "political, economic and military interests abroad, as negotiators of agreements, and as liaisons and advisors to policymakers" (Kelley 2010: 287–89).

Following the First World War, internationalist reformers proposed a "new diplomacy" of public negotiations and multilateral cooperation among sovereign nations in the League of Nations forums. Nonetheless, little changed in the conduct of international affairs during the interwar decades although nations expanded their physical presence in other nations in terms of embassies for diplomats-in-residence and consular services to protect private citizens' interests abroad.

After the Second World War, the ranks of nations' diplomatic corps began to diversify in terms of class composition, and, more slowly, in terms of gender.

By the end of the twentieth century, more nonstate actors participated in influential international diplomacy "beyond states," through social movements, nongovernmental organizations, public intellectuals, and others who shaped public opinion that, in turn, impacted states' policies and actions.

Fempolitik as defined by Valerie Hudson and Patricia Leidel asserts the equal participation of "women" and protection of their safety and security should be at the core of states' policies to protect their national and global security interests (2015: 278–81; 321–25). Fempolitik asserts that "women," in numbers roughly equal to those of "men," must be present in states' foreign-policy-making institutions and security operations at all levels of engagement and that women's gendered security interests must be considered "vital interests" in every aspect of states' international relations to attain truly democratic and stable forms of governance and to reduce international instances of violence and human rights abuses. While often constructed as the ideological antithesis of "realpolitik," fempolitik insists that incorporating women and gender equality into the conduct of international relations is both "pragmatic" and "rational," and represents "smart politics" and "smart economics" that improve security and economic development policy outcomes for states and global governance agencies.

Realpolitik is a German term used to describe realist IR theory that focuses on methods to restrain states' aggressive behaviors toward one another to maximize national security. Realpolitik asserts that states are motivated to act in the international arena based on calculations of masculine-gendered "hard power" as determined by their military and economic strength and industrial capacity, but sovereign states may seek a "balance of power" or engage in formal or informal institutional relationships with one another to reduce aggressive and competitive impulses in anarchic state systems. Diplomatic institutions that create efficient systems for communications between state powers are effective tools for balancing aggressive states' behaviors and encouraging coordination to address global security problems.

Practitioners of realpolitik were venerated in diplomatic circles during the late Cold War era. They downplayed ideological or moral considerations when conducting international relations as they sought states' alliances and agreements to manage international conflicts.

During the 1970s, German-American diplomat Henry A. Kissinger was considered the quintessential practitioner of realpolitik when he served as US secretary of state and US national security adviser to Presidents Richard Nixon and Gerald Ford. Kissinger relied on balance-of-power politics to negotiate the Paris Peace Agreements ending the United States' involvement in the Vietnam War and nuclear arms-reduction agreements that temporarily eased tensions between the United States and the Soviet Union, and to reopen diplomatic relations between the United States and the People's Republic of China, three foreign-policy goals that had eluded previous US governments whose foreign policies were guided by anti-communist ideological imperatives. At the same time, Kissinger's amoralistic foreign policies also earned him condemnation as a "war criminal," as he was held responsible for US foreign policies including a secret bombing campaign in Cambodia, the CIA-orchestrated overthrow of democratically elected Chilean president Salvador Allende and providing support for Pakistan's war against India in 1971. At the time of the Indo-Pakistan War, United States and global journalists severely criticized Kissinger's backing of a "brutal and non-democratic regime" against "the world's most populous democratic regime," based on Kissinger's realpolitik diplomacy (Schwartz 2011: 123; 132–33).

Introduction

Can you tell us why there is going to be a significant shift [regarding international issues] like "violence" and "peace" and "conflict resolution" on a sustainable basis [if more women are in international leadership positions]?

I do think that when there are more women that the tone of the conversations changes and also the goals of the conversation change. But it doesn't mean that the whole world would be a lot better if it were totally run by women. You know, if you think that, you've forgotten high school. . . .

The bottom line is, that there is a way [forward] when there are more women at the table, that there's an attempt to develop some understanding. . . . I think we're better about putting ourselves into the other guy's shoes and having more empathy.

INTERVIEW WITH MADELEINE ALBRIGHT, FORMER US
SECRETARY OF STATE, 2011

Today, we are living through challenging times, amid shifting geopolitical dynamics, increasing inequality, and serious environmental instabilities. Perhaps more than ever before, we are relying on our diplomats to chart a course to a safer and fairer world for present and future generations. Should current gender inequality in diplomacy persist, the resulting policy development will not adequately consider the needs of women—or worse, will be completely gender blind. Allowing this unequal, gendered landscape to persist would be immoral and ill-conceived. Immoral because all people have the right to equal participation in political and public affairs, regardless of gender. Ill-conceived because we already understand that policies and decisions that respond to the needs of all genders will have a better chance of success.

MARY ROBINSON 2017: XIV–XV

The history of women's involvement in international diplomacy goes back to ancient times. Women have played formal and informal diplomatic roles when leading their nations as rulers in their own rights, or when influencing male rulers' foreign-policy decisions from their positions as wives or mistresses, or members of important dynastic families or aristocratic classes (Enloe 1989: 93–95). In the recent modern era of the nineteenth and twentieth centuries, however, Western societies excluded "women" from nearly all formal diplomatic positions, that is, from representing their male-governed nations in official state-to-state foreign-policy negotiations or in global governance arenas, and ignored many gendered policy concerns put forward by women when conducting state-to-state relations.

Previous chapters have described the "separate spheres" ideology that Western nation-states adopted by the nineteenth century, and the male and female stereotypes that relegated "women" to the subordinated private sphere of home and family and reserved all privileged public sphere activities for "men." Following these gender conventions, the public realm of Western states' diplomatic relations generally excluded women's participation, although a few exceptional women broke through gender barriers. In non-Western states, women were similarly disempowered in the masculinized international political arena as Western colonial powers determined the international agreements and "laws" that governed sovereign state relationships and defined the protocols and behaviors that official states' diplomats, an elite male corps serving elite male heads of state and government policy makers, followed. These gender power relations generally guided diplomatic practices throughout the League of Nations era, although "women" pushed back against gender barriers and limitations. In addition, other democratizing changes in the diplomatic field were underway, including trends toward increasing professionalization of diplomatic ranks that rewarded merit rather than aristocratic status, that also allowed more women to enter the diplomatic ranks of their nations' foreign ministries, if only in subordinate roles.

After the Second World War, the upward trends in numbers of women entering their nations' diplomatic ranks continued, but without following a simple and linear progressive trajectory in any individual nation, or in the new global governance body of the United Nations (Cassidy 2017: 213). As historians Helen McCarthy and James Southern have explained, "establishing exactly how, when, and why women gained access to diplomatic careers in different countries is not straightforward, as every case has a unique history which requires in-depth research to construct in full" (2017: 23). "Women's" opportunities for diplomatic careers generally increased with the expansion of the UN system. With increased numbers, women's influence on government and global governance policies also generally increased, especially during and after the four UN World Women's Conferences, beginning in 1975. These developments involved women from Western and non-Western nations, although white and educated elite Western women wielded more power to set "women's" policy agendas within those global governance bodies through most of the twentieth century (Jain 2017: 65–66). UN forums and regional governance forums such as those organized by the European Union created spaces for women as political actors to raise awareness of gender power inequalities and to demonstrate how those inequalities affected global security concerns that were most important to still-male-dominated governments in the late-twentieth and into the twenty-first centuries. As historic reviews have revealed, women's "professional advances" in diplomatic fields in the twentieth century proceeded "alongside their political activism through international bodies like the League and UN" (McCarthy and Southern 2017: 28), to the point that, currently, "women have reached unprecedented levels of representation in diplomatic corps and esteemed international organizations worldwide" (Fliegel 2017: 187). One recent report in the *Economist* noted, for example, the rise in numbers of female diplomats in France, where the Foreign Ministry has set a target of appointing women to fill 40 percent of its top public service posts. In September 2015, the *Economist* reported:

> At the end of every summer, the French diplomatic service summons all its ambassadors from around the world to Paris for a week of brainstorming and fine cuisine. Usually, the assembled crowd is monochrome, middle-aged and male. This year, however, it was marked by a shock of silk scarves and coloured jackets: nearly a third of the ambassadorial corps was made up of women, compared to 19% in Britain and 26% in America.
>
> Little-noticed outside the foreign-policy world, France has transformed the place of female diplomats. Currently 48 of its ambassadors are women, a record; and women won 29% of all new ambassadorial appointments last year, up from 11% in 2012. "We've now achieved a

critical mass," says one of them. "Our presence has gone from remarkable to commonplace."

This chapter takes note of the rising numbers of women diplomats representing their nations' policies worldwide. It also examines women diplomats' impact on the goals and conduct of male-gendered state-to-state diplomacy. It proceeds chronologically, building on arguments made in previous chapters regarding gender expectations that women generally demonstrate different qualities than men when they hold leadership positions, and generally elevate different values and concerns in policy making. And it highlights a few individuals who have entered the diplomatic ranks at different points in the twentieth and twenty-first centuries, from different regions of the world. In more recent history, as numbers of women diplomats have risen, they have formed gender networks, sharing some common experiences and policy concerns with each other, but also forming important homosocial bonds, as elite male leaders have historically formed such bonds, which enable productive interactions with one another in institutional settings and positive outcomes in international policy negotiations (Fliegel 2017: 205–06). The examples shared here illuminate the experiences of some important international actors, who happen to be women. Because they are women, their names may not be widely known, but, as this chapter will argue, their contributions to building global peace and human security have been significant.

Women, gender, and diplomacy during the League of Nations era

During the League of Nations era, with few exceptions, "women" were not considered to be "constitutionally suited" to making the hard decisions of "high politics," regarding when and why to go to war, to forge military alliances and arms agreements, or to determine global trade and international financial arrangements. Although the League of Nations was an experimental forum for introducing "new" diplomatic practices, many male diplomats still expressed traditional attitudes from the days when "ideal" diplomats expressed "male qualities," that is, they were expected to be "impartial, imperturbable, and a trifle inhuman." Women, according to the traditional Western elite male perspective, too often expressed "dangerous qualities in international affairs" when they exhibited excessive "zeal, sympathy and intuition" (British diplomat Harold Nicolson quoted in Miller 1991: 75). These were criticisms that could have been leveled at the women who organized the 1915 Women's Congress for Peace at The Hague and devised "The Principles of a Permanent Peace" described in Chapters 3 and 4. These women threatened male policy makers because they operated outside the official masculine diplomatic corps and they rejected international diplomatic protocols for nations at war. The Western liberal feminist peace advocates who attended the Congress and then visited the government leaders who formulated their nation's war policies interjected their "feminist" and radical ideas for establishing global peace and human security into male governing circles, but their Congress's "significance for wider histories of gender and diplomacy is arguably unclear, given that the event had little direct impact on the progress of the war or on the post-war settlement" (McCarthy and Southern 2017: 17).

The "new" diplomacy that was coming into being during the League of Nations era did not fulfill its promises to be significantly more open, transparent, or fair (Kelley 2010: 290–91). But "new" forms of diplomacy did expand the number of forums devoted to interstate diplomatic relations, and therefore required larger diplomatic delegations and missions, located in Geneva at League headquarters and in nations around the globe as embassies and consulates increased in numbers of locations. These developments expanded opportunities for women's participation in foreign ministries, consuls, and in the League Secretariat, although most women entered the field of diplomacy in the lowest-level clerical positions (McCarthy 2014: 56). When a few women entered the professional diplomatic corps during the League era, they often remained in subordinate positions because of a concurrent development. As foreign ministries increased their diplomatic ranks, fewer aristocrats filled the positions overseas and in their nations' foreign offices. The growing prominence of "bourgeois" values in democratic states emphasized merit over inherited privilege, and states' foreign offices instituted specific training programs and examinations to select members of the new bureaucracies. New professionals entering these offices in the 1920s and 1930s criticized "traditional" aristocratic diplomats, with their "feminized" old-style elegance, refined manners, elegant clothing, and vanity. As diplomatic historian Rogério de Souza Farias has explained the transformations in the Brazilian diplomatic corps following the First World War, "new" diplomats, especially those working in consulates emphasizing economic and trade relations, were "blunt, pragmatic" and were often businessmen themselves. The "new" male diplomats thus reclaimed diplomacy as a masculine pursuit, even as women sought to enter the field. To be sure, women in many nations gained opportunities to enter diplomatic offices during the League era, as they gained rights to vote and participate in public spheres previously reserved for men. But commonly held beliefs about the "differences between the sexes" kept women at a professional disadvantage in diplomatic forums, as women were constructed as "overly" sensitive, by nature best "suited to home activities and raising children" as their "social destiny" (de Souza Farias 2017: 47–48).

A few British women whose contributions warrant highlighting them here joined the professional diplomatic ranks at the League of Nations.

Helena Swanwick served briefly on Britain's delegation to the League in 1924 and Dame Rachel Crowdy served as head of the League Secretariat Social Division from 1919 to 1931, as Chapters 3 and 4 have noted. Swanwick protested the limited gendered role women were supposed to play in international affairs, as she was assigned to represent Britain on the Fifth Committee on Social Questions when she felt she was intellectually more prepared for service on the Third Committee that focused on Disarmament, or, "the 'real' business of the League" according to elite male opinion at the time (McCarthy 2014: 120). As previously explained, Swanwick had developed arguments regarding the gendered impacts of war on women and children that were missing from policy debates taking place in male-dominated foreign ministries and global governance security councils during and after the First World War. Yet "someone," Helen McCarthy has noted, was needed to "drag these 'feminine' issues" that the Fifth Committee took up—trafficking of women and children, international refugees, global opium trafficking—"out of the sidelines and into the center stage of international politics." This was the role that Dame Rachel Crowdy took on as head of the Secretariat Section on Social Questions. Crowdy came out of a leadership role in the British Voluntary Aid Detachment (VAD) during the First World War, organizing nurses and other women who volunteered for the VAD's quasi-military operations, where she earned her title "dame" by Order of the British Empire that acknowledged her war service. As League Secretariat section head, Rachel Crowdy worked in collaboration with international women's organizations that contributed the gender-specific "data" they collected from women that they worked with in organizational chapters worldwide. From her elevated position in the League Secretariat, Crowdy could "tackle such evils" that affected women's lives "on a global scale." For those women with humanitarian zeal and ambition, the League provided opportunities to enact their foreign-policy agendas within the most elite enclaves of male power (McCarthy 2014: 121–24).

Women, gender, and diplomacy at the United Nations

While women played very circumscribed diplomatic roles at the League of Nations, some nations began to recognize the value of female emissaries when they sent delegations to the new-formed United Nations after 1945. Once again, women were in a distinct minority, but it was a minority that made its impact on UN values and operations from the UN's inception.

As Chapter 4 noted, there were just a few women sent to represent their nations with "full delegate" status to the first UN Organizational

Conference in San Francisco in 1945, from Canada, China, the Dominican Republic, and Brazil, but these women, and in particular the delegate from Brazil, Bertha Lutz, pushed the mostly male delegates to include important commitments to gender equality in the UN Charter. Lutz also overcame opposition from several other female representatives who attended the San Francisco Conference as part of the US and British delegations, who objected to the establishment of a UN Commission on the Status of Women (CSW). Lutz, along with her Latin American allies Minerva Bernardino and Amalia Castillo Ledón from the Dominican Republic and Mexico and Jessie Street from Australia, prevailed in their arguments that a CSW was necessary to overcome still-entrenched patriarchal attitudes among the mostly male government leaders and to promote women's rights in UN policies and in UN member states. While US delegate Virginia Gildersleeve, and British delegates Florence Horsbrugh and Ellen Wilkinson, did not want the women who participated at the United Nations "to be confined to the 'woman's" field' as they believed women would be if a CSW was formed, Bertha Lutz and Jessie Street vocally advocated for the commission, and their position represented the majority view. They also lobbied for inclusion of Article 8 in the UN Charter, opening all positions at the UN equally to men and women (Sluga 2013: 90). As a reward for her highly visible women's rights advocacy, Bertha Lutz "was swiftly named *Lutzwaffe* by some (masculine) wits on the U.S. delegation" (McCarthy 2014: 156).

World Young Women's Christian Association general secretary Ruth Woodsmall also attended the San Francisco Conference, as many NGOs' representatives attended to advocate for a greater role for NGOs in the new global governance system. She observed the debates among women regarding competing feminist strategies to achieve their common goal: gender equality in principle and practice at the new United Nations Organization. As Woodsmall reported to the women of her organization:

> The struggle to get women recognized in the Charter of the United Nations was led by Jessie Street (Australia), Bertha Lutz (Brazil), and Minerva Bernardino (Dominica Republic), aided by Amalia Ledon (Mexico) and Isabel Urdanta (Venezuela). These women spearheaded the movement to get a special clause included in the Charter specifying the eligibility of women to hold any position within the United Nations system (Article 8). . . .
>
> In arguing for the inclusion of Article 8 . . . Jessie Street pointed out that in practically every country in the world at the time women were excluded from occupying various positions just because the law did not specifically state that women were eligible. Bertha Lutz added that it had always been held that women were included in the general term "men," and that this also resulted in women being precluded from taking part in public affairs.

That such a statement on the status of women was necessary, she went on, was proved by looking at the number of women participating in the Conference. Only 1% of the delegates were women, and there were no women in the policy making body of the United Nations.

WOODSMALL, QUOTED IN GARNER 2010: 141

In the first decade at the United Nations, corresponding with the first years of India's postcolonial independence, India's Congress party government led by Jawaharlal Nehru sent two women to represent its national interests at the UN, and they both distinguished themselves in the global governance body. Hansa Mehta had been active in the independence movement, and when India officially proclaimed independence on August 15, 1947, she presented the Indian national flag to the new national representative assembly "on behalf of the women of India" (Ravichandran 2016). She was an elected member of India's national assembly from 1946 to 1949 and drafted the India Women's Charter of Rights and Duties, calling for women's equal civil rights, and rights to education and health care, equal to those of Indian men. As Mehta noted in her presentation of the Women's Charter to the Indian national assembly, "We have never asked for privileges. The women's organization to which I have the honour to belong [All India Women's Conference] has never asked for reserved seats, for quotas, or for separate electorates. What we have asked for is social justice, economic justice and political justice" (Ravichandran 2016). Mehta also served as India's appointed delegate to the UN Commission on Human Rights. There, she disagreed with Commission Chair Eleanor Roosevelt, and prevailed on the commission to change the language of the Universal Declaration of Human Rights from "All *men* are born free and equal" to "All *human beings* are born free and equal." She continued to champion women's human rights during her tenure on the commission, and as India's delegate to the CSW (Jain 2017: 71).

India's Congress government also appointed Prime Minister Jawaharlal Nehru's sister, Vijaya Lakshmi Pandit, as its national delegate to the UN General Assembly. Like her well-known political family, Pandit had been active in the Quit India campaign, and was jailed by the British government for her beliefs and civil disobedience. Also a leading member of the All India Women's Conference as Hansa Mehta was, Pandit was a staunch advocate for women's equal rights in India. She earned a global reputation, however, as a spokeswoman for the anti-imperialist sentiments expressed by independence movements in the Third World. As Priya Ravichandran has asserted in a biographical essay, "Vijaya Lakshmi Pandit was the face of Indian women on the international stage, and the voice of a country seeking its tryst with destiny, for an international audience. She was in many ways responsible for articulating, arguing and asserting India's foreign policy, and building its profile in a post-colonial world" (Ravichandran 2016). Pandit was present at the 1945 UN Conference in San Francisco. Recently released from jail, Pandit was part of a British delegation representing India. She delivered a bold speech demanding India's immediate independence to the delegations of the fifty-one original UN member states. A British diplomat at the UN Conference, Philip Noel-Baker, remembered later that "it was a glorious oratorical success. . . . But it was much more. It convinced those delegates who had been doubtful that, if India could produce such women, India could herself most assuredly control her national affairs. . . . A great blow was struck that morning for . . . the necessary decolonization of the world" (Mallik 2006: 7).

Following the 1945 UN Organizing Conference, Pandit toured the United States to build support for India's independence from colonial rule. As India's delegate to the United Nations in 1946, she delivered an infamous address to the General Assembly, standing up to South Africa's venerated leader Jan Smuts, criticizing South Africa's policy of *apartheid* that discriminated against Indian workers in South Africa. Pandit gave a rousing speech against imperialism, and called on all UN members to put into practice the principles articulated in the UN Charter:

India firmly believes that imperialism, political, economic or social, and in whatever part of the world it may exist and by whomsoever it may be established and perpetrated, is totally inconsistent with the objects and purposes of the United Nations, and of its Charter. The sufferings, the frustrations, the violation of human dignity and the challenge to world peace, freedom and security that Empire represents must be one of the prime concerns of this parliament of the world's people. Millions look to us to resist and end imperialism in all its forms, even as they rely upon us to crush the last vestiges of fascism and Nazism.

India holds that the independence of all colonial peoples is the vital concern of freedom-loving peoples everywhere. She looks with confidence to the United Nations to give to the exploited millions of the world faith and hope that their liberation is at hand.

VIJAYA LAKSHMI PANDIT, OCTOBER 25, 1946

Pandit's appeal led to a UN resolution condemning South Africa, in a hard-fought vote that expressed the will of the non-Western member-state majority at the United Nations. Throughout the gendered debate over whether to sanction South Africa's racial discrimination laws, male opponents of the resolution criticized the "emotional" arguments put forward by Pandit and other supporters of the resolution, even as they "expressed intense anger, frustration, and indignation, and resorted to personal insult on more than one occasion." In the end, "Pandit's fight against racism in South Africa became a proxy through which communities invested in the ideals of the UN framed their own struggles" (Laut 2016: 9–10).

FIGURE 7.1 UN 372908 *Vijaya Lakshmi Pandit, of India, president of the eighth session of the UN General Assembly, with UN secretary-general Dag Hammarskjöld in the Security Council chamber before the meeting of Steering Committee. September 16, 1953. Credit: UN Photo/AF*

Pandit went on to serve as India's ambassador to the United States and to the Soviet Union in the late 1940s, serving concurrently in these ambassadorial posts to the rival Cold War superpowers, as well as India's delegate to the United Nations. During the eighth UN General Assembly, 1952–53, Pandit was the first woman elected as president of the Assembly, "a major achievement in the masculine and Western dominated field of diplomacy." This was an especially unlikely accomplishment as she had to overcome Western gender *and race* stereotypes in Western males' "firmly established view of an Indian woman—a clinging vine subservient to all manner of caste restrictions" (Devenish 2013: 287). Pandit's election succeeded as she was "an acknowledged leader of the newly emerging Arab-Asian bloc." In another diplomatic triumph in her stellar career, she became India's high commissioner to Great Britain in 1954, "consolidating the former colony's new status as an independent and equal state within the community of nations." Her diplomatic career continued in a less-official capacity in the early 1960s when she represented her brother in talks with European leaders. In the mid-1960s she returned home to take part in India's national politics, as an appointed provincial governor (Plotke 2015).

The delayed advance of the woman diplomat in the United States and Great Britain

In the nations that have long considered themselves to be the leading democratic powers in the "free world," the United States and Great Britain, women's entry into their nations' diplomatic corps has been slow. In the United States, Ruth Bryan Owen was the first woman appointed to head an embassy abroad, appointed as US ambassador to Denmark in 1934 by President Franklin Roosevelt. Owen was a widow, and she was well-connected to President Roosevelt and his wife Eleanor, therefore overcoming the objections to married women serving in ambassadorial roles. And she was sent to a Scandinavian nation where women holding diplomatic roles was not an unheard-of concept; even during the League of Nations era (Linder 2001). The British Foreign Service Office had resisted opening diplomatic posts to women until 1946, worried that "foreign officials would not take female diplomats seriously, . . . female diplomats would be limited in their mobility . . . as a result of marriage and motherhood, and . . . women were physically and temperamentally too delicate for overseas service" (McCarthy 2016: 169). In 1946, British women were finally allowed to take the civil service exams to gain entrance into the diplomatic ranks.

Women serving in diplomatic posts through the US. State Department and the British Foreign Office in the early Cold War era both confronted gender barriers from the mostly male diplomatic ranks. In Britain, Helen McCarthy explained that "after 1946, female diplomats had to manage their femininity carefully, deploying it strategically in the context of inter-personal relations with male colleagues or professional contacts, but reining it in when faced with questions of structural inequality or sexual politics, . . . or in the ideological content of foreign policy" (McCarthy 2016: 179). The experiences of American diplomat Eleanor Lansing Dulles echo British women's experiences during these early Cold War years. Eleanor Dulles never rose higher than a "mid-level position" in the State Department Division of Postwar Planning, even though one of her brothers, John Foster Dulles, became secretary of state, and another brother, Allen Dulles, directed the CIA during the Eisenhower administration in the 1950s. Despite her "insider" connections to US foreign-policy elite, Eleanor Dulles was never able to rise to a senior position within the State Department "boys club." She had to employ gendered strategies to get access to policy makers in postwar Germany and Austria, entertaining as diplomatic wives had done in previous generations and acting as if she held a high rank, even when she did not. Dulles wanted to succeed on her merits, but gender barriers prevented her from attaining her goals (Dunn 1992: 123, 133).

Both the US State Department and British Foreign Office excluded married women from serving in overseas posts until the early 1970s. At that time, the US and British diplomatic services lifted the "marriage bars," a result of agitation by feminist government insiders and outsider NGO activists working together to expose gender discrimination and break down gender barriers. As more women who came of age during the post–Second World War era entered ambassadorial positions in both countries during the 1980s and 1990s, they rose further in the diplomatic ranks than their predecessors did as they benefited from rising consciousness supporting gender equality in both the United States and British societies, but they also represented their nations' foreign policies, and that fact restrained any radical feminist expressions of opinion. As Helen McCarthy explained regarding the British Foreign Office, "Female diplomats naturally played a part in forcing the Foreign Office to recognize that women's aspirations had changed. . . . Yet many disliked the 'militant' tone of second-wave feminism and continued to adopt the individualistic outlook of the post-war pioneer generation. . . . [F]emale diplomats preferred evolution" over revolution (McCarthy 2014: 285).

Women's roles in their nation's diplomatic corps have evolved, especially over the last few decades of the twentieth century and into the twenty-first century. The numbers of women holding leading "permanent representative" posts at the ambassadorial rank at United Nations, for example, have risen to forty-one out of 193 member nations; that is, 20 percent in 2016 of the whole body. In 2014, there were six women permanent representatives serving terms in the most elite ranks of the UN Security Council (Fliegel 2017: 187). Some of these women, such as Sweden's foreign minister Margot Wallström, specifically advocated for "feminist foreign policies" within their governments and at the United Nations, as Chapter 2 has explained. Others, such as British diplomat Baroness Catherine Ashton, the EU representative for foreign affairs from 2009 to 2014, her successor at the EU, Federica Mogherini, who previously held the position of Italy's minister for foreign affairs, and Wendy Sherman, US under-secretary of state for political affairs, have played leading diplomatic roles in multilateral negotiations of the highest consequence. In their cases, their feminine diplomatic skills were responsible for reaching agreement with Iran's Islamic government to halt their nuclear weapons-development project in July 2015.

Women, gender, and diplomatic relations with Iran

In moving forward toward a world where more creative and fruitful problem solving prevails in international relations practice, consider the role of women and their feminine and feminist leadership traits that brought about a positive development in the long-standing international problem of nuclear weapons proliferation in the Middle East. Consider the story of the women who brokered a compromise settlement between the United States, Western European powers, intergovernmental agencies, and Iran.

The United States and Iran had a history of contentious relations dating back to the early Cold War era. At that time, the US government, through covert CIA operations, intervened in Iranian affairs in 1953 to aid conservative forces that toppled the elected leader, Prime Minister Mohammad Mosaddegh, because Mosaddegh was suspected of pro-Soviet or communist sympathies. Following Mosaddegh's fall from power, the US government supported the elevation of an autocratic but pro-Western leader, Shah Muhammad Reza Pahlavi. The Shah held onto power and received millions of dollars in US foreign aid for over two decades. The Shah's reign ended when fundamentalist Islamic clerics led by the Ayatollah Khomeini organized a popular revolution that forced the Shah from power in 1979. The Islamic Revolution put the clerics in charge of the nation. When US president Jimmy Carter allowed the exiled Shah to come to the United States for medical treatment, Iranian revolutionaries struck at the symbol of US power in Teheran. They seized the US embassy building and held US government officials and employees hostage for 444 days. President Carter's decision to launch a military mission to rescue the American hostages failed miserably, and fueled the tense international conflict. Although the Iranian government released the US hostages after President Carter left office in January 1981, the United States and Iran have been on opposite sides of Middle Eastern regional conflicts since that time. The Iranian government issued many statements vehemently rejecting the United States' military and diplomatic presence in Middle Eastern nations and condemning US support for the Jewish state of Israel. Therefore, Iran's efforts to build nuclear weapons over the past decade were seen by the US government and its Western Allies as an aggressive threat to international security.

After these long years of conflict and deeply held grievances on the parts of the US and Iranian government leaders, and the International Atomic Energy Agency's attempts to monitor and block Iran's nuclear weapons-development programs, a recent round of negotiations broke through the international impasse in July 2015. What was the new factor that allowed the first step toward a permanent rapprochement? Women joined the UN and US negotiating teams. Federica Mogherini, the high representative for foreign affairs and security policy, led the negotiating team for the Western powers. Her diplomatic style, as described by Argentina's foreign minister Susana Malcorra, is distinctly feminine, and was effective in achieving results: "Her soft spoken manner has allowed her to forcefully push for compromise when needed and to be the voice of conscience when required. Federica has mastered the difficult balance between these seeming competing tracks," that is, she succeeded in showing her authority without becoming aggressive, opening herself to male criticism. Mogherini's predecessor at the EU, Catherine Ashton, a British Baroness and Labour Party politician, described as "self-effacing" and always willing to give credit to others, laid

FIGURE 7.2 **UN 564323** *Secretary-General Ban Ki-moon (center) meets with the members of the Middle East Diplomatic Quartet (from left): Catherine Ashton, European Union high representative for Foreign Affairs and Security Policy; John F. Kerry, US secretary of state; Sergey V. Lavrov, minister for foreign affairs of the Russian federation; and Tony Blair, special envoy of the quartet. September 27, 2013. Credit: UN Photo/Eskinder Debebe*

the groundwork of relationship-building with the Iranians with an interim agreement that led to a Joint Comprehensive Plan of Action two years later. Mogherini's deputy, Helga Schmid, and Wendy Sherman, US under-secretary of state for political affairs, also played key roles in advancing negotiations for a nuclear "deal" that froze Iran's nuclear weapons-development programs in exchange for lifting economic sanctions that were dragging down Iran's economy. Journalists have credited these women as the facilitators of the 2015 "P5 + 1" negotiating team that met with Iranian diplomats (P5 refers to the five permanent members of the UN Security Council: China, France, Russia, the United Kingdom, and the United States; plus 1 refers to Germany).

These women brought their expertise, technical knowledge, and political and diplomatic skills into the negotiating sessions. Although all the Iranian negotiators were male and they represented a government that institutionalized patriarchal power, the women negotiators were instrumental in forging a deal that slowed the pace of development and increased transparency regarding Iran's nuclear weapons program, steps that increased regional and global security. Future historians will build on

FIGURE 7.3 **UN 646117** M. Javad Zarif, minister for foreign affairs of the Islamic Republic of Iran, with Federica Mogherini, EU high representative for foreign affairs and security policy, meeting with representatives of the five permanent members of the Security Council (China, France, the Russian Federation, the United Kingdom, and the United States), plus Germany—the so-called "P5 + 1." September 28, 2015. Credit: UN Photo/Eskinder Debebe

journalistic accounts of the influence wielded by these women to add details to what is currently acknowledged and praised by world government leaders. This final example is included here to invite students of international history and international relations, who may not have previously considered the integral role of women and gender power relations in international affairs, to think more deeply about these gender issues and what feminist women's participation in policy making might mean for the future of world politics.

Summing up

This textbook began with the assertion that the influence of "women" and gender power relationships have been traditionally undervalued in the study and practice of International History and International Relations. This text has provided theoretical arguments and evidence drawn from many empirical studies to demonstrate that "women" have always been present, shaping international history and challenging Western-defined male-over-female gender power relations. But this historical evidence also reveals a path forward: scholars and global policy makers and elite national leaders, that is, the academics and the practitioners who seek to transform unequal and contentious international relationships and to create a more just and secure and peaceful world, must address gender inequalities and other linked inequalities and must challenge hegemonic masculine power that benefits only a small segment of humanity.

This textbook has presented a broader base of knowledge, gleaned from a growing body of gender studies scholarship, than is usually presented in international history texts, with the goal of deepening our understanding of the workings of the international system. The chapters in this book include feminist critiques of male-defined and masculine-biased IR theories. They have presented a synthesis of published scholarship that shows correlations between higher levels of gender equality in positions of political power and greater national and international security, lower instances of violence and human rights abuses, and more equitable sharing of the benefits of economic development including lower levels of extreme poverty and improved levels of health. When privileged masculine power-holders exclude women, feminine-gendered approaches, and feminist insights from government and intergovernmental policy-making bodies, and when they deny the negative impacts of male-over-female gender power relations on societies worldwide, there is a continual perpetuation of global problems that have long historic roots: war, violations of human rights, poverty, and environmental degradation, and so on. Or worse, these global problems are accepted as inevitable and unsolvable dilemmas of human civilization.

References for further study

Cassidy, J. A. (2017), *Gender and Diplomacy*, New York, NY: Routledge.
McCarthy, H. (2014), *Women of the World: The Rise of the Female Diplomat*, London, UK: Bloomsbury Publishing.
Sluga, G. and James, C. (2016), *Women, Diplomacy and International Politics Since 1500*, New York, NY: Routledge.

Web resources

Association for Diplomatic Studies and Training Oral History Interviews, over 2000 oral history Interviews with former U.S. diplomats. http://adst.org/oral-history/oral-history-interviews/ (Accessed August 23, 2017).
British Diplomatic Oral History Programme (BDOHP), established in 1995 to record the memories of retired diplomats who had achieved high rank,

Churchill Archives Centre, Cambridge, UK. Transcripts at http://www.chu.cam. ac.uk/archives/collections/BDOHP (Accessed August 23, 2017).

"Madeleine Albright: On Being a Woman and a Diplomat" (18 February 2011), TED Talk Forum, Interviewed by Pat Mitchell from the Paley Center. https:// www.youtube.com/watch?v=ioMpOr7Yx98 (Accessed August 23, 2017).

Bibliography

Amani, E. (October 30, 2016), "Gendered Diplomacy, Human Rights and the Role of Women in Making the Iran Deal," *Iran Human Rights Review*, http://www. truth-out.org/news/item/38163-gendered-diplomacy-human-rights-and-the-role-of-women-in-making-the-iran-deal (Accessed November 16, 2017).

Bindi, F. (October 7, 2014), "Women Leaders in Foreign Policy: When Federica Mogherini Found Her Voice," *Huffington Post: The Blog*, https://www. huffingtonpost.com/federiga-bindi/women-leaders-in-foreign_b_5946668.html (Accessed November 16, 2017).

Blair, D. (November 24, 2013), "Iran Nuclear Deal Takes Catherine Ashton from 'Zero' to 'Hero'," *The Telegraph*, http://www.telegraph.co.uk/news/worldnews/europe/eu/10471355/Iran-nuclear-deal-takes-Catherine-Ashton-from-zero-to-hero.html (Accessed November 16, 2017).

Cassidy, J. A. (2017), "Conclusion: Progress and Policies Towards a Gender-Even Playing Field" in J. A. Cassidy (ed.), *Gender and Diplomacy*, 210–18, New York, NY: Routledge.

De la Baume, M. (July 17, 2015), "The Women Behind the Iran Nuclear Deal," *Politico*, https://www.politico.eu/article/the-women-behind-the-nuclear-deal/ (Accessed November 16, 2017).

de Sousa Farias, R. (2017), "Do You Wish Her to Marry? Brazilian Women and Professional Diplomacy, 1918-1938," *Diplomacy & Statecraft*, 28: 39–56.

Devenish, A. (2013), "Performing the Political Self: A Study of Identity Making and Self Representation in the Autobiographies of India's First Generation of Parliamentary Women," *Women's History Review*, 22: 280–94.

Dunn, L. K. (1992), "Joining the Boys' Club: The Diplomatic Career of Eleanor Lansing Dulles," in E. P. Crapol (ed.), *Women and American Foreign Policy: Lobbyists, Critics and Insiders*, 2nd ed., 119–35, Wilmington, DE: Scholarly Resources.

Enloe, C. (1989), *Bananas, Beaches and Bases: Making Feminist Sense of Politics*, Berkeley, CA: University of California Press.

Fliegel, J. (2017), "Unprecedented: Women's Leadership in Twenty-first Century Multilateral Diplomacy," in J. A. Cassidy (ed.), *Gender and Diplomacy*, 187–209, New York, NY: Routledge.

Garner, K. (2010), *Shaping a Global Women's Agenda: Women's NGOs and Global Governance, 1925-85*, Manchester, UK: Manchester University Press.

Heath, R. (April 12, 2017), "Mogherini on Mogherini: EU's Head of Foreign Policy Reflects on her Time in the Job," *Politico*, https://www.politico.eu/article/federica-mogherini-performance-interview-self-assessment-reflection/ (Accessed November 16, 2017).

Heath, R. (April 12, 2017), "Mogherini's Mid-Term Report Card," *Politico*, https://www.politico.eu/article/federica-mogherini-report-card-midterm-grades-eu-foreign-policy/ (Accessed November 16, 2017).

Hudson, V. M. and Leidel, P. (2015), *The Hillary Doctrine: Sex and American Foreign Policy*. New York, NY: Columbia University Press.

Hunt, M. H. (1996), "Confronting Revolution in Iran, 1953–80," in M. H. Hunt (ed.), *Crises in U.S. Foreign Policy: An International History Reader*, 365–413, New Haven, CT: Yale University Press.

Jain, D. (2107), "Women of the South: Engaging with the UN as a Diplomatic Manoeuvre," in J. A. Cassidy (ed.), *Gender and Diplomacy*, 65–80, New York, NY: Routledge.

Kaufman, J. (2013), *Introduction to International Relations: Theory and Practice*, Lanham, MD: Rowman & Littlefield Publishers, Inc.

Kelley, J. R. (2010), "The New Diplomacy: Evolution of a Revolution," *Diplomacy & Statecraft*, 21: 286–305.

Kianpour, S. (August 6, 2015), "Iran Negotiations: The Women Who Made the Iran Nuclear Deal Happen," *BBC News*, http://www.bbc.com/news/world-us-canada-33728879 (Accessed November 16, 2017).

Laut, J. (2016), "India at the United Nations: A Postcolonial Nation-State on the Global Stage, 1945-55," Ph.D. dissertation, Urbana, IL: University of Illinois.

Linder, D. H. (2001), "The Contributions of Scandinavian Women at the United Nations, 1946-66," *Scandinavian Studies*, 43 (3): 165–208.

Mallik, A. (November 3, 2006), "Women Presidents of the General Assembly: An Uneven Past," *UN Chronicle*, 6–9.

Mayer, C. (November 25, 2013), "Meet the Woman Who Helped Negotiate the Iran Nuclear Deal," *Time Magazine*, http://world.time.com/2013/11/25/meet-the-woman-who-helped-negotiate-the-iran-nuclear-deal/ (Accessed November 16, 2017).

McCarthy, H. (2014), *Women of the World: The Rise of the Female Diplomat*, London, UK: Bloomsbury Publishing.

McCarthy, H. (2016), "Gendering Diplomatic History: Women in the British Diplomatic Service, circa 1919-1972," in G. Sluga and C. James (eds.), *Women, Diplomacy and International Politics Since 1500*, 167–81, New York, NY: Routledge.

McCarthy, H. and Southern, J. (2017), "Women, Gender, and Diplomacy: A Historical Survey," in J. A. Cassidy (ed.), *Gender and Diplomacy*, New York, NY: Routledge.

Miller, C. (1991), "Women in International Relations?: The Debate in Interwar Britain," in R. Grant and K. Newland (eds.), *Gender and International Relations*, Bloomington, IN: Indiana University Press.

"No Longer So Male and Stale: French Diplomacy," (September 19, 2015), *The Economist*, 48.

Plotke, A. J. (2015), "Vijaya Lakshmi Pandit," *Salem Press Biographical Encyclopedia*, Salem Press, on-line.

Posch, W. (February 2016), "Iran and the European Union," in *The Iran Primer*, Washington DC: United States Institute of Peace.

Ravichandran, P. (February 26, 2016), "Hansa Mehta (1897-1995)," *Women Architects of the Indian Republic*, https://15fortherepublic.wordpress.com/2016/02/26/hansa-mehta-1897-1995/ (Accessed November 16, 2017).

Ravichandran, P. (August 14, 2016), "Vijayalakshmi Pandit (1900-1990)," *Women Architects of the Indian Republic*, https://15fortherepublic.wordpress.com/author/binaryfootprint/ (Accessed November 16, 2017).

Robinson, M. (2017), "Foreward," in J. A. Cassidy (ed.), *Gender and Diplomacy*, xiv–xv, New York, NY: Routledge.

Schwartz, T. A. (2011), "Henry Kissinger: Realism, Domestic Politics and the Struggle Against Exceptionalism in American Foreign Policy," *Diplomacy & Statecraft*, 22: 121–41.

Sharp, P. (2017), "Diplomacy," in R. A. Denemark and R. Marlin-Bennett (eds.), *The International Studies Encyclopedia*, New York, NY: Oxford University Press.

Sluga, G. (2013), *Internationalism in the Age of Nationalism*, Philadelphia, PA: University of Pennsylvania Press.

Tharoor, I. (June 11, 2017), "The Trump Administration Should Read its Own Documents about Regime Change in Iran," *Washington Post*, on-line.

Walt, S. M. (2017), "Realism and Security," in R. A. Denemark and R. Marlin-Bennett (eds.), *The International Studies Encyclopedia*, New York, NY: Oxford University Press.

INDEX

www.ingramcontent.com/pod-product-compliance
Lightning Source LLC
Chambersburg PA
CBHW071844270326
41929CB00013B/2093